Beneath the Turbulence

D K LeVick

xulon PRESS

Beneath the Turbulence
by D K LeVick

Printed in the United States of America

ISBN 9781626977174

Unless otherwise indicated, Bible quotations are taken from The King James Version.

Also by Author D K LeVick **"Journeys Across Niagara"**
(Formerly published as "Bridges – a tale of Niagara" 2011 Readers Favorites YA General Fiction Silver Award winner)

www.xulonpress.com

Acknowledgements

Knowing that no man is an island, the work he produces is not his alone, but is the culmination of all parts of his life from the first word to the last letter of the final word. This is never truer than with this book. There are many who had a role in the writing of this book and my heartfelt thanks to them all.

Special thanks go to those whose imaginations ignited them concerning the things not seen or known. I want to thank all those who have invested so much effort and energy into exploring and documenting the fascinating study of ancient history, mythology and folklore, and looking beyond the closed minds of others to explore the 'what if's' of our world. I thank all the many scientists, whose minds far exceed my feeble attempts to understand their theories and work in areas of time travel and quantum physics. Those who have developed and discovered many secrets of the universe and dimensional concepts that allow a layman such as me to weave fiction around them. I thank all the numerous historians, archeologists and 'out of the box' thinkers who have dedicated their lives to exploring, uncovering and working the pieces of the 'puzzle' to what our 'true' history and purpose are.

I am deeply indebted to those who have directly contributed their time and energy to preview, review and question the rough drafts and notes leading to this work. Special thanks go to Doctor Adrian Sheremeta for being a 'check and balance' on the logical and technical aspects; to Pastor Rocky Berra for reviewing and editing from a scriptural perspective and to Ms. Patricia Hill for her quality editing and overall reader check.

I wish to acknowledge my brother, Dennis, for planting the seed, although realizing a divergent path and outcome than he envisioned.

Dedication

This work is dedicated to my wife – Grace Ann.
Writing is a roller coaster, a ride of constant ups and downs and rounds and rounds.
On a high one day – down in the pits the next.
Where is it going? How is it flowing? Is it coming together? Is it falling apart?
I wish to thank Grace for keeping me on the track – stopping me from flying off into space or wrecking at the end of the line. She listened to all my ramblings and theories and continually encouraged me, keeping me motivated to continue by her encouragement and her 'white fibs' that it was good when I knew better and wanted to shuck the whole thing.
And
This book is for all those who have wondered and questioned those things for which the answers are not obvious. We don't have the luxury of going back in time 2000 years – but we can go along on the journey.
Enjoy the ride.

Beneath the Turbulence. . .

Volume One
The Journey

Chapter One

David leaned into the railing, gazing into the turbulent waters below. Niagara was mesmerizing; its power overwhelming, and its promise enticing. In its depths, the demons stopped screaming. The waters, dark and mysterious, beckoned him into their embrace. Their thick, powerful tendons surged past, smashing and breaking apart against the protruding rocks, exploding in sprays of bubbling foam, dancing across the surface before racing to the abyss ahead.

David didn't need their call. This side of the water held no peace for him. Questions haunted him, day and night, and bitterness consumed his heart. The waters below held no questions and no pain. The *voice* told him to jump. He had no reason not to. It was urgent. . .insistent. . . .

. . . *Jump. . .Jump. . .*

He shook his head, and a new voice, quiet and calm, spoke softly in his head:

Beneath the turbulence – peace is found

Lifting his foot, he placed it on the lowest rail and slowly raised himself.

The first step is hardest; they say. Well, I've taken it; he thought, *so the rest should be easy.*

They weren't, but he had climbed three more and was standing on the second rail from the top when his cell phone challenged the river's roar.

Should I answer it? He wondered.

No – what for? Jump. . . Jump now! The urgent voice said.

Answer the phone. The quiet voice said.

Why? You have nothing to say to anyone, leave it be. . .jump!

Answer it. The quiet voice said.

"Hello," David snapped angrily into the phone.

"Is this Mister David Alden Kincaid?" This voice was real and masculine.

David Alden Kincaid? No one's called me that since my mother died, fifteen years ago. Who even knew that name?

"Who's asking?" David demanded.

"Hello David. May I call you David?" Not receiving a response, the man continued, "Thank you. My name is Doctor Thaddeus Lenkovitch. I wonder if I may speak with you about a matter of great importance?"

"Why? Am I sick?" *Then the joke's on you, doc. No pill you have will cure me of what I got,* he thought. "Whatever you're selling mister, I'm not interested in, goodb. . ."

"No, it's nothing like that David; I'm not that kind of doctor, and I'm not a salesman. I'm a Doctor of Archeology at Boston University."

"Archeology? What do you want with me? I'm not even dead yet."

"I only wish to speak with you, David."

"What for? I'm tied up at the moment."

"I would like to speak with you regarding something that has come up, something quite unusual and of great significance."

"What's come up that concerns me?"

"We shouldn't discuss it over the phone, David. I need to speak with you in person. It's extremely important."

"Important? I have nothing to do with archeology, doc. I think you have the wrong number."

"I appreciate your confusion, David, but trust me; I don't have the wrong number. You're the person I need to speak to. Indulge me, please, it won't take long. I promise you. I just need to ask you some questions, and then I'll leave you alone."

"Listen, Doctor Leninwitch or whatever your name is, I don't know who you are or what you want. I don't know anything about archeology, and I'm pretty busy right now; so if you got something to ask me, do it now, or I'm hanging up."

"David, I have something to show you. It's crucial, and it involves you. Please, I won't take up much of your time, and then. . ." He paused, ". . .and then you can finish climbing that railing."

David froze and slowly stepped off the railing. He looked in all directions but saw no one.

"Who are you?" He asked again.

"I told you; I'm Doctor Thaddeus Lenkovitch, Professor of Archeology at Boston University, and I need to talk to you, to show you something. It's very important, and it won't take long."

"And you want me to drop everything I'm doing and run to Boston so you can show me something? You some kind of nut?"

"You don't need to come to Boston, David. I brought what you need to see, with me. We could meet now if you like. It will only take a few minutes," he paused, "and no, I'm not a nut."

David didn't want to meet this mysterious archeologist, but he couldn't climb the railing now, not with this weirdo spying on him. That's not how it is supposed to go down. It couldn't be on someone else's terms; it had to be on his terms, in his own way, alone, with no prying eyes. *What does this wacko want with me anyway? What's he got that's so important?*

"Alright, meet me at The Wedge, in thirty minutes, and no monkey business, you hear?"

"The Wedge, yes, I'll be there. No monkey business. And David, thank you." The receiver went dead.

✦✦✦

David held back in the shadows, noting each person who entered the small diner on Main Street. Only a few did, and they all looked like locals. *Maybe he doesn't know where it's at,* he thought.

He had just about made up his mind to leave and forget the whole affair, when from inside the diner, a short, stocky man, wearing a blue windbreaker stood in the doorway and waved for him to come over.

How did he get there before me? And how does he know I'm standing out here?

David looked up and down the street. No one was around, and only a few cars were randomly parked. Then he saw him. In a car, by the curb, three doors down from The Wedge. The silhouette of a man's head outlined through the window, looking directly at him.

What the devil is going on?

A part of him told him to run – fast while another urged him on to find out.

The worse that can happen is you end up dead, and you were on that road already.

His curiosity was up; he wanted to see what this doctor of archeology had to show him that was so important to have him tailed.

He crossed the street.

"Hello David, I'm Doctor Lenkovitch. Thank you for meeting with me." Holding out his hand, the fingers were rough and calloused. David ignored the offered hand; keeping his own balled up inside his jacket.

He figured the man for his late sixty's; about five feet seven, having a slight paunch and a stooped back, presumably from too many years bent over, digging fossils. He sported an unruly, greyish-white mustache with a goatee beard that covered a weathered face.

"How long have you been following me?" David demanded.

"Not long, couple of days. Just long enough to be sure you're the right David Kincaid." The doctor said, continuing to hold out his hand.

"How many can there be?"

"There's actually fourteen we identified. I had to be sure. I meant no offense. We just have a problem, and we need you to help us understand it." He turned his hand over and opened the palm, "I'm not your enemy, David."

"Who's we?"

"Me and a few colleagues—and some others."

"What others?"

"Why don't we go inside to talk, David?"

"What others?"

The doctor hesitated, and he took a deep breath, "Government."

David's cocked his head forward and raised his eyebrows, wanting more.

"Homeland Security," the doctor said, lowering his hand.

"Homeland Security? That's who's in that car across the street?"

"Yes, that's correct. Come, let's go inside and sit down."

David turned, looking at the silhouette in the car.

"Are you with the government?"

"No, I'm not," the doctor was adamant, "and neither are my colleagues."

David didn't like this, but there was little to do except comply with the doctor's request. If he didn't, they wouldn't leave him alone but would keep pestering him until they got what they wanted—whatever that was.

"All right, let's get this over with." Brushing pass the doctor, he entered the restaurant.

***

"So, Doctor Lenkowitch, what's an archeologist doing with Homeland Security?" David asked, stirring a cup of steaming, black coffee.

Doctor Lenkovitch shook his head. "It does seem rather odd, doesn't it? But, when you think about it, we do the same thing. We both search for clues to put pieces together."

"Except, your pieces are for putting the past together, and theirs are for taking the present apart," David said. "Seems, while your actions may be similar, your goals are at opposite ends of the spectrum."

The doctor didn't answer, only stared at his tea. After a long minute, he raised his head and spoke in a low voice, "Sometimes, the line between the past and the present isn't clear. Would you like some sugar for your coffee?" He offered David a bowl packed tight with little pink, blue and yellow packages, everything except sugar. David didn't answer and only continued stirring the black liquid.

"My name is Len-ko-vitch David, but you can call me professor if you would rather."

"I'd rather not call you," David answered impatiently. "Now, what's this all about? What do you want with me?"

"Are you familiar with a 'tel', David?"

"Like a tattletale?"

"No, not that; I'm talking about in the world of archeology," he paused, taking a sip of tea.

"Horrible excuse for tea," he said, making a face.

"A tel is a mound that is excavated for archeological purposes. Buried under years of soil are the ruins of ancient settlements and cities. Sometimes these are stand-alone, and sometimes they are eras built on top of one another, like layers of a cake. That's what we do in archeology, find tels, dig them up and uncover civilizations—putting the pieces of ancient history together."

"I thought they're called archeological digs."

"Yes, they're called that, as well," the doctor said, taking another sip of his horrible tea. "Have you ever been to Israel David?"

"Yeah, once," he nodded.

"May I ask when?"

"Back in the eighty's sometime, around eighty-one or eighty-two. I'm not sure. Why?"

"October, 1981 to be exact."

"If you already know, why are you asking?" David snapped back, annoyed at the intrusion into his past.

"Just wondering why you went there?"

"I was studying the language and wanted to see the country where it was used."

"Why did you study Hebrew? You're not Jewish."

"I had credit hours to fill. I'd already studied Greek and figured I might as well finish it off with Hebrew." He stopped stirring the black coffee and put the spoon down. "Is that what you wanted me for? To ask me what I studied in college? That's what Homeland Security wants to know?"

"Those are extremely difficult studies, just to fill open credits. But no, that is not why I'm here," the doctor put down his cup and assumed his professor's demeanor. "I've been working a tel in Israel for a couple of years. It was a small village called Ammathus, along the southern shore of the Sea of Galilee. We'd excavated down through three distinct settlements built one on top of another, yielding some remarkable artifacts that have aided us immensely in understanding the history of the area."

"What interest does Homeland Security have in an ancient Jewish village?"

"None that I know of. Their interest lies in another direction."

"What interest do I have?"

"Early this year, we reached the third level down. It's from the turn of the First Century."

"Two-thousand years ago."

"Yes, exactly, and we uncovered artifacts supporting that era: earthenware, carvings, tools, etc. Carbon dating put them somewhere between 30 BC and 70 AD."

"So you found some old pottery; what's that have to do with me?"

"We were excavating under the remains of the wall of a building, when we found a pitcher. It had been carefully placed inside a box made of flat stones and was fully intact and sealed. Inside the pitcher was an object—this."

The doctor opened a metal case sitting next to him in the booth. Withdrawing a cloth, he placed it on the table. Gently opening it, he exposed a flat, smooth stone, brown in color.

"This is a clay writing tablet from the First Century. There's writing on it, can you read it, David?"

David looked at the writing; it was in Hebrew. He read it out loud.

חרצכמ ושי לש

"Jesus of Nazareth."

"Yes, that's right, 'Jesus of Nazareth'." The professor could not hold back his excitement. "Do you realize what this is? It's the first, direct historical evidence that clearly identifies Jesus as a person. This is earth shattering. And, it was carefully preserved and hidden as if someone knew it had to be protected for two thousand years until it was found."

"That's all very interesting, professor, but what does that have to do with me?"

"You're not a Christian, are you David?"

"That's really none of your business, is it?" David snapped. "But, since you seem to know everything about me already, no I'm not a Christian or anything else for that matter. So now that we've had our confessional, is there anything else you wanted to waste my time with?"

Thaddeus nodded his head, "Yes, there's one more thing I'd like to show you." Reaching into the metal case, he extracted a second wad of cloth.

"Beneath the pitcher, under a second layer of stones fitted together to form a box was a second pitcher. That pitcher was also fully intact and sealed to be preserved."

"And?"

"Inside that pitcher, was another clay tablet," he continued talking as he carefully opened the cloth, "this one. It's been analyzed and checked repeatedly for authenticity. Carbon 14 dating has verified, without any degree of doubt or uncertainty; it's from the year 30 BC, plus or minus four years, meaning it has been buried under tons of soil, in the ruins of that house in Israel, for twenty centuries." He placed the cloth on the table and revealed the tablet; he pushed it towards David.

There was writing on it, —in English:

David Alden Kincaid
31 BC

Chapter Two

David jumped back as if a serpent had sprung out of the cloth.
"What are you trying to pull, here? What kind of scam are you running?"

"It's no scam David; it's real."

"No way it is! You expect me to believe that you found that rock buried in some ruins from over two-thousand years ago, in Israel, with my name on it? English wasn't even in existence yet. You think I'm stupid? You carved that yourself! Sorry, doc, you're going to have to do better than that, I'm outta here." He rose to leave, and the professor grabbed his arm.

"I *can* do better than that, David—look."

He picked up the tablet and turned it over. Writing was on that side as well —in Greek.

Κάτω από τις αναταραχές-ειρήνης βρίσκεται

David's heart froze; his breath ceased as he slowly sank back down into the booth. *How can this be?* Those are the exact words the quiet voice had said to him only minutes earlier while he was climbing the railing at the Niagara River. *It just isn't possible. How could anyone know what I was thinking—before I thought it?*

The professor read the words out loud:

"Beneath the turbulence – peace is found."

He looked up, "Those words mean something to you, don't they David?"

"How. . .I don't under. . .Who are you?"

"I'm Doctor Thaddeus Lenkovitch, Professor of Archeology at Boston University as I've told you, nothing more."

"This can't be. It's not possible." Confused, David's mind grabbed at anything to bring a sense of sanity back, "The age of those tablets? There's no chance it's a mistake?"

"None. Both the tablets and the pitchers were anonymously submitted to four independent laboratories, each certified by the Departments of Defense, Interior and Homeland Security. They all agree, within plus or minus four years—they're from the year 30 BC." He paused, allowing this to register fully, "And the writing on the tablets has been verified as having been written centuries ago, definitely, not in the present era."

"But, how can that be? It's not possible."

"But it is, and once you accept that, we can begin to think about how it can be."

"And how is that?"

"There's the apparent answer."

"You're not implying that I wrote those, are you?"

"Do you have another explanation?"

"Yeah, they're fake! I don't know how you did it, but somehow this is all a scam — a set up."

"For what purpose, David? Ask yourself that. Why would I go through all this trouble just to scam you? For what? You have nothing I could possibly want. You're not wealthy—you have no family—possess no extraordinary wisdom or secret. You're an ordinary man, alone from what I can see, and if I recall correctly, one who was climbing a railing overlooking Niagara Falls just a few moments ago."

"Thanks for the resume!" David sneered, drinking down the bitter, cold coffee in one swallow. He looked at Lenkovitch, hoping for some flicker of sanity. "How do you explain this?"

"I only have one explanation, David."

"You seriously think that I wrote those tablets?"

"A message? Written in three different languages? Two of which are ancient and difficult to know, and the third, in modern English? And you just happen to be fluent in all three? And the only person who would understand the meaning of that phrase? And it's your name? You think that's all coincidence? Whoever wrote that knew when it would be read and by whom."

"Me?"

"You."

"You're suggesting that I somehow came to the present from two-thousand years ago?"

"No, I'm suggesting you went back from the present to two-thousand years ago."

"I can travel in time?"

"Well, at least once you did—or will."

"Believe me, I don't travel in time. If I could, I wouldn't be here now."

"I believe you David, but there are others who won't believe you."

"Others?" He looked out the window at the car across the street. "Him? Homeland Security?"

"Him. . .and others." His eyes darted to the counter where a lone man sat nursing a coffee.

"What's going on here?" David demanded, pushing back from the table. "Are you wired?"

"Calm down David, there are no wires. But your every move is being watched. You didn't see them, but they were there at that railing, ready to grab you if you ignored my call."

"I don't get it. Why? What do they want with me?"

"Think for a second David; what if you could travel in time? What power would you have? You could change history—no; you'd be history. You could destroy governments—societies—nations. You would be the biggest threat ever to face mankind: past or present."

"So, Homeland Security sees me as a threat?"

"As a threat – yes; and —as a weapon."

"But, I'm not either. I can't do that. I can't travel through time. Even, if I could, I wouldn't do those things."

"Wouldn't you? You wouldn't stop Hitler if you had the chance to? Or abolish slavery? You wouldn't stop nine-eleven if you could go back to nine-ten?"

The questions were too much for David, "It doesn't matter what I'd do because I can't travel in time."

They sat for a long moment without saying anything. The waitress refilled his coffee cup pausing longer than needed, giving David an inviting smile. It was wasted; he didn't even know she existed while he tried to absorb the bitter bile boiling in his stomach. When he finally spoke, he looked at the professor in a quizzical way.

"Why is Homeland Security involved anyway? How are they aware of your excavation and these tablets?"

"Oh, I wish it wasn't so, and it's my fault entirely. I told them." Lenkovitch shook his head, sadly, "You see my work is funded by a grant from the Department of Natural Sciences. Being required to keep them informed on a regular basis, I reported the discovery of the first tablet to them. Apparently, word spread quickly through the halls of government, and by the time the second tablet was discovered, it was too late, they had people on site. Before I knew it, Homeland Security showed up and took over the tel, stopped work, and confiscated my records." He sighed, "They interrogated me and my staff to no end. Meanwhile, they ran your name through their computers and found you."

"So they started tailing me?"

"Yes, they've watched your every move for the past couple of weeks. They were going to take you into custody, but I convinced them to let me talk with you first. They were reluctant, but finally relented; hoping you'll make a dash to your time machine or whatever you use to time-travel in, so they could catch you—and it."

"But I don't have any time machine."

"They think you do, and that's all that matters to them," he paused, "so, here we are."

"And where are we, professor? What happens next?"

"That depends on you. From what I can see, you have two options. One, make a dash for the railing at the river, and hope you can climb it before they grab you. Once they have you, they'll not let up until they've dissected you inside and out; then lock you up and throw away the key."

"And the second?"

"Come with me."

"Where?"

"To Boston, to the university."

"What's there?"

"My research—and my colleagues, who are anxious to talk with you."

"All of a sudden I'm popular. What about the meatball over there?" David nodded toward the back booth.

"They've agreed to give me latitude as long as you're with me. They're hoping you'll tell me about your time machine, or I'll find it without them having to resort to their own measures."

"Their measures?"

"They're the government David, and it's an age of terrorism—they have many measures and plenty of freedom to trample on our rights, all in the name of security, you understand. You have no family, so you can disappear quite easily if they choose."

David sat stunned and angry, mulling over this unwanted intrusion, on what was to be the last day of his life. He looked at Lenkovitch, then at the man in the back booth. He didn't see much choice.

"Okay, when do we leave for Boston?"

"Now."

***

As the car pulled away, taking David and the professor to Boston, a figure emerged from the shadows of a doorway, wearing a dark cloak with a hood pulled over his head. The streetlights catch the face inside. It's a beautiful face, smooth and perfect.

From it, malicious eyes glare as the car drove off.

Chapter Three

Rabbi Barosh Ben Goldberg clenched his fist for the umpteenth time in the last ten minutes. *When will it end?* He thought. *This senseless killing and maiming. So many dying and living in fear of death. How much more, God of Abraham, Isaac and Jacob, are we to suffer?*

The market square had been bustling with people going about their lives, shopping and quibbling over the price of figs and olives. Vendors plied their products and women planned their meals, when two women and a young girl had entered the marketplace and mingled with the crowds, separating and branching off in different directions. Within milliseconds of each other the body vests equipped with high-explosives, strapped tight under their cloaks, detonated. Six shops demolished. The ball bearings and nails packed in the casings had sprayed in all directions with devastating force, killing and maiming without discretion.

The final body count was twenty-three dead and nineteen injured. Among the dead—thirteen women and six children.

The newscaster did not identify the victims as Jews or the bombers as Palestinians. Rather, the victims are portrayed as a *mix* of citizens and the perpetrators as criminals. *Criminals?* Barosh shouted inside himself; *People who strap thirty pounds of explosives and nails onto themselves and their children are not criminals—they're terrorists! Terrorists trained by nations and governments determined to eradicate Israel from the face of the globe. One more day in a long, never-ending war of hatred that began centuries ago and continues to this day while the world looks away, pretending it's 'criminals', instead of national policies of genocide. Then, when Israel retaliates, it is portrayed as an act of war.*

He smashed the 'OFF' button on the remote and slammed it down. *How much more are we to suffer? You promised a messiah—when will he come? How much longer must we wait?*

The shrill ring of the telephone interrupted his private rant. Rummaging through his pockets, he searched for the annoying device. He had resisted having one, preferring the ancient handset on his desk that he could be absent from or simply ignore. But Thaddeus insisted he have it and so be available at his beck and call. But he drew the line at the idiotic array of tunes and chimes it played when it rudely interrupted him. If he had to have the annoying thing, then it would sound like a phone was supposed to sound, and not play the William Tell Overture.

"What?" He barked into the plastic box.

"Hello also to you my friend; I see you are just as happy as when I left you."

"Have you seen the news? Another bombing, this. . . ."

"I'm back."

". . .time in the marketplace of. . . ."

"Barosh—I'm back."

Barosh stopped, "Forgive me, Thaddeus. Yes, of course, you're back. How are you, my friend? It is good you have returned and concluded your business safely. Tell me, did you continue studying the Torah?"

"I did."

"Wonderful! And what headway have you made?"

"I'm still in Genesis, in the fifth chapter."

"Ah, the genealogy of the patriarch Adam. That is diligent study my friend, with so much 'begetting' going on," he chuckled. "It can be very trying, even for a rabbi such as me, but it can be quite enlightening as well, providing there are no outside interruptions."

"Yes, it is definitely interesting, especially the story of Enoch; and I've had no outside interruptions."

"That is good. We should meet so you can share with me what revelations you've uncovered and what mysteries remain."

"I would like that very much. Shall we say nine tonight, at my house? Do you think Allen would like to join us?"

"I'm sure he would, he has exceptional insight. I shall see if he is available."

"Good, Camille will have sweet tea ready."

The phone clicked off.

So, the mysterious David Alden Kincaid is found and he is here with Thaddeus, and the government has not interfered.

Ever since, Thaddeus had uncovered those mysterious tablets; Homeland Security has been his constant companion, determined to learn how much Thaddeus and this David Alden Kincaid know about time travel. They spent weeks questioning, poking and dissecting his life. Finally, they concluded Thaddeus was an innocent participant in the schemes of Kincaid and was not his accomplice.

Thaddeus did not think the government suspected anything of Barosh, knowing they've been friends for many years. Still, suspecting his phone and office were bugged, Thaddeus had started talking in code. With his archeological activities in Israel, it was a natural thing for him to study Jewish history and law, and who better to advise him than his old Jewish friend, Rabbi Goldberg? Referencing Enoch meant the mysterious David Alden Kincaid had been found and having "sweet tea" at his house, meant he was there. Barosh chuckled, knowing his old friend got his kicks out of playing James Bond.

His stubby fingers jabbed at the small phone, punching in Allen's numbers. The keys were so small, and his fingers so large, it took three tries before he got it right.

It picked up on the first ring.

"Shalom Barosh, how are you?"

"I am well Allen, and trust you are well also. Thaddeus has returned and is eager for us to resume our studies with him tonight"

"Has he progressed?"

"He's in chapter five of Genesis, about Enoch. He said he would have some sweet tea for us."

"Wonderful! I can hardly wait. My schedule is open. Perhaps I could bring some friends along who are also studying."

"I'm sure Thaddeus would welcome them. Nine o'clock then?"

"Excellent, I will see you then."

Barosh pressed the "END" button and returned the phone to his pocket.

So, it begins, he thought. *Will I, like Moses, look out from the mountaintop and only gaze upon the land of milk and honey; or will I, like Joshua, cross over into the Promised Land? Soon, old soul, we shall know God's will. But first, I must tell Mary I'll be seeing Thaddeus tonight and not to stay up for me.*

Chapter Four

Removing the headphones, Senior Agent Kenneth Rodgers sat back in the seat of the specially equipped van, and looked over at his partner sealing the tape inside the chain of custody envelope.

"So, what do you think John; are they up to something?"

"Nah, these nerds are just a couple of dried out corpses, buried in their moldy books. Those tablets just give them an excuse for playing "I Spy" for excitement."

Ken shook his head and wondered where the Department was headed when someone like John was being touted as an up and coming player. They wanted Ken to mentor him, but Agent John Markus Rosino was too filled with himself to leave room for any mentoring. *If John represents a rising star, then the Department's in serious trouble,* Ken thought.

"You'd be surprised what some of these "dried out corpses" do for excitement," Ken said.

"So, you're an authority on academic excitement, too?" John chuckled. "And, how would you know about that?"

"By doing what we're doing now—eavesdropping. These aren't the first professors I've watched, and not only in their dining rooms. In fact, I'd say I've listened to more of these "dried out corpses" than I have any other group. The universities are hotbeds for every wild and radical idea that pops up. And they don't only share ideas either. There's no shortage of sex clubs and swapping parties, not to mention the numerous affairs going on." He looked at Ken, who was listening intently, "They get pretty kinky."

"Yeah, like what?"

"Indulge your voyeurism on your own dime," Ken chuckled.

"So what do *you* think then? Are these nerds up to something?" John asked.

"Not sure, but I got a feeling they are. It doesn't add up; the professor comes back from New York, with Kincaid, and the first thing he does is call for a Bible study?" He shook his head, "No, it doesn't make sense, and why Genesis?" He paused, "Genesis is the first book of the Bible – the beginning. Could that be a code of some kind? And that stuff about Enoch, what's that about? Can you find that?"

"No problem, "John was a product of the 'now' generation, having grown up with a keyboard for a teething ring. Along with his "smartphone" he was a walking encyclopedia. Any question that arose he would have an answer within minutes.

"Got it. . .right here. . .Genesis. . .chapter five wasn't it?" He scrolled through the page and chuckled, "Just like the rabbi said, lots of "begetting" going on."

"Well, they didn't have fifty-inch flat screens in their tents to entertain themselves with," Ken chuckled. "Besides, they were on a mission from God—to "be fruitful" and populate the world."

"I should have been born back then." John said. "Man, can you believe this stuff? It says those old fossils lived eight and nine hundred years. Not much here on that Enoch guy, though. Only a couple of lines and it's kinda weird."

"How's that?"

"I'll read it to you and see what you think, *'And all the days of Enoch were three hundred and sixty-five years. And Enoch walked with God, and he was not, for God took him."*

"That's it?"

"That's it."

"What does that mean, 'God took him'? Took him where? Let me see that."

Ken scanned it and handed the phone back; his face wore a perplexed look. "All those people lived hundreds of years longer than this Enoch fellow did, where'd he go?"

"There's a reference for Enoch, in another book; one called Hebrews."

"What's it say?"

"I don't know; I can't find it."

Ken glanced at the screen in John's hand, "That's the Old Testament; Hebrews is in the New Testament."

"What's the difference?"

"The Old is before Christ, and the New is after Christ. You don't know that?"

"Nah, I never paid any attention to that religious stuff. New Testament. . .okay, here it is. . . Hebrews? Let's see, the reference is for chapter eleven. Okay, got it. I'll read it, *"By faith Enoch was translated that he should not see death; and was not found, because God had translated him."* Hey, that translation stuff sounds like time travel, doesn't it? Like Captain Kirk, 'Beam me up Scotty'. Maybe they had a time machine back then, and this Kincaid guy found it."

"I wouldn't believe such things were possible, except I've seen too much lately to question anything anymore. It's all just too coincidental for something not to be going on."

"So what do you think they're up to then?"

"Well, let's look at what we know: We have a professor, who just happens to dig up a message from two-thousand years ago; that was supposedly written by someone from this century. He meets the guy who supposedly wrote it; and brings him here. He calls his friend, who happens to be a Zionist, and now they're going to get together to study about some character, named Enoch, who supposedly never died. Yeah, I'd say they're up to something. They're not meeting at nine o'clock to have a 'Bible' study over a cup of tea. We need to know who these 'friends' are. Can you trace that call to that Allen fella?"

"Sure, I'll get on it. So, what do we do next?"

"What we're paid to do," he tossed the keys to John, "here, you drive."

"Where we going?"

"To a 'Bible study.'"

***

They parked directly across the street, making no attempt to conceal their presence. Hopefully, by keeping the professor aware of their presence, he would not forget his responsibility to them.

After testing the receiving equipment and getting a strong, clear signal from the bugs planted in the professor's house, they settled in to wait, listen and observe. Ken was eager to know who these "friends" were. He knew these academia types were strange but calling a "Bible study" at nine o'clock was pushing the envelope, and he doubted that Billy Graham was on the invitation list.

"Anything on that call the rabbi made?"

"Yeah, turns out this Allen is in our network and holds a Class 1 security clearance. They're sending his folder over. He is Doctor Allen Eberhardt, head nerd in the Science College of MIT and considered an Einstein clone in physics and mathematics. He chairs a number of brain groups and is listed as the number one world authority on quantum physics. The DOD, DOE and NASA have consulted him at times."

Ken's eyebrows rose while he listened, "I don't think this guy's coming to talk about "begetting" under the stars. There's more here than meets the eye, John. Get pictures of who's attending this 'Bible study'. My guess is "Enoch" is a code name for Kincaid, and this quantum physics genius's interest in him is other than studying the book of Genesis."

"Roger that."

"You know, the professor's giving his game away."

"What do you mean?"

"Well, while it may be coincidence, him finding that tablet with Kincaid's name on it, and he contacts some friends about it. But apparently, they've set up a phone code. Why? Why do that unless they're up to something. We approached him about this mysterious tablet, and we've made no secret of following him; so it's obvious he's hiding something. His playing "I-Spy" is giving him away."

"Maybe, maybe not, he could just be a paranoid old man who has seen too many boogie men hiding under those rocks he's been digging up all his life."

"If he suspects his phone is tapped," Ken said, "then he may also suspect his house is bugged. I hope this "fossil" hasn't outfoxed us. How many bugs are in?"

"Just two; one in the main room and one in the study. Along with the phone tap, the techies figured that was enough."

"I hope they're right, are they both working?"

"Loud and clear, boss, 'good signals' on both. Got some music playing in the background but nothing interfering. I'd say we're in luck, and the old codger doesn't know we're listening."

"Well, let's keep our fingers crossed; I think that 'old fossil' isn't as dead as we think."

Chapter Five

David felt like a specimen under a microscope. The Professor had placed him in an Ethan Allen chair in the middle of a large parlor, populated with a plethora of overstuffed chairs and settees. Scattered amongst the chairs was a vast collection of artifacts collected over decades of sifting through the dust of centuries. Tchaikovsky's '1812 Overture' played in the background, and he was instructed to remain seated while they waited for the professor's colleagues.

Arriving, they greeted Lenkovitch, entered the room and took seats opposite David, where they sat, without talking, casting fleeting glances at him.

David vowed never again to visit a zoo.

After the fourth person had arrived, the Professor turned the volume on Tchaikovsky up, entered the room and closed the door behind him. He was beaming as if showing off a prize artifact from one of his 'tels'. Maybe he was – a living artifact dug out from under a two-thousand year old wall in Israel.

"Okay, we're all here. David, I'd like you to meet my colleagues, each of whom have a strong interest in the study of Enoch," he said this while putting his finger to his lips and motioning to the windows. The others nodded, knowing his meaning. David understood about the agents outside, *but what's with the Enoch thing,* he wondered?

Placing his hand on the shoulder of a burly man with a husky build, Lenkovitch began, "This is my dear friend, Rabbi Barosh Ben Goldberg.

Barosh is a highly respected and widely published scholar who teaches Jewish history and law here at Boston U."

The Rabbi stood and extended a thick, muscular arm, covered in coarse, dark hair and ending in a meaty hand with short, stubby fingers. His face was framed by long, curled locks running down each side and a full beard across the bottom. Positioned on the top of his head was a small yarmulke.

"Shalom, David."

David took his hand and nodded. The grip was strong and firm.

"Next to Barosh, we have Professor Alexander Wainwright, of the University of New York. Alex is the Chief Egyptologist and Keeper of Egyptian Antiquities at the Museum of Natural Sciences in New York City. I met Alex many years ago, when I was working a dig near the Dahshur pyramids. His knowledge and insight has been invaluable over the years and especially so with our current situation."

Wainwright remained seated and nodded towards David without offering his hand. David thought him petrified, like one of his Egyptian mummies. *Maybe he's handled one too many, David* thought. What d*oes Egypt have to do with this?*

Before Lenkovitch could introduce him, a tall, lean man having a pale, angular face, sprang up and stepped towards David.

"Hello David. I'm Professor Allen Eberhardt of the science department at MIT. I've been looking forward to meeting you—to see if you actually existed." He stretched out a long, sinewy arm while boring deep into David's eyes. "I'm most pleased that you do."

"So am I."

"Allen is being modest," Lenkovitch chuckled. "He's not *of* the science department; he *is* the science department. He holds two doctorate degrees, one in Quantum Physics and the other in Relative Mathematics of Negative Energy. He has credentials in areas I've never heard of. He's the Senior Fellow for both, the Physics and the Mathematics Boards at the Brookings Institute; is a sitting member of several 'think tanks' and is listed as the leading authority on Einstein's theories of time and space relativity."

Allen's hand was warm, almost hot as he shook David's.

Sitting next to Allen, was a petite, strawberry blonde David thought was far too beautiful to be hanging with this group. He wondered who's assistant she was when Lenkovitch introduced her.

"I'd like you to meet Doctor Jennifer Albright."

"I'm pleased to meet you, David," her voice matched her beauty. She offered David a surprisingly firm handshake.

"Jennifer is the Director of the Clifton Sorby Metallurgy Department at the Museum of Natural Science in New York. She holds her Ph.D. in Metallurgy Physics from Harvard, and is a Board Member of the National Science Foundation in Washington. In her spare time, she's the Chief Consultant of Astro-metals at NASA."

So much for being someone's assistant, David thought.

"And that is our group," The professor locked onto David's arm and steered him to the center of the room.

"Gentlemen and Lady," he nodded to Jennifer, "I present to you, Mr. David Alden Kincaid."

David didn't know what was expected of him. They looked at him as if he had just stepped off the last bus from the Twilight Zone and had purple antennae sprouting from his head. He felt like the proverbial square peg in a round hole. What did these eggheads want from him? He didn't know, but he knew what he wanted from them—answers.

"It's nice to meet all of you, but I honestly do not know what this is about. I'm not a scientist, and I don't have a Ph.D. after my name. . . ."

"That's okay David, we know," Rabbi Barosh interrupted. "You're thirty-seven years old; an only child and both your parents are deceased, died three years ago in an automobile accident—we offer our condolences." He paused while the others nodded their heads. "Your family roots trace to Russia on your father's side, and Italy on your mother's. . .Sicilian, I believe. Russian-Italian, an interesting mix of cultures to be raised in."

"I've always considered myself an American. I know little about either, my Russian or Italian heritage."

Barosh looked at him with disapproval, "Roots are important, Mr. Kincaid, we must always remember our roots. I find it disturbing, the newer generations have lost their roots—their heritage, truly appalling, something. . . ."

"That's enough, Barosh," the professor interrupted, "David is our guest, and he's not interested in your theories about family roots, I'm sure."

"Of course, please, accept my apologies Mr. Kincaid; I sometimes get carried away." He continued, "Let's see now, where were we? You're a Mechanical Engineer, graduate of the University of Buffalo and, interestingly, you hold a minor in ancient languages, being fluent in both Greek and Hebrew. Have I missed anything?" He looked at the others and then turned back to David with cold, steel eyes, "Oh, yes, there is one more thing; you recently quit a good job, and. . . you have an attraction for Niagara Falls."

"Barosh! That's totally uncalled for," the professor rebuked him.

"I'm sorry, Thaddeus, but if we're going to make sense of this whole thing, we need to get everything on the table, don't we?"

Anger boiled up in David. He wasn't one to permit such intrusions into his personal life—but he had unanswered questions, and it was either this group of eggheads or that group of thugs outside who could answer them. He didn't think he'd get many answers outside.

"You apparently know a few things about me," he replied tightly, "but do not presume you know me. I'm here of my own accord, and I can leave just as easily. If your intent is to insult me, I'll leave now; otherwise tell me what exactly 'this whole thing' is that you want to 'make sense of'?"

"I apologize for my colleague's rudeness," Allen answered, "I assure you, our intent is not to insult you, but we were hoping you could tell us what this is about."

"If you're referring to that rock with my name on it, I haven't a clue."

"Well then, that settles it," Jennifer said.

"Settles what?" David asked.

"Whether or not you have a time machine of course, Mr. Kincaid" she replied.

"A time machine? Where would I. . . ."

"Before we proceed any further," Lenkovitch interrupted, touching his finger to his lips and pointing towards the window, "let's retire to the study where Camille has some wonderful tea brewing."

"A splendid idea Thaddeus," Barosh replied, jumping up. "David—after you."

***

The study was every bit as large as the parlor but appeared smaller due to the enormous amount of clutter. If there were windows, they were buried behind bookshelves overflowing with volumes, manuscripts, folders and binders. Each wall was layered in books from floor to ceiling. Only the doorway was uncovered, and a rolling ladder rode on a track ringing the room. Scattered notes and yellowed sheets of paper stuck out from the pages of numerous tomes and formed a small mountain on a desk in the corner. To one side, six mahogany chairs ringed a matching, ancient conference table. Next to the table was a serving credenza, where a decorative English pot reigned like a monarch ruling over its kingdom of cups, saucers and spoons. An ageless woman was arranging fine, white porcelain china around the monarch.

"Here, let me help you Camille," the professor said. She gave him a quizzical look as he began filling a cup with the steaming tea.

"Do you take anything in your tea David?"

"Uh, I'm not much of a tea drinker. Plain would be fine, I guess."

"Here you go," the professor placed a cup in front of him. "It may be a little bitter if you're not used to it."

Lenkovitch sat down and Camille brought him a chipped porcelain mug that'd seen better days. Barosh leaned over to David, "Thaddeus has a thing about that old mug; won't drink from anything else. Calls it his 'revelation' cup, and adds enough sugar to sweeten Lake Michigan. I think he owns a plantation somewhere."

After everyone had been served, Lenkovitch spoke, "Thank you Camille. That will be all. Close the door behind you, and switch the music to this room with the volume set to number eighteen please."

"Yes Thaddeus; good evening all."

From somewhere in the maze of books, Tchaikovsky flooded the room. David thought it was too loud to have a meeting. Lenkovitch leaned forward, addressing the group in a low voice.

"This morning I found a tiny device stuck to the underside of the table in the other room. A bug I believe they call them in the movies."

"Planted by our illustrious government, I'm sure," Wainwright said.

"Is that legal?" Jennifer asked. "Can they do that?"

"Since when do legalities matter to them, Jennifer?" Wainwright replied.

"I left it there, not wanting them to know I found it," Lenkovitch continued, "and I searched around and found another one, over there." He pointed to a book shelve across the room, where an unusually large pile of heavy books were stacked up like bricks. "I piled those books in front of it and moved the table down to this end. I checked everywhere for any more and didn't find any."

"You could hide the Queen Mary in here," Barosh said.

"Do we dare speak? How can we be sure they won't hear us?" Jennifer asked.

"We can't," Lenkovitch answered, "but I played a little detective work and placed a tape recorder next to the device and then spoke over here with the music playing. I found that, at a setting of sixteen on the stereo, I couldn't make out what I said over here when speaking in a normal voice. So, if we speak normal with Tchaikovsky set at eighteen," he shrugged, "they won't hear us."

"Are you certain there's no device on this table?" Wainwright asked.

"Unless it's buried inside the wood, yes, I'm sure. I went over every inch with a magnifying glass."

"Why don't we just go someplace else?" Jennifer asked.

"If we did, they'll know we're on to them, and they may take David. Besides, where would we go that they couldn't interfere?" Lenkovitch answered.

"Thaddeus is right," Wainwright said, "as long as we've identified all the bugs, there's no better place to be. They have equipment that can listen anywhere. With the windows here covered with all these books, it's almost soundproof, but let's not discuss any specific plans here."

"I meet with them daily, and I'll be able to determine if they are hearing us or not. Are there any objections?"

Receiving none, he asked, "Well then, how is the tea?"

"Wonderful, shall we get on with it?" Wainwright said.

"Yes, of course," Lenkovitch replied. "I've spoken with David at length, and he is very certain that he has no knowledge of the matter at hand."

"Is that correct, Mr. Kincaid?" Jennifer asked.

"The only Mr. Kincaid I know was my father, and yes, I don't have any idea how my name got on that tablet," David looked around at the group.

"Listen, I don't know what you folks are about, and I sure don't understand what's going on here, but you can be assured I don't have any time machine, and the travel I've done is measured in miles—not years." He tasted the tea; it was bitter.

"Are you sure that tablet is genuine and dated accurately?" He asked.

"Absolutely," Wainwright said, "They've been checked and verified by the best experts and authorities. There's no doubt as to their authenticity."

"Then how do you explain it?" David asked.

"That's easy, David," Eberhardt answered. "You did it."

"What! I did it? Two-thousand years ago, I did it?" David shot back.

"Give or take a decade or two." Eberhardt chuckled.

"Do you not hear very well? I told you; I don't have a time machine...." David's eyes grew heavy and began blurring.

"....and I've....never.....travelled...in......tim...," His eyes closed, and his head dropped.

"I don't like this; it's not right," Jennifer said.

"We've been over it Jennifer, we have to be sure," Wainwright replied.

"I still don't like it. It's unethical."

"You've made your point," Wainwright said, annoyed.

"We're beyond that now, so stop quibbling," Barosh snapped. "We don't have the time to be polite." He nodded at the professor, "Proceed, Thaddeus."

"David," Thaddeus spoke in a low, easy tone. "David, can you hear me?"

"Yes, I hear you."

"How do you feel David?"

"I'm very tired."

"It's okay to feel that way. You've been given something to relax you. It won't harm you. You'll wake up later and have no memory of our conversation. I'd like to ask you some questions, and I'd like you to answer them truthfully. Is that okay, David? Can you do that?"

"Yes, I can do that."

"Good," he looked at the group. Alex motioned for him to continue. "David, were you ever in Israel in the 1st Century?"

"When?"

"In the First Century David, around the year 30 CE."

"No."

"Have you ever been anywhere in the First Century David?"

"No."

"David, do you have a time machine?"

"I have a watch."

"I mean a machine to travel through time."

"No."

"Okay, good," he glanced at Barosh, who motioned him on. He took a deep breath and continued, "David, why did you climb the railing at Niagara Falls?"

The interrogation continued for the next hour. They asked and pried about his reasons for climbing the railing and were startled when David spoke of the voice in his head telling him to jump.

"What voice, David?"

"The *beautiful one.*"

"Why does he tell you to jump, David?"

"To end it."

"To end what, David?"

"Pain."

Like a surgeon Thaddeus cut away the layers of scar tissue, finally reaching the source of the "pain" in David's heart

"Nicole. . . ."

"Who is Nicole, David?"

"My fiancé."

"Where is Nicole, David?"
David didn't answer.
"Is Nicole gone David?"
No answer.
"Did Nicole end the engagement. . . .?"
"Nicole is dead."
"I'm sorry David. Did Nicole die in an accident?"
"No."
"Was Nicole sick David?"
"No."
"How did Nicole die David?"
David didn't answer.
"David, how. . . ."
"She was murdered."
"Oh!" Jennifer inhaled.

He explained how she was on her way to meet him when she was stopped. They had robbed and raped her and then, for no reason, had shot her. Thaddeus fumblingly attempted to comfort him.

"She's in heaven, David and is at peace."
"There's no heaven."
"Why is there no heaven, David?"
"Because there is no God."
"David why is there. . ."
"That's enough Thaddeus! Leave him be." Jennifer insisted.
"David, one last question, will you climb the railing again?"

Chapter Six

Watching them leave the house, Ken felt a knot in his gut knowing he had screwed up and taken the professor too lightly. The old man wasn't the pushover he appeared to be. He was a fox – a sly old fox who was covering his tracks.

"Man, that stunk," John grumbled, "I couldn't get anything. He must know we're listening."

"Whether he does or not, he suspects it. We should have placed more bugs."

"Hey, it's not my fault. . . ."

"I'm not blaming you John; it's my fault; I didn't take him seriously enough. But that's water under the bridge now. Did you get anything?"

"Well, I got a lot of Tchaikovsky. I don't know where those speakers are, but they must be close to the bug. The best was when the woman spoke. Her voice seemed to cut through the music a little."

"Or maybe she was sitting closer."

"Whatever. She's a real looker."

"Did you get a picture of her?"

"Oh yeah. Hard to believe a Ph.D. of metal comes in a package like that."

"The days of looks and no brains are long gone, fella," Ken said. "Did it seem that the rabbi wanted to provoke Kincaid?"

"They're all kind of strange, I thought."

"Wainwright and Albright came from New York. They didn't make that trip for a Bible study. What is there about Kincaid that brings these people running with only a phone call?"

"It didn't sound like they knew him before tonight."

"Agreed. Whatever they're up to, he's not part of the group. But they've done their homework on the guy, and dropped everything to meet him. Climbing that railing at the river. . .I wonder. . . ."

"What? Enlighten me, oh wise one."

"Well, that reference the rabbi made concerning Kincaid climbing the railing."

"Yeah, so what? Apparently he doesn't think much of suicide."

"Maybe or maybe he wasn't going to commit suicide? What if that's how Kincaid travels through time?"

"By going over Niagara Falls? Come on partner; you smoking the loco weed? Where's the time machine. . .at the bottom?"

"We don't know that there is a time machine, John. Maybe it's something different, some other kind of thing. Like, that TV show, the one where they jump into a stargate or something."

"Yeah, I saw that once," John said. "They jump through this shimmering thing into another world."

"Maybe Kincaid jumps through some kind of shimmering thing at the river. We don't know what's going on John; so we have to keep our minds open to anything. Ask yourself, why would anyone, who can travel in time, want to kill himself?"

"Maybe he doesn't like people, no matter what time they're from," John laughed.

Ken gave John a snide glance, "I could understand that," he said. "Anything else?"

"Only that the lady was objecting to something, and unless I'm wrong, I think Kincaid fell asleep."

"Yeah, it did get quiet and broke up early. Maybe he's tired from the drive from Niagara."

"Maybe. . .or wait a minute! Maybe. . ." John said, getting excited, "maybe he's not there! Maybe he went somewhere in time right there."

Ken jerked his head around, looking at John, "He doesn't need a machine and can travel through time at will? Maybe."

"Let's bust in and see if he's there or not," John opened the door.

"No, that won't gain his cooperation and would only prove to them that we've been listening. Besides, if he's gone, it wouldn't do us any good anyway; it's too late. Lenkovitch said they would meet again, tomorrow night. We need to get more bugs in there."

"We can try, but with the professor inside and suspicious, it'll be tough," John said.

"I'll get authorization for phone bugs. Get the cell phone numbers of each of them. And get that tape over to the techies. Let's see if they can pull something out of it. We'll meet with the professor first thing in the morning, and see what he has to say for himself.

Chapter Seven

David woke early the following morning, confused and disoriented. *What happened last night? Did I fall asleep? In front of those people? How could I do that? Why didn't they wake me?* He had never done anything like that before, and he hadn't been tired.

He made his way into the parlor. No one was around. Looking at the table, he recalled the Professor saying he had found a bug there.

Had he really? Or was it for show? What would a bug look like, he asked himself? *Creepy little thing with eight legs and antennas. Knock it off, these people are serious. They don't take kindly to wise guys who don't have a string of initials after their name.*

Searching under the table, there it was, stuck to the underside, a little, brown button. It didn't have eight legs, but he was sure it had an antenna somewhere.

"Good morning David, did you lose something?"

Jumping at the sound, David banged his head on the underside of the table.

"Be careful David. I didn't mean to startle you."

David crawled out from under the table.

"Did you find what you were looking for?"

"Yes...bugs." He rubbed the lump growing on his head, and a sheepish grin spread across his face. "I have to apologize for last night, professor. I don't know what happened. I guess everything just caught up with me."

"You don't recall anything?"

"I remember we were talking about the tablet and then nothing. I hope I didn't offend everyone."

"You did nothing wrong, David. Come with me, please."

In the kitchen, away from snooping bugs, Lenkovitch said, "I'm not sure where this is going, but wherever it is, we need to trust one another." He hesitated, took a deep breath and continued, "Last night, we violated your trust and did something that we felt was necessary, but of which I'm ashamed."

"What are you talking about?"

"You were given a truth serum. It's called SP-117. It has no taste, no smell, and no side effects, except that it knocks you out."

The hair on David's neck stood up.

"You drugged me? I thought the bad guys were outside! Who are you people? Why would you drug me?"

"David, you have every right to be upset, we had no right to do what we did, and under any other circumstance, I would never have allowed it. But this isn't a normal circumstance, we don't know what we're dealing with, and we have to be sure."

"Sure? Sure of what?" David yelled.

"Sure of everything. . .of what's happening. . .of the tablets. . .of Alex and Jennifer. . .of me. . .of you." Lenkovitch paced back and forth." I know it was wrong, but too much is happening and all so fast. There's no time to learn about one another in a normal, civilized way. The window is closing fast, and those men from the government are getting nervous. There's just no time; I'm sorry."

"So what was it about me that you didn't know that you had to drug me to find out? I told you; I don't know anything about those tablets."

"Yes, you did, and we believe you. It was a hard way to establish that, but there it is. There's just too little time."

"You didn't answer my question, professor. What did you need to know? What did your truth serum pull out of me? Whether or not I have a time machine?"

"That. . .and. . . ."

"And what? Tell me."

". . . .and why you wanted to take your own life."

David's chest deflated, his spirit sputtered and stalled.

"We're all sorry for your loss, David. Forgive us; we had no right to intrude into your personal life." He paused and looked at David hoping for understanding, "But we had to know."

"Why? Why's it so important anyway?"

Lenkovitch spoke low, "We had to know if you would still do it."

David closed his eyes, "And did you find out?"

"We did."

David looked out the window, past the sky. "And. . .will I?"

The professor put his hand on David's shoulder, "Would you like some tea?"

"No thanks professor—no more of your tea, but I could go for a cup of coffee."

"I'll have Camille brew some up right away."

"I'll watch."

***

The man knocked on the Lenkovitch residence, said he was from AT&T, showed his identification and said they were checking a series of line interferences. He asked if he could come in to check their line. Camille called Thaddeus.

He wasn't allowed in.

***

When the 'Bible study' group began arriving that evening. Ken and John were parked across the street in the van.

"They get anything off that tape?" Ken asked.

"Not much; they said it was masked and muffled too much, but what they did get is quite fascinating, especially the part at the end, it seems you may be right about that railing. Here, take a look." John handed Ken a single sheet of paper. On it was a series of incomplete sentences:

". . . .please close the. . . .behind. . . ."

"Yes Thaddeus, good night folks."

". . .are you convinced. . .genuine. . ."

"David. . . you hear me?"

"That's enough, leave the man. . ."

"I'm sorry Jennifer. . .have to know. . .

"Oh my God. . .We didn't know. . ."

". . .do you believe. . .God. . ."

"Thaddeus, no more, we know what we needed."

". . .when you go. . .you climb. . .railing at Niagara Falls. . ."

"Yes."

"What's going on here?" Ken asked. "What were they doing that Albright objected to? And what didn't they know that shocked her? 'Do you believe?' Believe what? 'When you go—you climb the railing,' that's pretty clear. That railing is involved in this some way. It must be a doorway of some kind. Have the office place twenty-four/seven surveillance on it." Anyone so much as spits at it, pull them in."

"Got it," John punched numbers into his cell phone, "maybe we should go inside and get to the bottom of this."

"Not yet, we need to know more first. We don't have a warrant or an imminent threat to justify one. Let's be patient. Our man couldn't get in to plant any more bugs, but at least we have the remote phone tap. This time we'll find out what's going on in there."

Chapter Eight

A rriving early, Allen pulled Thaddeus aside.
"A while back, I was on a project for the Department of Defense, and I discovered that my meetings had been recorded without my knowing it. It upset me immensely, and I insisted that I wanted to witness their devices removal. They informed me they hadn't used any devices but had set up a listening station using the handset of my telephone. It acts like a microphone, and no one has to come in to do anything. They can do it all remotely."

"Can they do that with a cellphone too?"

"I don't know, but I don't see why not."

Thaddeus nodded, "Okay, pass the word, everyone turn their cell phone off or, better yet, leave it in their cars." He walked to the small writing desk in the corner of the room, where an old style, rotary phone sat with a handset in its cradle. It was hardwired to a connection box on the wall. He yanked the wire from the wall.

Jennifer wondered if they should meet elsewhere, but Thaddeus again rejected the idea. The government has too many ways to listen, and their best bet was to keep one location clean. He feared the agents would grab David if he left the building.

Thaddeus had met with the agents earlier that day, giving them an edited version of what had occurred the night before. He told them David was beginning to feel comfortable, and they were making progress."

"How did that go over?" Allen asked.

"Well, one agent, Rosino, wasn't happy. He wants David, but the other one, Rodgers, is willing to work with us. Luckily, he's the one in charge."

"What about their listening in on us, any indication?" Alex asked.

"They didn't let on, but based on the questions they asked and on one weird thing they wanted, I don't think they're hearing much."

"What did they want?" Allen asked.

"They insisted on seeing David, to prove he is here."

"Where did they think he was?"

"I don't know, but they said they would exercise a warrant if they didn't see him."

"What'd you do?"

"I told them, he would be in the upper window five minutes after they left."

"What happened?"

"I stood in the window and gave them the 'official' salute," David said.

"We have to do something to keep them at bay. Let's talk later," Allen said.

***

Once everyone was settled in, sipping Camille's tea (David cradled a cup of black coffee), and with Beethoven performing loudly, Thaddeus spoke.

"Before we proceed, we need to clear the air. If David's going to sit at our table, he needs to trust us, so I told him what happened last night and apologized for it. We had no right to intrude into his personal life as we did."

Jennifer and Allen echoed Thaddeus's sentiments, voicing their apologies. It didn't make David feel any better about them. They had peeled a layer of his inner self away and saw something they had no right to see, something not even David wanted to see.

"I'm sorry if we offended you, Mr. Kincaid," Barosh said, "but I'm not sorry for what we did. The stakes are too high, and I, for one, needed to know the things we asked."

"I agree," Alex added.

When Thaddeus had made his confession that morning, David had wanted to leave, and take his chances with the thugs outside, even turn them loose on these nerds. Giving him a truth serum certainly was not legal, and the government would make mincemeat of them.

But it would be even worse for him, out there. They would probably drug him too, and they wouldn't apologize for it, all in the name of national security. He had nothing to tell them, but if they believed he did, to what lengths would they go? Waterboarding, like at Gitmo? *No, they wouldn't go that far—would they?* For right now, he was better off with the nerds, at least until he knew what was going on.

"As I understand it," he said, "your little venture into I-Spy 101 gave you nothing more than what I've been telling you from the beginning: I don't know anything about travelling in time."

He paused and watched as Jennifer nodded agreement, but the others only stared back.

"So, if I'm not a time traveler, and did not write those tablets—who did?"

"But David, who said you didn't write them?" It surprised him it was Allen who spoke.

"You did! Your illegal interrogation proved I didn't do it."

Allen answered meticulously, measuring every word as if listing the factors of a mathematical equation, "That's correct. . .it proved. . .you. . . didn't do it. . .yet."

David was stunned, "Yet? What's that supposed to mean? You still think I did it?"

"No. . .we think you. . .will do it."

"But, you said you believed me that I don't have a time machine."

"That's true; we believe you have no such device."

"Yet, you think somehow I came here from two-thousand years ago?"

"No, we believe you came here from now, but you're going to go back to two-thousand years ago."

"You do, do you? You actually believe I'm going back in time two-thousand years? Well, you know what I believe? I believe you are all nuts; that's what I believe! Just how am I supposed to do this magical trick, and why would I, anyway?" David asked, laughing at them. "I cannot believe this, of all people, scientists and Ph.D.'s', believing in Hocus Pocus. You've been watching too many 'Star Trek' reruns and need to get a grip on reality."

"Reality? What's reality David?" Allen asked as if talking to a child. "Reality is that anything is possible. That's the first thing you need to accept. A 'magical trick' you call it? What's magic? Show a native, in the jungles of the Amazon, a small box that has moving pictures and talking people inside of it, and they will make you a god and worship you. They'll call it magic; we call it, a cell phone. Not magic, David. . .reality."

He paused, with a slight smile gained from many years of lectures, "We must not be so arrogant to think we know all there is to know in this world, or beyond. That has been man's biggest mistake through the ages. Every generation thinks they've reached the limit of knowledge in the world around them. Tell Christopher Columbus that one day he could fly across the Atlantic in hours, and he would have you burned at the stake. Magic is only what we don't understand. Reality, is that anything is possible. . .we just haven't gotten to it all, yet."

"But, traveling through time? That's the stuff of science fiction and. . ."

"And two-way wrist radios were the stuff of 'Dick Tracy' in the comic strips just a few years ago," Allen cut him off, "and today, they're obsolete. Like I said anything is possible, no—probable. Until you accept that, your mind remains locked. Look at what you've seen in your lifetime alone. Your laptop has computing power a hundred times greater than the best scientific computers of just a few years ago. Paradigm shifts occur constantly as knowledge and technology advances exponentially. Anything is possible. . .we just haven't gotten to it yet. That's reality David."

David looked around at the group, "You guys have built a time machine, haven't you? That's what this is all about, isn't it?"

"No, we have not built a time machine, and I honestly doubt if such a machine could be built," Allen answered, "but we may have found a time machine, and have figured out how to use it and how such travel was done."

David looked at him, confusion riddling his face, "Wait a minute. You doubt if one could be built, but you may have found one? That's an oxymoron. And you said 'how such travel was done'. By who? People have traveled in time?"

"We don't have all the answers David, but what we're certain of, is that intelligent beings have traveled across dimensions beyond our present states of awareness and knowledge."

"Man, talk about double talk. 'Intelligent beings'? 'Dimensions'? What exactly are you saying? People appearing and disappearing into thin air? That's science fiction."

"Science. . .yes; fiction. . .no," Allen said, "It's not as fanciful as you may think. There are numerous renderings in every culture and race around the world of beings appearing and disappearing without explanation."

"Legends – myths—fables! Those are not real. They're just made up to explain things they didn't understand," David protested.

"Exactly!" Jennifer said, "And what is it, they didn't understand? Some event, some phenomenon that was beyond their knowledge and defied their reasoning. I think we've just come full circle, haven't we, David?" She smiled.

"The amazing thing about mythology and legends," Thaddeus said, "is how much is in common, regardless of the civilization or the era. People around the globe with no means of communication and at different stages of civilization have remarkable similarities and congruence of events running through them. The names may change, and the places and times vary, but the events and many details are the same. That's not coincidence."

"Wait a minute," David said, "if they couldn't understand what was happening, and had to create stories and myths in order to explain it, then how could they be doing it? Your logic is flawed."

"An excellent question, Mr. Kincaid," Alex spoke, for the first time. "Now you're getting to the root of the issue. If people are so primitive that something is beyond their comprehension, how then, could they have done it?" He looked around the group, satisfied that he had the floor.

"And the answer is the same then as it is today."

"And what's that?" David asked.

"Look at the technology we have today; airplanes, electricity, computers, or stay with Allen's cell phone. We use them daily, accepting them as a normal part of our life. Even five year olds have them. Yet, to those natives in the Amazon jungle, that phone is—magic." He held his hand out, with the palm up, "On one hand, a common device used by millions," he held out his other hand, "on the other—magic—both occurring at the same time in history. How does a jungle tribesman describe a jet he watches flying high in the sky over his piece of jungle, leaving a long plume behind it? He would see the gods flying across the heavens! Science and mythology occurring at the same time. I ask you, Mr. Kincaid, how can this be?"

"That's easy, different levels of technologies existing at the same time."

"Bingo."

"Not that fast. There weren't advanced technologies back then; everyone was primitive. Maybe one was in the Bronze Age while another was in the Iron Age, but that's not on the same level you're talking about. We know what the technological levels of the ancient civilizations were."

"Do we?" Alex smirked. "Do we know how primitive Egyptian people, living in mud huts, having none of today's construction, engineering or transportation technology, built the pyramids; when today with all our knowledge and equipment—we can't reproduce them?" Alex was animated and began pacing while words gushed from him like water from a ruptured pipe.

"Or do we know how they positioned them in the desert to be mathematically precise within centimeters, in full alignment with the earth's coordinates, when they did not even know the earth had coordinates? And I haven't scratched the surface yet, my friend. Not only the pyramids of Egypt. There are similar mysteries all across the globe. Do we know how Stonehenge was built and laid out so precisely? Do we know how the Mayans, on the other side of the world, built and constructed pyramids in the same mathematical alignment as the Egyptians did, when they didn't know each other existed? Or how they constructed a calendar more accurate than ours today? These were primitive people who didn't know the earth was round or about orbits and rotations. Do we know how the massive designs and zoomorphic figures on the mountains of Peru were made? Figures that are perfect, but can only be seen from high in the sky? I could go on and on, Mr. Kincaid; there are hundreds of things that are right in front of our eyes that we do not understand how or why they got there."

"In truth, we know remarkably little about the history of our world," Thaddeus said. "We like to think we do, but we build our knowledge on a few names from the past and the events surrounding them. Alexander the Great. . .Adolf Hitler. . .Napoleon. While this is not wrong, it excludes other information and facts that we conveniently dispose of in the wastebasket labeled, 'mythology and religion'."

"Are you suggesting there were advanced societies in ancient times, co-existing with primitive ones?"

"What we're saying," Allen replied, "is there is indisputable evidence that, throughout history, there's been an advanced society that has influenced, directed and controlled emerging civilizations across the globe."

"The aliens visited earth theory," David smirked, "'2001 – A Space Odyssey'. Nothing new there."

"Just because there are movies about these theories, doesn't change the evidence or answer the questions that still exist," Jennifer rebuffed. "We watch a movie; therefore, we close the book on the subject?"

David turned to Barosh, "You believe this stuff Rabbi? How does it equate with your faith and beliefs? Was God an alien?"

"Are you kidding?" Alex jeered before Barosh could respond, "God is the perfect definition of an alien. An intelligent being from outer space having supernatural powers."

Barosh gave Alex a worn look, "Are you finished Alex? I'd like to answer David's question if that's okay with you."

Alex nodded his head, "By all means Rabbi, proceed."

"No, David, God is not an alien from the plant Xylon or any other such place. But, 'aliens' may very well have come from God; only we call them 'angels' or 'messengers.' The Tanakh has many examples of the patriarchs and the prophets seeing visions of strange beings coming and going, many times from the heavens. Jacob wrestled with an angel; Abraham ate lunch with three such beings; Ezekiel witnessed them, and Elijah ascended with them. Enoch was taken and never died. In Judeo-Christian literature, they're called 'angels'; 'Nephilim'; 'holy ones'; 'the children of heaven' or the 'sons of God'. Some were good; some were bad. There's no contradiction, only different names."

"In Europe they called them 'Grigori'," Alex added. "The Celtics called them 'fairies'; the Irish referred to the 'Tuatha de Danaan' – 'the shining ones'. In Scotland they were called 'sidhe'. The Germans called them 'Alfs', and the Norsemen—'Loki' and 'Fenri'. And it doesn't end there; Hindu and Buddhist myths refer to the 'Asua' and Persian lore designates a class of divinity called 'Ahura Mazda' 'those who came from the sky'. Native Americans refer to the spirits and the ancient ones who fly through the heavens. The Hopi Indians say the 'Kachinas' came down and showed them how to build their civilization. The Babylonians, Greeks, Chinese. . . we could go on and on. All claim that their civilizations were started by beings appearing from nowhere."

"There are many theories and beliefs," Thaddeus added, "some believe the alien theory; others adhere to a religious belief of angels. In our group, we do not impose our personal beliefs on one another. Which way one leans doesn't change the fact that, within primitive societies, extraordinary accomplishments, completely outside the realm of possibility, were achieved, with someone or something either doing them or lending a helping hand along the way."

"Beings appear and disappear, bringing knowledge and abilities to different civilizations," Jennifer added, "and the deeper you dig, the greater the similarity of events, histories and even names becomes evident. It is amazing how the physical descriptions of those beings are identical or similar across the face of the globe from people who never knew the other existed."

"And those are the ones we know about," Allen added.

"What does that mean?" David asked.

"We're limited by our dimensions," Allen said. "We exist in three spatial dimensions, width, length and depth. We understand and can explain things in these dimensions with ease but find it impossible to understand anything in a fourth, fifth or higher dimension."

Seeing the confusion on David's face, he explained.

"Think if you lived in a one-dimensional world, consisting of length only. There is no such thing as a second or third dimension, meaning nothing has any width or depth. Everything around you would be a flat line, varying in length. Now, if a being from a three-dimensional world entered your one-dimensional world, you would only see a line—a slice of the three dimensional being. For example, if it was a three dimensional pyramid, all that would be seen would be a line, the length of which would vary dependent on where along the height of the pyramid, you saw it. We would never be able to visualize it as a pyramid, only as a series of different length lines and would never understand it. The "scientists" of your world would reject it as not being real. They would debunk it, laugh at it, and it would be folly for us to believe in a universe consisting of three dimensions. Well, that is exactly what happens when we talk about a fourth or fifth dimension. Yet, it is proven they exist."

David looked at Barosh, but before he could ask, Barosh answered his question, "God is the creator of all dimensions—He consists of dimensions far beyond our comprehension."

"Okay, I follow that, but what does this have to do with those tablets and – with me?"

"There are other dimensions we have not discussed yet," Allen said.

"Time?" David asked.

"Yes, time; intelligent beings, traveling back and forth through a temporal dimension known as time." Allen answered.

"Having a common purpose, and working with the civilizations on earth, through the ages, to achieve that purpose," Alex added.

"And that purpose is what?"

"That's a subject of much debate," Allen said. "One person's opinion is as good as another's. We disagree among ourselves what that purpose is, but one thing we all agree on is that they exist."

"Then why aren't they here now?"

Alex shrugged his shoulders, "Who knows that they're not?"

Silence cloaked the table while David absorbed what had been said. These were not stupid or ignorant people. They are some of the most intelligent, educated and well-connected people in society. They create the latest technology and sciences. They weren't some Hollywood morons creating aliens or fallen angels, or traveling through time using special effects, to make a buck. They're the world's leading scientists, moving outside the boundaries of arbitrary constraints.

"Okay, let me see if I can sum this up; there was—or is—some race of intelligent beings from someplace—or another, who existed—or exist—at some time—or another, who had—or have—super powers and abilities and knew—or know—how to travel across time; and you think you've discovered how they did it. Do I have that right?"

"Pretty much," Allen answered.

"Have you tried it yet?"

"No," Allen said.

"So, I take it that's where you think I come in?"

"Yes, that is where we think you may come in."

Chapter Nine

"Listen folks, I don't know what you think you've found or what you're planning, but let's not have any misunderstanding; I'm not going to be a guinea pig in whatever crazy scheme you're hatching, so just get any idea you have of putting me into a test tube out of your minds."

"No one is going to make you do anything David," Thaddeus assured him, "whether by fate, destiny or just pure coincidence, you're part of the group, and what involvement you have will be strictly your choice."

"Whoa! Hold it, right there; I am not part of this group. I do not belong here. I don't know how my name got dragged into this, but I'll tell you this—if there was a rail line to the year zero making stops every hundred years along the way—I ain't riding that train."

"I told you he doesn't belong," Alex said. "We're wasting valuable time. We should send him away."

"Just wait a minute Alex, we shouldn't. . .," Thaddeus was cut short by Barosh.

"No, Alex is right; if Mr. Kincaid is going to be a part of this, then he needs to decide that." He looked at David, "I understand it's a lot to digest and I'm sorry it's coming at you so abruptly, but whether this is destiny, or just a weird coincidence, we do not have the luxury to wait while you figure it out."

"I agree," Allen said, "we need to complete preparations and time is moving 'pun intended'. David, we need to know if you're on board or not."

David looked at the faces around the table. Each stared back, expressionless.

"With all due respect folks, it *is* a lot to digest, and I don't even know what being 'on board' means. You brought me here, remember? So, indulge me a little before you 'send me away' to those wolves outside. You owe me that."

Taking their silence as consent, he turned to Allen.

"You said you have figured out how time travel was done by these super beings, whoever they were, right?"

He paused, and Allen nodded,

"But you have not tried it yet, and it sounds like you're getting ready to, right?"

Again, the nod of the head.

"And you wonder if I may be part of whatever you're planning? How am I doing so far?"

"Keep going," Allen said.

"And the only reason I'm here is because somehow my name got put on a tablet from 2000 years ago, and you think the person who wrote that name was none other than yours truly?"

"It is the most logical answer," Allen said.

"So, you're expecting I'll go back in time to the dark ages."

"Actually," Barosh gave a hollow laugh, "a little further—to the time of the Roman Empire."

"Okay, why me? Why am I the chosen one? Is it because I can speak Hebrew and Greek?"

"Maybe you can speak Hebrew and Greek because you were chosen," Barosh said.

"What the devil does that mean?" David flared. "I learned those languages because I was chosen to learn them? By someone from two-thousand years ago? No, I made the choice to learn them—me, not some "spaceman" who built the pyramids."

"There're many things we don't understand David," Barosh replied. "Sometimes the answers lie hidden, and we can't see them through the turbulence." He held out his closed hand to David; opening it —inside was the tablet from two-thousand years ago.

Staring at him, in Greek, was the phrase spoken by the quiet voice, when he confronted the swirling waters of Niagara:

beneath the turbulence – peace is found

A sledgehammer slammed him squarely between the eyes. Was it possible? A thought put into his head from two-thousand years ago— by himself?

"Someone, long ago, knew that one day, you'd need a message. And that message had to come from a one hundred percent reliable source; someone who knew your state of mind when you climbed that railing. That someone sent you a message telling you where your peace was to be found, and it's not in the waters of Niagara Falls."

Barosh placed the tablet on the table.

"That someone was. . .you. You were chosen; I don't know why or by whom, but you were."

David looked beseechingly into Barosh's eyes, "Chosen for what?"

"To find the proof," Jennifer said.

"Proof? Proof of what?"

"Proof of whether or not Jesus Christ was the Son of God," Allen said.

"What? I'm supposed to prove that Jesus was God?"

"No. . .to prove whether he was or was not the Son of God."

"But, I don't even believe in God."

"So?" Jennifer shrugged. "There're five different opinions about that sitting at this table. We're not doing this because we have a predetermined outcome, David. We're not religious fanatics out to prove Jesus was God or a group of atheists out to prove there is no God. No, this is beyond personal beliefs. Each of us is following a path that appears to have been predetermined. Most of us didn't know one another two months ago. None of this was planned by us, and we don't know what the outcome will be. I daresay we were all chosen, although perhaps not as obviously as you."

David thought for a minute, and then looked at the five scientists.

"You know I'm an atheist. In light of what you just said, I'd like to know what each of you do believe, and who you think is doing this choosing you're talking about."

"There's no point in. . .," Alex protested, but Allen cut him off.

"No, that's only fair. Seeing what the stated mission of our group is, David has every right to know where we stand on the subject. As he stated, we owe him that."

Turning to David, he opened his hands, "I believe there is a higher intelligence that is directing us, and that intelligence is the ultimate authority of the universe. The universe holds too much order, system and wonder to have just randomly begun and exist on its own. Whether it's Genesis or the 'big bang', I don't know, but somewhere there's something that started it all and keeps it wound like a Swiss clock. I resist being labeled as being this or being that, I only know I look forward to the day when it will be revealed to me what that intelligence is."

"Well, it's obvious where I stand," Barosh jumped in, "there is one true God, from where all has come. As far as Yeshua is concerned, (Jesus the world calls him), I believe he was a man, a prophet even, although one who went astray. He is not the messiah he claimed to be. And I believe God is guiding us to expose his charade that has deceived the world for two thousand years."

"As for me," Thaddeus spoke up, "I've seen too many gods, too many beliefs and too much religion from too many civilizations, to know what's true and what's not. I'd classify myself as an agnostic. I don't know if there's a true god or if he's the invention of human minds to answer those questions that plague humans. As for Jesus, until that tablet was found, I hardly gave him a thought, just one more figure from the past among so many," he slowly shook his head. "And I have no idea if we're chosen for this task or not, but it certainly is suspicious."

"Rubbish," Alex barked, "the evidence is clear. There is a race of super intelligent beings that came to this planet from somewhere, thousands of years ago. Mankind and civilization are the result of their experimentations." He looked at Barosh, "If anything, Jesus was an alien and it's these aliens who are directing our activities, probably to restore their place amongst us."

"That begs the question of where did these aliens come from?" Barosh interjected, "That theory leaves open the existence of. . . ."

"That's enough! We don't dispute or debate another's beliefs or opinions," Thaddeus scolded. Barosh nodded while Alex looked amused.

Only Jennifer remained.

"I believe there is a dimension of existence beyond our senses, and that dimension embodies our definition of god. It's the same dimension or spirit across all the different religions, peoples and times; just called by different names. Someday we'll put our differences aside and embrace this spiritual dimension as the god of all religions and all people. Jesus was a good man, a holy man, but no different than other holy men, such as Confucius or Buddha."

David looked from one face to another. Despite their wide range of opinions and beliefs, he saw openness to discovering the truth. He thought it was particularly intriguing that none of them claimed to be a Christian follower of Jesus.

"Well, one thing is clear; the outcome isn't predetermined."

Light chuckles and smiles followed. Then Barosh asked, "David, we understand you are an atheist, and no one here questions or challenges that, but I wonder if you would mind telling us why?"

"I don't mind," David said. "I don't see where God is relevant in today's world. He doesn't fit. He was a creation of mythology and superstition by primitive minds, to fill in those huge questions Thaddeus mentioned; "Where did I come from?" "What are the stars?" "Why does it storm?" "Why is my baby sick?" And the granddaddy of them all, "What happens when I die?" But, science is filling in those gaps, one by one. Evolution explains how life began. Physics explains matter, and astronomy explains what the stars are. Everything you've said tonight supports this. God was invented to answer the things people didn't understand. Religion is something that only causes dissension and trouble between people. And it's all about where we happened to be born. Our parents went to this church; therefore we go. If we had been born on the other side of the world, or even just down the street, we'd be believing in a different god or going to a different church."

"There're lots of religions in the world," he continued, "and they speak nice words of love and acceptance, but they all hate one another; fighting and killing to see whose god is the toughest. I find it hard to believe it still goes on, when science has proven it's nothing but myths. And how is the Christian God so superior, above human emotions, when he sends people to a fiery hell for eternity! Talk about carrying a grudge!"

"Ah, the gospel according to science," Barosh sighed. "I'd be cautious about putting all my eggs in one basket, my friend; science may not have all the answers you seek."

"Thank you David," Allen said, giving Barosh a look of rebuke. "As you can see, we each hold different beliefs, so we appreciate your openness and willingness to share yours with us."

"Who would care for a refill?" Thaddeus asked. "Camille has prepared some fresh tea, along with some delicious scones."

"I'll stick with coffee," David said.

***

"With all the people in history who've affected life down through the ages—why choose Jesus?" David asked, after settling in with a fresh cup of coffee. "Why not Confucius or Buddha as Jennifer implies? In fact, why stay with a religious figure at all? Why not Alexander the Great? Socrates? Or Albert Einstein? Or even those ancient beings you claim are responsible for everything? Go right to the heart of it, if you're going to go at all?"

"That's a good question David," Thaddeus answered, "and there are two answers. First, if you examine history, there is no other person who has had a greater impact, good or bad, upon mankind than Jesus of Nazareth. I challenge you to find one. There have been more religions, more discoveries and, unfortunately, more wars, more unrest, more human suffering and death, resulting from those few years he walked the earth than from any other person in history. Determining the proof of whether he was or was not the Son of God would be the most significant event in human history and would have far more impact around the world, than any of the others you named. He claimed to actually be God."

"Okay, I can buy that. What's the second reason?"

Everyone looked at Allen.

"We don't have a choice in the matter," he answered, lowering his eyes.

"Why not?"

"As I said earlier, we are new at this and only beginning to learn and understand the science. While we've pieced together how time travel was done by the ancients, we haven't figured out how they controlled it," he sighed. "It's not as easy as Hollywood makes it look with dialing in a year on some chronometer and pressing a button on the mad scientist's time machine."

"I don't understand," David said.

"We're stuck with what year it falls on, and that year happens to be 30 CE," Allen replied.

David scanned the faces around the table before staring at the deep mahogany grain of the table. Finally, he looked up and nodded.

"Okay, you got me hooked; how did 'they' travel through time?"

Allen glanced around the table; Jennifer and Thaddeus both nodded their heads; Barosh opened his hands and shrugged. Allen looked at Alex, waiting for a sign. Alex stared at David for a long minute before giving a single nod of his head.

"Okay, let's show you what we have," Allen said.

Chapter Ten

Allen began talking, spinning theory and science in a dizzying spiral. His voice was relaxed and comfortable as if giving a well-polished lecture to a freshmen class at MIT. But it was also fragmented and fumbling as if talking to a student who did not belong in the class. David had the sense he was trying to condense a lifetime of teaching and research into a few concepts that David could comprehend.

"Ever since I was a boy, growing up in Kansas, I've been fascinated by the concept of time travel. I used to trudge down the dirt road and wish I could push a button and instantly be where I was going. You know, like in 'Star Trek'—*Beam me up, Scotty*?" It was during those long walks that I realized I was traveling in time. My trips were measured, not only in miles, but also in minutes. The school was a mile and a half, or twenty-one minutes away. Every minute that passed was time travel, and from that day on I was obsessed with it."

"In school, I found I could do a little math and devoted myself to understanding Einstein's theories of space, time and relativity."

"Could do a little math!" Jennifer interrupted. "Allen is too modest, David. He was a child prodigy in mathematics and physics. He had his Master's degree before most boys were out of puberty, and he earned his Doctorate in "Negative Energy" at the ripe old age of twenty-one. He's authored four books, none of which did he write, but are compilations of his notes and findings that are considered the *holy grail* of the emerging science of "Quantum Physics".

Allen raised his hand in protest, "Jennifer, please, you embarrass me." He turned back to David, "When I began my work, time travel was considered scientific heresy, and I avoided talking about it for fear of being dismissed as a fringe scientist by my colleagues. As you said, it was the stuff of science fiction. Today, it's accepted as fact and is a fundamental principal of space travel."

"Largely due to your work," Jennifer chimed. Allen ignored her.

"Time travel is not that hard to understand. We're engaged in it all the time. In its most basic, time is the rate of change in the universe. It's an ongoing, never-ending process. The universe moves, planets rotate and orbit, things fall apart. Nothing remains the same; all is in constant change, which means all is in constant movement; in relation to time. Everything is about dimensions and those things that impact them, meaning space, acceleration and gravity. In our current state of awareness, we have three dimensions in the physical world—height, width and length. Time is a temporal dimension, one that we can't see, touch or smell, but which we can measure. For example, our time on this earth is measured in years, and the earth is measured in many thousands of years."

"Although we measure the passage of time as a constant rate, using seconds, minutes, hours and years, this does not mean time moves at a constant rate. Just as, water in a river, rushes or slows depending on the breadth and depth of the channel, time flows at different rates in different places. In other words, time is relative, and our measurement of it, is relative. To travel to the store, we measure it in minutes; but we don't travel at the same speed the entire trip. Everything has not only a measure in physical space, but also in time space, as well. Time travel is nothing more than travelling through this dimension. It all comes down to the relationship between time and space. Time cannot exist without space, and space cannot exist without time. The two exist as one: the space-time continuum. Any event that occurs in the universe has to involve both space and time."

"I understand traveling in time and the physical dimensions together, but how can someone travel in one dimension without traveling in the other dimension?" David asked.

"Excellent David, and that's the heart of the matter, isn't it?" Allen smiled. "Einstein proved that traveling forward in time was possible. His relativity theory set the speed of light as the universal speed limit and showed that distance and time are not absolutes but instead are affected by one's motion. This has been proven with space travel and our GPS system. The satellites travel at a different rate than we do here on earth and adjustments have to be continually made, or everything goes out of kilter. As you approach the speed of light, you travel faster in time. Science fiction writers have had a field day with this, stories about astronauts aging a few weeks while back on earth, decades have passed."

He paused to refill his teacup. "So, as you can see, time travel into the future is easy, all you have to do is travel really fast," he chuckled, taking a sip of tea and nodding his head in satisfaction, "Excellent as always, Thaddeus, my compliments to Camille."

"But traveling back in time, now that's a different story all together. Remember, we're not in space; we're here, on Earth. How do we travel through time going backwards when we're anchored to the gravitational field of the earth, which limits our ability to change the speed of travel?" He paused, allowing the question to take hold.

"Einstein's theory of Relativity does not allow for travel into the past. In order to consider it, the laws of space and time must be revised by a set of new laws of physics that change the rules. Now, we cannot just arbitrarily go around changing the laws of physics, but we've found that we can in the case of Quantum physics of microscopic randomness. When we get down to that level, the universe is jumpy and discontinuous, and it's unknown how gravity behaves. There are a number of theoretical possibilities, such as traveling faster than the speed of light, finding black holes, cosmic strings, or Alcubierre drives, etc., but each of these have substantial hurdles to overcome." He paused, "How are you doing?"

"Okay. I don't understand the science behind what you're saying, but I grasp the concepts."

"Good, of course, you're an engineer. Let me continue then. Nothing is smooth or solid. If you look closely enough, you'll find holes and wrinkles in everything. It's a fundamental physical principle. On the sub-atomic level, these openings are vast and are comparable to the distances between stars and planets on the universal level. This is true, not only in our three physical dimensions, but also in the time dimension. There are tiny crevices, wrinkles and voids in time. Down at the smallest of scales, smaller than molecules and atoms, we get to a state called quantum foam, where tiny tunnels or shortcuts through space and time form. The bottom line is that space and time collapse, and time travel could be achieved using Einstein-Rosen bridges. You've probably heard of them as wormholes."

"Wormholes? Yes, I have, but I thought that was strictly a science fiction buzzword."

"Oh, they're real. Research clearly shows they exist, shortcuts through space, connecting two distant points in time, at an instantaneous intersection. Einstein's general theory of relativity allows for their existence since it states that any mass curves in time-space. To understand this, think of two people holding a bed-sheet between. . .wait a second. Thaddeus, would you hold up your dinner napkin by two corners of one side?"

Thaddeus did as instructed.

"Now Jennifer, take hold of the opposite two corners and stretch it out between you. Yes, that's it, good." He walked over to the professor's desk and picked up a baseball sitting in a small cradle on the desk.

"Hey, be careful, that's Mickey Mantle's fiftieth home run ball from nineteen-sixty-one and the famous "M&M" battle to beat Ruth's record," Thaddeus cautioned.

"Don't worry Professor; we won't send it into space. Now, if I place this baseball on the napkin, it will roll to the middle of the napkin, causing the fabric to sink down at that point." He placed the ball next to Jennifer's finger, and it rolled to the center of the cloth, forming a depression.

"In this simplified demonstration, time is depicted as a two-dimensional plane (the napkin). Imagine the napkin is folded in half, and it was possible to have a ball on that side also with gravity in reverse pushing a ball up similar to the ball on the top pushing down. The two balls would meet in the middle. This is similar to how a wormhole might develop. If the wormhole were large enough, a marble could move to the wormhole and pass through to the other side. Instead of traveling the dimensional length of the napkin on both sides, you could travel from one spot on the napkin to another in an instant."

He replaced the baseball in its cradle.

"Safe and sound professor and thank you both. Now, here's how a proposed time machine could work: one end of the wormhole is accelerated to some significant fraction of the speed of light and is then brought back to the point of origin. Another way would be to take the entrance of the wormhole and move it to within the gravitational field of an object that has higher gravity at the other entrance, and then return it back to its original position. In both of these methods, time dilation causes the end of the wormhole that has been moved to have aged less than the stationary end. This means that a traveler entering the accelerated end would exit the stationary end in backwards time."

"But, you said earlier, you doubted a time machine could be built?"

"I did, and I do. Notice I said this is how a *"proposed"* time machine *"could"* work. Among problems with the laws of physics, a significant limitation of such a mechanism is that it would only be possible to go back in time to the initial creation of the machine. No, I do not believe such a device could be built, but we know wormholes exist. Therefore, the key to time-travel is threefold; one—find a natural wormhole, or shall I call it a gateway; two—know when it will open long enough and large enough to pass through; and thirdly, overcome gravity to be able to pass through the gateway."

"Sounds overwhelming."

"Indeed. Those are formidable obstacles to overcome," Allen said.

"So, what are we doing here, if we can't overcome those obstacles?"

Allen smiled, "David, who said we can't?"

Chapter Eleven

"So, I guess that means you've found a wormhole, and you're looking for an 'Alice' to crawl into the rabbit hole," David said. "Is that what *"being on board"* is about?"

"We believe we know where and when a gateway will open," Allen corrected him, "but we're not looking for anything. When Thaddeus found that tablet with your name on it, you came to us. We're not looking for an 'Alice' as you so harshly put it, to crawl into a rabbit's hole."

David looked at him with bewilderment, "Wait a minute; I didn't come to you! You brought me here, remember? Everything you people have done was to get me to be your guinea pig. Smooth talking me to do this thing for you. For crying out loud, you even drugged me!"

"No, you're mistaken about that, Mr. Kincaid; we have no intention of smooth talking you into anything," Alex spoke sternly, "you can leave anytime you want. You just happened to pop up. What we're doing, if anything, is helping to facilitate what you're going to do."

"Facilitate me? That's the craziest thing I've ever heard of! Facilitate me? To go back in time? Excuse me, was I out there, trying to thumb a ride back to the Roman Empire? I've never wanted to go anywhere in time, in my life, and I still don't."

"You're missing the point David," Allen said, "history has a record that you did go back and wrote those tablets; therefore, you will. You cannot prevent something you already did. You can't change history."

"You're telling me, I have no control over this? That's crazy. I could get up and walk out right now if I choose to. Or what if I went back and decided not to write any tablets? Then what? That would blow your whole theory." David demanded, confused and annoyed.

"David, you just don't understand, it's not a theory. The tablets are real. You will write them because history shows that you did," Allen replied. "You can walk out of this building forever, or you can go back in time determined you won't write anything—but one way or another, you will, because you already did."

"But I didn't, so how can I have done it already?

"You haven't done it yet David—but you will, therefore, you did."

"What kind of circular logic is that? You actually believe I'm going to go along with whatever scheme you're hatching? That I don't have any say in this? That it's destiny in which I have no will of my own?"

"This is time in reverse, not forward, David. It's okay to say you won't do something tomorrow that you haven't done, but you can't say you won't do something yesterday that you already did."

"But. . . ."

Thaddeus placed his hand on David's shoulder, "David, calm down; whatever you do, will be of your own doing, not ours or anyone else's. I don't know about these things; all I know is we're presented with choices in life, and we make them. If it turns out that the choices I make were already predestined, then what is that to me? I wasn't forced into making them; they were still my choices, which I made of my own free will, even if someone knew what I was going to choose. You can put yourself in the loony bin if you allowed yourself to dwell on it, so why beat yourself up over it?"

"We make our destinies by our choices," Barosh added, "God has a plan for each of us, and we make choices as we go along to either follow that plan or not. It appears that you made a choice at some point to have gone back in time. Now, that may not be at this time. Others may forge a path that you'll come along and follow at some other time. Maybe you'll get locked up by Homeland Security for five years and make that choice after they release you. We're not going to make you do anything. However it happens; the proof remains you made such a decision at some point in your life, and you did, in fact, go back in time."

He looked at David, and smiled, "And, it also proves one other thing, David."

"What's that?"

"That you're not going to climb the railing overlooking the Niagara River anytime soon."

"Your confusion is valid David," Allen said, "this is a subject there is much debate about. Theories of time travel are riddled with questions and puzzles about fate and paradoxes. Compared to other studies in physics, time is not understood well, and time travel confounds even the best of minds. Philosophers have been theorizing about the nature of time since the era of the ancient Greek philosophers and earlier."

"Much earlier," Alex added, "thousands of years before Greek philosophy, time travel was an advanced science, and there was extensive knowledge regarding it, not only in Egypt, but in many parts of the world." He shook his head sadly, "Unfortunately, most has been lost or destroyed. Do not ever think our knowledge of history is complete; we know little of what actually happened on this planet."

"Anyone who studies the nature of time travel," Allen continued, "cannot help but question and theorize about its philosophical implications. There are many in the scientific community who believe that time travel into the past, even if the technology were available, is impossible due to paradoxes. Any theory that would allow time travel would first have to address the issue of causality. Do you know what I'm speaking of David?"

"No, not really."

"Stepping away from the science, let's take a look at the philosophical perspective. The premise of pushing a button and going back to yesterday violates the law of causality—cause and effect. One event occurs and leads to another. It's an endless one-way chain. In every instance, the cause occurs before the effect. There are no exceptions. Just try to imagine a different sequence, say for example, a murder victim dies of his gunshot wound before being shot. It violates reality as we know it. Thus, many scientists dismiss time travel into the past as an impossibility. They argue that the kind of time machine I described earlier would violate the fundamental principle that governs the entire universe - that cause happens before effect, and never the other way around. And, just so there's no misunderstanding, I firmly believe that law. Things that happened cannot make themselves un-happen. If they could, then there'd be nothing stopping the whole universe from unraveling and descending into chaos."

"How do you answer them, then?" David asked.

"Simple, they're wrong. What the skeptics fail to recognize is that something will always happen that prevents a time paradox from occurring."

"Just what is a time paradox?" David asked.

"Time paradoxes are philosophical time travel *"what ifs?"*, and have been a major theme in numerous science fiction books and movies regarding the subject. Robert Heinlein, Jules Verne and Isaac Asimov, to name a few, have popularized the idea of someone going back in time and doing something that changes history going forward. The adage of—if you could go back in time to assassinate Adolf Hitler and thereby prevent the destruction of fifty million people, would you? It sounds noble, and most people would say "yes" they would, but the question shouldn't be "would you"; rather, it should be "could you", and the answer is—no, you couldn't. You can't change what's already happened."

"Here's an example of a paradox, one that is widely debated. It's called the "grandfather paradox", and goes like this: a young man hates his grandfather and wants to kill him for whatever reason. But, his grandfather is already dead, so he builds a time machine and goes back in time to kill his grandfather. He meets him at a time before his father has been born, meaning the young man can't be born. What will happen? If he kills his own grandfather before his father is born, then he also will not exist, thus negating the entire sequence of events. We call this an 'inconsistent causal loop'."

"So, if the young man attempts to kill his grandfather, what will happen? Can he do it? Here is where the debate gets hot and heavy. Some believe, the instant he kills him, all time will unravel, and everything and everyone will disappear, like an enormous inverse "big bang" collapse. Others say the previous history will be erased, and a new history will begin. Still others believe there are parallel time dimensions and the former history will remain in one dimension and a new history will begin in a second, parallel dimension."

He paused and shook his head, "They're wrong, all of them. We're not multiple beings living multiple, parallel lives. We're distinct individuals. And history cannot just be ripped up and redone. What's happened—has happened, period, end of discussion."

"So what will happen?" David asked.

"It lies within the context of the word 'can'," Allen said. "Let's suppose the young man has a rifle, and it's a clear, calm day, and he has a straight shot at his grandfather with the crosshairs square on his head. Can he kill his grandfather? Considering the facts, it would appear that he *can* kill his grandfather. He can, but he doesn't, and he doesn't because he *can't*. These are not contradictions; they are both true given the relevant set of facts because it is logically impossible to change the past—an effect cannot occur without a cause."

"Then what would happen?" David asked again.

"I don't know, but something will. His gun may jam; a bird may fly in the way, or he'll slip on a banana peel just as he squeezes the trigger. I guarantee there will be some logical force in the universe that will interfere each and every time he tries to pull that trigger that will prevent him from killing his grandfather."

"Some philosophers answer the paradoxes by arguing that even if backwards time travel could be achieved, it would be impossible to change the past in any way." Alex said.

"And that is what we believe," Allen resumed. "Cause comes before effect, at least in this universe it does. There is a single fixed history which is self-consistent and unchangeable. Everything happens on a singular timeline which does not contradict itself. It's called the self-consistency principle, and it states that the historical timeline is totally fixed, and any action taken, by a time traveler, is actually a part of that timeline; so it is impossible for the time traveler to "change" history, in any way. In fact, the time traveler's actions may be the cause of the initial events, which leads to the potential for circular causation and the predestination paradox."

"Like my name written on a tablet from two-thousand years ago?"

"Precisely," Allen confirmed, "at some point in your future David, you will go back, and you will write those tablets because you did. When that time is may be of your choosing." He looked at David expectantly, "Unless that is; you didn't write those tablets, and someone else went back and wrote your name on them."

David looked down at the table, embarrassed, "I wish that were true, but no, it's not. No one could have written my thoughts on that second tablet; no one except me. Tell me, how is it that Thaddeus found those tablets, coincidentally while you were investigating time travel?"

"It wasn't a coincidence," Allen answered, "we weren't a group at the time, and in fact, it was the tablets that precipitated the group being formed. "

"That's correct," Thaddeus added, "When I uncovered the tablet, I contacted Alex, who I had worked with and known for many years, ever since sixty-nine when we worked together on a dig in Tel Aviv. Alex was particularly interested, and he asked if he could share the information with someone he'd been working with on a theory of his involving the pyramids and time travel. I agreed, and that's how Allen became connected."

"And," Allen added, "Jennifer was working with me on a possible means of passing through gateways in dimensional travel. We started communicating as a group and putting our notes together. When

Thaddeus announced that he had located you and was bringing you to Boston, we all took leave from our businesses to meet here." Allen looked around the table, "It is strange how we've come together, almost as if some higher intelligence is directing us. Individually, we had each uncovered a piece of the puzzle, which by themselves led nowhere, but when brought together, formed a picture beyond our wildest imagination. One that, I daresay, is putting us on the brink of revolutionary science, and maybe a total rewriting of history."

"I thought you said history couldn't be changed."

Allen chuckled, "Thank you, I stand corrected. A total rewrite of 'recorded' history is what I should have said. We're not going to change history, just set the record straight about what actually happened."

"So, since it appears my tablet is part of this puzzle, fill me in on the rest, please," David said. "What are these other pieces of the puzzle? Allen, you had said you'd located a wormhole, can we start there?"

"Other physicists and scientists call it a wormhole," Allen replied, "I prefer to call it a gateway. Understand David, we have a long way to go; there is much to learn; so what we are doing is crude and incomplete in the eyes of the ancient beings who used them. But we have to start someplace."

"Using the most powerful computers and modeling available, I could not produce a gateway. I could prove they existed and could calculate many things about them, such as the negative energy needed to hold one open, for example. But I had no idea how to locate one. It was Alex who discovered that piece of the puzzle and unraveled that mystery. Alex, would you care to enlighten David?"

Alex looked at David, his eyes boring into him, and when he spoke; his voice was like a steel chisel.

"No, I don't believe I would. Before we go any further with Mr. Kincaid, we need to know exactly where he stands with us. I think we've 'indulged' him long enough. He remains skeptical—that doesn't work with me. He indicated he would still take his life—that also does not work for me. It would not be wise for us to disclose anything further to someone who is not committed and is potentially unstable. Even if he walked away with no intention of saying anything, those people outside want to know what he knows, and they would get that information from him."

He turned to David.

"Do not be insulted by what I say, David; it's not personal. This is extremely serious for us, and I don't know if it is to you, but you've heard enough to decide what your connection is, and I don't intend for you to learn anything more until we know just what that is. If you remain skeptical, that is your choice, but then you should leave us now before you know any more. But for you to remain, I for one, need to know you're not a fly in the ointment."

Silence engulfed the table. David looked around and saw five expressionless faces looking back at him; no one raised an objection to Alex's mandate. Alex was right, he'd been skeptical from the beginning and even hostile to some degree (not that he didn't have a right to be, they'd drugged him for crying out loud), but he would feel the same if he were in their shoes. He'd been given an ultimatum. He needed to commit or to leave. Barosh broke the awkward silence that followed.

"It's been a long night, my friends; we've discussed much and I'm afraid we may have overwhelmed Mr. Kincaid. May I suggest we call it a night and allow him time to think things through?"

"Yes, I agree Barosh," Thaddeus said, "a good night's sleep is in order. Shall we plan on the same time tomorrow evening?"

"I suggest we meet earlier; we have much to do, and we've lost much time," Alex said. Then, turning to David, he added, "We have been open and divulged much to you, David."

"I have a lot to think about, but whatever I decide, I won't betray your confidence."

"Good, if I don't see you tomorrow then, I shall rely on your honor," Alex said, rising from the table.

"Shall we say seven o'clock?" Thaddeus offered. Everyone nodded and rose to leave.

On the way out, Allen asked Thaddeus in a low voice, "How is it going with your new friends across the street?"

"They seem to be patient with us. I think they're waiting to see what happens next, or if we try to make a run for it."

"Do you think they're hearing us?"

"I haven't found any more bugs, and no one has been allowed in, but who really knows?"

"We must be careful my friend; my office has gotten new inquires, and strange people are being seen where they never were before."

"Yes, that doesn't surprise me. The agents said they were checking us out. Once we know where David stands, it'll be time to play our hand."

"Let's hope they don't play theirs first."

Chapter Twelve

"AT&T confirmed the phone is disconnected from the inside," John said, "they sent a repairman, but he wasn't allowed inside."

"The old man yanked the wires," Ken said, "what about their cellphones?"

"They turn them off. Smarter than we thought they were. I got the transcript of what the techies were able to extract from last night's 'Bible study'. There's something going on. Here, read this stuff." He handed Ken the few pages of chopped up dialogue.

"...I'm going. . .two-thousand years. . . You're all. . . ."

"...a time machine. . . .built. . ."

"Sounds like there is a time machine, after all," Ken mused.

"Exactly. . .and what is it they didn't understand? . . . ."

". . .it's not only in Egypt. . .the pyramids. . . .leveled for miles. . . .millions. . . .missing. . ."

". . . .history. . . . .controlled. . . ."

". . .traveling back. . . .common purpose. . ."

"What are they talking about? I think the good professor's been holding back on us."

"Have you. . . .yet?"

"Have you what, yet? Have you drunk your tea yet, or have you planted a bomb yet? We have to know what they're talking about in there."

"I'm. . .part of. . . . I don't belong here. . . .dragged. . . . .hundred years. . ."

"Does that mean this David came to the present day, against his will from hundreds of years ago? By whom? Why? Who is this guy?"

"I agree. . .we have to know. . . . ."

". . . .send me away. . .super beings. . ."

"Chosen for. . ."

". . .authority directing us. . ."

". . .directing these activities. . . .restore their place. . . ."

". . . .a predetermined outcome. . . .you're going to go. . . ."

". . . .more wars. . . .and death resulting. . . ."

". . .pieced together. . . .pressing a button. . ."

"Who are these people they're talking about? *"Super beings"?* It's hard to judge their conversation with only these bits and pieces, but it's clear the professor and his cronies aren't what they pretend to be. There's another party involved that's looking to *"restore their place"*. Place in what? And just how does this Kincaid fit in? He sounds like an operative."

"We should bust in and get to the bottom of it," John said.

"No, they feel secure and are talking, and we don't want to shut that down."

"We could get the same information through interrogation."

"Maybe, maybe not, doesn't always work. Besides, our hands are tied since that Gitmo stuff went down."

". . .engaged in. . . . . .universe. . .things fall apart. . . .nothing. . .the same. . . ."

". . . .we're still on. . .Earth. . . .anchored to the. . . ."

"Be careful with that, Allen. . . .the great "M&M" battle."

"What was the 'M&M battle'? Can you find anything on that? And what was he touching? *'We're still on earth'*? I tell you John; this is downright creepy. Are these people from another planet?"

"Oh, it gets better. Keep reading," John taunted.

". . . .phantom energy. . .weighs less than. . . .anti-gravitational. . .violates. . .laws. . . .negative. . .energy would. . . ."

". . . .pushing space apart. . . .rip everything. . .ending every. . ."

"Whatever you do. . .we're following. . . forced. . .no control over. . . . fighting. . . ."

". . .we make our destinies. . .you made a choice. . .forge a path that. . .will follow. . . .in time. . ."

". . . to climb. . .that railing. . .soon."

"I want security increased on the whole group. Put a tail on each of them twenty-four/seven and have a full A-1 background performed, as well. I want to know everything there is to know about them. Every time they've spit and passed gas in the last twenty years. They're either planning something or else they're all a bunch of loonies."

"I still say we take them in."

"Who's the head man? What organization is it? Those are what's important, John. We need to know the top guys," he paused and added, "and, there's that railing again. Any activity going on out there?"

"Nothing, just ordinary tourists watching the Falls. Apparently, one poor sap tried to climb it to get a better look at the falls and had an accident in his pants when our two guys descended on him. Don't think he'll be climbing on things for a while."

"Look at this stuff, it's amazing," Ken said, reading.

"*. . .one event happens. . .and leads to. . .endless. . . .string of events. . .being shot. . . .they are wrong. . . .their minds. . . .to accept. . . .our ancestors. . . .governs the entire universe. . .never the other. . . .we firmly believe. . . .make themselves to un-happen. . .unraveling and descending into chaos. . . ."*

"This sounds like something out of Nostradamus! Who are these people?" Ken shook his head. "It's an old, dusty archeologist and a rabbi for crying out loud! Nothing in their backgrounds indicates anything like this. It just doesn't make sense—doesn't add up."

"There's still more chief, look at this:"

"*. . .someone going back. . .doing something that changes history. . ."*

"*. . .determined to go back and kill. . .regardless of the. . .when the bullet hits. . . .unravel and everything. . .will disappear. . .a new history will begin. . ."*

"*. . . there is a. . . .history, which. . . .part of history all along. . .the time traveler. . .cause of events. . .which leads to. . ."*

"*. . .higher intelligence is directing. . . beyond our wildest imagination. . . on the edge of. . .a total revision of history."*

"*It's been a long night. . .May I suggest we call it a night?"*

"*I won't betray your confidence."*

"*Good. . . .I shall rely on your honor. . ."*

"Have those tapes sent to Washington and let them listen to them. They have the best equipment for canceling out background interference. Let's see if they can make some sense out of this."

"On their way. What's next?"

"Time for a little chit-chat with our professor friend."

Chapter Thirteen

D avid couldn't sleep.
His head swirled, chasing images rising like mountains one instant and dissipating into fog the next. Everything was upside down, topsy-turvy. It was overwhelming—time travel—paradoxes—wormholes—all this science mixed with mumble jumbo.

Beneath flowed the waters of Niagara. Why had this happened to him? His mind had been made up, committed to what he was prepared to do. Then, overnight, he was Alice through the Looking Glass. He didn't want this.

All he longed for – was peace, to quiet the angry voices in his head. Why Nicole? She'd done no wrong. She was kind, loving and caring. She cried over injured birds and wept for stray puppies. She had made him whole, and she had been brutally plucked away—leaving him with an enormous emptiness.

He yearned for peace.

But, instead of that peace, a different *piece* had come—a piece of ancient clay. He didn't understand it; it made no sense and was straight out of the Twilight Zone. But understand it or not, it was here, and he had to decide what to do about it.

He wondered what the beautiful Ph.D.'s role was in this. She hadn't said much. Or Alex's for that matter. It was a strange mix of people, he thought. Whatever they were planning, apparently time was critical—it was going to happen soon.

He wondered about Homeland Security and how long they would keep sitting on the sidelines. What would they do when they made their move? *What can they do?* David thought. *I have nothing to give them that I haven't already told the professor and his group. But they won't believe me and will make life miserable in the meantime. Why me? I just want to be left alone so I can go on with my life.*

Go on with your life! The quiet voice said. *You wanted to end it!*

That's his choice, and his business—not yours! The loud voice said.

Beneath the turbulence –your peace will be found.

The words ran like a ticker tape across his mind. They would determine his future but which turbulence? Niagara's? Or Allen's?

Don't be stupid! You can't go back in time two-thousand years! The voice scolded.

Why not, just because you don't understand it? The quiet voice said.

Even if you could, you don't belong there.

You wanted to end your life. . .so why stay here? Why not find out? What do you have to lose?

The quiet voice was right—he had already rejected this world—had found it wanting at best and evil at worst. No one would miss him here; Nicole was gone, and he had no family.

Peace comes with answers—you'll find answers there. There are no answers in Niagara's waters.

A different time—a different place. If there were answers, maybe they were there.

What if you're wrong about God? The quiet voice continued. *What if he's real? Isn't it worth the time to find out? Maybe the man, Jesus can shed truth on that.*

The group had said they wanted to find the "proof" as to whether Jesus was a man or the Son of God. Isn't that a purpose to live for? To go back to that time, having today's knowledge and hindsight of what is written about him, would be the greatest purpose any person could have—whatever way it turns out.

Find the answers, David—and you'll find your peace.

"Yes," he said, "why not? I don't know what they're planning, but I want to know. I'm not ready to die—not just yet—I want to know."

Chapter Fourteen

C amille kept them outside while she fetched Thaddeus. While waiting, John's fingers felt along the bottom of the porch railing and left a little bump behind.

"Good morning gentlemen," Thaddeus said. "Sorry for the delay; how are you both today?"

"Shall we go in professor?" Ken asked.

"But of course, please follow me," Thaddeus ushered them into the parlor.

"Perhaps we should go into your study, where it would be more private," Ken suggested.

"Oh, this will be just fine," Thaddeus said, "please, make yourselves comfortable."

Thaddeus waited for them to settle into the large, overstuffed chairs.

"So, Agent Rodgers, what can I do for you today?"

"You know what we want, professor. Where are you with Kincaid?"

"Well, I believe we're making progress," Thaddeus answered.

"Don't play games with me, professor. I don't have the patience for it. I'm way out on a limb giving you this latitude. My people are growing increasingly impatient, and right now I'm the only one standing between you and the entire government coming down on you. So I suggest you think carefully about how you want to work with me."

"You're right, Agent Rodgers, and I truly appreciate your leadership. I have no intention of playing games with you; there's just not that much to report yet."

Ken didn't reply, waiting for Thaddeus to continue. John's fingers searched the chair for a hard surface that wasn't smothered by cushions.

"Mr. Kincaid swears he knows nothing about any time machine," Thaddeus said.

"How does he explain his name on those tablets?"

"He says he has no idea how his name came to be on them."

"Well, we know how to make him. . . .," John blurted out before Ken held up his hand, stopping him.

Thaddeus knew he needed to give them something. "But, he has said there is a thing called a 'timegate,' that is stepped through, like a doorway."

"Do you believe him?" Ken asked.

"Well, he's quite sincere, and he *was* climbing that railing."

"You think this 'timegate' is what he was going to step through at the railing?" Ken said.

"I do. I don't think he's the kind of person who would take his own life, and why would he if he could travel in time? I don't see what other reason there could be," Thaddeus replied hoping to buy a little time himself while they played detective at the river. "He's extremely defensive whenever I ask about that railing, and he said quite plainly he'd be going back to climb it again. Sounds crazy, but a possibility all the same. I assume you're watching it."

"There could be a reason for suicide," Ken said.

"What would that be Agent Rodgers?"

"His fiancé was murdered," Ken said, watching him closely.

"Oh, how horrible!" Thaddeus stood, shocked, "The poor man! I don't know what to think now." He slowly sat down, pondering, "Unless. . . ."

"Unless what, Professor?"

"What if. . .he attempted suicide, for this reason you stated, and unknowingly jumped through this 'timegate' thing, and instead of going into the water, he went into time?"

"That'd be an unlikely coincidence, professor," Ken replied.

"True, but it wouldn't be the first breakthrough in science discovered by coincidence. In fact, most breakthroughs have their beginnings in either coincidence or accident."

"We've checked him out thoroughly, his birth, parents, childhood etcetera. He has a clear, traceable history, all of which confirms he's not from some other time or place, and didn't just appear from out of thin air. He's from our century."

"Well, that would support the possibility then, wouldn't it?"

Ken stared at the professor and switched the subject, "What about the others?"

"Others? What others?"

"The others in your group, that's an odd assortment of friends you've been meeting with the last two nights."

Thaddeus knew the wrong answer would blow the whole thing. He didn't know how much they knew, but he was convinced they didn't know much, or they wouldn't be playing this cat and mouse game with him. He had to be careful; a little truth was needed to keep them at bay.

"Yes, I suppose it may look like a strange group, but it's not all that strange. In my business, I have many acquaintances who are involved in different types of research and specialties. When I found that tablet, I confided in an acquaintance, a fellow archeologist I've worked with in the past, as someone having the expertise to help unravel the mystery. And, of course, my friend Barosh, being a Jewish rabbi, has a wealth of information regarding that era."

"And the others?"

"Allen and Jennifer? It turns out that they were acquaintances of Alex's, who he brought in to add their expertise."

"A Nobel Prize winning physicist in quantum physics and relativity? And a leading expert in metallurgy? That's some strange expertise for a clay tablet, professor."

"For a clay tablet—yes, for time travel—no. They have years of study, and interest in dimensional physics, in their respective fields as it relates to the possibility of time travel," he smiled. "That's the advantage of me proceeding with my investigation, Agent Rodgers. I have access, to the best minds and resources to help us get to the bottom of this."

"I can assure you professor; the Department has resources as well."

"Yes, of course, there are always different approaches to solving a problem, isn't there? Allen is an expert in the potential of time windows and can easily decipher Mr. Kincaid's story from fact to fiction."

"And what insight have they added so far, professor?"

"Well, Allen tends to be wordy and goes into lectures, expounding on various theories, but it's all designed to elicit different reactions from Mr. Kincaid to see if a chord is struck. And a few have been, and with the railing as a potential window, we may have a significant breakthrough," he paused and looked Agent Rodgers directly in the eye, "I'm sure you've checked them out and have found them to be above board in all things, and a change in midcourse would be terribly disruptive with Mr. Kincaid's questionable state of mind."

Ken studied the professor's face for a long minute. He knew he was holding out on him, and he was inclined to shut him and his little group down, but he wasn't ready to spring the trap quite yet. *I need to find out who is behind this,* he thought.

"What has Mr. Kincaid asked about us?" He asked.

"Not a lot, he avoids talking about you. He knows you're there, and I sense he's on edge about it," Thaddeus replied.

"Good, let him worry. A little fear may loosen his tongue, and we can get on with this business. Do I assume you'll be meeting this evening?"

"Yes, we would be meeting sooner, but," he shrugged, "we have responsibilities that also must be attended to, and the breaks give Mr. Kincaid time to think about things a little."

"Do you have the transcript from last night?"

"Of course, it's right here," Thaddeus handed him a folder with an edited version of the previous night's discussions.

"Very well professor," Ken said, taking the folder, "but don't take much longer, my superiors aren't as understanding as I am."

***

Once outside, Ken turned to John, "Were you able to plant anything?"

"Just one on the porch. The old Coot never took his eyes off of me long enough to find someplace in the room," he paused and looked at Ken squarely, "How long are we going to play this game with them? I've heard enough to bust them all, right now."

"Patience John, this type will usually hang themselves. Don't get nervous, they can't do anything without us knowing it. Someone is directing them; that's whom we need to get."

"Whatever you say, boss, whatever you say."

Chapter Fifteen

That evening, Barosh was subdued, not his usual, robust self.

"What is wrong, my friend?" Thaddeus asked him, privately, "Are you ill?"

"Ill at heart, old friend."

"Mary?"

Barosh nodded, "She doesn't understand and has closed her mind, refusing to see the vision. She is convinced only bad will come from it."

"It is difficult for her," Thaddeus said, placing his hand on his friend's shoulder. "It is only out of concern for you that she refuses to see. Allow her, her concern."

***

Settling in around the table, no one spoke. Only the sounds of clinking tea cups and spoons competed with Wagner's – 'Ride of the Valkyries'. In the awkward silence that followed, everyone looked at David.

He stood.

"It's true; I was going to take my life. I know some of you see that as weakness and instability, and you're entitled to your opinion. For me, it was neither. I wasn't unhinged or steeped in self-pity; I simply had no reason to exist. 'Suck it up', some say. Well, maybe that works for them; it doesn't for me. Just living a meaningless existence wasn't enough. I'll not defend it to you. It is what it is; take it or leave it, I don't care."

"I don't understand this thing with those tablets. I have a lot of questions, not the least of which is, how did my name and my thoughts came to be written on them? It's a mystery to me, and it's unsettling, to say the least. You're telling me that I did it or will do it, two-thousand years ago. It's easy to say those words; it's a lot harder to accept them. You're intelligent people, and it is clear you believe in what you are doing, so I have no reason to suspect dishonesty or foolishness."

"So, where does that leave me? I don't know why my name is on that tablet, but it is, and I want to. . .no. . .I need to know why. If I was there twenty centuries ago, it had to be for a reason. . .a purpose. Yesterday, I had no purpose. Now, I do, and I need to see this thing through, wherever, or should I say *whenever*, it takes me. A few days ago the farthest thing from my mind was some crazy idea of traveling back in time, but now, after listening to you, it doesn't seem quite so crazy. I may not understand it, but I need to find out what my purpose in all of this is."

"I'm not climbing the railing. I'm not ready to die. Not just yet. . .not for another two-thousand years anyway."

Alex was the first to stand and extend his hand to David.

"Welcome aboard, David. Shall we get started then; we have much to do?"

***

"David. . .what do you know about the pyramids?" Alex asked.

"Not much, about what most people know, I guess."

"And what would that be?"

"Well, let's see, they are in Egypt; built by the pharaohs thousands of years ago, as their burial tombs."

"That's it?"

"Yeah, I guess it is," he said. "Oh, they were built by slaves, and Charleston Heston set them free. You know, "let my people go.""

Alex failed to see the humor, "Yes, it makes good theater, seeing hundreds of slaves pulling a massive block of stone up a ramp on the side of a pyramid—but it's all rubbish. It would have taken thousands, not hundreds of slaves, to move just one block, and the ramps to enable it would have been an even greater engineering marvel than the pyramids themselves. They tried, you know. Hundreds of people on one small block, couldn't budge it," Alex shook his head.

"The world has been fed a diet of lies and deception about the pyramids and has swallowed it hook, line and sinker. It's insulting to the ingenuity of these great structures, the lack of respect they receive."

Pushing back from the table, he stood, "It's all there, in front of our eyes; the *ancient ones* left it all in place for us to see and we refuse to. The pyramids have stood as open diaries of their civilization, and we reject their existence." He paused, looking directly at David, "do you realize there is no modern engineering feat that comes close to the pyramids?"

"Well, I'm not an expert, but that seems a bit of a stretch. Some incredible structures have been built, and some of the ones being built in Dubai are not only marvels of engineering but downright jaw dropping."

Allen chuckled, "Uh oh, wrong answer David, you just pushed Alex's button."

"Because the pyramids are made of rocks, people tend to dismiss them. There are over two million blocks in the Great Pyramid of Giza alone, some weighting upwards of seventy tons. That pyramid stood four hundred-eighty-one feet high with each side measuring seven hundred-fifty-six feet with a maximum deviation of less than one inch. The sides are curved in to match the curvature of the earth and rise at a precise angle of fifty-one degrees, fifty-two minutes, having a deviation of less than five-hundreds of one percent of degree. Quite amazing, since people didn't even believe the earth was round until thousands of years later? And it is intentional as it makes the relationship of the pyramid's height to its base, exactly the same relationship as a circle is to its radius, something you, as an engineer, know as *pi*. Interesting, wouldn't you say, since *pi* wasn't supposed to have been discovered until four-thousand years later, by the Greeks?"

"The pyramid's base is square to a deviation of less than two hundredths of a second while the slope of each side is within millimeters of one another. This achieved more than five-thousand years ago by primitive people who had no means of cutting, shaping, transporting or placing such blocks period, much less so precisely. Inside the pyramid, chambers and shafts are cut, precisely through each layer of granite blocks that defy today's technology."

"We've never witnessed the glory of the pyramid. The entire surface was covered with smooth, polished blocks of white Tura limestone. That's twenty-two acres of limestone blocks, eight feet thick and weighing over sixteen tons, cut and transported to the site and put in place with a mean variation of one-hundredth of an inch. That's on a slope, hundreds of feet high. How'd they do that David, when we can't do it today? The Egyptians called it the *Ikhet*, meaning 'Glorious Light', and it was so bright in the Egyptian sun; they could not look at it. The peak was crowned with a capstone, known as the 'pyramidion' which was either solid gold or was gold inlay.

"Most of the blocks came from a quarry over five-hundred miles away. Five-hundred miles David! For the three Giza pyramids, how were ten million blocks, each weighing forty to seventy tons perfectly cut out of the quarry, transported hundreds of miles, raised hundreds of feet in the air and set in place with the precision of a razor blade, by primitive people who had only axes and adzes made of bronze, in a period of perhaps twenty years?"

"I don't know," David mumbled.

"Of course not, but don't feel alone—no one does. I could go on with more facts about the construction of each of the three major pyramids in Egypt that would confound your modern engineering mind, but their construction is only the tip of the iceberg, just the beginning of the marvel. There is a much greater mystery to them. How the pyramids were built is a question that's asked repeatedly, but a better question is: 'Why were they built?' Why are they scattered randomly across the open desert? Such a massive construction effort. . .why?"

"I can tell you for certain why they *weren't* built. They weren't built to be tombs. Not only have no mummies ever been found in them, but they wouldn't go to so much detail, precision and work to build a tomb in the desert. And, it's my opinion; they never contemplated such a thing because. . .they never planned on dying. They intended to live forever."

"To understand the pyramids David, we need to put aside the material marvel they are and look at the cosmic marvel they are, something Allen showed me."

"The Great Pyramid was aligned, by its architects, to be exactly one-third the distance between the equator and the North Pole and is an exact mathematical relationship of the dimensions of the earth. This is truly remarkable for people who didn't know the earth was round, much less the true size and shape of it! Its north-south axis is aligned to within three-sixtieth of a single degree of true north. David, that's more accurate than the Greenwich Observatory in London! To position a structure that covers over fifty-three-thousand square meters to that precision is not possible today; so how was it done then? The pyramids are a precise mathematical model of the earth. Again, it begs the questions, not only how, but why? Why be so precise for a mausoleum sitting in the middle of the desert? Calling the Great Pyramid a tomb is like calling the Buckingham Palace an outhouse. I could spend the next week with scores of facts that would prove false any contention that they weren't built as tombs by the Pharaohs of Egypt. We haven't the time for that, and it's not necessary to show you what they are not built for—I'd rather show you what they were built for."

He pulled out a folder and laid some aerial photos and plot diagrams on the table.

"This is a map of the Memphis area of the Nile Delta, and it shows the layout of the pyramids along the Nile River. See the three Pyramids of Giza here? And further south here, are the pyramids of Dashour. Between them, there are a number of minor pyramids. To the east is the Nile Delta with the Nile River running through the middle here," he traced the curving path of the river with his finger. He turned the map upside down, "Now, does it look familiar at all?"

David studied the map showing the winding Nile Delta, the fertile discharge of the Nile into the Mediterranean Sea and the pyramids Alex had marked.

"It looks like an upside down map," he said.

"Humph, modern education," Alex said in disgust. He pulled out a second map the same size as the first and laid them side by side. The new map looked similar to the first one, but it wasn't a map of earth.

"This is a map of the sky the Egyptians called the *'Heavenly Duat.'* On the left side is the Milky Way, and this here is the Orion constellation, the constellations of the Little Bear, and the Great Dog. Notice anything now?"

"It's similar to the first map," David said.

"Yes, that's right, similar, but not exact. The degree of similarity baffled me. I felt I was close to understanding what I had devoted my life's work to, but things were just a little off. That's when my work took me to Allen, so I'll let Allen pick it up from here," Alex motioned to Allen and sat down.

"Archaeologists are forensic detectives," Allen said, "they dig and sift through the remains of dead civilizations searching for bits and pieces of evidence to recreate a civilization, and they're very good at it." He tipped his head to Alex and Thaddeus.

"But, they tend to lack an understanding of the impact of astronomy on their work. They become so engrossed in the earthly side of the puzzle that they lose sight of the cosmic side. Alex was on the right track and was close to unraveling a crucial piece of the puzzle. He only needed a little something called 'precession'."

"Precession is a fact of physics and astronomy and is caused by the extremely slow wobble of the earth in its orbit. It takes twenty-six-thousand years to complete a single cycle. The wobble only affects the position of the stars as seen from the earth. Precession algorithms are well known, and when applied they act like a star clock for the planet. Knowing the exact rate of precessional change and the co-ordinate of a star, we can determine its altitude and rising point on the horizon for any date in history. In other words, we can see what the heavens looked like at any given time in history."

"So, when Alex came to me with his theory concerning the Constellation Orion and the pyramids but was baffled because it seemed to be close but was off just enough to be wrong, I set the computers to reconstruct the skies over the Nile Delta in ancient times and compared it to the pattern on the ground. It became apparent that he was onto something. At first, things were conspicuously tilted away from the pyramids and the Nile. Then, as I allowed the computer to slowly apply precession, it went back in time, century by century, and the orientation of the Constellation Orion's belt slowly rotated counter-clockwise until perfect correlation was achieved with the Nile Delta mirroring the Milky Way! The three pyramids lined up exactly with the three stars comprising the belt of Orion, the Dashour pyramids exactly aligned with the stars Hyades and Aldebaran, and all the remaining pyramids and clusters of smaller pyramids aligned with specific stars."

"Stars designated in the ancient writings!" Alex jumped in. "It was exact, David! When Allen's computer reconstructed the skies over Giza during the true era of the pyramids, everything was in perfect alignment. Recall, I mentioned the shafts cut through the courses of stone of the Great Pyramid. For many decades, it was thought these were ventilation shafts, which made no engineering sense and went against the Egyptian custom of not ventilating tombs for the dead. These shafts are small in size and represent massive engineering and construction feats as they cut through the core of the pyramid at highly precise angles. Well, two of the shafts align precisely due north and the other two align exactly due south, tracking the 'meridian' which is an astronomical line dividing the sky north and south, like an equator in the sky. And that's not all. Each of the four shafts, with pin-point precision target a particular star. In the Queen's Chamber, the northern shaft targets *Kochab*, known to us as Beta Ursa Minor. The southern shaft targets the star *Sirius*, which just happens to be the brightest star in the sky and, to the ancient Egyptians, is the goddess *Isis*, mother of all Egypt. In the King's Chamber, the northern shaft targets the Pole star, *Thuban*, known to us as Alpha Draconis, and the southern shaft targets *Al Nitak*, which is the lowest and brightest star in Orion's belt. This star was identified with *Osiris*, the god of resurrection and rebirth and the 'bringer' of civilization to the Nile Valley."

As he spoke, Alex pointed out each star on the map and correlated it to a cut away diagram of the Great Pyramid showing the internal shafts with lines to the stars.

"Notice the constellation Orion, David. These three stars are Orion's belt. Notice how they are positioned with the smallest one, slightly offset. Now, notice the position of the three Giza pyramids."

"They look almost the same."

"Not almost—exactly. Now, notice these pyramids here and here," Alex touched different spots on the map and then on the celestial map. "There's a major star in the exact location of each pyramid. David, the pyramids were not randomly scattered about the desert, each was positioned and precisely aligned to make the entire Nile Necropolis a terrestrial image of the Milky Way heavens. The three pyramids at Giza are literally Orion's Belt on the earth and the Nile Necropolis is *Osiris*."

"Now look here," he trailed his finger from the Pyramid to a site straight down from it. "This is the Great Sphinx. You know it; everyone does. It's the oldest standing monument in the world. It's carved out of solid limestone bedrock. Every stone is massive, with the biggest being two-hundred tons. David, you're an engineer; so tell me, how do you move and place a two-hundred ton block? The, so called experts, speak in vague terms of 'earth ramps' and 'unlimited manpower.' Rubbish! They refuse to accept what is right there in front of their eyes. There is only one crane in the entire world capable of lifting a load like that, and it's a multi-story building itself."

"The Sphinx had the body of a lion and the head of a man, crouching there, for thousands of years. Why David? What's it doing? What's it for? Why was it built? It's not placed randomly but is precisely aligned with the rising horizon to the east. Precisely David, not close—but exact. Again it begs the questions, 'Why bother? Why use such unwieldy sizes and materials? Why such precision? Why such meticulous design? Why?"

"The Giza Pyramids and the Sphinx were built in accordance to an overall architectural master plan; they are not stand-alone monuments, but each is a part of a unified plan based upon geometrical and surveying principles related to astronomical observations. Why bring an image of heaven and place it on the earth?"

He paused and looked at David with the exuberance of a child in a candy store, "And David, there's one more question. Not only how, and why, but most importantly of all—by whom?"

"On that note," Thaddeus said, "I suggest we take a break, stretch and get some more tea."

"I second that," Jennifer added.

Chapter Sixteen

"The answers aren't found in the ruins and siftings of primitive peoples," Alex resumed, after the short break. "Try as one may, it's not possible to answer these questions with known civilizations. The only answer is the existence of a race surpassing the civilizations of those times. It's become fashionable, to dismiss this race as mythology and make them into Hollywood superheroes. This causes many archeologists to deliberately misinterpret or deny the artifacts they uncover, not wanting to be ridiculed by their peers. The prime example is the pyramids. It's an accepted fact that they cannot be built with today's technology and science, yet we flippantly say primitive people built them using ineffective slave labor and bronze tools, then dismiss the meticulous alignments and dimensions as 'coincidence'. Amazing!"

"Some believe that the Giza pyramids stand as a memorial to a highly advanced antediluvian civilization, destroyed by a 'great flood'," Thaddeus said.

"Not the old Noah's ark myth?"

"Thank you, David, you just proved my point," Alex scoffed. "It's a fable, a myth, a child's story, so, we dismiss it. Yet, these stories are common among every civilization across the globe and have impossible similarities between them. There are over three-hundred ancient writings from around the world detailing a global flood, and it's foundational in the oldest cultures of the world. Every ancient civilization has a beginning from beings, remarkably different from the normal populations, possessing extraordinary powers and knowledge. They're described repeatedly as *'shining'*, *'glorious countenance'*, having skin and hair *'white as wool'*, who appear and disappear in *'bright lights'* or *'blazing fires'*. We choose to dismiss these as fables, and allow the answers to the world's mysteries, to hide in plain sight."

"Inside of every myth lies a kernel of truth. Myths are explanations of things primitive people witnessed and didn't understand. How would an ancient Sumerian describe a missile, streaking across the sky to its target and exploding in a ball of fire? Would he say things like *'chariots of fire'*, *'lightning bolt from the gods'* and *'pillar of fire'*?"

"The Aztec's God-king was named Quetzalcoatl," Thaddeus said, "and when he left, a bright star dawned in the east, which was discovered to be Venus. He was described as having glowing skin and hair. China, Europe, North and South America, each have ancient ancestors who were glowing gods that descended from the heavens and taught them the knowledge of tools and science."

"The evidence is overwhelming," Alex said. "Is it all coincidence that stories of gods and revered heroes are the same from one continent to another, when they had no knowledge of each other?"

"Mythology has always been viewed and interpreted in the context of religion and culture," Allen said. "It needs to be revisited from the perspective of science. Someday I'm going to perform a mathematical analysis of mythology. The results may be quite revealing."

"We know little of the world's true history," Alex resumed, "we only know what we think we know or choose to accept and disregard the rest if it doesn't fit into our neat little packages. Do we even know what the world looked like thousands of years ago? Whole continents have appeared and disappeared. Do we know if the true builders of the pyramids even came from Egypt? Or could they have settled there because their land was destroyed, a land we know nothing about? The answer is – no; we do not."

"We know they existed. Who they were, is beyond the scope of our group," Allen said, "the question we're dealing with is: 'How did they come and go?' They left us clues, starting with the pyramids themselves."

"The *ancients*," Alex said, "called the pyramids *'Mer'*, meaning 'house of ascension' and *'Per-Neter'* meaning *'House of God'* or *'House of Energy'*. Viewed from a religious perspective these terms get glossed over, but what would a place of 'ascension' and 'energy' mean viewed from a scientific view?"

"The word 'pyramid' itself is Greek and means *'fire in the middle,'* David said.

"Precisely, they were described as the *'celestial stairway for the king to ascend to heaven'*. The Pyramid Texts state that the *'king belongs to the sky'*. It's interesting that, while there is evidence bodies of the earliest pharaohs were inside the pyramids, no bodies have ever been found in them. Where did they go? 'Grave robbers' is the pat answer. But, even when a pyramid hadn't been broken into—there were no bodies! We accept the pat answer because we don't want to consider the other possibility."

"Which is?" David asked.

"That the pyramids were places for travel between dimensions. In other words, they were – gateways. They had cosmic knowledge that baffles today's astronomers. The sky, the Milky Way, the stars, and the planets with their cycles, were all understood far beyond today's knowledge. They had extraordinary knowledge of mathematics, geography and physics. They not only knew the earth was round, but also knew its dimensions, coordinates, alignment in the heavens, its cycles, orbits and rotations. They knew and understood the language of the heavens. The stars spoke to them. They had an advanced working knowledge of precessional astronomy and were highly skilled in celestial surveying and geometry. They understood celestial mechanics, holding to incredible precision. A science we're only beginning to scratch the surface of."

"Accepting the existence of a race of super beings enables us to correctly interpret their writings. They left many, which have been considered religious mumbo jumbo, such as the *'Book of the Dead'*, the *'Book of Two Ways'*, the *'Book of Gates'* and the *'Pyramid Texts'*. These were written as hieroglyphics, in stone, to ensure their survival, and constitute the most ancient literature known. Reading them, it's clear these beings saw the waters of the Nile as the terrestrial version of the *'Winding waterway in the sky'* – the Milky Way—and they built a 3-D image of it here on earth."

"It's incredible, isn't it? Human arrogance refuses to accept that we are not the most intelligent beings who've walked the earth. The ancient sky religion wasn't a worship of the stars; it was an identity with the stars. They came from the stars, and wanted to go back to them. The twelve Zodiacal constellations weren't only known; they were instructions, and everything they did was aimed at following them."

"It's also clear that the general population did not have this knowledge. It was restricted to a small group of elites—and handed down to the kings and priests of each civilization. The earliest writings show this *'heavenly'* class as different from normal humans. They had elongated heads and were of massive stature. The people worshipped them as gods that came from the stars and returned to them. By the time of Tutankhamun, the Giza pyramids were already well over a thousand years old, and the memory of who had built them and why had been lost. Where did these beings go? Did they return to the stars? It was clear that those left behind didn't have the same skills and knowledge. Substandard pyramids were built that have vanished already while the great three still stand."

"Where and how did it start, we don't know," Alex continued, "but we know that there was a time when the sun's position along the zodiac was close to the star *Hyades* at the 'head' of the *Constellation of Taurus*. A unique celestial conjunction occurred at the moment of sunrise. The *Constellation of Leo* and the meridian-transit of the three stars of Orion's belt, all aligned. This was near the beginning of the Age of Leo and was called the *'First Time',* by the ancients. According to their writings, they've been going back and forth ever since."

"The fundamental concept of the sky religion was that while the king was alive, he was the reincarnation of *Horus*, the god king, and was hailed as the son of *Osiris* and *Isis*. Upon his death, he would begin the *'journey in the sky',* to rejoin with *'Osiris'*—and become a star in the constellation of Orion. Through all the writings, there is reference after reference, text after text, and detailed steps to follow to become *'Osiris-Unas'*—a star. It involves being *'made ready'*, and standing in the *'breast of Leo'* at the *'vernal point'* of the equinox."

"What's that?" David asked.

"In astronomical terms," Allen answered, "the *'vernal point'* is the highest position the sun occupies on the spring equinox, against the background of the Zodiacal constellations that encircle the path of the sun. The vernal point is not fixed because of precession, so it sweeps around the dial of the zodiac at a very precise and predictable rate. Here's the key, this journey towards Leo, would have been a journey through a succession of ages from the age of Taurus, around three-thousand BCE to the Age of Leo—*back* to the *'First Time'*, around thirteen-thousand BCE. This is a journey against the flow of precession, or in other words— backwards in time. And, the computer for precession took us back to the year thirteen-thousand BCE, the exact half-way point of a full precession period and precisely when Leo aligned with the Great Pyramid and the Sphinx. That David is not a coincidence."

"So, where's the time machine?" David asked.

"Here," Alex said, pointing at a spot on the map, "and here and here. It's the whole Nile Necropolis, David. They had constructed a live replica of the 'cosmic kingdom' in the Memphite region, and the whole thing, as the terrestrial image of the Milky Way, is a time machine."

"Where's the *'breast of Leo'*, they stood in?" David asked.

"When the celestial Horus-King stood *'between Leo's paws'* he was in the Constellation Leo, up in the Milky Way. On earth, the living Horus-King, stood between Leo's paws too—the paws of the Great Sphinx—*the 'breast of Leo.'*" Alex tapped the Great Sphinx on the map.

"The Sphinx lies exactly along the east-west axis of the Giza necropolis with it gaze fixed precisely due east. It is an 'equinoctial marker' with its eyes targeting the exact position of sunrise at dawn on the spring equinox. The Sphinx was built to be a copy of the Constellation Leo. This is what the builders of the Great Pyramid were doing when they targeted the southern shafts of the Kings and Queens chambers in the Great Pyramid on the Orion and Sirius stars. By setting up such precise time markers, they were providing a 'zero' point for calculations that was used for determining points of past time—for dialing in time if you will."

"Are you telling me that standing between the paws of the Sphinx will cause time travel?" David asked.

"It's not quite that simple," Allen said, "but it's a piece of the puzzle. It's a gateway. The Sphinx gazes east, directly at the equinoctial rising point of the sun in any and every epoch, past, present and future. When the sky begins to lighten, on the spring equinox, the constellation rises on the horizon. At the precise moment that the sun breaks over the earth, exactly 90 degrees to the right, precisely at the meridian, the three stars of Orion's belt will form a pattern in the sky that is identical to the ground plan of the Giza pyramids. The King's and Queen's Chambers in the Great Pyramid, will be perfectly aligned to the stars Orion and Sirius, and. . .in that instant, the gateways will open."

"Gateways?" David asked, "There's more than one?"

"Three, that we suspect, probably more. As Alex said, the entire necropolis is a dimension machine. In addition to the gateway at the Sphinx, we believe there's gateways inside the King's and Queen's Chambers. We don't fully understand the gateways inside the pyramid, as to what dimensions they open to. I don't believe they are time dimensions, and think they open more often than only on the spring equinox. There are four crucial astronomical moments in the year called cardinal points, consisting of the winter and summer solstices and the spring and autumn equinoxes, and each was extremely relevant to the ancients. I think the gateways open for each. But, we can't investigate them as the pyramids are guarded closely and the insides are off limits to us. What we do know, as Alex explained, is that the Horus-King gateway between the paws of the Sphinx is a gateway back in time."

"How do you control when you go to?"

"We can't," Allen sighed, "at least, not yet."

"You said the gateway will open at 30 CE; how do you know that?" David asked.

"By tracking the 'eastwards' direction along the ecliptic path of the Constellation and installing algorithms to apply precession, the computers can calculate where the vernal point is at any year in the past and where it will be in the future. Here, let me explain it this way. Remember the napkin the professor and Jennifer held stretched between them?" David nodded, "Well, recall how the baseball settled in the middle of the napkin and how it flexed the napkin at that point?"

"Yes, I remember; that's where the wormhole or gateway you described would go from one dimension to the other."

"Exactly, that's the vernal point of the dimension. With the napkin stretched out and fixed, that point is established. For the upcoming equinox, the computers affirm that point will be 30 CE with a deviation of plus or minus two years. But, suppose Jennifer was to lift one corner of the napkin, the ball would move and reposition itself to a different point on the napkin, right? By controlled flexing of the corners of the napkin, it would be possible to position the ball at any particular spot on the napkin. The same holds true with the time dimension. By flexing that dimension, we could make the vernal point any particular date in history we chose."

He sighed deeply, "So far; I haven't been able to figure out how to flex the corners. What I've been working on is a form of "exotic matter" known as Casimir energy. This energy, which is also called 'phantom energy' or 'negative energy', weighs less than zero and would have an anti-gravitational effect, keeping the wormhole's walls apart and allowing moving them around. I'm getting close and will have it figured out soon."

He chuckled, "Some of my colleagues believe 'negative energy' may be pushing space apart and is so anti-gravitational that it will rip the universe apart, destroying everything. I don't subscribe to that theory as it would have happened by now. Every time a discovery is made in our universe, overnight a crowd of 'gloom and doom' experts pop up out of nowhere, screaming the world is coming to an end."

Quiet settled on the group as David absorbed these revelations. He looked at Thaddeus, grabbing for some semblance of familiarity. Thaddeus only shrugged and smiled.

"Pyramid type buildings are scattered all around the world," he said, "in Asia, Mexico and South America. The purposes of these structures have been a mystery to modern archeologists for centuries, yet each has similar myths surrounding them, which are ignored as only fables. Quetzalcoatl *'ascended to the heavens'* from the Mayan pyramids in Tiwanakuthe. Mexico City is built over the ruins of the Aztec Tenochtitlan meaning *'the place where men become gods'*. The Babylonians and Assyrians built Ziggurats, which were steeped pyramids, and were used as *'portals by the gods on their visits to earth'*. They were considered to be *'bridges'* between heaven and earth as well as horizontal bridges between the points of the earth itself. The Nile necropolis is not the only place where this occurs."

"Not by a long shot," Alex said, "the Mexican pyramids mirror the Egyptian pyramids in regard to precision of placement and alignment with the stars. We believe the ancient pyramid and monument sites in China, Russia and India would reveal similar patterns if we were allowed to investigate them. Then there are the Nazca formations in Peru that exactly line up with zodiac constellations and have meridian focal points, and there are similarities in many other sites such as Stonehenge, Ankor Wat and Easter Island."

"It's clear some or all of these are gateways for dimensional travel," Allen said.

David looked at Barosh, "What do you think about this Rabbi?" David asked, "How does this line up with your beliefs in your God?"

Barosh thought before replying. "There is a passage in the Dead Sea scrolls that reads: *"When the gods of knowledge enter into the doors of glory, and when the holy angels depart towards their realm, the entrance doors and the gates of exit proclaim the glory of the king. . .when they depart and enter by the gates."* There are many instances in the Tanakh and even in the Christian scriptures that speak of men and beings coming from and going to the heavens. This ancient race that Alex speaks of could very well be servants of or sent by God. We do not understand or know everything. We know only what we have been allowed to know."

David sat back and shook himself, "Whew, this is like an Indiana Jones movie." He turned to Alex, "You said that the Horus-King was *'made ready'* to begin the journey. What did you mean by that?"

"Oh, you caught that, did you?" Alex chuckled, "I wondered if you did. Recall that Allen had earlier said there were three things required for time travel—finding a gateway—knowing when the gateway would open—and passing through the gateway. Well, if you were to stand between the paws of the Sphinx during the spring equinox, nothing would happen—you have my word on it. In order to pass through this non-physical gate, the physical body must be *'made ready'*." He turned and opened his hand to Jennifer, who had said little during this discourse.

"I guess that's my cue," she said.

Chapter Seventeen

David had wondered how the metallurgist fit into this puzzle. He wasn't sure he wanted to find out. The smile accompanying his attempt at humor didn't conceal his uneasiness.

"There's something about that phrase, *'made ready'* that sends chills up my spine," he said. "The ancient Aztecs had a ceremony where they *'made ready'* their victims before offering them to the gods; they cut their beating hearts out."

"No one's heart is getting cut out David," she laughed. "Actually, we're turning hearts into gold." The others chuckled, but David didn't get the point.

Maybe they are mad scientists after all.

"Let me explain what being *'made ready'* involves," she continued. "Over the past few years, my work has concentrated on the noble metals, particularly platinum and palladium, researching and developing new alloys and uses. When the Apollo missions brought rock samples back from the lunar surface, I was asked by NASA to analyze and categorize their mineral and metal composition. They were fairly generic in nature and didn't deviate much from similar materials here on earth."

"That changed when a rock from Apollo 17 was delivered. It came from the 'Taurus-Littrow' site and was a *'breccia'* rock, which is made up of fragments of other rocks. These common rocks are formed by the impacts on the moon's surface over the millenniums, creating the craters and ridges you see. Imbedded in this rock was a strange blackish material that exhibited noble metal characteristics but refused to be categorized.

Using a technique known as 'crucible reduction,' the material settled to the bottom, meaning it was heavier than lead and it had the characteristics of gold, yet it didn't analyze as gold. When struck with a hammer, it shattered like glass. I was perplexed; gold does not shatter. Was this a new form of gold—from the moon? Further analysis showed it contained iron, silica and aluminum. Each of these dissolve with sulfuric or hydrochloric acids, yet acid didn't touch it." She paused and leaned forward.

"And that's the easy part; here's where it really starts to get spooky. GC (Gas chromatograph) and NAA (Neutron Activation Analysis) testing also didn't classify the material, so I ran it through a GES (gas-emission spectrometer) using a fifteen second burn time. Even though, I could see the sample glowing in front of my eyes, the analyzer indicated there was nothing there!"

"I retested, this time using a longer burn cycle and a special electrode. This is an extremely difficult and expensive test, but it was worth it and utterly blew my mind. The first part of the burn was the same as the previous test; I could see the material glowing, but the instrument registered nothing. But then, it registered—as a different material—the element palladium! As the burn increased, it changed again, into platinum, and then it became ruthenium, rhodium, iridium and osmium. I repeated the test several times and the results were consistent; the material consisted of all these noble metals but at different times and in forms not recognized by science. I was baffled and became obsessed with the material."

"Under strict atmospheric control conditions, I tried an annealing procedure, using thermo- gravimetric analysis for measurement. The end results defy everything I know about metals. An ultra-white powder was produced. When cooled, it weighed over three-hundred percent of the initial weight, but when heated, it weighed less than zero! Even the measuring dish weighed less! When I removed the sample from the dish—both returned to their original weights." She stood and began pacing.

"I began running every test I could think of, including cryogenic and high-temperature superconductor coding. Normally, gold doesn't have properties of a superconductor, but this 'white-powder' gold defied conventional metallurgy science. Removing gravitational effects, not only was it a superconductor—it would actually levitate! I realized the powder was so incredibly white because it actually repelled gravity!"

"The levitation aspects and the missing weight especially excited me. I couldn't see how weight could be lost and then return again. I speculated that the weight was there, and I just couldn't detect it. That the molecular structure of the material changed allowing it to translate into a different dimension and that it took what part of the sample dish it rested on with it."

"Took it to where?" David asked.

"I don't know," Jennifer shook her head. "Anyway, the samples from NASA weren't sufficient for me to continue my research and I was bound by a confidentially agreement regarding them. I needed freedom to pursue my research unhampered. I returned the samples to NASA along with my reports and turned my focus to determining how to produce the white powder myself from yellow gold."

She smiled, looking at David with an embarrassed expression, "Does this sound familiar?"

"There's something swirling around in the back of my mind; I can't quite put my finger on it; black magic or something."

"That's right, black magic, wizards and witches! It's right out of the medieval ages. Except what I was doing was the reverse of what the wizards and witches were trying to do. The word you're thinking of is—alchemy."

"Yes, that's it, alchemy—the quest to turn lead into gold, except you're trying to turn gold into white powder."

"Not trying, David—did. I've been quite successful at making the white powder and have continued my research into the extraordinary and unique properties of the material. I named the phenomenon 'Asymmetrical Deformed High-spin Nuclei', or in layman's terms, 'monatomic gold' and began a thorough study of the material. I learned enough to publish an article in *American Scientist* regarding the effects of gravitational-quantum mechanics on monatomic noble metals. This was followed by a paper I presented at the *National Science Academy* on the unique and unusual properties of monatomic noble metals. My article caught the attention of Allen, who then attended the conference to meet me. He discussed his work in dimensional translation, and we began collaborating together, sharing our research. It was after this that Alex contacted Allen regarding his theories of the Nile Necropolis being a cosmic configuration of gateways. We all became students of the ancient texts and writings, shared our work with each other and soon the pieces began falling into place."

"Where's the connection between your white powder and the gateways?"

"Good question," Alex responded, "and to answer it, we go back to the Pyramid Texts. They describe a mysterious substance called *mfkzt*. References refer to it as an extremely valuable 'stone,' but it's not described as any stone or metal we're familiar with such as turquoise or granite. Actually, in some inscriptions it's referred to as 'bread' and as 'light' and in the 'Book of the Dead,' it's called the 'food of the gods.' There is a description in the Pyramid Texts of how the pharaoh will be resurrected into the Afterlife. It will be in the 'Field of Mfkzt,' where the pharaoh presents to the god *Amun-re* a loaf of something that has the following inscription: *'The presenting of the white bread that he may be given life.'* In another description, the pharaoh offers a similar loaf to the god *Sopdu*, with the inscription: *'He gave the gold bread. . . so the mouths rejoiced.'* There are other inscriptions and scenes depicted that show the same theme, calling it the 'food of the gods'. Whatever this *'food'* was it provided life for the traveler. Part of the preparation for a departing pharaoh was to partake of the *'white bread'* made from gold. Sound familiar?"

"You're saying this 'white bread' is Jennifer's 'white powder.'"

"We are," Alex replied.

David turned to Jennifer, "Do you think that's what the alchemists were trying to make?"

"I believe it started out that way," Jennifer said, "the descendants of the ancients tried to duplicate their divinity, but they couldn't and the original purpose got lost, and turned into a carnal lust for gold, which failed."

"The ancient sciences placed astrology and alchemy on the highest levels," Alex said, "exceeding even mathematics. They both became corrupted and defiled from their original purposes. Just like the history of the ancients became mythology, the science of astrology became 'black magic' with fortune telling and the science of alchemy became the twisted quest to transform lead into gold."

"The Philosophers' Stone was believed to be the missing link to achieving the transformation," Jennifer resumed. "A seventeenth-century alchemist stated it clearly: *'Our Stone is nothing but gold digested to the highest degree of purity. . .it is fixed and incombustible like a stone, but its appearance is that of a very fine powder.'* Kind of says it all, wouldn't you agree?"

"In 1904 an archaeologist, on an expedition to the Mount of Moses in the Sinai desert, discovered the ruins of an ancient Egyptian temple," Thaddeus injected. "In it, they found flasks, tables, trays, alabaster vases and cups, along with a large metallurgist's crucible. Buried beneath carefully fitted flagstones they uncovered *'a considerable amount of pure white powder'* which, unfortunately, blew away in the desert wind. Now, why was an Egyptian temple isolated out in the Sinai desert? Why would a metallurgist's crucible be in a religious temple? And what was the white power that was so carefully hidden away?"

"You think that temple is where this stuff was made?" David asked.

"It was one location," Jennifer said, "there were probably others as well."

"Why way out in the desert?"

"The material was special and made in remote areas for security," she replied.

"They also uncovered a large amount of weapons and armor in the temple. This indicates it was heavily guarded and protected," Thaddeus added.

"No one has ever understood what the writings were referring to concerning the *'food'* the gods needed for travel to the stars," Alex said. "It was thought to be a religious rite for travel in death, or that there were errors translating the words 'stone', 'bread', 'gold' and 'food.' But with Jennifer's discovery of monatomic gold, it's not contradictory."

"You're suggesting they ate this white powder?" David asked.

Allen answered, "Just suppose for a second that someone had the properties of monatomic gold flowing through their blood stream while standing in a gateway at precisely the instant it opened. Could the material alter the composition of the person's body to enable him to translate through the open gateway? There may be no noticeable change in the person's outward appearance, but what change may have occurred inside on a molecular level?"

"How would it get into their blood stream, an injection?"

"No, that wouldn't be necessary. Simply mixing it as a liquid drink, will work."

"You think that would work? That drinking this stuff would actually change someone's body, and they'd vanish into some other dimension?"

"We don't think it David," Jennifer said, "we know it. You see; we've done it."

"You've actually done this? You've translated?"

"Oh no, not me, not any of us; we're not that brave. No, it was a lab mouse. I named her Sally, after Sally Ride, the first woman in space. I gave Sally a specified amount of solution and placed her in a controlled atmospheric chamber. I observed her for 30 minutes under normal gravity; there was no difference in her looks, actions or responses. She moved around and ate as normal. Then, I reduced the gravitational field of the chamber. Sally began glowing! At first it was like a shine, but it quickly grew brighter and brighter until there was a bright flash. When it cleared, Sally was gone!"

"Where did she go?"

"I don't think she went anywhere. I think she was right there in the same spot, only in a different dimension, one that I couldn't see. When I returned the test chamber to normal gravity, there was a bright flash again, and Sally suddenly reappeared."

"Had she traveled in time?"

"No," Allen said, "she had gone into another dimension; one we can't sense. Jennifer called me, excited over it. We reviewed the test and explored all the possibilities, and decided to repeat the test."

"We set up video recordings and repeated the test," Jennifer resumed, "and just like in the first test, Sally began glowing until she again disappeared in a bright flash. When restoring gravity, she returned. The third time, we waited ten minutes before restoring gravity to the chamber. When we did, Sally didn't appear."

"What happened to her?"

"We surmise she ran off somewhere during those five minutes."

"Ran off? Ran off, where?"

"Wherever she was."

"But where was she?"

"We don't know."

"Would you like some more coffee, David?" Thaddeus asked.

David looked at his empty cup suspiciously, "No, I think I'll pass."

Alex laughed, "Don't worry; we're not spiking your coffee with white powder."

David failed to see the humor, "It wouldn't be the first time, would it?"

Alex stopped laughing.

Chapter Eighteen

"As I said," Allen picked up the conversation, "we're just scratching the surface in this science. The ancients' far surpassed our knowledge. They moved in dimensions about which we know nothing. We believe they used gateways to travel between points on the earth and even off the earth. Some of the things we've identified, such as the Mayan pyramids and Stonehenge are gateways connecting together, like travel corridors."

"Okay, so you think drinking Jennifer's golden cocktail will enable translating between dimensions; how certain are you that you'll travel through time in the Sphinx gateway? How do you know you won't fly off into the Twilight Zone like Sally did?"

"That's a key question," Alex replied, "one which we've spent many hours studying. We have no desire to disappear into the Twilight Zone. The Pyramid Texts are clear in stating the Horus-King traveled back in time to a preselected date. There are several references along those lines. They had the ability to manipulate the time dimension to select the dates they wanted; so we know it's possible."

"And we'll have that capability soon," Allen said firmly.

David turned to Barosh, "Okay rabbi you've not said anything. Once again, how does all this talk about eating white gold set with your faith? Seems it's getting a little on the fringe."

Barosh was in thought for some minutes before answering, "There is a passage in the Torah that has baffled scholars for ages, and because of this, it is often ignored and brushed aside. It's found in the book of

Exodus and concerns itself with the newly freed Israelite people having just escaped their captivity in Egypt. Moses had gone up onto the mountain, and the people grew impatient and made an idol, a golden calf, to worship."

"Yeah, I remember that in "The Ten Commandments" when Charleston Heston came back and he smashed the tablets."

"Yes, that is the scene, but the scripture I'm referring to is what happened after that. Moses does an extremely strange thing; it goes like this: *'And he took the calf which they had made, and burnt it in the fire, and ground it to a powder, and scattered it upon the water, and made the children of Israel drink of it.'"*

"You're kidding?" David asked.

"No, you can read it yourself. There are questions and mysteries concerning this passage that have never been answered. How did Moses turn the gold into a powder? Gold should melt not turn into a powder. How is it then scattered *"on"* water? Gold should sink, not float. Finally, and most peculiarly, why did he make the people drink it? There's no further mention of this in the scriptures. It appears as an isolated, stand-alone event."

"But, notice what happens next. Moses commands the sons of Levi to do the following: *'. . .go in and out from gate to gate throughout the camp, and slay every man his brother, every man his companion and every man his neighbor. And the children of Levi did according to the word of Moses, and there fell of the people that day about three thousand men.'"*

"Now, the question that begs to be answered is, out of hundreds of thousands of people, three-thousand men were killed, how did the sons of Levi know who to kill? There is no explanation given. A superficial explanation is that they were the ones who fought back, but that doesn't hold water. Any man who is going to be killed will fight back. Besides, it's too ambiguous; guilty ones would have slipped through, and innocent ones would have been killed. It's a mystery that has never been answered. . .that is until now."

"Jennifer's powder?" David asked.

"Yes, if we put this incident in context with what we now know about the white powder and its mysterious properties to change molecular composition, it could make sense. Keep in mind, Moses was raised in Pharaoh's family, and as Alex has shown, the Pharaohs were familiar with and used the white powder; it was for them. So it is highly likely that Moses knew about the powder and how to make it. Consider these scenarios (and there could be others). What if the Israelites who opposed Moses refused to drink the 'Egyptian water', which would be likely as they were in rebellion against Moses? Now, what if those who did drink had a molecular change occur inside their bodies that gave an outward sign to the sons of Levi, and they were 'passed over'? Or, what if all the people who drank were temporarily translated to a different dimension, leaving behind the ones to be killed? Granted, it would have taken divine intervention for either of these to occur, but that is consistent with God and the Passover itself."

"The point is, just because there is a belief in God does not mean everything is understood or must fit within the constraints of our perceptions or intellect. In fact, it is quite the opposite; my belief in Almighty God opens my mind to accept things I do not understand. After all, we are human—and God is all powerful. He created all things, most of which we do not yet understand."

"So your faith doesn't hold all the answers?" David asked.

"No, of course not, why should it?"

"It must be comforting to have faith like that," David said. "By the way rabbi, have you memorized the entire Bible?"

"No, only the Torah. . . the prophets. . . and the writings."

"How do you know Jesus wasn't an alien?" Alex asked. "Think about how many times he referred to himself as the 'bread of life' and that unless you ate of him 'no man shall enter into heaven'. What did he mean when he told Nicodemus he had to be 'born again' in order to enter heaven? That sounds like a translation to me. After his resurrection, he 'glowed brightly,' and told the women not to touch him because he hadn't 'ascended into the heavens' yet. And when he did ascend, angels (aliens?) appeared out of nowhere saying he would return the same way. There are a lot of statements and things he said and did that point to what he actually was—an alien—one of the ancients. The Apostle Paul wrote, 'flesh and blood cannot enter into the kingdom of God' and that you had to be changed into spirit first. How? By monatomic gold?" He looked around, scanning the group.

"You are well versed in the New Testament Alex," Barosh said.

"I read all old writings Rabbi, and I keep an open mind about all religions to glean out those kernels of fact inside of them. Moses had to cover his face with a veil because he shone so brightly the people couldn't look upon him. Maybe he wasn't up on a mountain, maybe he was in a different dimension—or in a spaceship. Doesn't this fit in with your account there about the people drinking the water and somehow changing? Remember, Sally, our mouse glowed brightly before translating."

"Your points are well taken Alex," Allen interrupted, "which brings us back to our present course. David, you've heard a lot, what do you think about this?"

"It's overwhelming and pretty wild," he answered, "but, the pieces seem to fit together as weird as they are." He looked at Jennifer, "How long does the cocktail last?"

"I've been experimenting with that, with a second mouse, Enoch I named him. I gave him a single dose, like Sally, and I put him in the chamber weekly to test the response. So far it's been seven weeks, and he translates each time. I've also monitored his responses and reactions when he reappears and other than a little disorientation, he doesn't seem to have any ill effects from it. Just shakes his head and looks around for something to eat."

David turned to Allen, "Are you positive of the date the gateway will open to?"

"I've run the calculations forward, backwards and inside out; and the computer comes up every time to 30 CE, plus or minus two years. Yes, I'm sure."

"I hope so; hate for you to have made a mistake and we come face to face with a Tyrannosaurus Rex."

An awkward silence descended. He looked around the table, and they avoided his eyes.

"What? Did I say something wrong?" He asked. Getting no responses he searched for some common ground. "The spring equinox is in less than four weeks, isn't it?"

"That's correct," Allen said.

"That's not much time to go to Egypt. I assume that's where we're headed, right."

"That's right," Alex said.

"So, what's the plan? How are we going to do this?"

"David, there's no 'we'," Allen broke the silence, "We're not all going, that wouldn't be practical or sound science for all of us to do this."

"I thought that was what this is all about."

"I must stay behind to evaluate what happens," Allen said, "and there remains some critical work that needs to be done." He looked up and nodded towards Jennifer, "For the same reasons, Jennifer cannot go."

"I'm too old for such a journey," Thaddeus spoke. "It's come twenty years too late for me. I couldn't survive it, as much as I wish to do so."

David's spirit fell; it was going to be him and Alex going together, the one person he didn't feel comfortable with. How dependable would he be? Chasing aliens all over? His mind was already made up; no matter how 'open-minded' he said it was.

"I'm passing on this," Alex said, "because of the date. I'm taking a rain check until we're ready to go to the time of the ancients. I want to meet them and learn what they are, where they're from and where they went."

David slumped down, isolated and out of place. He understood Allen's and Jennifer's reasons for remaining; they had to stay to record and manage this thing as well as solve the remaining riddle. But he was confused about the others. Wouldn't they jump at the opportunity to travel back in time? After all, they were archeologists. An opportunity like this is what they've devoted their lives to. They dig and sift through the trash and garbage of ruins and cultures on their hands and knees for years, looking for one broken piece of pottery or scrap of history. Now, they'd pass up a chance to actual be there?

He was on his own. He was the guinea pig, after all. He looked at the rabbi, who hadn't said anything, sitting there, with his hands cupped together in front of him. *It must be gratifying to be removed from all this,* David thought. David wondered if finding Jesus was the real purpose of this trip. Did they really care about revealing Jesus for whom he was or was that just rationalization because that's the year Allen's computers spit out? He began to feel the real reason for the trip was to determine if all their theories would actually work. Uneasiness settled over the group. He surmised how they viewed him; first it was Sally, then Enoch, and now—David. He was just another lab mouse to them.

"I'm the Alice in the rabbit hole," Barosh said.

David jerked upright, startled by the proclamation. "You? You're going? I never thought you'd. . . ."

"Oh and why is that?"

"Well, you're a rabbi. And you've made it clear your mind is made up regarding Jesus."

"And it is, about being the messiah, but he was still a Jewish prophet, and to see and speak with him would be remarkable. But, it's not only about Jesus. To go back and see my people at one of the most turbulent and historical times in our history is a chance of a lifetime. This was when the Romans controlled the world. I have many questions that need answers. The Dead Sea Scrolls, the Zealots, Jerusalem, all to be explored and understood, to uncover and bring back. Most of all to see and pray in the Temple before it was destroyed! What rabbi would not risk giving their life for that?"

David stared at the rabbi, and then repeated his words, "Risk giving their life? What does that mean Rabbi?"

Again silence filled the room. He looked around the table, and he began understanding maybe there was something more to their reluctance in going on this journey.

Not receiving a response, he asked the question that hung in the air, "Tell me, how does 'Alice' come back out of the rabbit hole?"

Everyone looked at Allen, "The mechanics of coming back are the same as going, only in reverse; be in the gateway during the spring equinox, with a solution of monatomic gold altering your molecular make up."

"Something tells me that's not all," David said.

Allen spoke haltingly, "There are some concerns."

"Let me guess, first there's the question of how long the cocktail is good for. Will it still be effective two thousand years away?"

"Yes, that's correct," Jennifer replied, "we don't know if the molecular alterations to the body are permanent or temporary. But that can be resolved by taking a packet of the powder for the return trip."

"That's not the real problem, is it?" David asked. "The real problem is opening the gateway to the right year coming back, isn't it?"

"That is a concern," Allen said.

"Let's see," David said, "it would be the spring equinox of 30 CE, right? Can your computer predict what year the vernal point will be, that far back?"

"It can," Allen said, "without question; the algorithms are consistent across time and once set up, it doesn't matter what year it calculates to."

"So what year will the gateway open to then?"

"Well, it's not that simple David. There's a bigger problem."

"Which is?"

"You recall I mentioned earlier that the gateway will open to the year 30 CE. . .," Allen took a long pause before finishing the sentence, ". . .plus or minus two years."

David realized immediately what this meant, "Oh my God! You're not sure it's the year 30 are you? It could be between 28 and 32 CE, and each year would have a different vernal point return date, so there'd be five different possible dates of return!"

"Actually twenty-five," Allen replied sheepishly, "each of the five years would themself have the same plus or minus two giving five possible return dates for each year."

David's jaw dropped, and he looked at Allen mortified, "Twenty-five possible dates! It could be anywhere."

Allen hesitated before answering, and then he carefully picked his words. "Not 'anywhere,' but "any time". . .yes. Most of the dates open further back in time. I've run the calculations; they go from 112 BCE plus or minus two years to 1247 BCE plus or minus. The algorithms are correct, and the computer gives consistent results." Allen sighed, shaking his head, "As you can see; I have work to do. That is why I cannot go; I need to be here to ensure a return to the present. I have to learn how to tweak the time dimension to adjust the vernal point, and I need to be certain of what date it opens to this year, in order to set the proper return to one year from now."

"Why one year?"

"Well, it cannot open to this year because we'll already be using this year to send the travelers, and we cannot send and receive the same bodies at the same time. I need the year to complete the investigation. If the return was before that, it would be a paradox. I would not want someone standing in the gateway in the year 31 CE if it's adjusted for the year 32 CE."

"You wouldn't?" David sneered. "If either end of the wormhole is off by a year, who knows what time era they'd be transported to?"

"I wish I could be more specific, but I cannot—not yet anyway."

"Maybe it's too soon to be doing this," Thaddeus said, "maybe we should wait until we have more answers."

"That's what we wanted to do in the beginning as you recall professor," Allen replied, "but finding those tablets caused us to reassess that, and now with the government bloodhounds on our tail, we don't have that luxury. But then, that's up to those going, isn't it?" He placed his hands on the table and said, "David, you wrote the year '31 CE' on that tablet we found; I think that means you were telling us what year you went back in, so we open the gate for the year 32CE. You knew of our dilemma and gave us the answer."

"So, it's come full circle to me again. How will we know you'll be ready on your end?"

"I'll be ready; you have my word on it."

"No disrespect Allen, but your word won't do me any good when I'm dinosaur bait." David paused, reflecting. "So let me see if I got this straight. To return, one year from now, we need to be standing in the gateway of the Sphinx; drink Jennifer's magic cocktail, and pray that you've figured out what year we went to and how to manipulate the vernal point for that year to open at one year from now, is that right?"

"That about sums it up," Allen answered.

"And if any of these don't happen, then we don't come back a year from now, but to some era or time that's most likely even more distant and primitive."

Silence descended on the table like a thick fog. Finally, Barosh spoke.

"When the sun breaks over the horizon, on the spring equinox, one year from now, I will be standing between the paws of the Sphinx, waiting for my friend Allen to open the gate and bring me back."

David stared at the table.

I wrote that date on that tablet, he thought. *I knew they would find it and left them a date.*

beneath the turbulence – peace is found

David looked at Allen. Allen's face was determined and his eyes steady.

"The gateway will be open, Barosh, to return you here one year from now." Allen said.

David looked at Barosh. Barosh's face was calm and his eyes steady.

"Okay, Rabbi, when do we leave for Egypt?" David asked.

Chapter Nineteen

E ntering the large conference room, the buzz around the immense oval table quieted down, and all eyes followed Agent Rodgers and Rosino. Taking his seat, Ken scanned the faces staring back at him, feeling the tension in the air. In addition to Larry Caldwell, his immediate supervisor; there was Jimmy Norton, the Department's Technology manager; DHC Director Thompson, along with an aide; and three faces Ken did not recognize.

"Okay, shall we begin then?" Director Thompson said. "Agent Rodgers, I believe you have a report to present."

"Yes sir," he began as John handed three identical folders to their supervisor. "First, I apologize for not having enough copies of the report; I was not expecting the additional attendees."

"That's quite alright, Agent Rodgers. Susan, will you make copies of this for everyone?"

"Yes sir."

"Please proceed Agent Rodgers."

"Yes sir. This morning Agent Rosino and I met with Professor Lenkovitch. He's made progress in his interrogation of the subject and he. . . ."

"Have you met with Kincaid yet?" One of the unknown faces, a squat fireplug of a man, barked at him. Ken looked at the man and then at his supervisor.

"I apologize Agent Rodgers; introductions are in order," Director Thompson said.

Pointing to the man who spoke, he said, "Introducing himself in typical fashion, is Sherman Mason, Assistant Director of the Federal Bureau of Investigation. Next to him is Dennis Colbert, Junior Secretary of Defense, and seated to my right is Ms. Elizabeth DeVane, Special Assistant to the President. You're free to discuss openly and to answer their inquiries."

"Yes sir."

Ken looked at Mason, "Agent Rosino and me sat with Mr. Kincaid this morning. We spoke with him at length. He was polite but cautious, obviously wary of. . . ."

"Let's cut to the core, Rodgers," the fireplug interrupted, "can he do this magical trick of his? Does he have a supposed 'time machine'?"

Ken paused for a moment, assessing Mason; *be careful*, he told himself; *this guy climbs the ladder by crushing people.* "Yes, he claims he can, but. . ."

"Then I say we take him now, immediately! Get him into our custody and that machine too," Mason retorted, half rising from the table, "I'll have a SWAT team over there. . . ."

"Sit down Sherman, and allow Agent Rodgers to finish his report," the Director said. "Continue Agent Rodgers, you were saying?"

"Yes sir," Ken slowly resumed, keeping his eyes fixed on Mason. ". . . .but he claims there is no time machine and that he travels in time by stepping through, what he calls 'timegates.' These gates are located at various 'dimensional nodes' around the world."

"Agent Rodgers, how long does this man claim he's been stepping through these timegates?" Secretary Colbert asked.

"Not long, only a couple of months. He claims he stepped through the first one by accident and since then has gone through two more. He said the first one took him to the. . ." Ken paused before continuing, ". . .to the *'beings'* who control the gates."

"For crying out loud," Mason snorted, "the man's a lunatic!"

"He says these *'beings'* showed him where additional windows are located and how to 'step' through them,'" Ken continued, ignoring the barking fireplug.

"What exactly are these *'beings,'* Agent Rodgers?" Director Thompson asked.

Ken took a deep breath, "Kincaid says they are an ancient race possessing superior intelligence, existing before humans and having super powers and abilities. He said they account for the UFO sightings, the unexplained mysteries of history and unusual phenomena around the world, such as the 'Bermuda Triangle.'"

111

"Hogwash!" Mason stormed. "Nonsense from a deranged mind. Obviously, a mental case. I bring him in, and we'll find out just what he's up to. 'Timegates' and 'ancient' supermen for crying out loud!"

Director Thomas gave Mason a stern look, and then asked Ken, "Do you believe him Agent Rodgers?"

Ken reflected a long moment before answering, "I believe there's something, sir. He's holding back and is not entirely forthcoming, but he presents a compelling sincerity. There's sureness and stability about him that goes counter to him being mental. Everything we've checked out has proven true. He's not looking for any publicity or personal gain from saying such things." He looked at the others, "And, of course, there are the tablets."

"Yes, there are those," the Director said, and seeing Mason begin to object, quickly added, "and they've been verified as authentic by numerous sources. There appears little doubt they are genuine and as such cannot be dismissed."

"Then that's all the more reason to bring him in," Mason said. "He represents a serious threat to our security. Heaven knows what he could do—or is doing."

"There could be a problem with that," Ken said. "He is well aware of the threat we pose and claims he's taken steps to ensure his freedom."

"Steps? What steps?" Mason demanded, "What could he possibly do?"

"With all due respect, sir, that's the problem," Ken replied, "with his claimed ability to travel in time, he could conceivably do anything. We have no way of knowing what or even when he could have done something. He's made it clear to us that he has no intentions of doing anything to our security or defenses. He said he has no interest in politics or governments of any type, and that his interest is strictly academic and philosophical."

Ken paused and shook his head, "It's a different way of thinking. We're trained to think and act in order to prevent an incident from occurring in the future. But with this situation, it may have already happened in the future. If we accept what he claims at face value, then the possibilities are endless of what he could do." He looked around the room at the solemn faces, and knowing he had their attention, he continued.

"He said, as a safeguard to his freedom, he has put things in place that would be 'fatally detrimental' (his words) to the present administration if he does not go back to undo them before a certain date transpires."

"What the devil!" Mason blurted out, "Who does he think. . ."

"Agent Rosino," Director Thompson interrupted, "do you confirm this?"

"Yes sir. That's exactly what he said, sir. Told us he had gone back in time before the election and had something in place that would destroy the current administration if he didn't go back to undo it. He referred to it as a 'ticking nuclear political bomb.'"

"Well, we're not going to sit back and let him pull this nonsense on us, are we?" Colbert asked.

"He also said these *'beings'* have placed a 'timegate' at his disposal, giving him immediate access to step into it at the first indication of interference from us." John said and seeing the concerned looks around the table, he added, "He sounded like a terrorist to me sir."

Ken gave him a sharp look.

"And you would propose we should do what, Agent Rosino?" the Director asked.

"That we storm the building and take him and the professor into custody immediately, sir."

"Exactly!" Mason blurted out.

Only the sound of Ken sighing heavily broke the silence.

"There's another thing sir," Ken said.

"Go on Agent Rodgers," the Director said.

"Lenkovitch, the professor, told us, in case we didn't believe Mr. Kincaid, he has taken some measures of his own to ensure their freedom."

"There's no end to this insanity!" Mason stormed, "What is that kook threatening, to bring back Attila the Hun?"

Ken didn't respond.

"Go on, Agent Rodgers," the Director said.

"Lenkovitch claimed he's made several copies of a file detailing the entire affair, to include the government's suppression and concealment of the tablets. He said should anything happen to any members of his group; these files are set to be automatically released to the public. His words were 'the greatest historical, cultural, spiritual and technological discovery in the history of the world, covered up by the United States government, would create a global crises for the administration.' He repeated they had no desire to do anything to harm the administration, but would in order to ensure their freedom."

"Do you believe him Agent Rodgers?" Ms. DeVane asked.

"Yes Ma'am. We followed up, and his housemaid had, in fact, mailed five packages to different cities, two days earlier, which we were too late to track down. He's no fool, Ma'am."

"They can't seriously believe they can blackmail the United States government while we sit back and allow this nutcase to run around willy-nilly!" Mason said.

"Actually, they don't. They said they understood we would wait only so long, despite their warnings, and they didn't want to be at odds with their government. They said they would fully cooperate with our investigation in four weeks after they return."

"Return? Return from where, agent?" the Director asked.

"Athens sir," Ken answered.

"Athens?" the Director repeated, "What's in Athens?"

"A 'timegate' sir, one that will take them back in time to. . . ." Ken paused.

"To what, Agent Rodgers?"

"To the year 400 BCE sir, to. . . .to meet with Socrates."

"Socrates! This is incredible!" Mason blurted out, "I cannot believe we're sitting here listening to this nonsense. We're wasting time."

"What about our devices?" the Director asked, looking at Norton, "Have you gotten anything yet Jimmy?"

"I'm afraid, not much sir. What little we were getting has pretty much dried up. They've taken strong measures to keep us from listening in on their discussions. What we have picked up tends, in general, to confirm they've had discussions about 'gateways', the pyramids and some ancient histories. We've found nothing relating to any current governments or situations in the world. There are bits and pieces about testing some metals and a white powder, but we haven't been able to figure that out yet."

"White powder!" Mason exploded, "my God! That's anthrax! That a WMD! They're planning a mass attack!"

"We've considered that," Ken's supervisor said, "there's nothing in their backgrounds to indicate such action. We've checked them out thoroughly. They're scientists and dirt nerds with no known political agendas. The rabbi has Zionist leanings, but has never attended any of the groups we monitor or joined any radical causes, and he's there only as the professor's closest friend. He's scheduled to travel to Israel in two weeks on a trip he's made often in the past. Nothing unusual and nothing to indicate any WMD sir."

"We need to be very vigilant, Larry," the Director said, "The possibility cannot be taken lightly."

"Yes sir, we're on that."

"I still say we move on them now," Mason said, slamming his fist on the table, "Anthrax for crying out loud! Blackmailing the government! The DOD concurs, isn't that right Dennis?"

"Absolutely, we should put out a full net and bring them all into custody immediately," Colbert said.

"No one is going to do anything until the President is fully briefed on this," Ms. DeVane spoke up, "this case is now officially under the control and direction of the President of the United States, and no further action will be taken without the President's express approval. Is that understood?" She looked from one face to another and received nods, except from Sherman Mason.

"Assistant Director Mason," she said, "is that understood?"

Mason stared at her for an eternity before curtly giving his head a single nod.

She continued to stare at Mason while talking, "No agents from any other organization are to be involved or assigned to this case. The Department of Homeland Security will continue to handle the investigation and surveillance, understood?"

Again, reluctant nods.

"Agent Rodgers, please continue your surveillance and interaction with the subject and include me on all reports and correspondence. This is my private cell number. Use it with any development, understood?"

"Yes ma'am."

"Mr. Norton, please continue working on breaking through the recordings; we seriously need to know what they're talking about in there."

"Yes ma'am; I'm doing my best."

"This meeting and its subject matter are restricted to this room, and "For Your Eyes Only" security, and is not to be leaked or released to anyone inside or outside of the government or anywhere else, to include our allies in Greece, without the President's express authorization."

She looked around the room for approvals, "Gentlemen while this whole thing may be difficult to accept or understand, and sounds like some science fiction story, we cannot afford to react out of anger or arrogance. This very well could be a monumental hoax, but until those tablets are shown to be fakes, and we know exactly what is going on, we must keep our emotions in check. Whatever this is, the potential downside must be weighed heavily, and I assume you each understand what I mean." She surveyed the room, her eyes burning into those around her.

"Very well then, unless there is something else, this meeting is adjourned," she said.

Chapter Twenty

D avid spent the next two weeks cramming.

It's an easy thing to say, '*Let's go back in time two-thousand years and see what's going on,*' but, unless you want to be worshipped as or sacrificed to the gods, a little preparation is in order. There are the obvious things, like clothing and language, and then there are the not so obvious things, like interacting with people living a first Century existence.

They had two things going for them. First, Israel was a trade center. People from all nations and cultures passed through Jerusalem, from Egypt, Greece, Asia and Rome. There would be a diverse mix of clothing, appearances and mannerisms, giving them cover. Second, they had the combined knowledge of Thaddeus, Alex and Barosh—two archeologists and a Jewish scholar. Between them, they were an encyclopedia of life in 1st century Israel.

"Everything will be different David," Barosh said. "This isn't like a vacation to another country. Two thousand years of civilization and technology will be wiped out in an instant. We'll be challenged in ways we're not accustomed to. For example, it'll be just as hot and dry as it is now, but we won't have the comforts of air conditioning, lightweight clothing, or pools of fresh water to cool off with. In fact, we won't have much water at all for drinking or bathing, and it won't be treated with chlorine and fluorine, cooled and sanitized. Forget all about the Surgeon's General recommendation of drinking eight glasses a day. There are no plastic bottles of water."

"Towns will be impregnated with the stench of decaying food and waste – animal and human. We'll experience humanity as we've never experienced it before. Personal hygiene will be limited. You won't be the Aqua Velva man, and there won't be Colgate toothpaste available at the corner convenience store. It'll take a while to get accustomed to," he chuckled and added, "but don't fret; in time; you won't notice the smell—or your own."

"I can't wait. You mentioned clothing; I don't suppose we'll walk around in jeans and a polo shirt."

"No, that wouldn't do, so we have a new wardrobe for you," Thaddeus said while opening a cardboard box. "These were for Alex, who was on the fence about going. They're not 5th Avenue, but they'll grow on you."

"Literally," Barosh laughed, removing what looked like a pile of rags, "our cover is we're Israelites on pilgrimage to Jerusalem, and that's not far from the truth. We'll be dressed appropriately, not upper class, or we'd draw attention to ourselves, from outlaws or Romans."

He withdrew a long swash of material.

"First, the loincloth," he said holding it up, "this is your *Fruit of the Loom*, and before you wrinkle your nose at it— many of the men won't be wearing anything," he chuckled, "and that option will always be available to you. Here, I'll show you how you wear it." He wrapped the cloth around Thaddeus waist, bringing it up between his legs, and tucking it in.

"I've never seen a grown man wearing a diaper before, especially over his pants," David laughed.

"I think he looks rather stunning," Barosh mocked.

"Is there any particular reason I'm the model?" Thaddeus complained.

"You got such cute cheeks," Barosh tweaked him.

"This is ridiculous. I re. . . ."

"Over the loincloth," Barosh ignored his protests, working a grey nightshirt over his head, "you wear this tunic." Pulling Thaddeus's arms through the sleeves, he unfurled it down to his ankles.

"All you need is a tasseled nightcap, and you'd be a dead ringer for Scrooge," David laughed.

"It's not Calvin Klein, but it's made from the most advanced materials, providing warmth, cooling and comfort. It can be worn long or shortened, like this." He pulled it up between Thaddeus's legs and tucked it in around his waist." He next extracted a long strip of cloth, "We had this belt made for tying the inner tunic around your waist. It's light, strong and, most importantly," he turned it inside out; "there are a series of hidden pouches woven into the fabric that have ties. These are for carrying the things you don't want to lose."

"What kind of things are those?"

"The packet of white powder Jennifer will give you for the return trip home for one, plus money and medicine," Alex answered.

"Medicine? What medicine?" David asked.

"You don't want to get sick or catch some foreign disease," Thaddeus replied. "Tomorrow, you'll get a series of inoculations for typhoid, fevers, and a host of other potential problems, as well as the strongest Tetanus available. But, with all that, we're in a bit of a quandary regarding the health risk."

"Why's that?" David asked.

"Well, the world will be two-thousand years younger, cleaner, devoid of the built-up of pollution and chemicals, and you'll benefit from two-thousand years of immunity in your genes. Also, many of the potential malicious strains of disease will be either two-thousand years weaker or not on the scene yet, so you'll have a healthy immune system."

"Unfortunately, we don't know what benefit that will be in a first century world. The world will also be dirtier due to poor sanitation, unclean water quality and lower hygiene standards that your body is not conditioned to. We don't know what strains of disease there could be that have become extinct over the centuries, which you may have no immunity to. For example, just how strong and contagious was leprosy? It's mentioned in many ancient writings, as a fairly common aliment. What your immunity will be to it, we don't know. You'll carry a supply of powerful aspirin and antibiotics to help protect you should any illness present itself. You'll also have a large quantity of water purification tablets. Without them, the water there would probably kill you."

"When in Mexico, don't drink the water, my mother always said," David joshed.

"A word of caution," Alex said, "the medicine is for your use only. Don't give it to anyone there, or you could run the risk of a paradox."

Unfolding a large, tan garment, having alternating brown and black stripes up and down its length, Barosh resumed, "This is your outer cloak. Take care of it. It's your primary protection from the elements. During the day, it's your coat, and at night it's your blanket. While it looks like an ancient Hebrew mantle, it's actually made of highly advanced, synthetic material, interlaced with microfibers of silver and titanium that retain body heat at night, yet breathes and deflects heat during the day. It's water repellent as well and is a marvelous piece of technology. Inside are pockets woven for carrying items. If anyone should question you about the material or its texture, say it's the newest weave from Alexandria."

He pulled out a long, wide strip of supple leather. "This is your outer belt, used to secure the cloak around your body. They called it the girdle, and this pouch loops around it like this."

"And these are your shoes," Alex said, setting a pair of, what looked like boards with leather and rawhide strips hanging from them, on the table.

"You've got to be kidding!" David said.

"They're a lot more comfortable than they look," Alex said. "We've put a lot of effort into these. They look like normal sandals, but that's where the similarity ends. When strapped up, the leather sides have hidden ankle support, and the soles have a long-lasting traction tread and provide support, as well as arch relief. We took liberties to have toe guards and heel coverings built in for protection. You'll carry an extra pair since walking will be the mode of transportation. As with the cloak, if questioned about them, say they're the newest creation from Alexandria."

David turned them over in his hands, "They don't feel like my Nike's."

"And be glad of that. Your Nike's may help Michael Jordan float like a butterfly on the court, but they wouldn't last a month and would be like ovens in the desert," Barosh said. "Any man in the first century would sell his wife and kids to own these, so don't leave them lying around. They wore stiff leather, planks of wood or went barefoot. Their feet were calloused, hard and tough from years of sand and sun. Our feet aren't conditioned for the Sinai. Start wearing these now, to break them and your feet in. We'll have a long walk when we arrive, and sore feet with blisters won't get us to Israel." He lifted his foot to show he was wearing a similar pair.

"Finally, this is your headgear," Alex said, holding up a cloth of the same material and design as the cloak had been. He put it on Thaddeus's head to show how it was worn. "It's not the Scrooge nightcap you mentioned but a basic, oversized cap with a wide covering of material around it." The cap covered Thaddeus head, and the excess material came down over his shoulders like a mini tent. "You can let it hang down, tie it back like so, roll it up, or go bare-headed; all are acceptable."

"You look like a shepherd in the annual Christmas play," David snickered.

"No, not a shepherd, and not one of the wise men either—more like Joseph," Barosh responded with a deadpan seriousness. "Don't trim your beard any longer. Let it grow. Also, spend some time under the tanning lamp Thaddeus bought. You need some color, and you don't want to get sunburned there. You're wearing a ring."

"A gift from Nicole."

"I suggest you, either leave it or wear it around your neck under the tunic. It would be tempting for someone to steal it—along with your finger."

"Will I have any weapons?"

"Only a Zealot or an outlaw would carry a sword," Barosh answered. "Having one would be an open invitation for Roman interrogation, which is a polite way of saying torture and possible execution. So, that's out. You're an Israelite, on pilgrimage to Jerusalem, and wouldn't be carrying weapons. You'll have this good knife. Carry it under your cloak, and hope you never have to use it, except for cutting figs."

"I'd prefer a .357 under my cloak. This sounds more dangerous than I thought."

"Jerusalem is a mixing bowl of nations and cultures, so hopefully we'll blend in without notice. But there are always risks. The main threat, of course, will be the Romans and outlaws. If we can stay clear of those two—we'll be okay. Carry your least valuable things, along with a few coins, in your outer pouch. If you're accosted, don't fight, but give the pouch to them, and they'll most likely run away."

"What about money?"

"An interesting subject," Thaddeus said, stripping off the clothes. "Numerous economies were in play in the first century, having various forms of money. It was a profitable business exchanging one for another."

"Wasn't it the money changers Jesus flipped out over?" David asked.

"Yes, that's true; twice, in fact," Thaddeus said, and then added with a chuckle, "who knows maybe you'll actually get to see that." David's expression dropped and the color drained from his face.

"What's the matter?" Barosh asked.

"I don't know. It just kind of hit me what we're doing and what we might actually see."

Barosh nodded, understanding, "I know; it hits me, as well, and I feel the ground open under me. It's exciting, but frightening at the same time. I try not to think about it."

"Anyway," Thaddeus continued, "with the Empire's heavy taxation policies, it simplifies the problem; all money eventually went to Rome. You'll each be carrying a fortune. Most will be in Roman coinage consisting of gold aureus and silver denarii. These will be supplemented with silver Greek drachmas and gold Tetradachmas. You'll also have a large supply of Jewish coins. Many Jews wouldn't use Roman or Greek coins that had an image on them. They had their own coins bearing no images. You'll have silver Tyrian shekels and half-shekels along with a quantity of copper prutas, or mites. You'll each have more money than fifty Israelites would earn in a lifetime, so keep it hidden inside your inner pouches. Keep Jewish coins in the outer pouch, as those are what would be expected of an Israelite on pilgrimage, and you'll need them to purchase food and shelter and for the offerings at the temple, as well as the Tyrian half-shekel temple tax. A word of caution, gold coins were not common, so using them publicly would attract attention. When you exchange one, do it in private.

"Where are all these ancient coins coming from, the Denver mint?" David smirked.

"There are advantages to having two archeologists and a metallurgist on the team," Thaddeus said. "We had them made ourselves. We know what the coins from the era were, and they were stamped out by hand, with simple images and writings on them. Edges were rough and uneven. It was an easy matter to supply the gold, silver and bronze along with some examples to Jennifer. She was able to have them duplicated and aged. I daresay we've become quite accomplished at minting them. I don't know if it'd be called counterfeiting as they're not fakes, but are the real thing, even better. You'll have no trouble using them."

"In general, the Jews held a distain for coins," Barosh said. "They preferred to barter and viewed money as evil, used by the pagan authorities and the Pharisees. Many Jews refused to trade with Roman coins having the likeness of Caesar on it, and it was forbidden to bring a coin with an image on it into the temple. So the money-changer tables were set up to provide the exchange (at a tidy profit) for the Tyrian half-shekel for the temple tax. Herod the Great created uproar, when he minted a series of coins bearing the image of an eagle. It was seen as a symbol of submission to Rome, and of open defiance to God. Many believe it is for this reason that he was stricken and died a horrible death."

"Is that the same Herod Jesus went before?" David asked.

"No, that was his son, Herod Antipas. He took over, along with his brother, Philip after Herod died. Herod the Great was the one who killed all the newborns in Bethlehem."

"We'll be able to prove or disprove some of those stories," David said.

"Yes, that's exciting, isn't it?" Thaddeus said. "If I was only younger and in better health, I would be going with you. Such an opportunity, knowing the stories and their events and outcomes ahead of time, to witness what actually happened. I anxiously await your return to hear all that you have seen and heard. You will witness history David, and what you bring back will determine the future of history."

"That's a heavy responsibility," David replied.

"Yes it is, and you're the right man to carry it."

"Here are some books you should study," Barosh said, handing David an armful of volumes, "they provide the timeline and histories leading up to 30 CE for Israel, Egypt and Rome. There's information on the Jewish, Roman, Greek and Egyptian cultures and their way of life during the first century. This one here gives the values and exchanges for the coins you'll carry and references how much things cost at the time. Read this one closely as it explains the Torah and Jewish law and how it impacted everyday life then. There are many things that you would not think of, which if done wrong, would expose you as an imposter or get you killed. For example, you could get stoned for saying the wrong thing or touching a woman in a perfectly innocent way."

David's expression showed his anxiety and perplexity.

"Don't worry," Barosh said with a laugh, "read these and then follow my lead."

Chapter Twenty-one

Assistant FBI Director, Sherman Mason didn't like the President. He didn't like this uppity, blonde 'Special Assistant' to the President, and he didn't like being talked to as if he was some two-bit political hack.

I'm the Assistant Director of the Federal Bureau of Investigation, the FBI, for crying out loud! Who does she think she is ordering me around like some wet-behind-the-ears college freshman?

He knew how to handle Kincaid; he dealt with these nut cases every day. The country was full of them, claiming special powers, visions and psychic abilities. Lately, they've been coming out of the woodwork, and this broad was tying his hands in dealing with them.

'Travel back in time,' gimme a break! Just one more yokel who fell off the turnip truck.

His job was dealing with the likes of them. He built his career by doing just that, and by God, he was good at it too.

You squash them. Stamp them out, one-by-one, like a pestilence of cockroaches, and this presidential lackey isn't going to tell me to stand down!

The buzzer on his desk interrupted his silent rant.

"Send him in," he said, without asking anything.

The large, oak door swung open and a well-built man, wearing a charcoal-grey suit walked in.

"Have a seat," Sherman said, without standing, "thanks for coming."

"No problem, sir."

"Do you know why I asked you here?"

"No sir, but I assume it has to do with the Kincaid case."

"Tell me agent, what is your take on the whole affair?"

"Well, it's certainly strange sir," he shifted in his seat.

"Relax Agent; what is said here remains here. Feel free to speak your mind. I took it you didn't agree with everything that was said yesterday."

The Agent looked at the solid man sitting across the wide, cherry wood desk. There were no papers, folders or files visible, no pencils or pens and notably, for today's world, no computer keyboard or glowing screens. Only the cupped hands of Director Mason occupied the top of the large desk. This was in stark contrast to the walls, which were covered with citations, awards and pictures of various dignitaries, politicians and well-known businessmen, each strategically posed with Sherman. The American flag stood in one corner of the large room, and the Bureau's flag draped the other.

His instinct told him to be cautious; this man was dangerous and could crush his career without batting an eye. But, played right, he was the break he'd had been looking for. It had been obvious that Mason and the little floozy hadn't hit it off, and he hadn't been called here to congratulate her.

"Yes sir, I find it discouraging our hands are being tied."

"Precisely! I have the same sentiments myself," Sherman looked him in the eye, *slimy little weasel,* he thought, *trying to size me up. Well, that's good, that's exactly what I want you to do.*

"Tell me, Agent, What would you do?"

"Haul them in, the whole lot of them. It's obvious they're up to no good, and they shouldn't be allowed to continue."

"They're American citizens, and they have rights."

"Yes sir, as do the law-abiding citizens of the country, and our job is to protect their rights against dangerous terrorists like this."

"So, you consider them to be dangerous, Agent?"

"It's clear they're planning some sort of strike. The bits and pieces we've put together speak of missiles, explosions and changing history sir."

"You don't believe they can travel through time then?"

"No, sir, that's a smoke screen to cover their intent."

"Exactly!" Sherman said, rising from the deep leather chair. "But I can't intervene by order of the President."

"That's unfortunate sir, politicians aren't trained and capable of recognizing real threats and dangers as we are sir. They're more concerned with political capital and opinion polls."

Testing me are you?

"We must not underestimate the value of political capital; we each need to know which way the wind blows."

Sherman walked around the desk and began pacing the room.

"I agree with you that they aren't capable of distinguishing a genuine threat when it confronts them. They need our help, even if they do not realize it. And, that's the responsibility the American people have placed on us, isn't it Agent Rosino?"

"Yes sir."

"Yes, and I take that responsibility darned seriously as I know you do also, John. The country is looking for strong, astute men who recognize these threats and protect the people from them." He came around the back of John's chair and placed his hand on his shoulder, "The Bureau is always keen to finding clever, capable men such as yourself. There could be a bright future for you in the Bureau, especially if you were to expose and prevent a significant terrorist attack."

"I'm here to serve my country, sir."

"As am I, John, but my hands are tied. As the Assistant Director, I cannot go against the standing orders of the President of the United States," he paused, "unless, that is, there was a direct threat or action taken against America." He gently squeezed John's shoulder, "Then, he would offer congratulations and be thankful. . . forever in *our* debt."

"Yes sir."

"How does your partner feel about the situation?"

"He's cautious, giving them too much latitude. We disagree on that point, sir."

"I see. A commendable attitude, but one that could be too late in stopping a serious incident."

"I agree sir."

"As responsible guardians of America, I think we need to be especially vigilant and alert and not allow an incident to occur. It would go poorly for the agents on a case if something was to happen, and those agents did not prevent it."

"Yes sir."

"Sometimes, we have to step outside of the box to do the right thing."

"I fully concur sir."

"Good, then we agree," he handed John a small card; "this is my cell. It's a secure number. Use it without hesitation for any developments. I have a SWAT team on call twenty-four/seven. They can be activated within seconds of your call."

"Yes sir."

Sherman held out his hand to John, who stood to shake it. As he did so, Sherman moved him towards the door, which opened silently.

"Thank you Agent Rosino, the country rests a little easier relying upon your expertise and alertness. Of course, I rely upon your discretion. I don't see any reason for Agent Rodgers to be involved."

"Agreed sir. Thank you sir."

As John exited down the hall, Sherman smiled.

Well done Sherman; don't tell me, Ms. Presidential advisor, not to have my man on the job.

Chapter Twenty-two

David remained in Thaddeus' house buried under a mountain of books. Barosh contributed an endless supply.

I get through all of these, David thought, *and I'll pass the rabbi bar exam.*

Alex piled on as well Egyptians—Romans—Greeks—Persians—Arabians. The stack grew, and like an anemia cell monster, split into two, then four.

He poured over drawings, maps, and pictures of coins, weapons, utensils and clothing. He liked studying. Sciences, engineering, languages, had always fascinated him and kept him captivated. But, this was the granddaddy of cram courses, an ocean of cultures, rituals and histories; all in preparation for the final exam, to be held—two-thousand years *ago*—in three weeks.

The more he learned—the more anxious he became. Despite the religious overtone of the mission, the idea of traveling back to the world of the First Century was mind-boggling.

Thaddeus insisted he not leave the building, afraid the agents outside might seize him. He managed to keep them at bay, but it was an uneasy standoff, and it wouldn't be wise to tempt them. That worked for David; he had tied up any loose ends prior to climbing the railing. All he needed was his passport, which Thaddeus had Camille retrieve from his old apartment. No one would miss him.

He wore the sandals, or went barefoot on the hard wooden floors; stopped trimming his beard and eating desserts; and worked out twice a day. He needed conditioning, outside as well as inside, to prepare for the wilderness conditions of Egypt and Israel—twenty centuries ago.

Nights were hard, giving no rest. Tossing and turning, sleep refused him refuge. His head spun from the daily onslaught. Not only the mountain of information the three amigos hurled at him, but the wonder of what he was about to do. Upon accepting this craziness, the reality of it, hit him like a locomotive. He, along with a Jewish rabbi he hadn't known until a few days ago, was going on a vacation to Israel—two thousand years ago!

He was following in the footsteps of that famous explorer—'Sally' the lab-mouse.

Step right up here, Davey boy. Drink the magic potion; climb in that rabbit hole. Who knows what you will find there? Maybe you'll find. . . Davey boy.

Who *does* know? Knows what really will happen? Sure, they have their theories and ideas, and they run their computer models, calculating sunrises thousands of years ago. That's all fun and games, but who genuinely knows what will happen? Only 'Sally,' the mouse, knows, and she's not around to tell anyone. What if they were wrong? With just one of their assumptions? Would he emerge as dinosaur bait? Or be suspended in some unknown dimension? Or would he simply vaporize?

But, what if they're right? Then he would step out into the First Century—to meet Jesus—the man who claimed to be the son of God—the man who changed the course of human history!

Either way—sleep avoided his nights. He may as well have been lying on hot rocks, as on a mattress. How could anyone sleep with such thoughts assaulting him? He must be crazy, believing these mad scientists and their wild stories of pyramids, gateways and magic gold dust.

Compared to this, climbing the railing at Niagara was child's play.

Lying wide awake, staring at the ceiling fan making its slow, rhythmic circles, round and round. . . the voice spoke to him. The quiet voice. . . the one that had spoken when he had stood on the railing overlooking the turbulent Niagara River.

Still your spirit, David. . . you can do this. . . for you already have done it.
A message was left. . . a message for you. . . a message from you.
This is the time you were chosen for.
Beneath the turbulence. . . your peace is found.
David slept.

***

He found It incredible how quickly his life had changed. Despite the risks involved, the prospects of the journey excited him. He had serious doubts about Allen's ability to manipulate the time dimension. And, despite the experiments of 'Sally' and 'Enoch,' being the first 'human' lab-rat rattled him as it would any sane man. He calmed his quaking heart by clinging to a rock - that small piece of hardened clay having his name and thoughts carved on it.

That - and the quiet voice telling him all would be well.

He didn't underestimate the hardships. He was in reasonably good shape, but he'd never taken on the desert before without the advantages of modern technology.

Sure would be nice to translate in an air conditioned Humvee, he thought.

He found it humorous, to be seeking a holy man from among the many people he would have selected if given the opportunity. His childhood had been traditional Christian, which he had quickly disregarded, viewing Jesus in the same context he viewed Achilles and Hercules and a host of other, larger than life, myth-heroes, steeped in folklore and exaggeration. They were legends, claiming to be mighty men or even gods, usually made bigger than life by their followers. He had no doubts that Christianity fit into that definition.

Knowing little about Judaism, he didn't have an opinion of Jesus as a prophet, and it didn't matter as he held those, so –called prophets, in no great esteem either. Hairy, wild men, eating grasshoppers and wearing camel hair, coming from the deserts, spewing out threats and curses at everyone. The asylums are overflowing with them.

Amazing, people still believed such nonsense; he thought. *Well, Barosh can deal with that; it's a Jewish thing anyway, and he seems to be on a vendetta to expose the man.*

***

Most evenings, regardless of where they started, they would end up talking about Jesus. Their differing views about him made for lively conversation. The Christian religion has been a force of unparalleled influence in human affairs for two-thousand years, and the impact of what they would discover, would be earthshattering, whichever way it went. Entire religions, cultures and nations would be turned inside out. The basis of western civilization would be challenged. Wars and millions of lives that have perished would be questioned. Entire races had been annihilated by people carrying the cross as their standard. The heritage of North America and the powder keg of the Middle East would each be tested. Whether Jew, Muslim or Christian; believer, infidel or atheist; all would be impacted. People across the globe know the name of Jesus, and when mentioned, it stirs up intense love or intense hatred—along with a large dose of apathy. Anyone who views the history of mankind must come to a reckoning of the man, and what he was and is. What David and Barosh would discover about Jesus would be a paradigm shift in human history, and could, literally, turn the planet into an infernal.

"How difficult will it be to find him?" David asked one evening, "I don't expect we'll find an information kiosk set up, with a flashing neon sign saying, "Welcome to Israel – Meet Jesus here—one night only."

"You won't need an information booth David," Thaddeus scuffed, "if Jesus did even some of the things recorded about him—you'll have no trouble finding him. Israel isn't large, and his ministry was centered in Galilee, an even smaller area. In particular, focus your search around the towns and villages and along the shore of the Sea of Galilee. Capernaum was his center of operations. Large crowds followed him so he won't be hard to find."

"You talk as if you're sure he existed."

"There's little doubt of that," Thaddeus said, "despite what skeptics say. The evidence of history is clear and not only from his followers in the New Testament. Supporting documents have been uncovered, such as the gnostic gospels, as well as the historian Josephus who confirms he existed. Outside the Jewish community, Gentile historians, such as Thallus, Tacitus and Serapion have provided records that a man called Jesus lived in Palestine and died under the hand of the Roman governor, Pontius Pilate. In fact, there's more historical evidence that Jesus lived than for any other ancient person, Alexander the Great for example."

"He lived; there's enough evidence of that," Barosh added, "and he died, and that's where it ends. I'll prove that. He didn't rise from the grave, and he wasn't the "son of God" or the awaited messiah as he claimed to be. He was a misguided teacher, who declared himself messiah. His followers perpetuated the myth after his death. I shall show the world how it has been deceived and misled for so many centuries."

"Looks like you're on your own vendetta Barosh," David said, half amused, turning to Allen, "Do we know at what point in his ministry he'll be at?"

"That's a question we've wrestled with. There's, not only, the uncertainty of what year you'll arrive, but also the uncertainty of his age then. The textual accounts can be reconciled to create a reasonable timeline, but we don't know when that timeline begins. Where he'll be along that timeline depends on when we establish the starting date. The texts don't give the year of his birth, and no matter what Santa Claus says, he wasn't born on December 25th in 1 CE. He was probably born in September, around 3 or 4 BCE"

"I thought the calendar was based on Jesus's birth starting with year 1. How could he have been born prior to that?" David asked.

"Our calendar," Allen said "wasn't developed until over five-hundred years after Jesus lived. Pope John the First, asked Friar Dionysius, a monk who enjoyed his rum a bit, to create a standardized calendar based upon Jesus's life. His designations were known as 'BC' Before Christ and 'AD' Anno Domini.' These were recently changed, for the sake of political correctness, to 'BCE' for 'Before Common Era' and 'CE' for 'Common Era.'"

"Clues in Luke's account," Thaddeus said, "when fitted with known history, puts us close to his birth. It's widely accepted that Luke's information about Jesus's birth came directly from Mary, his mother. He was born during the reign of Herod the Great. The family escaped to Egypt, where they stayed until Herod died. Now, Josephus affirms Herod died in the year 2 BCE, so Jesus was born sometime before that. It appears the old friar had a little too much rum, and missed the mark by a few years."

"Keep in mind" Barosh interjected, "our calendar won't have been invented yet. People will be going by Hebrew and a host of other calendars from different nations. There wasn't any standardization."

"There's something you can clear up while you're there," Allen said.

"What's that?" David asked.

"The slaughter of the babies in Bethlehem, there's a lot of controversy as to whether that actually happened or not. There is no evidence of it anywhere in history, which you'd think there would be. Even Josephus never mentions it."

"Was there even a town called 'Nazareth'?" Alex asked, "It's not mentioned anywhere else in the Bible, Old or New Testament, and no historian lists such a town. It's not until the Eighth Century that its first mentioned anywhere."

"Why September?" David inquired.

"Jesus was most likely born in the fall of the year as the census of Quirinius was taking place requiring Joseph to travel to Bethlehem," Thaddeus resumed, "and the shepherds were in the fields."

"So? What do they have to do with it; I thought they were only decorations for the manger scene?" David asked.

"Actually their presence tells us a lot," Barosh said. "Jews took their sheep into the wilderness at Passover time and brought them back at the first rain. While in the wilderness, shepherds watched them, protecting them from wolves, thieves or just wandering off. The Passover occurs in the spring, and the first rain comes in the Jewish month of Marchesvan which aligns with part of October and November today. Luke describes Zacharias, a priest, performing his duties during the course of Abijah, and his wife, Elizabeth's, resulting pregnancy. Six months into her pregnancy is when Mary conceives. So when you factor the shepherds and Zacharias timing of performing the Abijah just prior to Elizabeth's pregnancy, it's a safe bet that Jesus was probably born in September."

"Okay, Christmas on Labor Day! That makes sense," David said and not receiving any response he asked, "You know *'labor'* day?"

"Well, anyway, here's what we think," Thaddeus resumed, ignoring David's humor, "he was executed when he was 33 years old so that occurred in either 30 or 31 CE which means It is most likely you will translate the year before or the year of his execution."

"Another consideration is the time of the year we're going," Barosh added, "the spring equinox for the year 30 CE occurred on March 22nd. Passover that year began on April 7th. According to the text, Jesus was executed prior to the start of the Passover. So, depending on what year we translate will have a large impact on the mission. Barring interruptions, it'll take us over a week to cross the Sinai. If we translate in the year he was executed, we may not get to Israel before the execution. It'll be best if we arrive the year before his execution."

"What if we miss him? Doesn't that negate our mission?" David asked.

"No, there's still the disciples and the supposed resurrection to investigate," Barosh said.

"As you can see, there's uncertainty," Allen said. "We're not certain what year you will translate to and we're not sure what year he was executed in. Because of this uncertainty, I plan on setting the gateway to one year ahead of now during the next few spring equinoxes, to cover the variableness of your return."

David gave Allen a skeptical look, "Provided you figure out how to 'set' those years."

Allen nodded, "True—but I will, stake your life on it."

"I am," David replied.

**

That evening Camille served a dinner of stew made with lentil, beans, barley, vegetables and intermixed with pieces of mutton. Heavy, dark-grained bread, accompanied the meal making for good bowl mopping.

"All that's missing is a little camel hump," Alex said, then seeing the look on David's face, added, "that's a joke David, but you may be wishing for a camel before it's over."

"Actually, I hope we can secure a couple of camels to carry us across the Sinai," Barosh said. Turning to David, he asked, "Ever ride a camel, David?"

David shook his head, "No, never."

"Ah, then you will be in for a treat," Thaddeus laughed.

"I don't suppose we could translate inside of an air-conditioned RV?" They laughed, tipping their glasses to David.

The mellow wine was generously consumed, relieving some of the stress and anxiety that was taking its toll on everyone. Following the meal, Camille cleaned off the table and brought in a large tray, overflowing with grapes, oranges, apples, pomegranates, figs, dates and nuts. It looked breathtaking and after the heavy, thick stew was more than pleasing.

"There won't be any ice cream, so get used to figs," Alex chuckled.

"Thank you Camille," Thaddeus said, "that'll be all for tonight."

"Yes Thaddeus; thank you and good night all."

"Good night Camille," the men said in unison.

"It was a lovely meal, Camille, thank you so much," Jennifer said.

"Yes ma'am; thank you.

"Oh, and Camille," Thaddeus said, "leave the wine, please."

***

Settling back with full glasses, David asked, "Assuming we do meet up Jesus, what would you have me ask him? How would you prove who he is?"

"Well, providing Barosh doesn't drive him into the wilderness as a heretic, I'd start with the miracles," Thaddeus said, giving Barosh a scolding glance.

"It would be better if you were able to witness some," Allen said.

"Miracles can be staged and faked, especially in that era. I'd just come right out and ask him, "Are you the son the God?" Alex interrupted.

"Well, I don't think that approach would get you very far," Thaddeus rebuked, "a little finesse might be in order."

"You're going to have to get around his disciples," Allen said, "it'd be best to hang back, and observe for a while. You'll have a tremendous advantage knowing what's supposed to happen ahead of time," He tossed a copy of the New Testament across the table to David, "Here, I suggest you study the four gospels and know the sequence of events as they recorded them."

"Just keep in mind the gospels are not biographies," Thaddeus added, "they're collections of reminiscences, events that stood out in someone's mind. Two of them are second hand. Mark's gospel is more of Peter's recollections, and Luke got his information from Mary and Paul, and Paul wasn't one of the twelve neither. Many events are out of sequence."

"I've read them," David responded while refilling his glass, "along with a mountain of books it has been "suggested" I study lately."

"Hey, no one said it was going to be easy. Pour me some while you're at it, would you?" Alex said, holding out his glass, "You should find out if he had any girlfriends."

"Girlfriends? You're joking, right?"

"No, he was a man wasn't he? He'd have the same feelings any man would have. Finding who his girlfriends were would tell you a lot about him," Alex said.

"Wasn't that already covered in 'The Da Vinci Code'?" David asked, "With Mary Magdalene and that story about having a child?"

"'The Da Vinci Code' was just that—a story, fiction, you're going to meet with the man himself—no fiction there. You don't think those men, who made him into a god, were going to write about his love life, do you?" Alex responded. "There was a group of women that followed him around and took care of him. Sounds like "groupies" to me, and when all the men deserted him, it was the women who stayed. What do you think Jennifer? From a woman's perspective, did he have a love interest?"

Jennifer sipped at her wine while she thought for a long moment before answering, "If I had to make a guess if he had one; it was probably male."

"Male! You think Jesus was gay?" Allen said, "Now who's joking?"

"Oh, it makes perfect sense, Allen. Now, I don't know if he had any sexual inclinations one way or another, but if he did, my guess would be they probably leaned towards homosexual," she placed her glass on the table and leaned forward, watching the male reactions around the table and smiling.

"I'll refer to the Bible, just as Alex did. Look at the way he talked about love; 'love one another', 'love your neighbor as yourself' and on and on, all about love and mostly said to men. He hung around with twelve men all the time. Doesn't that seem rather odd? And there's one man in particular he favored."

"You're speaking of John," Barosh said.

"Yes, John who Jesus called his "beloved" numerous times, and whenever John referred to himself, he said *'the one Jesus loved.'* Now if any man talked that way today, he would be considered gay in a heartbeat."

"Interesting theory, Jennifer," Alex said, leaning back and looking at Barosh, "What do you think rabbi?"

"Well, he was a Hebrew rabbi, and there's no tradition of rabbinic celibacy, but he could have chosen to refrain from any sexual lifestyle. It wasn't unusual for prophets and holy men to be surrounded with male followers; women weren't on an equal standing."

"He claimed to take on human form with all human emotions and sensitivities," Alex interrupted, "if he had no sexual feelings then he couldn't represent humanity, ignoring the strongest drives and motivations people have. The whole concept of God becoming flesh would be false."

"And where would that put you with your alien theory?" Barosh asked.

"No problem, there's plenty of evidence aliens interacted with humans."

"Well, you seem to have it covered no matter which way it goes," Thaddeus said, tipping his glass to Alex. "From my perspective, the idea that he had a romantic relationship with Mary Magdalene, or anyone else, is the stuff of fiction and is based on no evidence. It's true women attended to him, but that wasn't unusual, with no sexual context implied, and Jewish law was quite clear about male and female relations. Jennifer's theory is intriguing but not realistic. If I had to take a position on this, I'd say he was asexual. Sex was not his driving motivation. Whether he was the son of God or not, he believed he was, and that consumed him."

He looked towards David, "You've been quiet David; what's your opinion?"

"I don't have one, and to be honest, I don't care. Heterosexual, bisexual, homosexual, asexual; he could have been any or all of these for all I know. The relationship Jennifer mentioned that he had with the 'one Jesus loved,' sounds modern and would be interpreted as being gay in our world today, but who knows how people thought in those days. Whether he was a long-haired, hippie with his head in the clouds, a visionary who thought he was a king or just a peasant who heard one too many prophesies of a messiah while languishing under too much desert sun, I guess is what we'll hopefully find out."

"Well said David," Allen said, "but you left out one possibility."

"What's that?"

"That he really was the son of God," he tipped his glass to David and added, "I believe you are going to have a most fascinating journey. Just try to keep Barosh on a short leash."

"Going back to David's original question, I would focus on Jesus' presence," Thaddeus said, "what was it about him that made people follow him? It was more than just performing miracles. He didn't change the world; you know. He stayed close to home, never left Israel, never wrote a book, confined his ministry to the Jews and was then rejected by them. The fact is he should have dissolved into obscurity—why didn't he? How did the world undergo such a phenomenal impact, sustained for over twenty centuries? It was his apostles. Those men he personally taught and trained that went out into the world and turned it upside down, them and Paul. How did that happen? What effect did he have on them that they could do this? Except for Paul, they weren't mighty men, respected leaders or distinguished speakers. They were fishermen! I doubt if most of them could write. What was it about Jesus that transformed these oppressed, ordinary Jews into the movers and changers of history? That David is what you need to discover. Once you understand that—then you'll know what Jesus truly was."

"Bravo, professor!" Alex said, and they all tipped their glasses to him.

"There's one thing that will prove whether he is god or not, without any need for interpretation and leaves no doubt whatsoever," Allen said.

"What would that be Allen?" Barosh asked.

"Simple; the resurrection, dead people don't walk around," he answered, looking at them keenly. "After all, that's the crux of the whole matter, isn't it? Without the resurrection—Jesus is not God and is only a man, and all of Christianity is a lie."

He placed his glass on the table and spread his hands, "That folks, is the bottom line."

No one spoke, knowing the truth of Allen's words.

Chapter Twenty-three

"I was wondering," David said one evening after everyone settled in, "if the white powder alters my internal molecular structure enabling me to translate, how do my clothes and other things translate through? I wouldn't like popping out in the middle of the Egyptian desert in only my birthday suit."

Alex laughed, "Oh, too much information; there's a visual I do not want."

"Now Alex, I don't think it would be all that bad," Jennifer said giving David a coy smile. "But, it's a legitimate question and one I've looked at quite seriously. One of the characteristics of monatomic gold, which I haven't come to understand yet, is its ability to change the objects around it. You recall, in the initial experiments the sample dish had also lost weight along with the sample. I assumed the part of the dish that the sample rested on was being affected."

David nodded, "Yes, I remember that."

"I explored the theory on 'Enoch', hanging small items around his neck and attaching others to his tail. I also placed some small items on the bottom of the test chamber. When 'Enoch' translated, all the items attached to him translated also. Only one of the items placed inside the chamber translated. The one his foot was touching. The others did not translate. Each time I repeated the experiment, I recorded the same results. Some of the items that translated with 'Enoch' didn't return. I assumed; 'Enoch' had moved and was not touching them when the return translation happened. It actually became comical for me thinking of what it must look like if there was something over there, seeing this creature appearing and disappearing wearing these different things, and leaving some behind. Would he be considered a messenger from God? Anyway the bottom line is, hold onto your things, and they'll go with you."

"Those things are out there somewhere, in never-never land," Alex laughed, but when he noticed no one laughed with him, but were looking at David, who sat with his eyes closed, slowly shaking his head, he recanted, "Sorry David, just a joke. No harm intended."

"That won't happen to you and Barosh, David," Allen said, "you're not going into never-never land, some dimension we don't know about. You'll be in the same place you started from."

David opened his eyes and turned to Allen, "Now I know how the astronauts felt about 'Houston Control' when they blasted off. Bet they treated them to a steak dinner first."

"We'll take a rain check—for when you return," Allen replied.

"*Houston, we have a problem,*" David quipped. Everyone chuckled, except Allen.

As the humor subsided Allen said, "It does bring up a point you should be aware of."

"Every time you say that, I get chills up and down my spine," David said.

"Relax; it's just that the earth is not in a perfect orbit, year to year. There is some variation. Like a car going around a racetrack. It's always going in the same oval, but it's not in the same set of tracks on each lap around. There's a similar effect due to the motion of the earth as it orbits the sun, and there may be a difference in the position of where the earth was the year you enter the gateway and where it is the year you leave the gateway, two-thousand years earlier."

"What does that mean?" David asked.

"It means you may not come out of the translation in the exact, same spot you stepped into it. You'll be in the same place on the race track, but not necessarily in the same set of 'earth' tracks."

"Just how far apart are these 'earth tracks'? We talking feet or miles?"

Allen paused, "Well, I'll tell you some of my colleagues have taken this to an extreme, surmising that the motion between thousands of years could be large, perhaps outside the current earth's orbit."

"You mean we'd pop out in space?" David jumped.

"According to their theory. . . yes. But before you panic, they're wrong," Allen said firmly, "the theory of relativity rejects the idea of absoluteness in time and space, and so, there is no universal truth about the spatial distance between an event occurring on Earth today and an event occurring on Earth 2000 years ago."

"What's that mean?" David's expression was not happy.

"What I mean is with the theory of general relativity, the effects of gravity keep all coordinates on an equal footing because of a feature known as "diffeomorphism invariance". "

"And what's that mean?"

"It means you'll be okay. You'll translate at the same position in the gateway, within a slight variation, measured in feet."

David shook his head, "This is unbelievable. There are so many theories we're dependent on being just right for this thing to happen. If any one of them is off, then. . ., "he looked at Barosh.

". . .then we 'pop out' together David," Barosh laughed. "I think about the astronauts going to the moon or Christopher Columbus setting out for the New World. They also went based on a bushel of theories that, if any were wrong, could have left them stranded on the moon or sailing off the edge of the world. We're the new explorers David, on the verge of history."

"And you have a tremendous advantage," Allen said, "You have signed evidence that it was done—by you. Just imagine if before Apollo 11 lifted off, Houston Control focused their telescopes and saw writing on the lunar surface saying 'Neil was here'."

Whether a joke or encouragement, Allen's parody hit the mark, and David couldn't help but laugh, breaking the tension. Alex stood and raised his glass to the ceiling, "A toast—to David and Barosh—the new age explorers."

All except David stood and raised their glass, waiting. David looking at Barosh, who looked back with a steady gaze; David smiled, shook his head and stood.

"We must be crazy, but what the heck, here goes nothing," he clinked glasses with Barosh, "to Neil Armstrong, Sally the mouse and. . ." he turned and clinked Allen's glass, "Houston Control."

***

Over dinner, Alex asked David, "How well do you understand the political climate of First Century Israel?"

"Probably not as well as I should, but I think I have a decent handle on it," he answered.

"Good, would you mind giving us an overview?"

"Okay. Let's see; it's the height of the Roman Empire, and Israel lies on the outer eastern boundary of the empire, making it an essential crossroads to Rome for trade with the east. Rome had only recently established its dominance in Israel, when Pompey conquered Jerusalem sixty years before Jesus. Political shifts in Rome involving Julius Caesar, Mark Anthony and Octavian, resulted in Herod named King by Rome. He ruled until he died in 3 BCE. Rome then divided Israel into four regions of Judea, Samaria, Galilee and Perea. Jewish rulers were allowed to sit, but a Roman governor was appointed, who held real power. Herod's son, Agrippa took over Galilee and is ruling in 30 CE along with Pontius Pilate, the Roman Consulate."

"That's a fair summary of facts David, but it doesn't touch on the climate," Barosh interrupted. "It's a time of tremendous unrest for the Jews. They're oppressed, brutalized and murdered; their women defiled, their faith trampled and their way of life threatened. They've endured years of misrule by despotic leaders, and now the burden of a foreign government is imposing more demands on them, enslaving them with additional taxes and Caesar worship. When Pompey conquered Jerusalem as you mentioned, thousands of Jews were murdered and butchered. He lined the road to Jerusalem with crosses. Those murders are deep scars the people carry in 30 BC. . . they were their fathers and husbands."

"The Romans are tolerant as long as the taxes are paid. When resisted—they're brutal. The people despise the Romans. Herod was a warlord, evil and cruel. He wasn't a Jew, and only converted to Judaism as a way to gain power. Mark Anthony declared Herod the 'King of the Jews', as a reward for helping him seize power by killing thousands of innocent people. Upon ascending to the throne, he massacred hundreds of Jewish leaders and citizens to solidify his power. He killed on a whim, for personal gain or no reason at all. He killed the High Priest, confiscated the scared vestments and installed his own High Priest, a Babylonian, in his place. A pagan! Ruling the Temple of God! He executed anyone that he thought might be a threat to him. He deliberately minted coins with an image on them and placed the statue of an eagle in the Temple, not only to defy the people, but to defy God. Blasphemy! They hated him stronger than they hated the Romans who clogged their streets with their soldiers," he paused, shaking his head in disgust.

"Josephus, a Jewish revolutionary turned traitor, who became a Roman historian, tells us much about Herod. He murdered his favorite wife's father, drowned her brother in a swimming pool—and then murdered her! He executed his most trusted friends, his barber, and 300 military leaders—all in a single day's work. Not satisfied, he then killed three of his own sons. The story of him killing all the babies in Bethlehem wouldn't be out of character for him. And it didn't end with his death. On his death bed, he ordered 3000 of Israel's leading citizens locked up in prison and gave the order they were to be executed the hour he died. Why? Because he wanted to make sure, there would be mourning in the nation when he died."

"Good lord, what kind of monster was he?" Jennifer asked.

"Oh, trust me Jennifer, he was a monster, and his son Herod-Agrippa, who took over after his death, continued the bloodshed and misery. He's the Herod who had John the Baptist beheaded, and who Jesus stood, or will stand, before," Barosh replied, the fury of years of Jewish persecution bubbling inside of him.

"And if the abuse by their own rulers and the Roman oppression isn't enough, there's the total control and domination of their lives by the religious and judicial authority of the Sanhedrin. The Pharisees took the Torah and expounded on it, adding hundreds of oral rules, rituals and taxes to the Talmud that no man could comply with, yet they lived an arrogant, haughty life. The "once in a lifetime" temple tax they changed into an annual tax, and only accepted Tyrian half-shekels, which they exchanged for a tidy profit! Not only does the Sanhedrin dictate and control every aspect of life, they also have an army and have no compulsions or hesitation about using it. They are every bit as harsh and rigid in their interpretation and application of their laws as the Romans are in their collection of taxes. It's a lose-lose-lose life for the population; on one side, strict enforcement of God's commandments of no images, no other gods and costly temple observances—on another, a pagan, idol-worshipping, tax collecting brutal foreign power—all being overseen by despotic rulers who are diabolical murderers."

He pointed at David, "Be aware, my friend, the people will be angry, suspicious of outsiders. They are proud, believing they are the chosen people of the one true God, who will send a messiah to destroy the Romans. There will be zealots, outlaws and revolutionaries. Remember, we have the advantage of foresight, we know what will happen. In only a few years after our arrival, the entire nation will erupt in rebellion and hundreds of thousands will be murdered and tortured. Jerusalem will be burned, and the temple totally sacked and destroyed. It's a powder keg we're going into David, and we must be careful not to strike a spark."

Allen looked at Barosh, his face creased with deep frowns, "Barosh, do you think it wise for you to go on this journey? It may be too much for you to bear. Remember, you cannot attempt to change history."

Barosh shook his head, "Don't fret my friend, I will do nothing. I go to learn and to see the Temple before it is destroyed. What could I do anyway? Nothing could change what was prophesized to happen," he smiled, "besides; your Principle of Self-consistency would prevent any-thing from changing history. Anything I would do has already been done and is part of the history, right?"

"Let's not test the principle; it may be bad for you."

"So," Jennifer asked, "if that's the world Jesus lived in, what was he? A revolutionary? A prophet? Or a disgruntled carpenter who didn't want to pay his taxes?"

"Or, an alien," Alex suggested.

"Or, all of those things," Thaddeus said.

"Or, the son of God?" Allen asked.

Chapter Twenty-four

"How long are we going to let these wackos jerk us around?" John complained, removing the headphones and shaking his head, "I've heard enough classical music to last the rest of my life."

"It'll do you good," Ken replied. He gave John an exasperated look, "Can't you grasp the problem here? If he has this ability to travel through time, anything we would do he could already know about. I know it's a different way of thinking, but if you give the idea even the slightest possibility, then you see how volatile the situation is."

"You heard what they're talking about; millions of people dying."

"No one has been able to determine if those bits and pieces represent a threat. Where? Who? When? Jimmy says what they piece together make it sound like generic history talk, not any specific terrorist threat. And, so far, nothing has given any indication of terrorist activity from any of them."

"So, we just sit back and do nothing—until a nuke goes off somewhere? Based on "if" they can travel in time, which is nothing but hogwash! I thought our whole purpose was to prevent things from happening."

"Give it a rest John. Our job is to evaluate a credible threat; so far we don't have one. All we have are those tablets; otherwise we wouldn't even be wasting our time on this. Just what exactly would you propose we do? Put them in solitary confinement for 30 days? Pull out their fingernails until they tell us what it's like to meet Socrates? Regardless of what some may think, we're still in America, and such things aren't supposed to happen."

"How do you know he doesn't have a time-machine inside there?"

"For one thing, Kincaid was at the river, getting ready to jump. Whichever way you look at that, it tells us; he doesn't have one."

"How do you see that?"

"Well, it means either there actually is a time gate at the river or he really was going to commit suicide. Neither would be true if he had a time-machine in there. They've booked a flight to Athens, why would they do that if it was inside?" He sighed deeply, "And if they did have a time-machine in there, then it doesn't really matter what we do, does it?"

"What if this whole time travel stuff is all a sham, nothing but a cover for whatever they're really up to? There are wackos every day pulling one crazy stunt after another."

"I hope it is, John, because then, we're right on top of it, aren't we? They can't make a move without us knowing about it. We're monitoring every phone call and watching them every minute. We have them covered with an electronic grid; a gnat couldn't get through. They cannot communicate with anyone without us knowing it, and we can have SWAT and ATF teams mobilized in seconds. We'll make it real obvious that we're following them to Athens, as well as having additional teams there, looking for the first indication of a move. They can't so much as sneeze without us knowing it. If they're terrorists, then I want to catch the ones pulling the strings."

Ken stood and walked to the pictures of the tablets. Picking them up, he tossed them to John, "And we have these to consider. No terrorists have ever produced two-thousand year old markers to cover up a plot. Until we can debunk these, we have no choice but to tread lightly with this."

"They're probably fakes. You can do a lot with technology."

"Maybe, but the best experts in the world say they're real," Ken said, "our leaders believe in their authenticity, and that's who we're responsible to."

"Not all of them do."

"Who you talking about? Sherman Mason?"

"Him, and others, who see their responsibilities to the American people."

Ken looked at John hard, "Be careful John, don't get confused about who you work for. Our responsibilities are to the American people, *through* the Department of Homeland Security. My advice to you is stay clear of any interdepartmental politics. You can be crushed between those swinging doors."

"Don't worry about me; I can take care of myself."

"It's a lonely life swimming upstream John."

"I still think we should pull them in."

"That's not our call. That's the President's. It would do you good to remember that."

Exasperated, Ken shook his head, finding it difficult to understand John's refusal to grasp the situation. *Unless he changes his stubbornness and opens his mind, he's not going to be a good Agent*, Ken thought, *especially if he's playing inter-agency politics.*

Exasperated, John shook his head, finding it frustrating to sit back and let Ken be in charge. *These old timers are too cautious, more concerned about drawing their pension than catching terrorists. Their priorities all wrong. The Department is responsible for protecting the American people, individuals takes a back seat. Besides, if they were innocent, they wouldn't be under suspicion.*

It was obvious he couldn't depend upon Ken for stepping up when the time came. He'd have to do it himself. *That's okay with me*, he thought, *I won't have to share anything then, it'll be me alone that stops a major terrorist plot. I'll call Sherman tonight to bring him up to speed.*

Chapter Twenty-five

S ipping an excellent Remy Martin, with Bach's Ninth Concerto playing in the background, they went over the plans for the final time.

Knowing every move would be followed closely, the plan was devised so that when the sun broke across the horizon, on the sixth of April, Barosh and David would be standing between the paws of the Sphinx, without a DHS agent within 700 miles of them.

Alex was leaving for Egypt in the morning, on the premise of working a site there. Having spent his life working such sites as the Chief Egyptologist and Keeper of Egyptian Antiquities, this was not unusual. Barosh would fly to Jerusalem, a trip he has made many times and which has been scheduled for months. These trips shouldn't raise red flags with the agents, who were focused on David.

Allen and Jennifer would return to their homes and businesses.

The agents will be told the meetings have concluded, with everyone resuming their normal routines while David and Thaddeus prepare to go to Athens.

They would leave for Greece on the second of April. Hopefully, they had instilled enough trepidation in the DHS with their threats, to hold them at bay. And, the threats weren't all bluff. Thaddeus didn't trust any newspaper editor to sit on a package without opening it, so the envelopes Camille had mailed were a ruse—with the exception of a single large one.

She had discretely opened safety deposit boxes in five different banks around Boston. Inside of each, she had placed a folder containing a complete history of the affair, including photographs, names, numbers and a full accounting of surveillance and intervention by the government.

The single large envelope Camille delivered went to his most trusted lawyer friend with instructions to secure the envelope in his safe, protected by lawyer-client privilege. If he hadn't heard from Thaddeus by May 1st, he should contact the University's President, and inform him that he was being held against his will by the Department of Homeland Security, and the University should bring pressure to have him released. Further, if he still had not heard directly from Thaddeus by June 1st, he was to open the envelope and follow the instructions.

Inside were five letters, addressed to the chief editors of the major newspapers in New York City, Boston, London, Rome and Jerusalem. They are to be delivered via 'Overnight Express'. Each letter contained a one-page summary of the discovery made in Israel; a photograph of the tablets; the location, number and key to one of the safety deposit boxes.

If Thaddeus were to 'disappear', it would not be without a bang.

The agents would follow them to Greece, of course, (they were counting on it). There probably were agents in Athens already.

Good, Thaddeus thought, *the more the merrier. If the Feds were going to do anything, they'd have done it by now, and they won't take us into custody on foreign soil, creating an international incident. They'll keep their distance until they believe something's going down.*

On April 5th, during the busiest hour of the day, a car will pick up Thaddeus and David at their hotel to take them to the ruins of the Decathlon. Along the way, the driver will drive down a crowded, one-way street he is familiar with, and in the commotion of the crowds, while making a sharp left-hand turn, Thaddeus and David will exit the taxi on the far side and jump into a waiting vehicle, which will speed off in a different direction. While the agents follow the first car, they'll proceed to a private airfield where Alex will be waiting with a small plane for a fast flight to Cairo.

It'll take a couple of hours to cover the 700 miles to Cairo, where Barosh will be waiting to drive the final eight miles to the Sphinx. If all goes according to plan, they should arrive just after midnight. Timing is critical. They need to have enough of a window to allow time for any problems they may encounter with traffic or the authorities, but it can't be too large a window, or the authorities in Egypt might become suspicious. Alex had assured them he could bribe the guards at the pyramid site.

Allen was paranoid about the DHS learning the true location of the gateway. If the Egyptian government sealed off the site, it would create serious problems.

"To bring them back a year from now," he said, "we must have access to the gateway. I'll have it figured out, and I'll bring them back, but they wouldn't want to materialize surrounded by armed guards."

"Then, no one must know they ever went to Egypt," Thaddeus said. "We must continue to convince them the 'time-gate' is in Greece."

"Agreed," Alex said.

"That changes things. David will fly to Cairo alone then, and I must stay in Greece, to maintain the deception."

"Yes," Alex replied, "and you'll be amazed that David had disappeared there, leaving the agents searching in Athens for the non-existent 'time-gate', with no connection to Egypt."

"I suspect they will have a few questions for me," Thaddeus said.

"And you'll have fewer answers for them, my friend," he laughed. "Just an old archeologist who's eaten too much dirt over the years and allowed the time traveler to slip through his fingers. You always wanted to play Indiana Jones."

Clinking their glasses, they laughed.

***

Around the table that evening, the group enjoyed their last supper together. There wasn't much conversation, only nervous inquiries concerning the preparations.

"Do you have all your clothes together?"

"Have you read up on the Persians?"

"Is your money secure?"

"Are there any effects from the shots?"

"Are you feeling okay?"

"Are the sandals broken in?"

David felt like a boy going off to summer camp. Thaddeus was like a mother hen and Jennifer fidgeted over every detail. He'd like to think there was something personal in her concern, but he thought she just viewed him as the next generation of 'Enoch'.

"Remember, after you drink the solution, hold onto all your things until the translation is finished," she admonished for the third time.

"Will it work if I'm touching a Jeep?" David asked.

"Whatever you do, don't lose that powder packet, and don't break the seal until you need it a year from now. You may not need it, but we don't know that yet." She hugged him tight and whispered in his ear, "Take care of yourself David; I want to see you one year from now."

"Like Enoch?" He asked.

"No. . . like David," and she kissed him.

"Where's my mug?" Thaddeus roared, rummaging through the cups and saucers on the tray, "Has anyone seen my mug?" Not receiving a response, he went into the dining room, and they could hear him calling Camille and slamming doors and cupboards.

He came back, looking distraught, "I don't understand where it is." He mumbled, "Camille doesn't know where it is neither; how can that be?"

"Forget it Thaddeus," Barosh said, slightly annoyed, "there're more pressing things right now. It'll turn up."

"Maybe it translated, and some barbarian is drinking his grog from it," Alex said laughing.

Allen stood and addressed the group, "Well, this is it. In the morning, Jennifer and I will be driving back, and Alex and Barosh will be catching their flights. In a week, Thaddeus and David will leave for Athens. My friends, after tonight, none of our lives will ever be the same."

He raised his glass, "I offer a toast," everyone stood. "To a successful conclusion of our little charade with the DHS - to the fulfillment of our mission - and most important of all. . . to the safe return of our brave explorers - Barosh and David, one year from now."

Everyone clinked glasses and exchanged toasts and sat back down, except Allen. He looked back and forth between Barosh and David, before saying in a firm, confident voice, "We are on the threshold of the greatest moment in history. Not only to rediscover the ability to move through time and ultimately, other dimensions, but to bring to the world, proof of the existence or non-existence of a divine presence. Barosh. . .David. . .I give you my word. . .I will solve the mystery of moving the vernal point, and we will be waiting for you on the following spring equinox. If you're not there, we'll be waiting the following year and if not then, the following year. You be there, and we'll bring you back."

He sat down. Everyone was silent, and then David stood.

"Never did I think I'd be standing here, getting ready to go, not just on a trip, but into time – into history. My hat is off to each of you for your brilliance and hard work, and I believe you will do everything in your ability to bring us back, and I give you my word that I will do everything in my ability to give you the proof you seek and make all your efforts worthwhile."

"Well said David," Barosh said, and raising his glass to everyone, "I second it."

Only the soft, almost imperceptible sobs of Jennifer broke the silence.

Chapter Twenty-six

"I just don't understand how you can do this thing. You have responsibilities, to me and to your children. If you don't care about me, then think about them. How could you not love them?"

"How can you say such a thing to me?" Barosh shot back. She was pulling out all the stops now, that was the third time she had mentioned the children in the last ten minutes. "You know I love my children more than I love life itself!"

"What manner of love is this? Deserting them. . . not knowing where you are - what you are doing - or if you are alright or not!"

"I'm not deserting them or you. I'm going on a business trip, and, I'll be back!"

"In a year! What kind of business trip is that - for an entire year? Without any word from you? And no way for me to send word to you? What if something were to happen to one of them or to me? You would not know or be of any help to us! We could die (God forbid!) and you would not even know, or be here to mourn, much less to help, and how would I handle such a situation?"

Barosh sighed deeply, hearing the anger in his wife's voice, but knowing beneath the anger, a river of fear flowed.

"Mariam, I go on God's business, and He will watch over you while I am gone. It grieves me greatly that it must be this way, and it is the burden I carry each day I am away, but, it must be so. . . it is God's will."

"I do not challenge our God, Barosh, but I do not understand such a thing, or how it can be His will for you to leave your family for so long with no means of communication."

"We must not question the will of God, Mariam."

"It is not God's will that I question, but the will of my stubborn husband."

He sat down next to her and took her hand into his. "When Moshe was called by God, to lead his people out of bondage, he had to follow God's calling. He left his family behind and was the deliverer of the people."

"Oh Barosh, you are not Moses, and you are not the deliverer of our people," she said. "Besides, I do not want you to follow in Moses footsteps; I would not want my husband wandering 40 years in the wilderness. He never returned to his family."

Inwardly, Barosh smiled, if she only knew how close she was. He actually was going to follow in Moshe's footsteps, crossing the same Sinai Wilderness (hopefully without a 40 year detour).

"Why can you not tell me, your wife of 27 years, where you are going and what the purpose of this business is? I have never doubted you or betrayed you, why do you not trust me now?"

"Mariam, I trust you. I shall return in a year, and then you will understand everything. Have faith, my dear wife, I love you more than life."

"But, I don't understand why you can't, at least, tell me where you will be?"

"That is not possible," he stroked her face. Even with her fear and worry, her face reflected the warmth inside. She was every bit as beautiful as when he first asked her father for her hand twenty-seven years ago. Her skin was rosy and smooth, creased only by the wrinkles of her children - and her husband. The hazel eyes pleaded with him for an explanation she could hold onto. He had none to give.

"What you do not know, Mariam, you cannot tell."

"Barosh! I would never tell anyone about your business! You know that."

"I know, but this is different, there are some who will be extremely demanding about learning what you know. It is best, therefore, that you know nothing."

"Barosh! You're not doing something illegal, are you? You're not involved with the Zionist fringe are you?" Her fear turned to real anger, "How could you bring such a thing down on your house? On your children? On me? You have placed us all in danger!"

"Mariam, stop! I have done no such thing. I swear on my children; I have not. I am going away for research only, but there will be some who will not believe that and will be inquisitive of where I am. When they find no substance with you, they will forget you."

"Barosh, your words are alarming, and they scare me."

"Don't be frightened, Mariam, God watches over us," he put his arms around her and held her tight. "I will miss you so it will hurt, and Jacob, Joseph, Mary and Ruth also. But I shall return, never despair and never forget. . . I will return."

"What will I tell the children? And what will I tell the neighbors when they ask, 'Where is our father?' 'Where is your husband?' What will I tell Thaddeus?" She looked at him, appraisingly, "Or is he also going with you on this business trip?"

As a tenured professor, he had requested and received approval for a one-year sabbatical from the University. He'd put all his affairs in order, and made arrangements for all of Mariam's needs to be taken care of. Thaddeus had agreed to watch over her and help where needed.

He had faith in Allen and had confidence he would work out the solution, and that the gateway would be open to the proper time one year from now. But in case it wasn't, he had left a letter with Thaddeus to give to Mariam on that day which included, among other things, instructions for her to meet with Allen, who would know what to do next.

"No, Mariam, Thaddeus is not going on this trip, and he will be here for you."

He would miss his wife and his children immensely, but that pain and burden was not enough to prevent him from going on this journey - a journey that would change the future of faith and religion throughout the world.

Besides, he'd never be able to live with himself if he abandoned David.

Chapter Twenty-seven

Thaddeus and David sat across from the two agents, for what would be their last meeting. Thaddeus noticed Agent Rosino was tense and nervous.

Why are you so on edge? He wondered. *What's going down that we're missing? What game are you playing, my young friend?*

"Now, let's see if I got this right," Ken said, checking his notes. He'd already known the flights they had booked and the whereabouts of the other members of the 'Bible Study' group, but he wanted to read their faces again. "You say that you're both booked on the Delta Flight 683, departing at 7:24 tomorrow morning from Logan airport, arriving at. . . ."

"Agent Rodgers," Thaddeus interrupted him, "please, let's not waste each other's time. We both know you knew our flight itinerary before our tickets were printed. As you know, we arrive at Venizelos airport in Athens on the morning of April 4th, and we're reserved at the Cecil Hotel for three nights. Now, what is it, you really want to know?"

Ken smiled; he had actually come to appreciate the old man. He was crusty and cantankerous, and had an air of antiquity that precluded any thoughts of trivializing him. He'd seen everything, from civilizations spanning thousands of years; there was little that he missed.

"What I want to know professor, is what exactly happens with this 'time-gate' thing."

Thaddeus nodded to David.

"The time-gate will open exactly at sunrise on April 7th," David said. "With the proper preparation, we'll enter the gate and translate to the age of Socrates."

John rolled his eyes.

"Will this happen instantly?" Ken asked.

"Yes."

"Will you be in a different place?"

"No, only a different time."

"Where exactly is this 'time-gate'?"

David hesitated, thought for a moment and then answered, "It's in the ruins of the Decathlon."

"Where in the ruins?"

David didn't answer.

"Okay, what are these 'beings' that you met before?"

"Members of an ancient civilization."

"Here, on earth?"

"Yes."

"What civilization? Where was it? What happened to it?"

"It was a tropical paradise, located where Antarctica is today. Thousands of years ago, the magnetic poles of the earth switched, and everything was buried under hundreds of feet of ice."

"What a crock! Do you expect us to swallow this nonsense?" John blurted out. "You must think we're. . . ."

"That's enough Agent Rosino," Ken snapped, agitated.

"I don't really care what you swallow, Rosino," David spat at John, his expression pure contempt.

John's face turned a shade of purple as rage boiled inside of him. *Who does this two-bit nobody think he's talking to? Why does Rodgers let him talk to me that way? He actually seems to like these kooks. They're playing him like a fiddle. Sherman would never allow it.*

"Let's just stay on track, shall we?" Ken said. "Where do these 'beings' live now, Mr. Kincaid?"

"I don't know; I only seen them for a brief time."

"And now you're going to meet with Socrates?"

"That's right; he was executed in 399 BCE; the 'beings' said there is great wisdom to be learned from him prior to his death that would be beneficial to mankind."

"Have you ever met with anyone in history before?"

"No, this will be my first. Up to now it's been like an orientation."

"Is there anything in these visits of yours that has anything to do with attempting to change or influence history or governments?"

"I have no interest in politics or governments, Agent Rodgers. My interest lies with people and culture. I'm not concerned with changing history, only with why they did what they did. Besides, history can't be changed."

"You know we'll be there, during this 'translation'."

"Just keep a safe distance or you could be hurt when the gate opens if you're not prepared."

"I trust your organization's not having second thoughts about our agreement," Thaddeus said, "or plans on interfering. Should anything happen to either David or me, everything will happen as we told you. I mean that not as any threat to you, but only as protection of our safety."

Ken sat for a long moment and then nodded his head as he rose to his feet, "Very well, professor. We'll see you in Athens, gentlemen."

After the agents had left the room, Thaddeus turned to David, "A civilization in Antarctica?"

"I read about it in National Geographic."

***

"Sherman."

"This is John. They leave in the morning sir. Supposedly, this 'time-gate' is located at the Decathlon and will open at sunrise on the seventh. I'm sure there's an incident planned of some sort."

"Is the DHS doing anything to stop it?"

"No sir."

There was a pause on the other end, "It would be detrimental for America if they were to fulfill their mission. A disruption in their plans may be in order."

"Yes sir; I fully concur."

"Do you believe the old professor's threat about the dossiers?"

"Yes sir; I do."

"Then any action on American soil, before this 'incident', would make us the aggressors. Something not to be welcomed, wouldn't you agree?"

"Yes sir, over there would prove convenient."

"And you could arrange that, Agent? With deflection, say maybe to Al Qaeda?"

"Arrangements can be made, sir."

"Good. The two scientists have resumed their normal routines; Wainwright is digging in Egypt, and the Rabbi is praying in Jerusalem. So far, nothing suspicious, but you'll know the minute they do something."

"Yes sir; that's good to know." *So much for the FBI staying out of this,* John thought.

The line went dead.

Okay Kincaid; we'll see who swallows what!

Chapter Twenty-eight

David enjoyed the atmosphere of Athens. He'd been to Greece before, when he was making his grand tour of languages, and had found it a fascinating land of culture and history. He liked the ambiance of this hotel, situated as it was in the heart of old Athens and close to the Ancient Tonyet. He commended Thaddeus on his choice as the pedestrian street was crowded with the bustling business of living, lending itself well to their diversion.

Tomorrow was the 5th of April; the car would pick them up, and the journey would begin. He was nervous and excited, but he wasn't frightened. He was in harmony with himself. He didn't understand everything that was happening, but he knew this is where he was supposed to be.

Hopefully, they had convinced the agents into believing nothing would happen for another two days. He felt bad for Agent Rodgers; he seemed a decent man who was genuinely doing his job to protect the world from terrorists. It wouldn't go well for him once the ruse was known.

He didn't feel any remorse for the other one – Rosino. He was an egomaniac, using the guise of security to make a name for himself. He'd take his frustrations out on the professor, and David felt guilty about that.

Looking out the window, he marveled at the view of the Acropolis in the distance. He picked out Lycabettus Hill, Philopappus Hill and the Syntagma Square, places where the famed orators had debated and expounded on their ideas of democracy and human dignity. He couldn't help but feel their presence around him as he considered the journey he was about to embark on. His gaze followed a flock of pigeons, circling

Philopappos Hill just west of the Acropolis. In antiquity, it was known as the Hill of the Muses, after the fabled nine muses. There is where Orpheus had taught and where a monument was erected in honor of Philopappos, the Roman senator who loved Greece. He had lived in Athens and was a friend of the Roman emperor Trajan. It was under Trajan's rule that Jerusalem had been burned down, and the temple destroyed, not long after the man Jesus died. Funny, how things came full circle. It was fitting to David that he should be here before embarking on this journey. The pigeons swooped down, disappearing within the ruins of the monument, only to reemerge, soaring upwards.

David smiled, thinking they approved and wished him well.

***

They had made the trip to Logan airport unhampered. Arriving at the gate, he had expected to see the stoic faces of Rodgers and Rosino staring back, but he hadn't. Two men had openly followed them through the terminal, and he noticed they went through security screening without being screened. At the gate, they stood off to the side, watching intently until Thaddeus and David entered the boarding corridor. Walking down the aisle to their seats, there, two rows back, the stoic faces of Rodgers and Rosino stared back.

Rodgers nodded while Rosino glared.

***

During the flight, Thaddeus had extracted a package from his briefcase.

"Here, this is for you."

Inside, was a pliant, oilskin sheath, holding a small, black book about the size of a pocketbook with two thin pens attached. David opened the book and thumbed the pages. They were lined and felt strange.

"It's a special book," Thaddeus said. "The pages are made from a unique, synthetic, waterproof material that's tear and stain resistant. It's called 'fusion' paper and is virtually indestructible. It's the most advanced, technological 'paper' available. The two stylists are specially made for permanent, non-smudge writing on the material that will not fade or chemically react over time. Carry it, secured in your inner garments, and record what you see and hear."

David liked the feel of the book in his hands and smiled, "I will, thank you."

* * *

John liked the feel of the rifle in his hands and smiled. It was a piece of perfection. No frills, no shiny, polished wood, just cold steel and synthetic stock, each part designed and constructed to fit together into an efficient killing machine.

It was a Tabuk; an Iraqi adaptation of a Russian AK-47 assault rifle modified into a sniper's rifle. Chambered for the 7.62x39 caliber, it had a thicker gauge of steel formed over a larger and heavier trunnion, adding stability and accuracy. Equipped with a flash suppressor, muzzle brake and a Soviet designed sound suppression device, it was an assassin's dream weapon. The mechanism was designed for semi-automatic, precision fire instead of automatic suppressive fire. The barrel was light and finned at the rear, facilitating heat distribution, and had a skeletonized butt stock with a collapsible cheek piece. The rifle was fitted with 9 X 40 scope optics.

It was the perfect weapon for dispensing four well-placed shots; two into that arrogant, nutcase Kincaid, and two into that fossil of a professor.

He had located an empty, second floor apartment, 95 yards from the entrance to the Decathlon, for the ambush. Ken had another team situated on the east side of the Decathlon, keeping surveillance.

Wearing latex gloves, he set up the shooting site at the west window, where he'd have a clear, unobstructed view when they arrived. They'd have to park and walk, and he'd shoot them both, leave the rifle, vacating the scene before the other team even knew anything had happened. It would appear as just one more terrorist attack by the radical Islamic fractions.

It never entered John's mind that, as an agent of Homeland Security, his role was to prevent terrorist acts, not perform them. He viewed himself as a hero, protecting the motherland, and he would be well rewarded by Sherman.

It had been easy fooling his partner, setting up his own covert operation right under Ken's nose. *Your time is past, my cautious friend,* he thought, *it's a new era where the world recognizes those who have the foresight and courage to take action.*

In just two days, his world would change, and he'd get the recognition he deserved. The buzz of his cell phone interrupted his reverie.

"John here."

Chapter Twenty-eight

"Sherman. Status."

"Everything is in place, sir."

"Including deflection?"

"Yes sir."

"Good. I don't know if this has any relevance or not, but my man just reported that Wainwright chartered a plane for a flight tomorrow morning. It could be nothing, just to visit another of his sites, but he did it under a false identity, which is suspicious. The pilot hasn't filed a flight plan yet. I'll let you know as soon as I know."

"Yes sir, anything else, sir."

"Only that we've lost the Rabbi. He merged into the crowds and didn't return to his apartment. Be alert, something may be up."

"Yes sir."

The line went dead.

What are they up to? John wondered.

***

From the shadows of the alley, a dark figure watched John prepare his ambush. Looking out from beneath the hood covering his beautiful face, the eyes were malignant and evil. A smile sneered at the corner of his mouth.

Soon, David, soon, the threat you are will be over.

***

Sherman punched the buttons on his cell phone.

"Yes sir," a cold voice answered.

"Are you situated?"

"Yes sir; I'm staged in a second floor apartment, just east of his location."

"Do you have a good view?"

"Yes sir; he's set up in a window for a clear shot. Gives me a clear shot, as well."

"Good, take him out as soon as he kills the two of them. Cover your tracks well."

"Yes sir."

Sherman disconnected the call. *Now Director Thomas, let's see you get out of this one. This'll shake the entire government, and I'll step in to clean up your mess. Then I'll be in charge. Everything according to plan.*

Chapter Twenty-nine

Agents Rodgers and Rosino sat without talking, eating chicken salad from the hotel kitchen. Ken was worried. John appeared unusually pleased ever since arriving in Athens, and his sudden interest in making excursions into the city to 'sightsee', didn't fit his usual lack of interest in anything historical or cultural. Ken was sure he was up to something, not knowing what bothered him.

But he couldn't dwell on that right now, in less than two days the professor and Kincaid would take their drive to the Decathlon, and Ken would finally find out if this time-gate thing was real or not. His rational mind kept telling him it wasn't, and that something else was happening. There've been so many discoveries made in the past twenty years, anything was possible. He couldn't be as closed-minded as his partner was. There were too many mysteries in the world to dismiss things just because he did not understand them. The buzz in his pocket interrupted his thoughts.

"Ken here."

"Larry here. The subjects just left the hotel. A car was waiting for them."

"Are you on them?"

"We are; they're heading into the Market place."

"Stay on them. Don't lose them; we're right behind you."

"Got it."

"Let's go," he yelled at John, "they may just be out shopping, but then, maybe not."

Maneuvering the car through the crowded streets, John became anxious. "Something's going on," he said, "I feel it. That old croon isn't out buying grapes and olives. I don't see Larry anywhere ahead. Can't see, with all these people?"

"I feel it too," Ken answered, "Maybe they lied about the date, and today's the day the gate opens. Head to the Decathlon." He punched his phone. It was immediately answered.

"Brian here."

"Ken here. The subjects have left the hotel for destination unknown; they may be headed your way. Stay alert and let me know if you see them."

"Roger that."

As John steered the vehicle through the crowded streets, he began feeling sick to his stomach. *No, not today, please not today; that'll ruin everything.*

Ken's phone buzzed, "Ken here."

"Larry here. They left the Market area and are headed towards Philopappos Hill."

"Stay on them; we're behind you."

"Maybe they're doing some sightseeing," John prayed out loud.

"Yeah, and maybe my sister's Mother Theresa. They're trying to pull a fast one on us. Head to Philopappos Hill," Ken said while John's stomach did somersaults.

"Where's that?"

"West of here."

"Which way's west?"

"There, that way!" Ken yelled.

Philopappos Hill, being the highest of the three hills west of the Acropolis, loomed ahead. As John turned onto the road climbing the hill, Ken's cell buzzed once again.

"Yeah?"

"Larry here. They skirted around Philopappos Hill."

"We're already on it."

"Looks like they're headed north."

"Stay on them, don't lose them!"

"Roger that."

Turning around and heading back down the hill, John knew his plans were for nothing. How would he explain this to Sherman? These idiots were going to ruin his career. His cell phone buzzed.

"John here."

"Sherman. Wainwright's flight plan was logged this morning. Looks like you're going to have company over there, he's headed to Athens."

"Got it," John said in a whisper.

"Is everything all right there?"

John pushed the disconnect button.

"Who was that?" Ken asked.

"No one."

Ken looked at him and knew something was terribly wrong. He was about to say something when his cell buzzed.

"Yeah?"

"Larry here. They're headed up Pnyx hill."

"Got it, stay on them."

Pnyx hill, the birthplace of democracy, *fitting,* Ken thought as a lorry blocked their way. John leaned on the horn, cursing and yelling for it to get out of his way.

When they finally pulled up beside the two cars parked on top of Pnyx Hill, Larry was standing outside the vehicle.

"Where are they?" Ken demanded.

"Over there," Larry pointed, "when we got here, the car was empty. Sam ran after them while I waited here in case they backtracked."

"Good, stay here and keep watch," Ken ordered, "come on, John." He ran up the hill. Approaching the top, they saw the ruins of the Bêma - the podium — where the ancient Greek philosophers had made their famous speeches. Sam stood to the side while there, on the podium, was the professor—alone.

"Where's Kincaid?" Ken yelled, running to him.

"Right here," the professor calmly said.

"Where?"

"Here, in the year 400 BCE."

Anger surged in Ken, and he wanted to beat the old man bloody. "You lied to me!" He yelled, "You and Kincaid, you lied! I trusted you!"

John pulled his pistol and pointed it at the professor, "You stinking old kook; I'm going to blow your rotting brains out!"

Ken grabbed his arm, pushing it down. "Put that away, it'll only make it worse."

***

The car screeched to a halt, and David jumped out. The plane sat revving on the runway. Alex stood outside the open hatchway, waving him to hurry. His face broke into a wide grin as he grabbed David's hand in a hearty handshake.

"You made it! Come on, let's get out of here."

"I hope the professor's going to be okay."

"Don't worry, he'll be fine; the old man is enjoying this."

Chapter Thirty

John's stomach twisted in knots pushing bitter bile up his throat. They'd gotten the better of him, these two nutcases, with their ridiculous scam of traveling in time. His plans were ruined; he'd never face Sherman now.

They'd questioned the professor repeatedly, but his story didn't change. The time-gate was located at the podium on Pynx Hill and had opened for a brief moment. Kincaid had stepped through it, back to the year 400 BCE. It was never intended for the professor to go. The *'beings'* on the other side, only wanted David; he was a son to them.

He was sorry for the deception, but it had been necessary; they couldn't take the chance that David wouldn't be able to return. He assured them there's no plot or plan to do harm to any one—now or in the past. History was set and could not be changed, and the future would be determined by the living, not the dead. David was there to learn.

John knew it was all a crock. There was no such thing as a 'time-gate' and Kincaid had certainly not gone back in time 2500 years to see Socrates. They were terrorists, pure and simple and this wasn't over by a long shot, no matter what his feeble-minded partner believed. While they chased the professor around Athens, the real culprit, Kincaid, had escaped. Kincaid and. . .and. . .wait a minute!. . . Wainwright. . .and the plane!

John started putting the pieces together. *It was all a charade just to get them out from under our surveillance so they could carry out their terrorist plot in. . .in Egypt. . .Yes, of course! That's where the real threat*

166

is. . .in Egypt. Wainwright had secretly chartered a flight from Cairo to Athens, not to do anything here, but to pick up Kincaid and take him to Egypt, where the real plot was being hatched. The rabbi was missing. . .in Jerusalem. . .only a stone's throw from Egypt. That's where it was all going to happen, in Egypt, by the three of them. The professor was just a decoy. All those bits and pieces they heard in those meetings about changing history and annihilation and the pyramids. . .the pyramids! That's it! The pyramids. That's where it will happen. Well, hang on Director Sherman, this isn't over yet, Rosino is still on the case.

Taking the vehicle, he drove to the airport and using his government ID, secured a private flight to Egypt. He'd worry about Ken later after he single-handedly prevented a major terrorist attack, captured the terrorists and saved the pyramids.

***

The flight was uneventful. Alex and David went over the plans and arrangements and worried about the professor. Arriving in Cairo, just before midnight, Barosh was waiting.

"Shalom," he said, extending his hand to Alex, "I see you brought our young explorer. No trouble, I trust?"

"None, everything went as planned," Alex said, shaking the rabbi's hand warmly.

Barosh turned to David, grabbing his hand in his, "David. How are you? Were there any problems?"

"No, we completely fooled the agents; they're back in Athens."

"Good and how was Thaddeus? I do hope it doesn't go badly for him."

"He is good, Barosh, and in excellent spirits. How are you rabbi? Is all ready?"

"I am well David, and yes, everything is in order. Come, let us go and greet the Great Sphinx."

***

The plane wasn't fast. John wanted to get out and push it. He needed to get to Cairo. . .to the pyramids, before it all went down. He couldn't miss his chance; it would never come again. On the way to the airstrip, he stopped at the apartment, grabbed the Tabux and the ammo belt packed with twelve, twenty round magazines.

167

240 rounds, enough to take care of you, Mr. Kincaid. You and your terrorist buddies, he thought.

He'd hot-wire a vehicle once he landed, and race to the pyramids. He couldn't waste time to hire one, and he didn't call ahead to have one waiting, not wanting to tip anyone off about his whereabouts. This was his show, and his alone. He'd never been to the pyramids, but he knew they were just a few miles south of Cairo and shouldn't be hard to spot. There'd be signs pointing the way.

He couldn't wait to get his hands on Kincaid. He wondered what they were planning. The pyramids were large and solid, not easily destroyed. They had lasted for thousands of years and their destruction would be the greatest terrorist act ever. It would shake the foundations of the world.

Could it be nuclear? He wondered. *A nuclear explosion? Yes, that must be it. They were going to set off a small nuke. A suicide mission? Why not, those people have been blowing themselves up, and for a lot less than the pyramids. Or maybe they were going to set it in motion, and then high tail it back to Israel where the rabbi had a safe house set up for them. That sounds more like Kincaid. He was too much of a coward to take his own life. They thought they had everything figured out, but they didn't figure on me. I'll be the one to stop them. . . me. . . Special Agent, John Markus Rosino. Forget Sherman, he's small potatoes now. Everyone will want me after this. The world will be at my door. I'll be the greatest hero of all time. Hollywood will be screaming for my story. I'll be on Oprah and Leno! The President will award me a medal!*

***

Crouching on the desert floor, its posture, timeless and serene, the feline, guardian-god of the Great Giza pyramids, rose massive and powerful above the dunes. Taller than a six story building and as long as a city block, battle scared and bloodied, the Sphinx towered over the desert while steadfastly gazing at the horizon, patiently waiting the equinox.

The guardian shows its age. Its lean flanks are deeply cut and carved by the desert wind and sand, and it carries the scars and wounds of ageless battles with human degradation. Attempts have been made to heal it, giving it a cement collar for its wounded head, and brick bandages for its battered paws. Despite the wounds, it remains a vigilant sentinel, unwavering, keeping watch. The Egyptian moon, shrouded by a wisp of passing clouds, plays across the sentinel's face and torso. Its mood remains unchanged as it watches the seasons and years march by in the eternal parade of time. It knows time well, for time is its mother and the constellations are its siblings. Behind it, the pyramids repose, pointing to the heavens, declaring the might and intelligence of the masters who built them—masters, the modern world denies.

Standing between its massive legs, David stares up at the proud face of the Egyptian god gazing eastward. Silent and patient waiting the coming of the equinox. He stares further, past the royal Menes, into the heavens, and despite the artificial lights of man, he sees the celestial river of the Milky Way. He marvels at the replica on the desert's floor. A shiver runs through his core, feeling the weight of history engulfing him. Who were these beings, that they knew so much and could do such extraordinary things?

True to Alex's word, his bribes were successful, and no guards are around the great monument. Staying in the shadows, avoiding the lights, Barosh hands David a suitcase.

"Well my friend, are you ready?"

David lowers his gaze from the heavens to the bearded face of the rabbi, "Yes, I'm ready."

***

David laughs; dressed in his 'travel' clothes, Barosh looks like a desert nomad and not like the educated scholar David knows him to be. Looking down at himself, he laughs again, and Barosh joins in. He looks into Barosh's face, and their eyes lock, "Whatever may happen we are now in the embrace of time."

Barosh pulls out an envelope and hands it to Alex, "Would you give this to Mary for me? Tell her, I carry her in my heart."

"I will my friend," Alex says. "It is time, you must drink now."

He unscrews the cap from a thermos and pours the contents into two large paper cups, handing one to David and one to Barosh. Pulling a flask from his pocket, he raises it.

"A toast—to time—to history—to truth—and to your safe return."

David and Barosh tip their cups to Alex's flask.

"And to the well-being of our friends left behind, who will take the heat," David says.

"Ah," Barosh adds, "and to Allen's success."

"Hear, hear to that," Alex says.

They tip their cups and drink.

"Alright, hold it right there! Don't any of you move!"

They freeze, staring into the dark, trying to identify the harsh, demanding voice. Had the guards betrayed them? Did they want more money? The clouds move across the face of the moon sending light flickering in and out across the Sphinx. A man, moves out from the shadows, into the moonlight. . . Agent Rosino!

He holds a nasty looking rifle, and it's pointed directly at them.

"Put down those cups nice and easy like; make a wrong move and you won't need a time machine; I'll blow you into the future without blinking an eye."

They set the cups on the edge of the great Sphinx's paw.

"Well, well. . .what do we have here? The little weasel, Kincaid, along with his co-conspirators. Rabbi Barosh I presume? And you must be Wainwright. How cozy. Just the three of you. Thought you could outfox me did you Kincaid? With that little farce back there in Athens. You may pull the wool over the eyes of that fool partner of mine, but not me; I'm too wise for your little charade. Move over there, all of you. . . now!" He motions them into the center of the paws.

"So, what's the plan, maggots? Gonna blow up the Sphinx? And what's with the garb? Going to a masquerade party? Or are those your terrorist's clothes?" His voice takes on a hard, mean edge, "What are you maggots up to? Come on, speak up."

No one answers. The sky is just beginning to lighten behind Rosino's back, and the Constellation will be rising soon. David wonders if he drank enough of Jennifer's cocktail and he wonders what would happen if he hadn't. Would he 'half' translate?

"Answer me!" John jerks the menacing weapon at them. "If someone doesn't talk right now, I'll shoot you, one by one, starting at the legs and working upwards. And don't think anyone will come running to your rescue either; this baby's quiet and flameless, no one will hear or see a thing. I'll just have a grand old time shooting up a bunch of terrorists, and when it's over, they'll give me a medal for doing it. Now speak up."

"We're waiting," David says.

"Waiting?" John barks, "Waiting for what?"

"For Leo."

So, there are more involved; I knew it; John thought. *Well, I'll just bide my time and capture the whole gang of them.* He moves towards the Sphinx's paw, placing his back against the stone, and smiles.

"And what is Leo bringing to the party? The bomb? Or the detonator? Well, let's just wait for Leo, shall we. And meanwhile, you can tell me what your plan is. How does that sound?"

David watches the sky; dawn is beginning to break on the horizon. He glances at Barosh and sees the same worried look on his face. Alex takes a step to the side, trying to outflank the agent.

"You stay right there Wainwright, or I'll shoot you where you stand. I don't need you anyway; I got the little maggot here. He's all I need." He moves to where the cups rest on the ledge, and glances at them, "And what do we have here? Were we making a little toast in celebration of your victory when I interrupted the party?" He picks up a half-filled cup, "well, your party is over because the victory is mine. I've foiled your plot, and I'll drink to that," he raises the cup to his lips.

"Don't drink that!" David shouts.

"Watch me."

John drained the cup.

"You fool!" David yells, "Move away! Get away from the Sphinx!"

The horizon is glowing golden, and the Constellation is rising as the spring equinox approaches.

"You call me a fool? How stupid can you be? You don't call me a fool, Kincaid; you're the one who is looking at the business end of this rifle."

"Agent Rosino, I'm begging you, step away from the Sphinx, please. Move away quickly!"

"And leave you to your fun, not on your life maggot. We'll just wait here for your friend Leo to show up while you tell me what this is all about."

Dawn breaks and the constellation rises resplendent in the east as flames of fire shoot out across the horizon, igniting the sky in renewed life and glory.

"Please, Agent Rosino, for your own sake, move away. I'm warning you, please, move away."

"You're in no position to be warning me Kincaid. Now start talking what this is all about; I'm losing my patience fast."

The leading edge of the sun shoots over the horizon, sending its rays into the heavens while the constellation charges across the heavens, declaring the spring equinox has arrived. Between the paws of the mighty Sphinx, crouching and offering a knowing smile, a glow begins and grows wider and brighter. It's coming from the men themselves standing under the Sphinx's steady gaze. Alex backs away as the light grows in intensity, overpowering him, forcing him to shield his eyes with his arms. Suddenly, a brilliant flash explodes, throwing Alex to the ground, his eyes slamming closed from the brilliance of it.

As the light slowly dissipates and the dawn spreads its rays across the solemn face of the Sphinx, it seems pleased, having a self-fulfilled look.

Alex slowly opens his eyes, and as they clear and focus, he stares into the shadows between the great Sphinx's paws.

There is no one there.

Chapter Thirty-one

They kept him in interrogation for weeks. Using every technique they knew, barring out and out torture; pressuring him to tell where the 'time-gate' was?—How it worked?—How many are there?—Where was David Kincaid?—who did they work for?—what was their plan?

He told them he didn't know how it worked. All he knew was. . . one instant David was there, and the next he was not. He told them no one else was involved; they worked for no one, and there was no plan.

He told them about certain dossiers, containing letters and photographs, sitting in multiple safety deposit boxes that will be opened on June first if people don't see him personally first.

He spent hours with a team of 'bad guy' interrogators relentlessly questioning and threatening to lock him up, take away his possessions and destroy his reputation. They were replaced by the 'good guy' interrogators who offered financial rewards, fame and recognition if he would show them where the time machine was and how it worked.

Thaddeus held firm to his story. A gateway was at Pynx Hill, and David had gone back to 400 BCE, to meet with Socrates.

"So, Professor, can we go through this magic gate too?"

"I don't see why not; as long as you know how."

"Good, now we're getting somewhere. When can we do this?"

"In another three hundred years or so, give or take a decade or two."

"What does that mean?" They demanded.

"According to David, that gate only opens every three hundred years."

"Yeah, right," they scorned, "then how did he come back before?"

"Other gates, in other places, that open at different times."

They threw a tablet and pencil at him, "List them for us."

"I don't know them," Thaddeus said. "David said the keepers of the gates directed him where and when to be somewhere."

"This is ridiculous!" The interrogator shouted, "Where's David?"

"I told you; he's in Athens, 2500 years ago."

"Where's Agent Rosino?"

"Why, I have no idea; I did not know he was missing."

Between interrogations, he was kept in isolation, alone, and then he'd wonder about Alex, Allen and Jennifer. He hadn't heard about them since that day, and his interrogators refused to answer questions regarding them. Thaddeus assumed they were getting some of the same treatment being the brains behind the theory - no, it wasn't a theory any longer - they had proven it now.

He wondered more about David and Barosh. Had they gone back to 30 CE? Or had they vanished? Destroyed by the power of the gateway? While his mind asked such questions, his heart knew the answer—they'd gone back. At least David had, after all, he left them a message.

What was it like? What a marvelous experience, to go back in time, knowing today's knowledge and history. Obviously, there had been no 'Grandfather paradox' as they had feared may happen, or he wouldn't be here today. Even though, it all happened only days ago for Thaddeus, it was over two-thousand years ago for David and Barosh, and any paradox would have occurred already.

They moved him repeatedly, always blindfolded, giving him no idea of where he was. They'd walk him to a car and drive for hours to some unknown destination. On three occasions, he had boarded an aircraft, with a hood over his head, and flown for several hours. They took his watch, and he lost the awareness of time, both in hours of the day and days of the month. He slept for short periods only before a new round of interrogation began. Without the rising and setting of the sun, or the luxury of a watch, time jumbled together into one continuous cycle of questioning. Considering what they'd just accomplished, he found this concept of non-time comical.

The university made a fuss about his detention without legal representation and turned their lawyers loose, along with a PR campaign for his release. June first loomed and the government couldn't risk exposure. Contacting his lawyer, they confirmed he had letters to deliver on June first, but refused to answer anything further, claiming lawyer-client privilege.

One day, they loaded him into a car, and after it was underway, the blindfold was removed. He was inside a limousine. The windows were blackened so he couldn't see out. He searched for window and door handles; there weren't any.

Across from him, sat Agent Rodgers.

"How are you feeling Professor?"

"Hello Agent Rodgers, I'm well, thank you—as well as can be expected, anyway. May I ask where we are going?"

Agent Rodgers didn't answer as they continued to ride in silence.

"Then, may I ask what day it is?"

"Wednesday, May 30."

Seven weeks! Thaddeus thought. *Seven weeks since David and Barosh went back, and two days before the deadline.*

"Am I being released?"

Agent Rodgers sat in silence.

"May I ask if my colleagues are okay?"

"They're being well cared for Professor, you needn't worry about them."

Thaddeus asked a few more questions, but Agent Rodgers had nothing more to say, and so they rode in silence the remainder of the trip. The vehicle came to a stop, and he heard the metallic click of the locks unlatching. The door opened and looking out; he was outside his own house. He looked at Agent Rodgers.

"You're free to go Professor. Inside your house, you'll find everything is in order, passport, wallet, watch; nothing is missing from when you were first picked up. I trust you enjoyed your stay with us."

As he moved to exit the vehicle, Agent Rodgers grabbed his arm, "Just one thing Professor, Agent Rosino—is he alive?"

Thaddeus looked into the agent's eyes and saw honest concern.

"I don't know," he answered, "but if I had to guess, I'd say he's alive – somewhere - sometime."

***

The house was as Agent Rodgers said it would be, with nothing out of place. It was clear they'd been through it, looking for anything to aid them. His mail was on a table in a neat pile. Each letter had been opened. They hadn't bothered to hide the fact they'd read it—a Federal offense. But then - they're the Federal.

Checking everything and assuring himself that all was in order, he put water on to heat. He longed for a cup of sweet tea—it had been a long time. Getting his mug, he sat down at the table to wait for the water.

What now? He wondered. *What happens next? David and Barosh are gone. I don't know where the others are, and I'm back where I began. What should I do next? Check on Mary, and then see if Alex is home, and find out what happened in Egypt. Check on Allen. It's going to be a long year of waiting.*

He ran his fingers through his sparse, silvery hair, staring at the empty mug.

Mug? My mug!

Where did it come from? It was missing that day before leaving for Greece. Had Camille found it? He picked it up, turning it around in his hands. On the bottom of the cup was writing. . .in Hebrew:

 יליבשב םישדח רפס

Book of Revelations

His heart raced.

It's a message, from David or Barosh.

He hurried into the study where row upon row of books, manuscripts, notebooks having hundreds of notes and fragments of paper sticking out, waited silently for him. Some were 10, 20, even 30 years old; written in Hebrew, Greek, Latin, English and French. The DHS would never be able to make heads or tails of them. They wouldn't attempt it - having no reason to.

He began pulling books out concerning Revelations—commentaries, concordances and various translations. Thumbing through them, he scanned each note and each inserted piece of paper. He couldn't believe he had so many books that involved Revelations. Time moved fast, and the minutes raced by.

Then, in the '**Interpreter's Bible**' - there it was.

At the beginning of the Book of Revelations, a folded sheet of note-paper was inserted. There was a coffee cup stain on it—David! The writing was in Greek.

Professor,

I'm writing this the day before we leave for Greece. I don't know if I'll have been 'translated' or vaporized, but either way, I'm sure I'm dead by the time you're reading this, just not sure what century I will have died in.

You see; it was clear from the beginning this would be a one-way trip. Because of the tablet, I have confidence I'll make the translation, but I cannot say the same about Allen's ability to bring me back a year from now. So, speaking for myself only, I won't be standing in the gateway a year from now. My life will end here – wherever or whenever here is. I don't mind telling you I'm scared. Like the astronauts going to the moon, only knowing they will not be coming back. But I rather have it this way than possible dinosaur bait.

Don't be sad - after all - I had already made that decision when I climbed the railing at the river the day so long ago. It's just a different railing I'm climbing this time.

The authorities will be questioning you, searching your home, your office and your mail. I left the message on your mug, knowing they wouldn't find it or think anything of it if they did. I knew you would - after all - it is your "revelation" mug.

If I've 'translated', then I intend to fulfill my mission (destiny?). I look forward to it – you see; I have a purpose now, and for me – that's everything. Since we know I left (or should I say – will leave) those tablets you found, under the wall of a building in Ammathus, it's safe to assume there's an opposite wall.

***Dig there, professor.** If I leave my name under one wall of that building, I'll leave the 'proof' under the opposite wall. I don't know what that 'proof' will be, but even though I'm an atheist, I go into this with an open mind, and I give you my word, I will not distort what I learn - I will give you the truth as I find it.*

Remember me,

David Kincaid

P.S. Tell Jennifer not to wait for me – she'd have a long wait.

It was there – In Israel - the proof! The truth – waiting in Israel!

Trembling, his hands shaking, he picked up the phone, and made arrangements to leave for Israel immediately. He knew he would be followed and watched closely, but that didn't matter any longer. He had nothing to hide. There were no more games – no more deception – there was only the truth to be known – once and for all – for the entire world to hear.

***

Work had stopped on the 'tel' while the Professor was missing. Upon his arrival, he redirected their efforts to the opposite side of the site they'd been excavating. He ordered a film crew to document every minute of the entire excavation, without interruption. He contacted CNN and FOX news and promised them the greatest discovery ever found in archeology. They sent reporters who set up on the site with lights and cameras. He wanted full coverage, so there would be no question of authenticity or fraudulent claims. He contacted Alex, Allen and Jennifer, and the group reunited on the site along with Agent Rodgers. All watched, day and night while the soil was removed, scoop by scoop.

And – there was an opposite wall. They worked without stopping, excavating down, extracting each spoonful of dirt carefully and meticulously, until finally; an associate called out:

"Professor, there's something here."

'Something' was a box made of stones; similar to the ones the tablets had been found in earlier. Thaddeus motioned the diggers aside and climbed into the pit. On his hands and knees, he carefully began removing the stones. Inside was an earthen pitcher, intact and engraved with the Star of David on the outside. Thaddeus's heart began racing; the Star of David did not come into existence as a Jewish symbol until centuries after this pitcher had been buried! It was a sign from Barosh, from two-thousand years ago!

Thaddeus made sure the camera crews had a clear view and were recording everything. A crowd had assembled, knowing something extraordinary was happening. Gently he cupped the pitcher and removed it from its stone tomb where it had rested for 20 centuries. The top had a lid on it, sealed with wax that was dried, cracked and broken away. Thaddeus gently picked at the wax, pried and wiggled the lid, slowly working it away from the pitcher. He never would have been so careless with such an ancient artifact—but this wasn't normal.

The lid came off.

Inside was what looked like an ancient sheepskin. He gingerly touched the parched material, carefully unfolding the edges. Inside the skin were two stained, iron spikes and a dried oilskin sheath. Carefully extracting the sheath, he held it in his hands. His heart raced even faster, having seen this same sheath when he had given it to David, only nine weeks and two-thousand years ago. Then, it had been soft and pliable, now it was hard and crinkled. Opening the sheath, Inside was a small black book. Tears swelled and began rolling down his face as he reverently removed the book from its protective skin. Cradling it carefully, he gently stoked his fingertips across the cover. At the sight of the book, his associates and the camera crews fell back, in shock and amazement.

The book was in good condition, intact and easily readable. He knew this would unhinge the scientific community—a book of twenty-first century technology but which would 'carbon 14' test to twenty centuries ago.

Have fun playing with that one kids.

He opened the book. On the inside cover was writing in Hebrew. He read it out loud:

"And I went unto the angel and said unto him, 'Give me the little book.' And he said unto me, 'Take it and eat it up; and it shall make thy belly bitter, but it shall be in thy mouth sweet as honey. And I took the little book out of the angel's hand and ate it up, and it was in my mouth sweet as honey, and as soon as I had eaten it, my belly was bitter. And he said unto me, 'Thou must prophesy again before many peoples, and nations, and tongues and Kings.'

Thaddeus knew the passage; it was from the Book of Revelations. They were sending him a clear message. Holding the little book in his trembling hand, he turned the page.

The writing was in English.

It was a title page:

The Journal of David
31 CE
David Alden Kincaid
Rabbi Ben-Barosh Goldberg

Beneath the turbulence. . .

Volume Two
The Journal

The Journal of David
31 CE
David Alden Kincaid
Rabbi Barosh-Ben Goldberg

1

I was falling – bouncing – skidding – tumbling - sliding.
I couldn't see, blinded by a brilliant explosion of light. The explosion was not around me; it came from within me—I was the explosion!

I was on a slope, hard and smooth. Scraping and clawing at the glossy surface - trying to stop the fall - to no avail. The soles of my sandals caught, and like the front brakes on a bicycle, threw me head over heels—slamming me back onto the unyielding surface as I continued to slide.

I heard screaming, and then realized I was screaming.

Suddenly, my legs jammed into my hip sockets as I jolted to a stop. I had landed on a ledge and lay inclined against the hard surface. Out of breath, bloody and bruised, I took inventory. I hurt everywhere, my knee throbbed, but nothing felt broken or dislocated. Touching my face, my hand came away wet and sticky - blood. Feeling my nose - it wasn't broken. Working my hand through my beard, a sharp pain ripped through me as my fingers discovered a deep gash running the length of my cheek. Moving my mouth back and forth; it worked – not broken.

The blindness slowly receded, and vision, although blurry and distorted, returned. The surface was white, shiny, hard and smooth. Wiping my hand across the surface, it left a red smear, defiling the purity of the whiteness.

Where was I? What happened?

My mind was clear. I recalled pleading with Rosino, when everything started glowing, getting brighter, before exploding in a silent ball of light. I was standing between the paws of the Sphinx. There was no boom, no thunderclap, only that tremendous flash, no - flash was too mild a word – detonation - a detonation of light, and then I was falling.

The translation had failed – I'm in another dimension!

I looked at my feet. I stood on the edge of the same material I laid against. I was grateful for the extra coverings on the sandals, or I might be missing some toes. Looking around, I saw pieces missing in the surface, leaving small gaps. It was in one such gap that I stood.

Slowly and carefully I turned around until my back pressed against the smooth surface.

The sight staggered me. The sun was a golden-orange conflagration, boiling over the horizon, igniting the sky in pillars of fire. An effusion of glowing purples, reds and yellows, pushed the blackness of the night into the distant heavens. Stray whiffs of clouds glowed fluorescently as they raced across the sky, fanning the fire. High above, the last stars twinkled, one by one quenched by the fire of the sun. Lowering my gaze, sharp and distinct, framed by the blazing sun, the majestic Sphinx crouched, gaze fixed on the rising disk as the fire washed across its flanks. To my left, the imposing structure of a pyramid rose from the desert floor, glowing like a ruby, reflecting the fire of the sun. It emitted an eerie radiance, casting fiery shadows across the dark, sweeping dunes. It was smoother and more defined than it had been minutes earlier. Layered in white and glowing like the sun, its peak blazed like a flaring match. I felt suspended. Feelings of motion swept through me as if standing at the bow of a large sailing ship in a sea of blazing swells. I swooned, and if not flattened against the surface, I would have fallen.

The smooth stone continued below me, stopping at a line of darkness. Above the line, was a brilliance of light; below the line, all was blackness, awaiting the sun's magical touch. Following the surface to the top, the bright, white purity changed to a blinding radiance, capturing the full force of the sun's power. I couldn't see the peak, my eyes slamming shut against the blazing light that shone in the sky like a thousand searchlights.

I knew I lay on the side of the Pyramid of Khafre and to the left of me was the Great Pyramid, except it wasn't the same pyramid I'd looked upon just moments before, which was dark and coarse, weathered by erosion and stripped of its polished surface. This pyramid was proud, robust, cloaked in a white coat of shiny limestone that I knew would be shaken loose by the great earthquake of the 1300's.

The translation hadn't failed! I was back in time—at least to sometime before the 14th Century.

But, why was I here? I had been standing between the crouching legs of the Sphinx. Then I recalled Allen explaining how the wobble of the earth, varied slightly, in its orbit, like a racecar making laps, and that we may not translate to the exact same spot. Congratulations Allen, I didn't pop out in space! But why'd it have to be here, on the side of a smooth pyramid?

I looked around for Barosh. I worried he hadn't translated that he hadn't drunk enough solution before Rosino showed up with that gun? Was I alone? In Egypt - in some bygone era? Panic rose in my throat like vomit.

Calm down, I told myself, *first things first, and the first thing is to get off of this pyramid without breaking your neck or else it won't matter where I am.*

I figured I was about a third of the way up, leaving around a hundred feet to the bottom. Turning back around again, I felt along the surface for cracks or bumps - there were none, only the seams where the blocks came together every two feet. It amazed me how these megaton blocks of polished limestone were placed on this slope; each cut so precisely and fitted together so perfectly. This wasn't done by primitive people.

The safest way down was to move from gap to gap, like the one I stood in. The trick was to get to each gap without sliding. Moving to the far edge of my gap, I raised my right foot off the ledge, feeling for a seam with the side of my sandal. My right hand found the seam above, and was able to obtain a slight hold. Lifting my left foot from the safety of the gap, I dragged it across the block until it too, found the groove. I tested the hold. It wasn't much, but it held. Clinging desperately to the seams, I carefully slid my left foot down the stone until it found the next seam. The right foot followed. Now came the moment of truth as I released my left hand from the edge of the gap I had stood in, and slid it to a seam. I was completely off the gap now, clinging to the side of the pyramid, like a spider. Every muscle was tense and strained as my fingers tried to penetrate the stone. I didn't slide.

The next gap was three blocks down and a couple of feet over to the right. I wanted to be directly above it, so if I lost my grip, I'd fall into it as I had before. Belly-sliding along the seams, until I was positioned above it, I began moving down the side, seam by seam. If the slope had been any steeper, I would not have been able to keep my hold.

After what felt like an eternity, my foot touched the solid edge of the gap. Relaxing my muscles, my legs began quivering uncontrollably. I had moved down about eight feet.

Regaining control of my legs, I continued moving, gap by gap, slowly but steadily, down the side of the massive monument. The sun continued to rise in the sky, and soon the entire pyramid was aglow. The light reflected all around me, blinding my eyes to anything beyond my immediate surroundings.

I was resting in a gap, calming my jumping leg muscles again, when a voice startled me.

"David? Is that you?"

Barosh!

I turned to the voice and saw a dark shadow, flattened tight against the glowing side of the pyramid, thirty feet above me to the left.

"Yes Barosh, it's me, David!"

"Thank God! I feared you had not made the trip."

"And I, you. How are you? Are you injured?"

"Praise God, other than some bruises, I am good."

"Thank God you are okay. I feared I was alone."

"Ah, an atheist thanking God," he laughed.

"Now is not the time for sarcasm, Barosh."

"David, we did it! We went through the gateway—we're back in time."

"Did you see the view?"

"Glorious! Although, I will lodge a complaint with Allen. He did not prepare us for pyramid climbing. Can you tell how far it is to the bottom?"

"No, the light and glare are too strong, but it can't be much further. At least, it had better not be; I don't think my arms and legs can take much more of this."

"Ah, mine are like Jell-O."

I looked down and stared into the glow below. As my eyes focused, I could see through the whiteness, and it gave way to a darker stone below. "Barosh, it looks different below, darker, rougher."

"I can't see that, David, but I will follow in your steps. Praise God! Just a little more and we'll be on solid ground."

I continued down, with a renewed spirit and enthusiasm, knowing I was not alone.

Finally, my foot stepped onto the darker stone of the pyramid I had seen. There was no further whiteness below me, and I could see the desert floor, not more than thirty feet below. The rest of the way was rough ledges that could be traversed without difficulty. The smooth, limestone facing was missing.

Waiting for Barosh to join me, I heard music.

"Barosh, do you hear that?" I called. "It sounds like singing."

"Yes, it's chanting."

He continued moving down until he stood on the same ledge as I and moved to me.

"Shalom, my friend," he said, embracing me, "it is good to see you. I worried that I had lost you."

Barosh stepped back, looking me up and down, "It appears you are intact, although that's a nasty gash on your face."

"It will heal, and is a small price to pay for having traveled so far."

"How true," Barosh laughed.

"Do you think we went all the way back to the first century?"

"I don't see why not. Allen was sure regarding the vernal point of the gateway, and seeing that it opened as he said it would, and here we are; I don't think we stopped along the way."

"Barosh, did you see the sunrise? It was glorious! I felt I was floating."

"Yes, it was the most beautiful thing I've ever seen. Seeing the world. . .," he stopped, "there's that chanting again."

A breeze had risen with the sun, carrying the sound to us.

"It's coming from there," I pointed.

"The Sphinx," Barosh said, "they worship the spring equinox and the rising of the constellation. We must get down, before. . ."

POP!

The sound broke the stillness of the dawn and was close.

"What was tha. . ."

POP! POP!

"Those are gunshots! But how. . ."

"Rosino!" Barosh shouted. "Come on, we must hurry."

2

Descending the remaining thirty feet of the massive structure went quickly and without incident. The blocks were rough, having small ledges. My heart racing and my mind reeling from those shots we'd heard, climbing down was only a blur. It had to be Rosino; there was no other explanation. He had translated along with us.

What had he done? What havoc could a twenty-first Century policeman, armed with a rifle, do in first century Egypt—was there even a limit?

Stepping onto solid ground, what should have been a feeling of elation was overshadowed by fear of what I'd find around the corner.

"Come on," Barosh said.

We covered the ground to the edge of the pyramid in short order. I grabbed Barosh's arm, pulling him back.

"Hold it Barosh; he'll shoot first and ask questions later. I'll go - he knows me." Peeking around the edge of the massive wall, the risen sun lit up the base of the pyramid, revealing a scene that sent chills up my spine. Rosino was on the ground less than a hundred feet away; one leg outstretched with his back against the pyramid. He cradled his rifle, and sprawled, on the desert sand, in front of him, were two men. They weren't moving.

"Agent Rosino," I called, "Agent Rosino, don't shoot, it's me, David Kincaid."

Rosino jerked, swinging the rifle in my direction.

"Who's there?" He yelled, panic filling his voice. "Stay away! Stay away or I'll shoot!"

"It's me — David - David Kincaid. Don't shoot." I waved my hand around the corner.

"Step out here where I can see you, Kincaid! Now!"

"Don't shoot. I'm stepping out, okay? Don't shoot." I slowly stepped from around the corner. "It's me — David. I'm here, with Rabbi Barosh."

"You don't look like Kincaid," Rosino yelled, pointing the rifle at me. "You look like them."

"It's me, Agent Rosino," I said opening my arms. "See, it's me, David Kincaid."

"Get over in the light, Kincaid. Where's that other maggot? Get him out here where I can see you both."

Barosh stepped from around the corner; his arms raised, "I'm right here, Agent Rosino. Rabbi Goldberg. Don't shoot; we're going to help you."

"Get over here, so I can see you." Rosino yelled, motioning with the rifle. "Where am I? What's going on here?"

"Put the gun down Agent Rosino. We're not going to hurt you," I said, moving over, "and, stop yelling, we can hear you."

"Long as I got this rifle no one's going to hurt me," he said, looking muddled and disorientated. "Is that Leo?" He asked gesturing towards the bodies sprawled in the sand.

"No, they're not Leo," I said, "Leo's not a person."

"Then who are they?"

Barosh walked over to the bodies. They were dark skinned, wearing white linen loincloths and leather sandals wrapping high up their calves. Polished, brass helmets covered the clean shaven domes of their heads. Each carried a short sword on his waist, and a small, circular shield on his arm. Two long spears, having sharp, flat heads, lay in the sand.

"If I had to guess, I'd say they were Nubians guarding the pyramids."

"Well they didn't do a very good job of it," Rosino sneered.

"Lucky for you, they didn't. Although they weren't expecting to face a rifle," Barosh said.

"Why are they dressed like that? How did I get over here, anyway?"

"We don't have time to explain it right now," Barosh said firmly. "There'll be more guards, and those worshippers are going to be here soon."

"What worshippers?"

Ignoring Rosino, I asked Barosh, "Do you think they heard the shots?"

"Not being that far away, and with the noise they're making. They were only pops anyway."

"That's right," Rosino sneered, "only pops. This baby pops just fine, and no one will hear the pops when I blow holes through both of you too."

"What about the bodies?" I asked, again ignoring Rosino.

"Leave them."

"But. . ."

"We can't worry about them, David. When the others find them, they'll think they were killed by raiders or struck down by the gods, whatever, but we need to get away from this pyramid."

"No one's going anywhere until I know what's going on here," Rosino barked.

Barosh turned to him, "Listen Rosino; you're not home in the twenty-first century, and no one is coming to rescue you. You're in the first century, and those people over there are sun worshippers, who don't take kindly to outsiders interfering with their gods. David and I are your only hope now, and we're leaving. So you can either come with us, or stay here and take your chances with those primitive people who may not like it that you killed two of their people."

"I got a rifle."

"Yes you do, and you've shown just how stupid you can be with it. Just remember, at some point, you'll run out of bullets, but they won't run out of spears and swords," Barosh spoke firmly. "Now, David and I are walking out of here, and you can shoot us in the back if it'll make you feel better, but remember, you don't know anything about where you are, or more importantly, how to get back to the twenty-first century. We do. So make up your mind, because we're leaving."

Rosino thought for a long minute before finally lowering the rifle, "I can't walk. I broke my ankle getting off of that stupid wall."

"Let me see it," Barosh said, bending over his leg.

"Owww!" Rosino yelled.

"It's not broken; it's only sprained. You're lucky you got down from there alive," Barosh said. "Come on, we'll help you, grab my arm. David, get the other side." He grabbed hold of the rifle, "Give me that thing and hold onto us."

Rosino jerked the rifle back and growled at Barosh, "Don't touch my rifle. You just grab hold of my arm, and don't either of you forget I have the rifle. As soon as we're settled, I expect to get some answers."

Once on his feet, with Barosh on one arm and me on the other, using the rifle as a cane, he barked, "Ok, which way?"

"That way," Barosh pointed to a small group of mud huts, a couple of hundred feet away. "That looks like a worker's compound; let's see if we can sneak in."

***

We were in luck.

The compound was deserted. Apparently everyone attended the ceremony at the Sphinx. A morning breeze had picked up, and the blowing sand quickly filled in our tracks. Entering a hut on the outer edge of the compound, we settled Rosino on a small wooden stool and pulled the flap over the opening.

"We don't have much time; I don't imagine that ceremony will last much longer," Barosh said, watching through the opening for returning workers.

"I want some answers," Rosino barked, cradling the rifle. "What's going on here?"

"Let's look at that ankle while we talk," Barosh said. "David, look around and see if you can find some clothes for Rosino. He can't be walking around in a suit."

"Walking around where? No one's taking my clothes," he snapped. "Where am I? What ceremony, and who were those clowns back there?"

"Be quiet and listen to me," Barosh snapped back, "we don't have time to play good guy, bad guy with you, so I'll only say this once. First, lower your voice, or you'll get us killed. Second, your bullying and threats don't mean anything to us anymore. We've back in time two-thousand years ago, in first century Egypt, and. . . ."

"Two-thousand years! Are you craz. . ."

"I told you to shut up and listen," Barosh spat back, pulling off Rosino's shoe and ripping the pants leg up."

"Owww! Careful - what are you doing to my pant. . . ."

"Hush!" Barosh hissed, jerking the leg out and removing the sock. "Your ankle is swollen, but I don't feel anything out of place. We'll wrap it tight, and see if you can stand on it."

"Here, I found these," I said, tossing him a white linen loincloth and tunic. "I'll look in the other huts to see if there's anything in them."

"Be careful," Barosh said, "don't stray too far. Look for some sandals." He turned back to Rosino, who sat holding the garments as if he was holding a bag full of roaches, "If you're coming with us, then you'll have to wear them; you can't be walking around looking like James Bond."

191

"Coming where?"

"As I said, you're in the first century, around the year 30. Obviously, you're in Egypt, where you were before you translated."

"Translated? You mean all that talk about a 'time-gate' was for real?"

"Look around and you tell me," Barosh said.

"But, how. . .what. . .?"

"You were standing in a time dimensional gateway at the Sphinx, and you drank that solution David warned you not to drink. When the gateway opened, well. . .here you are."

He shook his head in disbelief, "Where's that other guy, what's his name. . .Wainwright?"

"He didn't drink the solution; so he didn't come."

Rosino stared, dumbfounded. Barosh might as well have been Santa Claus, the tooth fairy or the Wizard of Oz, as being a twenty-first century rabbi, bandaging his foot in first century Egypt.

"I hit the mother lode," I said, dumping everything on a straw mat. "The next hut over is some kind of general quarters, and there's stuff all over. Here's a good cloak, and another tunic along with a sash. I didn't see any sandals, but I got a head coverings, a pouch, and, best of all, I found this," I held up a wooden staff. "I think it's a crutch; see the 'tee' here on this end and the other end has this wide piece on it, like a small ski. It's made to walk on the sand without sinking in."

"Excellent David," Barosh said. "Well Rosino, what will it be? You coming or not?"

Rosino had an almost childish expression, "Can we get back to our time?"

"We can."

"How?" He demanded. "Tell me."

"Give me the gun, and I'll tell you the way."

"No!" He snapped. "The gun stays with me."

Barosh nodded his head, "Okay, the gun stays with you—and the way back stays with us. Are you coming or not?"

"Where are you going?"

"Israel."

"Israel? What's in Israel?"

"The way back."

Rosino wasn't happy, either way he was trapped. I could see him mulling it over. Realizing he had no options, he stood up, but his eyes said he would extract his revenge the first chance he had.

"How do I put these rags on?"

3

"Where are we headed?" I asked as we slipped out of the compound.

After Rosino had changed clothes, Barosh wasn't sure what he would pass as. The dress was Egyptian, but not worn in the Egyptian style, and he had no Egyptian features. Barosh told him to keep the cloak loose, and his head covered, and above all, not to speak. He was to be deaf and dumb.

"The dumb part should come easy," Barosh said.

Barosh bundled Rosino's clothes together and carried them under his arm. Rosino insisted on keeping his wallet and DHS badge. Barosh said the badge wouldn't do him any good here, but to keep it hidden if it made him happy. Rosino refused to let go of the rifle, and insisted we go outside while he dressed. Barosh finally convinced him he couldn't be walking around carrying that rifle in the open. Reluctantly, he wrapped it in linen, tied a cord around it, and strapped it on his back. He secured the ammo belt under his cloak. It was heavy with bullets.

"We'll head to the Nile," Barosh answered, "that's our route anyway, and the Delta isn't far. Let's put some distance between us and those dead guards and find someplace where we can lay low while we figure this out."

Rosino picked up the hang of using the crutch quickly; the ski shaped bottom skidded across the surface of the sand without digging in. Unfortunately, his feet—didn't learn as quickly. Wearing Barosh's extra pair of sandals, he couldn't pick up the hang of walking in sand.

The sandals kept digging in, causing him to stumble often. He fell twice, emitting angry curses.

As Barosh had said, the Delta wasn't far. We began seeing its lushness, painted across the horizon like a green stripe. The desert changed from windswept sandy dunes to grainy hills, interspersed with large rocks.

We had descended to the bottom of a deep dune, when Barosh stopped, knelt down, and began scooping sand with his hands.

"What are you doing?" Rosino demanded.

"Digging, now be quiet."

Rosino didn't like being told anything by Barosh, but he knew protesting would get him nowhere with the stubborn rabbi. He watched, angry and confused.

After scooping out a large hole, Barosh tossed in the bundle of Rosino's clothes, and started pushing the sand on top of them.

"Hey! What are you doing?" Rosino screamed. "That's my clothes! Get them out of. . ."

"Be quiet!" Barosh snapped, "They don't belong here. You're wearing your clothing now."

"You son of a. . .," Rosino cursed as he fumbled with the rifle, trying to pull the cord over his head. I grabbed him in a bear hug from behind, holding both, the rifle and his arms immobile while he squirmed and kicked trying to get loose.

"Let go of me, you lousy. . ."

Barosh jumped up, took two fast steps to Rosino, and slapped him hard, across the face. "Enough!" He roared.

Rosino's face contorted into boiling rage, as a string of vile curses and spit erupted from his mouth, "I'll kill you, you son of. . . ."

Barosh slapped him again, harder, "Enough, I said! No more from you!" Rosino's face blazed a fiery red. His eyes burned with hatred, ignited by the hard slaps, but he stopped struggling.

Barosh removed the knife from the inside of his cloak. Rosino's anger turned to alarm, his eyes following the glint of steel.

"No one wants you here," Barosh hissed, moving behind Rosino, "and no one will miss you if you disappear—because you've already disappeared. You're a non-person here. Stop all your noise and orders or the next hole I dig will be for you."

"What are you doing? You don't dare harm me; I'm an agent of the Department of Home. . ."

Reaching around Rosino, Barosh grabbed his chin, jerking his head back and placed the blade against his throat.

"I said, shut up! Don't say another word. Move and you'll slice your own throat. You just don't get it, do you, Rosino? There is no Department of Homeland Security; it hasn't been created yet. There is no United States of America. You're not an agent of anything anymore. You're a nuisance; that's all you are, a big, loud-mouthed nuisance, and we don't have any time or patience for you. Now, David is going to slowly relax his hold, and as he does, I want you to cross your arms across your stomach and slowly sink to your knees. Nice and easy like. Don't move too fast or my hand will slip. You understand? Good. Go ahead David, but be ready to hit him hard if he moves."

I released my bear hug enough that Rosino could hug his stomach, and he slowly sank to his knees with Barosh keeping the blade tight to his throat all the way down.

"That's good, Rosino. David take out your knife. Now, cut the cord on that gun and take it." Rosino jerked, and Barosh pulled Rosino's head back as far as it would go without cracking, keeping the blade directly on the skin. "Don't move Rosino, or you'll die here and now, and I'll bury you along with your clothes."

Cutting the cord, I pulled the rifle away.

"Make a move Rosino, any move at all, and before you're heart beats twice, this blade will have cut right to your spine, got it?" Rosino's chin made the slightest of quivers indicating he understood.

"David, smash that gun against that big rock." Rosino quivered, and his eyes strained to the edge of their sockets, in desperation.

Raising the rifle in the air, I brought it down hard on the protruding rock. The long barrel bent. I raised it again and slammed it down again – and again – and again, beating Rosino's twenty-first century killing machine against first century granite. When I had finished, the rifle was a mangled twisted mess of steel and nylon.

"Bury it with those clothes," Barosh ordered and I eagerly complied.

"Okay, come here and hold your knife at Rosino's heart. If he tries anything – kill him. Can you do that?" I knelt down next to Rosino and placed the point of my knife at the side of his chest.

"I can."

"Now Rosino, there are two knives posed to kill you. I'm going to lower mine away from your throat, so you can breathe, but it will be right at your chest, ready to pierce your heart in an instant. If you think you can move on me, well, maybe you can, but you can't move on both of us before a knife is pushed into your chest, understood?" Rosino nodded. "Okay then, here goes." Barosh slowly lowered his knife and released his chin.

"You no good, lousy. . ." Rosino growled.

"Hush! I'll talk—you'll listen. That gun was a death sentence for all of us. We're visitors here, Rosino; we don't belong. You can't be running around killing people from two-thousand years ago. You've already killed two, and we're lucky they died with no consequences. Now you'll kill no more. On the other hand, you could die here, and it would have no effect on history, other than to make some buzzards happy. That is what will happen if you don't begin to understand what the situation is. You're in an ancient time, where there are people who have very primitive opinions about life. They will kill you and feed your bones to the jackals thinking they're doing the gods a favor. Your only hope of survival is to blend in and not look, say or do anything that will arouse suspicion. You're a liability to David and me, so I'd just as soon kill you now and get it over with."

He paused and gauged Rosino for his reaction, who continued to stare; anger, fear and pride melding together into one malevolent look of hatred – but he listened.

"David and I know, not only how to survive here, but how to get back home. You don't think we came here without having a way back, do you?"

Rosino shook his head.

"Good. We're not going to share that information with you. That's going to be our little secret. I know you would like to kill us, and as long as you had that gun, you probably would have, at least one of us, without knowing what you were doing. But now, you can think about this: If you decide to kill us while we're sleeping or to do anything that would betray us, you'll also be killing yourself. You'll be stranded here—alone. I don't suppose you know how to speak Greek, Arabic, or Egyptian for that matter, do you?"

Rosino shook his head.

"I thought not. How long do you think you'd last without being able to understand or speak to anyone? In a primitive time, when outlaws and soldiers are rampant? Killing and torture are the new normal. You'll die here, and in all probability, in a not so pleasant manner. Do you under-stand that Rosino?"

He nodded.

"We know you don't like us, but that only makes us even because we don't like you. You weren't invited on this trip. You're only here because of your pride and arrogance; so before we let you jeopardize our journey, we'll kill you first. The only reason I'm not killing you now is because God would not want me to do that without first giving you the opportunity to live. Do you believe me?"

Again he nodded his head.

"Whether any of us like it or not, you're here. So, here's my promise to you – as long as you play ball with us, we'll do everything in our power to protect you and get you back to your world. But there'll be no more orders or yelling from you, no more arguing when we tell you to do something, no more of you thinking you're the boss. That's all gone now. You will take your lead from us and follow our example. We are your only hope for salvation. You may not like that, but you have to accept that. If you don't, then you'll die here, alone, without a country, without honor, and no one will even know." Barosh leaned forward and said quietly, "But just think if you accept, then when you get back to your own time—you'll be a hero, a celebrity, a time-traveler—the world will be at your doorstep."

Barosh slowly stood up and backed away from Rosino but kept his knife in view. He picked up the crutch and tossed it.

"David, move away easy, and Rosino, you stay right there on your knees. Don't move." As I slowly rose and backed away, Barosh continued to talk, "David and I are going to leave now. We're going to find a place ahead where we can figure out our next move. You can either follow us or not. It's your choice. If you follow us, then get rid of that ammo belt and bury it, and you follow on the terms I laid out. If you don't, then God be with you. Shalom, Agent Rosino."

We began walking away, towards the fertile Nile Delta, leaving Rosino kneeling at the bottom of the desert sand dune.

After traveling a couple of hundred yards, we stopped and looked back.

Behind us, cresting the top of a large sand dune, through the sweltering heat waves, the head and shoulders of the former agent of the non-existent, Department of Homeland Security, for the non-existent United States of America, hobbled on his crutch.

We waited for him.

4

The transition from desert to delta was startling. A line of demarcation paralleled the course of the Nile River as it flowed and drained into the Mediterranean Sea. One moment I stood with both feet sweltering on the lifeless, burning sand of the desert; the next, I stood on the moist, black soil of the Nile.

Without the Nile, Egypt is a desert; hundreds of miles of hot, sweeping dunes, drifting and blowing, creating tempests of choking, blinding death. The sand holds no moisture; no rain replenishes its dead depths; no grasses, trees or brush grow in it. Few creatures can survive its harsh heat and cruel sting. It encroaches steadily, swallowing the river, inch by inch.

Meanwhile, deep in the heartland of Africa, the skies open, deluge after deluge soak into the moist, abundant rain forests, and the gods smile bringing *akhit,* 'the season of the flood'. The Nile rises - overflows its banks and reclaims the scorched, baked fields, quenching the parched land. Layer upon layer of black, alluvium soil, is deposited. Life is given back to the land, the creatures and the people. From June to September, the river banks swell sending millions of tons of the rich, mineral saturated soil into the marshes and fields of Egypt. The lines are drawn; to the west lies the 'land of the dead', comprising mounds of abrasive desert sand, tombs and funeral temples; to the east lays the wilderness of the Sinai. Between them lies the 'land of the living', the rich, fertile Nile Delta, thick with fields of grain, farms, villages and temples to the gods.

The Egyptians rely entirely on the Nile's annual flooding. They worship the gods who bring the 'black gold', and know that they are the 'people' the gods favor. They also know they are at the god's mercy. When pleased, the Nile snakes across the desert in rich, green loops and curves, and the vibrant nation flourishes. When displeased, the gods withhold the waters, and the Nile withers and shrivels, and famine spreads across their world.

Fields of grain, wheat, millet and barley stretched unbroken in all directions, fanning out in rich meadows and marsh lands. *Shemou*, 'the harvest season', was underway and labor gangs, of *Fellahin*, hurrying to gather the crops before locusts, hailstorms or the heat claimed them, swarmed through the fields like bees around a hive.

Barosh led the way, setting a course northeast, avoiding the south, where the ancient city of Memphis bustled. We couldn't risk drawing attention to ourselves while getting a sense of the land and the people, and while we decided how to handle the Rosino situation. I was confident Rosino would play ball with us - until he got what he wanted – then he would extract his revenge.

Avoiding large groups of people, we steered towards a small cluster of huts, huddled together in a protective cocoon, alongside thick Tamarisk trees, lining a secluded bluff. A group of women, garbed in black cloaks and head coverings, were squatting and chattering around a large kettle suspended over an open pit.

"Don't say anything; I'll do the talking," Barosh said.

"Shalom," he said bowing and holding both hands in front of him. The chattering stopped while an old woman, wrinkled like leather, rose to her feet.

"Greetings sir, you travel far?" The voice was strong; the words slow. She looked inquisitively at Barosh, appraising him and not averting her eyes when she spoke.

"We do, mother."

"And to where does your travel take you?"

"To Israel, we go to worship our God."

She looked Rosino up and down, obvious questions on her face, but it would violate politeness to ask them.

"You have far to travel, sir. Will you rest here?"

"We would."

"Over there. Many who travel, rest there," the old woman pointed to a stand of Chestnut trees, "Would you eat?"

"We would mother."

The old woman nodded and spoke to the others around the fire, "Give these pilgrims food. They are holy men. Where are your manners? Do you want the gods to deliver you to *Hapi*?"

The women scampered; filling three clay bowls with a thick, steaming gruel from the large kettle, and tearing off chunks of flat bread. They filled clay cups with a dark, foaming liquid and handed it to each of us.

"Thank you mother," Barosh said, handing her a Denarii, "God bless you."

The old woman took the coin, tested it with her teeth and nodded her head before stuffing it somewhere in her clothing. She resumed her place with the others around the kettle, and as we walked away, they broke out in lively conversation about us.

Approaching the trees, a group of men eyed us sharply. Barosh nodded to them as we walked past, moving to a spot out of hearing range. He squatted on the ground, motioning for us to follow while speaking quietly.

"Don't touch the food until I've blessed it, and then eat, whether you want to or not." He set his plate and cup in front of him and opened his two hands.

"Barukh atah Adonai, Eloheinu, melekh ha-olam, ha-motzi lechem min ha-aretz. *Blessed are you, O Lord our God, King of the universe; blessed is He who brings forth bread from the earth.*"

After praying loudly, in Hebrew, he dipped the bread into the bowl and scooped a mouthful of the stew. I dipped also, and after watching us, Rosino reluctantly followed. The group of workers, who had been watching us, turned back to their conversation.

"Well, the money passed," I said, and Barosh smiled, nodding.

"What is this garbage?" Rosino asked his face full of repugnance.

"I'd guess it's barley with a heavy dose of garlic and onion in it. Looks like a few pieces of fish are thrown in as well," I chuckled. "Good, huh?"

"Screw you Kincaid," he said.

"I suggest you eat it," Barosh said, "you'll need the nourishment, and there's no Burger King around the next pyramid. It's not all that bad, maybe a little heavy on the garlic." He turned to me, "Did you understand her?"

"I did. It seemed to be a form of Greek and Arabic."

"Excellent, I was praying you understood her," Barosh said. "It's *koine*, an Arabian dialect of Greek, influenced by Semitic and Berber. It's going to be the common language everywhere."

"Hey, this stuff almost tastes like beer," Rosino said, drinking the foaming liquid.

"That's because it is beer," Barosh replied. "It's the number one drink here. I take it you don't object to that?"

"You need to wash this rot down with something," he sneered. "They drink more of this than water?"

"Keep your voice down," Barosh admonished, "English won't go over too good here, and drink the beer; the water here – will kill you."

"No water? We can't drink beer all the time, can we?" He asked.

"They do," I said, nodding to the group of men, "but no, we can't drink beer all the time. We brought two bags of water with us, and we have pills to treat the water here," I reached under my cloak and brought out a double zip lock baggie full of tiny, white pills. "One of these purifies a gallon of cleaned water."

"How do you clean it?"

"We Strain it. The water from the river and streams has silt, debris, and a host of living things like snails and worms in it, as well as possible animal and human feces."

"That's disgusting! How do people live, drinking that?"

"They don't. The average life expectancy is just over 40, and – they drink beer," Barosh said.

"How many pills do you have?" Rosino asked.

"Enough to last until we go back, and if we run out, then we'll boil it."

"And just when do we go back?"

I looked at Barosh, who nodded his head.

"In a year," I said.

"A year!" Rosino exploded, startling the group of men under the trees, who all turned to stare.

"Keep your voice down," Barosh admonished him, while grabbing his arm, "there's no point in yelling about it. It's out of our control. There is nothing you can do about it."

Brushing his arm off, Rosino stood in open hostility, "You expect me to stay here, with you two idiots, running around like Halloween freaks, for a year?"

"Whether we expect you to or not doesn't matter. We're here for a year, and we have no control over it," Barosh said. "Now sit down, before you start something."

"Who has control?" He yelled.

"Allen Eberhardt," Barosh answered, trying to placate him.

"That egghead scientist?"

"The same."

"And how does it happen? What does he control?"

"A gateway, like the one we translated through to get here."

"Where's the gateway? How do we open it now?"

Barosh shook his head, "We can't open the gateway."

"Where's the gateway? Show me, I'll get it open!"

"No, you can't open it."

Rosino's face turned red, and his eyes grew large. He looked like he was going to burst or beat the two of us to a pulp. Every fiber of his being rebelled against the condemning words he heard. His eyes shot back and forth between Barosh and me. We both stood up, putting our hands inside our cloaks.

"Don't think those flimsy knives you're reaching for, scare me. You'll never hold a knife to my throat again," he said through gritted teeth. Screaming a cry of despair, he kicked the bowl, sending it smashing into a tree and bringing a howl from his mouth as the pain of his forgotten sprained ankle shot through him. The group of men jumped up, murmuring excitedly.

"Tell me," he growled, "just what are we supposed to be doing for the next year, anyway?"

"We're going to see Jesus; that's what," I said.

He stopped, taken aback and baffled, "What? Jesus? Are you out of your mind?"

"No, we're going to Israel, to meet Jesus, just like David said," Barosh answered.

"You're kidding?" When we both shook our heads, he couldn't contain himself. "That's what this is about? To meet Jesus?" He bellowed, his whole body agitated. "You mean the 'in the Bible', Jesus? There's no terrorist plot? No assassination? No mass annihilations? All this, to meet Jesus!"

He hobbled back and forth, like a wild man. The group of men had stopped babbling, and were grabbing tools or picking up sticks. They were afraid and anxious about this strange man jumping and hopping about, screaming hysterically, in a strange language.

"Quiet him down before we have a riot on our hands," Barosh said to me while he approached the group of men, with his hands held open in front. I heard him say something about 'a holy man' and a 'vision from god' while pointing at Rosino. The men backed away, turned and ran, shouting about the gods being displeased.

Meanwhile, I was wrestling with Rosino, trying to restrain his jumping around while continually talking to him. Barosh came back and grabbed him, spinning him around. He raised his hand to strike him, and Rosino's hand shot out like a cobra, instantly stopping Barosh's hand in midair while his other hand, balled into a fist, slammed hard into Barosh's face, sending him sprawling.

"Don't you ever raise your hand to me again," he snarled, "next time I'll kill you."

Barosh shook his head, regaining his composure. "Okay," he said, standing, "that makes us even. But stand still and be quiet. Stop making a scene or you'll get us killed." An uneasy tension filled the silence that followed. I could see the wheels turning in Rosino's head.

"Wait a minute," he said, "I know what you're up to. Mass annihilations! The world turned upside down! Chaos and inferno! All those things we heard you talking about—are real. I knew you were terrorists all along; you never fooled me for a minute. I know what you're doing. You're not going to meet Jesus—you're going to assassinate him! You'll turn the whole world upside down! Pit everyone against everyone, mass murder and world upheaval. That's what this is all about."

Barosh looked at him with a mixture of amazement and contempt. He slowly shook his head, "You're an idiot."

"No, I'm no idiot. I know what you're doing. I got you figured out."

Barosh began collecting his things, "I suggest we move and get away from here. Those men may have gone to alert the authorities, and there could be guards already looking for us."

5

Traveling in silence, we'd gone a couple of miles, skirting three clusters of huts until Barosh felt we'd moved far enough away from any potential fallout of Rosino's outburst.

People were everywhere, busily engaged in the massive harvest. Most never looked up as we passed; those that did quickly returned to their toils. Many strangers traveled through the Delta during the harvest time, and we were just three more.

We kept Rosino between us so he would attract the least attention, and few people seemed to notice him. He hadn't complained about his ankle, and in fact, had not made any sound at all since leaving, absorbed in his thoughts, nurturing his hatred of Barosh and me while massaging his assassination of Jesus theory.

I worried about that theory. If he truly believed we were on a mission to assassinate Jesus, what would he do? I didn't know what his religion was, but I assumed his background was Christian, which may or may not mean anything to him. I didn't think he was a believer in much of anything except his own self-worth. I had no doubt that, if he thought he could get home on his own, he would kill us both, especially if he could go back as some kind of hero saving Christianity. Only his fear of being stuck here alone would keep us alive.

I feared him, his anger, his mental state and of what he was capable of. It was an immense relief knowing his gun was destroyed.

I wondered if we shouldn't have killed him when we had the chance. The way he watched us, keeping his guard up, told me he wondered the same thing.

We skirted around fields thick with laborers wearing loincloths and small kilts, mowing the stalks with their short sickles. I marveled at their skill, cutting the grain quickly, at uniform lengths, leaving behind stubble a few inches high.

They were followed by reapers, bundling armfuls of the cut stalks, carrying them to the large threshing area, where they tossed them onto the granite stones, bundle after bundle until the area was two to three feet high with them. Heavy wooden sleds, fitted with wide curved runners and dragging rows of iron bars behind, pulled by teams of oxen, rode over the bundles, threshing the stalks. Back and forth they squashed and trampled the stalks, knocking loose all the kernels of grain before moving to the next threshing floor piled high with fresh bundles.

A line of men, carrying long wooden 'winnowing' forks worked the floor next. They tossed the threshed stalks high into the air, allowing the wind to separate the light husks and straw from the heavier grain. There was a rhythm and beauty watching them work in unison, pushing a swirling cloud of blowing straw and husks before them. Upon reaching the end, a mountain of straw and chaff stood, and the men refreshed themselves with long draughts of beer before moving on to the next area.

The straw was gathered up and hauled off to be used for bedding and brick making while the thick layer of grain remaining was scooped up and sifted through sieves into large vats. Scribes, distinguished by their shaved bodies, white pleated skirts and light shawls draped over their shoulders, meticulously measured and recorded the harvest on papyrus scrolls. The vats, two at a time were loaded onto donkeys, taken away to the enormous storage silos.

Everywhere, overseers carefully watched and monitored the work. Anyone who slacked was quickly reprimanded or removed. They also kept a watchful eye on the gleaners, those women and children, who picked through the harvested fields, for the grain left behind by the reapers, making sure they didn't wander into fields not yet harvested. Barosh stopped at one field and watched them intently.

"What is it Barosh?" I asked.

"In the Tanakh, there is the story of a woman – named Ruth. She was a Moabitess, whose husband was a Jew and died. Ruth would not abandon her mother-in-law, Naomi. Instead, she left her own country and followed Naomi to Israel. In order to survive Ruth followed the reapers, gleaning in fields just as these women do here. It's a story of great love and faithfulness and of God's great design."

"Is it related to our mission, Barosh?"

"She told her mother-in-law, '*where you go, I will go; And where you lodge, I will lodge; your people shall be my people and your God my God.*' Barosh turned and looked at me.

"Ruth ended up marrying Boaz, the owner of the fields, and it is from their lineage that the great king of Israel David came, and. . .," he paused, "ultimately, Jesus, whom we seek."

An overseer was watching us closely. We stood out in our Hebrew cloaks and bearded faces. Travelers were not uncommon, in the Delta, and as long as they kept moving, they weren't bothered.

"Come Barosh; we're drawing attention."

We continued skirting field after field, seemingly without end until we approached the shores of the Nile. It was a veritable jungle of papyrus and palm, henna, fig and sycamore trees, surrounded by thick undergrowth. We followed a trail through dense, heavy reeds and sugarcane rising high over our heads. Entering a grove of towering date palms with wide, fibrous leaves and loaded with fruit, the copious canopy, blocked the sun's rays, and we were able to rest under it, without scrutiny. Barosh shared his water with Rosino, who drank long and deep, without saying anything.

***

Moving out from under the trees, I smelled the pungent fresh water of the Nile before seeing the river. It sparkled a deep, royal blue, ringed by ebony shorelines and adorned in lush, rich vegetation. It teemed with life. Birds of all sizes and shapes, perched, circled, and swooped down across the surface. Large cranes and pelicans walked stiff-legged in the shallows and fish rippled the surface. Although being the dry season, the river was wide, flowing serene and silent. We would need to cross, but not here and not now. Now, it was only to be admired, and the scent and taste of it savored. I could understand why people would worship this river; it was abounding life in the midst of lifeless desert.

"Where to?" I asked Barosh.

"Follow the river; we're bound to come to a crossing."

The river took a wide turn, and following it around, we came upon a small, tightly packed encampment of tents. Only a few people were around, signifying it was a camp of fellahin, out working the fields. Several women, wearing only light, linen shirts, busied themselves around a large fire pit, preparing the camp's meal. Two were on all fours, grinding grain on a slate with a round granite stone. Another was kneading dough, forming it into flat, thin loaves of *battaw*, which she passed to a woman who was baking the loaves on a large copper disk suspended over the fire. One woman cut onions and turnips, and two others cleaned a pile of fish.

"Wait here," Barosh said. He approached the group and extended his greeting. After some discussion, and an exchange of coins, he came back.

"Okay, follow me." He led us to a tent at the edge of the camp.

"For five denarii, we can stay here and have a daily share of food along with three cups of beer apiece."

"Whose tent is this?" I asked.

"The woman I was talking to and her family."

"What about them?"

"They'll sleep out there. She wants the money, and made it clear that her word goes."

Looking around, there was little to look at. The tent wasn't much of a tent, just a covering on four poles with open sides. Two mats, covered with straw, were along one side of a non-existent wall, while three mats were on the other. A small collection of bowls and cups, along with scattered pieces of linen, completed the furnishing. There was no table or chairs.

"Where are the beds?" Rosino asked.

"You're looking at them," Barosh said, and before Rosino could protest, he added, "If you prefer, you can sleep in the trees, with the spiders and snakes."

Receiving no answer, Barosh said, "Take that mat there, and rest your ankle."

"That's a lot of money for one night," I said.

"It's for seven nights. They're a group of migrant workers, and we got it until they move on in seven days." When Barosh saw the questionable look on my face, he added, "We need the time for Rosino's ankle to heal, and for us to make arrangements."

"Arrangements for what?" Rosino asked.

"First, to cross the river, and second, to see if we can find a caravan."

"Caravan? You mean like with camels? What for?"

"To cross the Sinai." Barosh said.

***

That evening, when the men returned from the fields, there was a slight commotion as the woman explained the arrangements to them. I could tell they didn't like it, but true to her word, she called the shots, and they were too tired to argue with her. Besides, the clinking of silver coins was convincing.

We weren't invited to join the group at the campfire for dinner, but three girls brought us bowls filled with a steaming stew, loaves of *battaw* and cups of beer. As they scampered away giggling, I glanced at Rosino, whose eyes were following their semi-nude bodies.

"Don't even think about it," Barosh said to him, "you'll get yourself killed, along with us."

Rosino looked at Barosh with contempt, "Give me some credit Goldberg, I'm not a pervert. Besides, I got other things to think about." He poked around in the bowl with a piece of bread and asked, "How do we know this stuff won't kill us?"

"They seem to live on it okay," Barosh said, nodding towards the sounds coming from the campfire. "You may have to develop a taste for it, but other than that, it's cooked, its vegetables, bread and fish, and like you said earlier, you got the beer to wash it down with. Cheers!" He raised his glass in salute.

As we ate, we discussed the plans for the next few days.

"I'm going to ask around where we can cross the river, and where we can find a caravan. Rosino should rest that ankle as much as possible. David, you stay here in case anyone comes around asking questions."

"I'd rather go with you," I replied, not wanting to be alone with Rosino.

"That wouldn't be wise, leaving Rosino alone, without being able to communicate. If authorities or guards came around, they could drag him off, and we wouldn't be able to get him back."

"That wouldn't break your heart any," Rosino said.

"Honestly? No, it wouldn't, but God wouldn't approve." Barosh said, wiping his bowl with the last piece of bread, "You need to draw and clean some water in the morning, David. I'll barter with these folks for food to take with us."

"We need to get some clothes for Rosino," I added, "this semi-Egyptian garb isn't making it, and he can't cross the Sinai like that."

Two of the girls came back carrying a plate loaded with figs and grapes, as well as a pitcher of beer to refill our cups. They picked up the dirty bowls and skittered away, giggling.

"What do we need a caravan for? Can't we just cross the Sinai ourselves?" Rosino asked, devouring grapes.

"Well, for one thing, it's too far to walk with your ankle – over 200 miles. We don't know the routes around the mountains, and even if we did, it will still take a couple of weeks on foot, and we'll need to carry a lot of food and water," Barosh answered. "For another, there are outlaws and revolutionaries looking for easy marks. The Jews, on pilgrimage to Jerusalem, were easy prey. It'll be safer traveling in a large number who know the routes."

"And lastly," I added, "there's the Roman Legions, who are patrolling and moving around. We don't want to run into any of them alone."

"Roman Legions?" Rosino repeated. "You mean like in the 'Gladiator' movie?"

Barosh turned to him, and despite Rosino's shortcomings, I could see he felt compassion for him.

"This whole thing is overwhelming to me, Rosino," Barosh said. "Being here, at the dawning of history, seeing these people and this different way of living, and I've had months to prepare for it. I can't imagine what it must be like for you to be thrown into this world of two-thousand years ago without having time to prepare for it."

"But you're here, and you have to come to grips with it. Look around; it's somewhere around the year 30. Not 1730 or even 1930 – just plain 30. The Roman Empire rules the world, at least what they know the world to be. America won't be discovered for hundreds of years yet; Christopher Columbus won't even be born for another fourteen-hundred years; there are no planes, no cars, no electricity, and no gasoline engines. Right this minute, only a couple of hundred miles from where we're sitting, Jesus Christ is alive and walking around. That's for real; it is not a movie or a church play, but is as real as that bowl you're holding in your hand." Rosino had stopped eating and was listening intently.

"We're here, with no way back until one year from now. I'm sorry you're getting hit with this, but you have to understand exactly what our situation is. If we don't do things the right way, we won't make it back, and we'll die here. We have a tremendous advantage because of our foreknowledge of events, but we must use it wisely."

Rosino stared at Barosh, and for the first time, I thought he was beginning to grasp what he had gotten himself into.

"Yes, David means Roman Legions – soldiers - carrying swords and spears, just like in the movie 'Gladiator' - only it's no movie. They're very real; they don't speak English; their swords and spears are real, and they have no qualms about using them. They are killing machines."

Barosh changed his speech, speaking to Rosino in a confident and quiet voice, "We're here to meet Jesus. We're not here to kill him. History cannot be changed. What's happened - has happened, and it cannot be undone; that is the law of the universe, and, we have no desire to want to change it if we could. If you can't or won't believe that and insist on thinking otherwise, then think about this: If Jesus were to die prior to his execution, which cannot happen, but just suppose it could, then what would that mean to us? We'd be committing instant suicide. Everything you know would be erased. The histories of Europe, the Middle East, America, wars, the Crusades, genealogies—all would change. Whole lineages, including our ancestors, would cease to exist. It would all tumble like a gigantic domino set. So, even if it were possible, which it's not, who in their right mind would do it? And, despite what you may think, we're not crazy. We're not here to commit historical suicide. Lastly, if we were on a mission to assassinate Jesus, then why are you still alive? Why would we risk our mission? We would have killed you back at the sand dune. We have no desire to kill you, and as I gave you my word, we're going to do everything possible to return you to your own world." Barosh stood.

"Come on David, let's walk and settle our stomachs while Rosino thinks on these things." He looked at Rosino, who looked lost and forlorn, "We're here together, like it, or not, and if we want to go back, we must stick together."

6

After filling the second water jar, I stood up on the river's edge, stretching the kinks out of my back, and breathing deep, luxuriating in the moist scent of the Nile.

Gazing up and down the river, all is quiet and peaceful. Flocks of kingfishers circle and swoop, cutting and diving along the surface. Across the river, two large Benu birds stride like gods through the shallows while high overhead, the sky is dotted with a covey of Barbary falcons, circling and waiting for a careless shrew or river rat to expose itself.

A large ship whispers past. Standing rowers, along the length of each side of the ship, bend in unison, pulling long oars through the gentle current. At the helm, a bare-chested, muscled man keeps the ship within the deep channel, avoiding the sandbars that rise to snare it as it glides smoothly across the surface. Its cargo is from the heart of Africa - ivory tusks, ebony panther skins, brightly colored ostrich feathers and coveted coconuts - is piled high, lashed securely to the deck.

An involuntary grunt escapes my lips as I hoist the two large jars of water, for the walk back to the tent. A child, no more than two or three, stares up at me from the river's edge where he has been playing. The boy has a full, head of hair matching his wide eyes, both as black as the Nile's loam, in which he sits. His face breaks into a wide smile and his laughter rings out with the same joy and innocence all children, from all time holds. His mother, bent over among the reeds searching for snails, stands up at the sound, turning to check on her small son. Her arm bracelets jingle and jangle as she brushes the hair away from her face, and she too smiles at me.

I smile back, hoist the jars securely, one in each arm, turn and start up the path to the tent.

"Aieeeeeeeeeeee!"

Coming directly behind me, the scream shatters the air, causing me to jump. Spinning around, I see the young mother, who seconds earlier was smiling at me, running in panic towards her son, whose arms and legs dangle from the mouth of an enormous crocodile.

"Aieeeeeeeeeeee!"

Dropping one jar and raising the other above my head, I run at the creature, bringing it down hard on the monster's head. The jar smashes into pieces as the reptile bellows in pain, opening its mouth to snap at me. The mother grabs her child's feet and pulls; while the crocodile slams its mouth shut and jerks its head once before turning and slowly walking back into the river.

"Aieeeeeeeeeeee!"

Standing at the river's edge, she screams again and again, venting her agony, watching the crocodile slide beneath the surface while, in her hands, she holds the legs from the torn body of her baby.

My own legs give out and I drop to my knees, shaking and trembling. The women from the camp come running, and gather around the hysterical mother, backing her away from the river and the harsh price it had extracted.

Left alone at the river, I stare at the large footprints of the cold messenger of death and see where they covered my own prints, made while filling the water jars. But for a matter of seconds, it would have been me in the monster's mouth. Raising my head, I look out at the river, serene and uncaring as it has been for thousands of years and would continue to be so for thousands more. And I remember another river I had stared into, not that long ago, and. . .

. . .I cry.

***

In the shadows, a man wearing a long, dark cloak watches. From deep within the hood, pulled far over his head, malignant eyes glow like burning embers.

Next time David. . .next time, he muses.

***

The camp is quiet that evening. There's none of the usual chatter and banter about the day's activities and squabbles. No one talks. Those who eat—eat in silence.

The young mother sits alone and cries through the night. Her husband tries to comfort her.

"It is the will of *Hapi* - god of the Nile - father of gods - who brings joy among us. You must not weep, but be honored he chose our son. We must go to *Kereha*, and give our thanks and prayers to him for such a blessing."

Not consoling her, he leaves her to her grief.

Before dawn, while the camp sleeps, the moon casting eerie reflections and shadows across the silent river; the young woman rises from her crying. She gathers her baby's things and walks back to the river. Kneeling in the black mud, she spreads out the small woven mat her son had slept upon. Placing his bowl and cup on it, a handful of grain, his clothing, and his toy rattle made of bone around the edges—in the middle; she places her son's legs.

He will need these things on his journey she whispers.

Raising her face to the moon, masked by wisps of gauzy clouds, she stretches her open hands to the river. Softly she sings a song to *Osiris*, the god of life and death; brother-consort to the goddess *Isis* and father of the mighty *Horus*. She sings her song and calls upon *Osiris* to answer her prayers. The rhythmic lapping of the river, gently stroking the shore's edge, accompanies the soft, sorrowful sounds of the young mother's song.

When dawn arrives, breaking over the horizon like a flaming fireball and the camp stirs, the young mother's soft song is missing from the rhythmic lapping of the river, and the small woven mat sits alone.

7

Barosh used the next few days well. Initially, he had found it difficult finding anyone who would talk with him, other than the nod of the head or the polite exchange of greetings. It was harvest season; work was plentiful and hard. People had no time or energy for idle chatter with foreigners, especially with the followers of the 'one God'.

He found an old man, too feeble to accompany his sons to the fields, who they left behind each day. Over cups of beer and slabs of fish, swathed with a thick, brown sauce, stuffed between pockets of *battaw* bread, the old man welcomed the escape from his solitude and was an endless source of information.

He had no concept of years as a continuation of time. His calendar was divided into three seasons, centered around the annual flooding of the Delta. It was currently *Payni*, the second month of *Shemu*, in the fifth year of the counting, and he had no interest in knowing anything further about time (Barosh wasn't sure what he counted, other than it had to do with how much taxes he would have to pay).

He told Barosh there was a river crossing a day's walk from the camp. The river is narrower there, and a ferry shuttled people and animals back and forth.

Caravans passed through on a regular basis, traveling between Alexandria and the Far East. The favored routes were through Memphis to the south and Heliopolis to the north. Some left from Pithom. When asked about Roman soldiers, the old man's eyes narrowed into slits.

"Roman dogs!" He spat. "Many are in Alexandria, Ramses and Memphis. They violate our women, mock the gods and do whatever they want. They are pigs and steal our riches for their masters in Rome!"

"Are there soldiers in Heliopolis?" Barosh asked.

The old man drained his beer and nodded, "Heliopolis has many. They have a fortress there. It is not good to go there having a beautiful daughter or wife. Pithom is safer."

Barosh thought of Abram traveling through Egypt and disguising his beautiful wife, Sari, as his sister, out of fear the Pharaoh would have him killed to claim her for his own.

Some things never changed.

Rosino's ankle had responded well to the rest, and he was able to walk around without the crutch for short periods of time.

We drew water from the river; strained and treated it; drank it and we didn't die. The river was the source of both death and life.

***

With full skins of water and a supply of dried fish, figs and nuts, we left two mornings after the crocodile incident. The loss of the small boy and his mother had put a cloud over the encampment. *Hapi*, the god of the Nile, had wanted the boy and had sent the giant crocodile for him. They accepted the child's death as part of their world.

But the smashing of the water jar on the crocodile's head had angered *Hapi*, making him reject the boy as evidenced by leaving his legs behind. And the self-sacrifice of the young mother was something they could not accept. It was not the will of *Hapi* to take her and was offensive to him. Their ill fortune with the Nile god had started with the arrival of the foreigners, who worshipped the 'one God', and it had been the foreigner who challenged and angered the great crocodile. People avoided us, and murmured when we passed. Barosh sensed we should leave before the camp's fear turned to open hostility.

"Well, I'd say we're doing just terrific," I mumbled to Barosh as we packed up. "First, we're running from the pyramids for murder; then we're stealing some workers clothing, and now we're running from the Nile gods for offending a crocodile, all the while having to watch our backs from an egotistical cop on a vendetta from two-thousand years ahead."

"I am not running from any gods David; let's make that clear," Barosh said in a firm, stern voice. "There is only one God, Jehovah. I run from no false gods. We didn't know what we would find here, and we must be prepared to adapt. Now, we have to cross this river anyway; so it's best we do it and leave these people to their grief before it finds a wrong outlet. We've lost too many days already and need to get to Israel and find Jesus. I fear we may already be too late." He placed his hand on my shoulder, "Give Rosino some time. Put yourself in his place. Think of how you felt when you first heard of this and then imagine just waking up one day and being here."

For all his strength and conviction, Barosh had a depth of compassion I didn't comprehend.

***

We traveled north, following the river. Once on the other side, we'd head towards Pithom before settling in somewhere for the night.

"We'll skirt Heliopolis to avoid the Romans there. Hopefully, we can hook up with a caravan in Pithom." He glanced at Rosino, working the crutch.

"With any luck Rosino, we might be able to find a camel for you."

"Great," he grumbled.

Coming around a wide bend in the river we passed a *saqiah,* where a donkey had worn a deep circular trench in the riverbank walking round and round, turning the wheel rotating the large waterwheel, in the river. We stopped and watched the clay jars, fastened to the circumference of the waterwheel, submerge empty and resurface filled, to empty into a wooden trough feeding the irrigation ditches. The vast, fertile wedge of the Delta may have been formed by the spreading mouth of the Nile, but it was nurtured by the sweat of man and beast.

Resting under the trees gave us relief from the sun's heat and allowed Rosino to soak his swollen ankle. While we drank and ate, Barosh watched the Egyptian children helping the donkey on the *saqiah*, pulling water from the Nile to nourish the land.

"There is a passage, in the Torah," Barosh said, "when God called Moses to be the deliverer. He told him:

'. . .if they will not believe also these two signs, neither harken unto your voice that you shall take of the water of the river, and pour it onto the dry ground; and the water which you take out of the river shall become blood upon the dry land.'"

"I'm in awe David, knowing that such things took place here, on this river. No matter how I had prepared for this journey, it's overwhelming. This is the same place where Joseph's brothers had come begging, during the great famine, throwing themselves at the mercy of pharaoh's over-seer for grain to survive. They were too blinded to see that the overseer was the same brother they had bound and sold into slavery. After years of imprisonment and mistreatment, Joseph was now second to only pha-raoh himself, yet he held no hatred or bitterness towards his brothers, declaring:

'I am Yosef your brother, whom you sold into Egypt. Now there-fore, be not grieved nor angry with yourselves that you sold me hither: For God did send me before you to preserve life. . . .Haste you and go up to my father, and say to him, 'Thus says your son Yosef: 'God has made me lord of all Egypt; come down to me, tarry not. And you shalt dwell in the land of Goshen. . . .'''

"And then Pharaoh said,

'. . .take your father and your households and come to me, and I will give you the good of the land of Egypt, and you will eat the fat of the land.'''

"They came and lived here for four-hundred years, multiplying and prospering as the pharaoh had said. But by the time of Moses, their fortunes had changed; a new pharaoh had come, who didn't know Joseph; and the land of Goshen had become a, 'house of bondage', for the Hebrews, their lives made bitter with hard work;

'in mortar and in brick and in all manner of service in the field.'''

"We're back to the "Let my people go" story again," I said laughing.
"This wasn't the land God had promised to Abraham," Barosh ignored my sarcasm. "You see how they must work to water the land? God told Moses,

'For the land where you go to possess, is not as the land of Egypt from whence you came out, where you sow your seed, and water it with your foot, as a garden of herbs: But the land where you go

to possess, is a land of hills and valleys, and drinks water of the rain of heaven.'"

"Moses was sent by God to deliver His people from the bondage of this land."

He paused, and I could tell he was struggling with something. Turning away from the children and looking at me, his eyes reflected his deep passion, and when he spoke, I knew the words were coming from his most inner depths.

"I keep wondering what God has sent me here for."

"We're here to find Jesus," I said, "and you're going to expose him."

"Yes, that's right, but inside there's another voice speaking to me."

"What's it saying?"

"I don't know. . .that's the problem."

***

The ferry was located a short distance ahead. We knew we were getting close by the wide, furrowed trail cut through the marsh and reeds, crowded with laborers and travelers. Few paid any attention to us.

Men, carrying tools, hurried along giving us dismissive side glances and mumbling amongst themselves. The banks of both sides of the river were beaten down flat by thousands of feet and hooves.

Approaching the landing, the ferry was in the middle of the river, headed to the opposite shore where people waited to cross over to this side. It wasn't much more than a large platform, surrounded by a wooden railing with openings at both ends; men worked long oars, moving the heavily loaded raft across the river. The current carried it downriver past the landing, where a series of pilings extended out into the river, and the platform slid into them perfectly. A rope was attached from the shore, and the ferry was pulled in to the un-boarding landing. While everyone exited, a second rope was connected to the side of the platform, and after the last person had exited, men worked a large crank pulling the platform upriver to the boarding landing.

We waited for two crossings before it was our turn to board. The operator wanted 7 copper debens each, to board. Barosh offered him Jewish putahs, and the man adamantly shook his head rejecting them. Barosh then offered him a silver denarii for all three of us instead, and he happily took it.

Moving to the front of the platform while the ferry filled, we watched a group of feluccal fishing boats clustered together upriver. Each small skiff held two men. The boats all worked together, hauling in a large net between them. It appeared they had a good catch by the way the heavy net pulled on the boats.

The crew was preparing to begin the trip across, when the operator began yelling and waving his arms for them to stop disconnecting the side mooring rope.

Pointing upriver, a large ship under both sail and oar came around the bend in the river. It was majestic, sporting a large, square sail, braided and interlaced with golden trussing ropes on its edges and a golden disk, set between two large horns, embroidered in its center. The ship had multiple decks, cabins and trappings. A tall figurehead of *Hathor*, daughter of the Sun god *Re*, goddess of love, with long curving horns extending far above the animal head, adorned the bow, facing backwards towards the brightly painted decks.

On each deck, richly dressed (and in many cases—undressed) men and women lounged and sprawled, enjoying the glory of the Nile and of each other. Eight standing rowers on each side of the huge ship worked long, black, silver-plated oars. In time with the fast cadence of the rowing drum, they dug deep into the Nile. The combination of the river's current, the sail's push and the intense rowing sent the lotus-love boat skipping along the surface at a high speed. It bore down directly on the fleet of small fishing skiffs struggling to gather in the heavy, fully-laden net.

High on the bow of the ship, the bare-chested pilot stood defiant, pumping a red baton faster and faster, directing the cadence to increase, and signaling the helmsman to steer the ship directly into the boats.

The fishermen began shouting and cutting the net away in panic. People on the ferry shouted and pointed while the operators held the platform tight to the shore.

The colossal ship rammed the first fishing skiff sideways, crushing it under its high bow like a walnut, and swept over the next two like a tidal wave, swamping them and sending their crews into the river. The rudder, although raised high, caught the net and pulled it behind it as it sped through the fleet, dragging three more boats under the surface. The ship rammed another skiff and brushed another while the crew quickly cut the net away from the rudder and lowered it back into the river clear of the fleet.

The ship sped past the ferry. The pilot stared straight ahead, pumping his red wand, wearing a satisfied look on his face, knowing he had given the passengers an added thrill. In the ship's wake, a tangled maze of over-turned skiffs, men and net thrashed on the surface. Nude men and women on the decks of the big ship, unashamed and arrogant, pointed joyfully at the melee behind them. The screams of the fishermen, entangled in the wreckage and nets, mingled with the laughter from the receding lotus love ship.

The screams turned to terror as the crocodiles moved in.

On the ferry, there was neither - screaming or laughter. An eerie silence had settled over the spectators. The crew disconnected the mooring rope, and the rowers began moving the platform across the river. It was almost as if what we had just witnessed had never happened.

I was in a different place and a different time, where injustice and death were accepted as normal by those not favored by the gods.

8

A day's journey from the river found us resting at another fellahin camp. Heliopolis was not far ahead. We could see the smoke rising above the city from the many cooking fires and businesses. When the wind shifted, we could smell the city—it wasn't a pleasant smell.

Being late in the day, we decided to wait until morning to continue. The Delta was black at night and held many dangers. No one, doing honest business, moved in the Delta at night.

Barosh negotiated a price for food and drink, and we were given a place in the camp. We would sleep on the ground, but I hadn't found much difference from the ground and a mat covered with a little straw anyway.

Rosino's ankle was healing. The same couldn't be said for his spirit. He'd grown markedly quiet since Barosh's talk, asking few questions and giving short, curt answers when spoken to. I didn't know what was going through his mind, but he understood his situation now. It was clear he didn't like it, and that he blamed us for it.

"We'll leave right after sunrise," Barosh said. "People will be going to work, and we should be able to slip around the city unnoticed. The old man said there were many soldiers in the city. Once past, we'll head for Pithom."

"How far is Pithom?" I asked.

"Two or three days walk, depending on how fast we can travel. How's the ankle, Rosino?"

"I'll survive."

"Yes," Barosh said, "but can you travel all day on it?"

Rosino didn't answer.

That night, an orange glow pulsed on the horizon over Heliopolis. Looking away from the city, the stars lit up the sky with layer after layer of sparkling diamonds and lights. There were tens of thousands of them and the deeper I looked, the more I saw. I knew constellations were looking down on me, but I was too ignorant to know them. I could only be over-whelmed with astonishment at the magnitude and order of the universe. This is the same sky I looked at two-thousand years ago - in the future. It was so much bigger here. We are such a small part of it. So many worlds we know nothing about. What keeps it all in place? What stops it from unraveling? What was really out there? I wondered who those 'ancients' were who knew so much and could do such things beyond human capa-bility? Where did they come from? Were they aliens, as Alex claimed, or were they angels as Barosh believed? Was there a difference?

I fell asleep wondering.

***

Bypassing Heliopolis was uneventful. The road was crowded with people going and coming. Young women and girls wearing the traditional linen half-skirts, balanced tall loads of green vegetables and clay pots on their heads hurried by. Many had babies on their backs. Laborers, car-rying tools, hustled to the fields for the day's harvest; and craftsmen and merchants, carrying their goods, rushed into the city to the markets. They paid little attention to us.

Crossing the main road leading into the city, set-back, on each side, massive temples loomed, honoring the gods of the Delta. Heliopolis, 'the City of the Sun', is a cult center, home to the *Ennead Cosmology* of nine gods protecting Egypt and bringing life to it.

Each deity demands its own temple. On one side of the road was the temple of *Atum*—the 'ancient One,' self-created from the 'Watery Waste' of *Nun*. On the other side, a cluster of three temples stood, each dedicated to an offspring of *Atum*. The temple of *Shu*—god of the air; the temple of *Tefnut*—goddess of moisture; and the temple of *Geb*—god of the earth rose resplendent in the Egyptian sun.

Attendant priests, wearing long, white linens, and devoid of any hair, swung smoking castors of incense, purifying the temples with the scent of terebinth resin. Prostrating themselves before the gods, they anointed them with unguents while chanting hymns of adoration.

In another temple, the falcon headed god *'Horus'*, is washed and perfumed, food is burned in offering to it while the alabaster god smiles benignly on the passing fellahin rushing to the fields to labor. An obelisk, surrounded by tall, stately palms whispering secrets about the ancient beings that inhabited this land, plays host to families of black and white striped Hoopoe birds. Wearing golden crowns, they swoop and dip around the trees and columns, filling the air with cries of "oop-oop-oop" as they feed on the abundant insects.

The gods stand in the center of each temple, protected by granite columns and roofs. Not being places of public worship, the temples are cared for by priests, and only on holy days are they open for worship. The people are sealed off from them, and the priests communicate the will of the gods using oracles.

I wondered what good a god was when people had no access to it. It seemed ironic that the gods needed shelter and protection from the elements while the people went about their lives, despite the elements. Were the people being kept from the gods? Or were the gods being kept from the people, to hide their impotence?

Moving away from the city; the agricultural backbone of the land again dominated. Everywhere, fields of grain were in one stage of harvest or another. We passed groves of fig, date, persimmon and pomegranate trees. The land produced profusely, and it was carefully harvested, measured, stored and rationed out; for the Nile was known to withhold its bounty when the gods were offended.

A commotion arose; people scrambled and ran to both sides of the road. Shouts of alarm filled the air, and then a scream followed by curses and more shouts. As the crowd cleared in front, a horseman charged directly at me.

He was a Roman soldier, the first we had seen, and as he bore down on me, he was staring straight into my eyes. He had a beautiful face with dark, evil eyes. Cursing and yelling, he sat atop an enormous black horse, frothing at the mouth and layered in sweat. I froze in place and a cold chill swept through me.

Someone grabbed and yanked me to the side, just as the rider brushed past in a flash of red and bronze.

A man, carrying two magnificent, faience vases in his arms, staggered trying to get off the road.

"Out of the way!" The rider yelled as the horse knocked the man to the ground and trampled over him. The man held tight to his vases, protecting them. They shattered as he fell on top of them.

I looked at the man lying on the ground; his calf was torn open and blood ran down his face. The broken shards of Egyptian blue and black, laced with intricate designs of yellow and copper silica, bordered in silver trim, lay scattered across the road. They had been exquisite, the best work he had ever created and would have garnered him enough debens to sustain him for over a year. Six months of work, destroyed, leaving him injured and destitute, without means of paying taxes to the same power that just took away his ability to do so. He wailed and called upon his god, *Nekhbet,* to avenge him.

Nekhbet was in a temple, being perfumed by a priest, and didn't hear his pleas.

It could have been me trampled by the horse instead of the man. I turned to thank Barosh, surprised to see it was Rosino who still gripped my cloak. He was staring at the receding rider. When he finally turned back it was clear by his face, he knew he had just seen a Roman soldier, and this wasn't the movie '*Gladiator*'. He looked at his hand gripping my cloak and released it as if holding a snake.

***

The road followed a wide, man-made canal. When the rains stop and the Nile begins receding, the backwaters dry out quickly, and the rich, moist, black soil can turn into baked, black slabs in the moisture stealing Egyptian sun.

Irrigation is essential for the survival of the nation, and irrigation design was a significant factor in the success of Egyptian civilization. It produced the surplus crops that fueled the social development and culture of Egypt.

Throughout the Delta, a series of canals and ditches were built, creating a large triangular region (much like a pyramid) of lush growth and aerated farmland. The planning and craftsmanship, from such a primitive people, was astonishing. Wide, deep canals, extending upwards of sixty miles, were excavated and are navigable for shallow draught boats for at least seven months of the year.

A wide-beamed ship, fitted with tall, triangular sails, loaded down with obsidian from Ethiopia, glided down the middle of the canal. Behind it came a second ship, running slower, having a deeper draft, loaded with gold and copper from the distant mountains, and behind that, yet another. From each ship, a long rope extended to shore, harnessed to groups of three men, who walked a well-worn path, pulling the boat through the canal.

Egypt had become a province of the Roman Empire in 30 BCE, a mere sixty years earlier when Octavian defeated Marc Anthony and Cleopatra in the Battle of Actium.

Marc Anthony was rewarded with death, and Cleopatra with an asp. Octavian was rewarded with a new name – Emperor Augustus, and the world was rewarded with the end of the Roman Republic and the beginning of Roman dictatorship. The Egyptians were rewarded with the harsh reality of being stripped of their wealth and pride.

Rome relied heavily on Egyptian wealth and trade. Not only was Egypt the main source of grain, it was rich in granite, greywacke, decorative limestone, and provided the gypsum so desperately needed for making plaster. Rock formations, richly laced with copper, gold and semiprecious stones, such as turquoise, were found in the wadis in the eastern desert and the Sinai. Gold from the mines of Nubia, flint, sulfur for cosmetic substances, as well as combs, faience vases, stone figurines and jewelry, all traveled on the canals, delivering Egypt's wealth to Rome. Egypt was the heart of the eastern and African trade routes, making it the most prominent of Rome's overseas provinces. Egyptian craftsmen were the most skilled in the difficult glass making and shaping techniques, creating the highly prized luxury items so much in demand by the Romans.

And the country was a ripe target for hefty Roman taxes.

As such, Rome took a keen interest in Egypt's political situation. Egyptian revolts and unrest led Rome to send its legions to secure the country. They quelled rebellions, chased bandits, collected taxes, and squashed opposition with brutal force.

**

Rosino's ankle caused us to rest often, and it was almost three days before we reached the outskirts of Pithom. Barosh feared we had missed seeing Jesus.

He went ahead to scout the city while we stayed in another fellahin camp. Rosino's ankle had taken a turn for the worse, having pushed too hard without rest.

Returning before dark, Barosh carried three staffs and a bundle of clothing under his arm.

"These will come in handy with the walking ahead," he said, handing both of us a staff.

He tossed the bundle of clothing to Rosino, "Here Mark, try these on."

Rosino gave Barosh a quizzical look, "Mark?"

"'Rosino' isn't going to work here. Markus is your middle name, right? Mark works for me."

In the bundle was a Hebrew tunic, underclothes, slashes, headgear and an outer mantle.

"How did you get those?" I asked.

"Asking around, I was directed to a small Jewish community on the edge of the city. They greeted and welcomed me there, although it was touch and go for a while. The elders asked me where I was from and what news I brought," he laughed. "I didn't think they'd appreciate news from the twenty-first century."

"What'd you tell them?"

"The truth, that I was from a far country beyond the western borders of the empire of Rome, and that me and my companions were on pilgrimage to Jerusalem. I told them there was great unrest in my country, with revolutionaries infiltrating and creating upheaval. They fully understood and said it was the same here in this country and also in Israel. We read the Tanakh together, and afterwards I was able to buy these clothes from them."

"These things smell," Mark said.

Barosh chuckled, "Have you smelled yourself lately? Maybe they'll be an improvement."

"What did you learn?" I asked.

"Caravans form and cross the Sinai from here on a regular basis. One is forming now. We'll go tomorrow and arrange passage with them. There's only a small detachment of soldiers in the city. We're in luck; a Roman Cohort was here, staging for deployment east. They left three days ago."

"A Cohort? How many men is that?" I asked. "Were they going to Israel?"

"They said it was a small cohort of only five hundred men, and yes, they were headed to Jerusalem."

He stopped, and I could see the excitement in his face.

"What is it Barosh?"

"The soldiers are being assigned to. . .to the Consulate. . .Pontius Pilate! To be distributed throughout Judea." Grabbing my arm he squeezed it hard.

"Pilate, David! We truly are back when Jesus lived!"

Barosh sat down, cradling a cup of weak beer.

"It was incredible, reading the Tanakh with Jews from two-thousand years ago. So little has changed. I could have been home, in Boston, reading in the synagogue with Rabbi Begay. Holding that scroll in my hands, knowing it will be lost over the centuries. What Thaddeus would give to see it. My hands trembled touching it, and I felt the presence of the Almighty filling the room."

Normally I'd jump at the chance to scoff at Barosh and his blind faith, but I respected him too much now to want to alienate him—and liked him too much to want to hurt him. Besides, it'd be the height of folly to mock things unseen and unknown, when I'm sitting in an Egyptian fellahin camp—twenty centuries ago.

And to be honest, I was jealous. I've never felt like that about anything, and I fell asleep that night wondering what it must be like to have such a strong faith.

9

Rising before dawn, we headed for Pithom. Glancing at Mark, I chuckled.

"Something funny Kincaid?"

With his new clothes and staff, he looked like he just stepped out of the Bible.

"Nope, just seeing if any sheep were following you."

"Go to hell."

If nothing else, regardless what name he went by, he was consistent.

***

Passing a field, looking like a checkerboard of four foot square pits in the ground, a macabre scene was in progress. In many of the pits, two men, knee deep in muck, tramped up and down, back and forth, while men above threw armfuls of straw and stubble into the pits. It was a grim scene, these nude men; bodies caked in thick layers of black mud and straw, working the straw into the heavy muck. At other pits, men scooped out the gooey mixture, packing it into small wooden molds before placing them in long rows to bake in the Egyptian sun. Still others knocked the finished bricks from the forms, trimmed them off and stacked them in neat equal piles.

Barosh stopped to watch this ancient dance, and began reciting:

". . .Pharaoh commanded the same day, the taskmasters of the people. . .saying, 'You shall no more give the people straw to make brick as heretofore: let them go and gather straw for themselves, . . . for they be idle; therefore they cry, saying, Let us go and sacrifice to our God. Let there more work be laid upon the men that they. . . not regard vain words."

"I take it we're back to Moses again," I said.

"It was pharaoh's response to Moses's command of 'Let my people go.'"

"Looks like all Moses achieved was to bring more trouble on his people."

"Only temporary. You know how the story ended. One shouldn't challenge God."

"Tell me Barosh, if God controlled everything anyway, why did He let them suffer, just having a little celestial fun?"

His eyes bored into mine.

"Don't mock God David; He asks only one thing of us—to believe in Him. Unfortunately, sometimes He needs to get our attention first.

***

Unlike the temples and tombs, which were built from stone to last forever, the houses, large and small, are constructed from the sunbaked mud-bricks. The bricks are excellent insulators against the fiery Egyptian sun. The closer we came to the city the more homes we passed.

Clustered in groups, they are uncomplicated designs; the smaller ones shaped like beehives and the larger ones like loaves of bread. Many are connected together. They have small openings in the roofs for cooking; walls are painted white, and many have coverings of brightly colored linen hanging across openings and walls as decorations. Floors are covered with reed mats.

The city isn't much of a city, at least from a twenty-first century perspective. A single main street has several smaller roads branching off from it. I am surprised by the animals. Except for a few oxen and donkeys employed on harvest and irrigation, there has been a distinct absence of animals throughout the Delta. Land is too precious to allow livestock to graze. But here, in the city, they seem to coexist with people. A number of stone pens hold small groups of cattle while goats and pigs meander about freely. Not only do they wander aimlessly in the alleys and around the buildings, but they stroll in and out of homes and shops at will. Coops are stocked with ducks and geese, but chickens are underfoot. Flocks of pigeons swoop up and down while a variety of cats and dogs slumber in doorways.

The city is cleaner than I expected. Having braced myself for the stench of decay and waste, I am surprised by the robust aroma of vegetables and meats cooking, aromatic spices and fragrances intermingle with the smell of animals and the earthy smell of the Delta. Waste is collected and removed from the city. The Nile's soil is so rich with minerals and nutrients; fertilizer isn't needed, and the desert is not far away, making for easy disposal.

The people place a strong value on hygiene and appearance. Most have daily bathing, and many of the men shave their entire bodies. It seems everyone, male or female, wears the same clothing of simple, white linen, either as loincloths, kilts or full tunics. Children run about wearing nothing.

We stroll past shops and market stalls. The narrow streets are teeming with the sounds of vendors and women haggling over the quality and price of goods while the clip-clop of donkey carts echo down the alleys. Man and beast alike push carts, piled high with melons, eggplant, leeks and onions, and women balance trays of figs, dates and nuts on their heads.

Although we stand out from the local population, we aren't unique. Greeks and Romans, distinguished by their shirts, and short togas and their close cropped hair ply the markets. Nubians and other tribal peoples mix in, buying or trading wares, bartering goods not found in the Delta, such as turquoise, ivory, feathers, animal skins and wood carvings, for such items as flint, food, stone and copper utensils. A group of Asians, with short, wiry beards and long thick hair, wearing colorful, woolen cloaks, carefully watch a merchant tweaking brass weights on a scale, weighing a small amount of expensive incense on a copper measuring dish.

Rows of baskets, filled with brightly colored spices of reds, yellows and oranges, giving off rich aromas, line the streets. Shops, selling castors of porcelain, stone and bronze for the burning of incense are situated next to where the frankincense, myrrh and 'ud are measured and sold in small clay or porcelain jars. I stop to smell these fragrances closely, thinking of the wise men who supposedly brought these to Jesus. I especially like the 'ud scent which is different from all the others having a subtle fragrance that is pleasant and relaxing.

While none of the local population carry weapons, many of the foreigners carry swords or daggers in their belts.

***

Barosh knows where he is going. Turning off the main street he walks a short ways along a dusty side road and stops in front of a building where a man reposes on a couch, propped up by an abundance of pillows. He wears a flowing, royal blue haik, girdled with a wide leather belt. His face is narrow, sun-weathered and sports a trimmed, black beard flowing down past his chest. A thick, long turban covers his head, trailing past his waist. His hands are tattooed with an intricate pattern of symbols and lettering down to the tip of each finger. In his belt are a long, curved scimitar and two matching daggers. He is an imposing figure, even lying down.

"Shalom aleikhem," Barosh greets him, placing his folded hands to his lips.

"Salaam aleikum—Peace be to you, Hebrew," the man replies, not standing, "and to your companions," he nods to Mark and me.

"Shalom aleikhem," I said, folding my hands in front. Mark doesn't offer a greeting.

Staring at Mark, the man's left hand curls around the hilt of his scimitar.

"Our friend is unable to hear and speak," Barosh says, "please forgive his poor manners."

"He appears to be lame, as well as rude."

"An unfortunate accident, he is blessed to have survived."

He stares at Mark for a long moment before turning back to Barosh, "My name is Abdul Rahman bin Omar Hakeem. May I be of service to you, Hebrew?"

"I am Rabbi Ben Barosh ha-Rav. My companions are David Bar Kalaid ha-Rav and Mark Levi ha-Roshini. We travel to Jerusalem, to give praise to our God, and we understand you are the khabral-bashi of a train that travels to the east. We seek passage with you, Abdul Rahman bin Omar Hakeem."

Relaxing his grip on the sword, the man stands, straightens his haik, adjusts his turban, and bows his head to Barosh, ever so slightly.

"You may call me Abdul-Hakeem. It is true, Rabbi Ben Barosh ha-Rav that I am khabral-bashi for my people, the al-Rashaydah of the desert and yes; I prepare to travel east, but I do not travel to Jerusalem. I travel the 'Incense Route', crossing the Wilderness of Shur to Petra. From there, I travel south to Aqaba and then to Charax and Persia. You are most welcome to be my guests as far as Kadesh-Barnea in Amalek. Jerusalem is an easy two day journey from there."

"You may call me Ben Barosh, Abdul-Hakeem. We are most grateful for your hospitality."

Abdul-Hakeem looks at Mark, appraising him. "Is the one, without the voice and manners, able to make such a journey? It is a difficult route, and I travel hard."

"He is strong and able."

Abdul-Hakeem shifts his gaze to Barosh, "The camel waits for no man, Ben Barosh."

"We will not delay the camel, Abdul-Hakeem."

"Good, then we shall talk." He claps his hands, and immediately two men appear and take the couch away while another unfolds a large mat on the ground. Abdul-Hakeem sits down on the mat, and gestures for us to follow. We form a half-circle facing him, and another man sits, to the side, holding a small board having a papyrus scroll, stylus and ink vase on it. A bare-chested man, wearing a bright orange turban, brings a silk bundle which he sets on the ground alongside the caravan leader. Carefully, opening the cloth, inside is a black polished stone, roughly resembling the shape of a man.

Abdul-Hakeem folds his hands, bows his head to the rock, and then addresses Barosh.

"The wilderness holds great dangers, Ben Barosh. Bandits and revolutionaries are many, having swords thirsty for pilgrim blood, and we pass through the land of the Tarabin. The beasts of the desert seek to fill their bellies on pilgrim flesh. The evil one sends the scorpions and snakes to bite us, and the mountains cause us to wander in the wilderness. One can easily lose his way. There are great hardships in the wilderness. These are the things I must consider to ensure your safe passage. It is a great source of distress for me to give you protection from so many who would do you harm."

"We recognize your grief Abdul-Hakeem, and we are most grateful that your gods have given you such courage and generosity to guide us. Your reward in the afterlife will be celebrated, and we would be most honored to ease your burden in this life, for providing such generosity."

"Ah, and such an enormous burden it is. So many things to worry about, but to honor *Hubal*," he placed his hands together in front of his face and bowed to the black stone, "I shall endure such burdens for you, for, shall we say, three Tyrian shekels each?"

"Your munificence is pleasing to your god Abdul-Hakeem. So many dangers you face and such great distress it gives you. We are most grateful for your concern for our safety and beg your forgiveness for bringing such hardship on you. Our God, Yehovah, will keep us along the way as well. May we ease your burden with four denarii each?"

"Oh, praise to *Hubal*, if only I could for you, seekers of your god. But that is not possible with so many costs to sustain. Your god's protection is most welcome on our journey, but I find a sharp scimitar brings more comfort when confronting my enemies. I need guards to protect both you, day and night. The camel drivers demand so much these days, and there are the packers, and the food and supplies needed for such a trip. Ah, such hardships, so much to think about—but for you, my Hebrew friend who seeks to worship his god, I will do all this for two shekels each."

"I praise Yehovah for your sacrifice on our behalf Abdul-Hakeem. And two shekels are more than worthy in the eyes of your god. Alas, if only we could we would do so for you, but we are only poor pilgrims, traveling to worship our God before the ground sucks on our bones. To honor your graciousness, we will sacrifice and provide six denarii and 10 putas each?"

"Ah, joy to those who worship their gods, and to not offend your god, because Hubal demands I lend kindness to all who travel to visit their gods, I will sacrifice exceedingly and provide you protection for one shekel and two denarii each."

"You are most kind and considerate Abdul-Hakeem, and your god will praise you for your obedience to his commands, rewarding you in the afterlife. We accept your generosity of one shekel and two denarii each."

"Ah, it makes me a poor man in this life, but for Hubal's sake, so shall it be." The scribe wrote down our names and the sum on the scroll.

"Have you provisions for such a journey, Ben Barosh? You will require much water and food—for your camels. You do have camels, yes? And leather buckets, saddle bottles and tent cloth? You have these things? No? Ah, such things are so hard to find, and the cost! There are those who would profit without shame to provide such things, to pilgrims who seek their god."

"You are most wise and experienced in such affairs, Abdul-Hakeem; it would be most foolish for us not to prevail upon your great wisdom and knowledge."

"Ah, your words are like the rain on the parched desert sands Ben Barosh. This humble servant is not worthy of such praise. It will be most difficult, being so late, but at great sacrifice, I can acquire such needs as you will require for such an arduous journey."

The negotiations continued, and when it was finished, Barosh had purchased two camels for a Tyrian shekel apiece, and for a total cost of two shekels and four denarii, he obtained six saddle-bottles of water, food and water for the camels, a small tent, travel utensils and morning and evening meals for us each day. Abdul-Hakeem agreed to "buy" back these items for eleven denarii when we reached Kadesh-Bernea.

Barosh counted out the coins, and Abdul-Hakeem inspected them carefully.

"I have not seen coins of such quality Ben Barosh. How did you come by them?"

"They are from the newest smelt and are the finest produced in Rome. We were there when the money changer received them."

He bit each coin and nodded his head, "Excellent," he put them in his pouch. "Hubal willing, we will reach the Paran Cistern on the sixth day, where fresh water will be available. We must go around the Wilderness Mountain and through the Pass of Shur in the land of the Tarabin. Five days later we will reach Kadesh-Bernea. There we will show you the way to Jerusalem, and you will leave us. This business is concluded." He stood.

"Would you be so kind as to honor me with Al-Qahwa?"

Immediately, my body trembles at the mention of coffee. It had been so long since I fed my addiction; I want to jump up and embrace this tough Arab.

They carefully wrapped up the black stone god, and the scribe leaves with the writing board and table. The couch comes back out for Abdul-Hakeem, along with couches for us as well.

A young woman, with bangles of gold and copper jangling up and down her arms and wearing a bright, multi-colored shawl laced with gold and silver coins, sets a tray down on the mat. We recline in silence while she grounds the coffee beans and brews the coffee. The aroma fills my nostrils, and I have to hold myself back from grabbing the dalla and pouring the liquid down my throat.

The coffee is served in small, colored glasses having no handles. Spices, cloves, cinnamon and a syrupy liquid is added, giving it a golden color. It is terribly sweet, not at all like my black addiction, but as the first drops of caffeine touch my eager throat, it doesn't matter—I am reborn. Accompanying the coffee is a platter of dates and candied fruit. I wonder how large the inside of that building is, there seems to be no limit to what comes out of it.

"You like the Al-Qahwa, David Bar Kalaid ha-Rav?" Abdul-Hakeem asks, seeing my passion.

"My compliments Abdul-Hakeem, it is most delicious. Would it be possible to obtain the superb bean for our journey?"

"Praise *Hubal* for the simple joys of this world. Your compliment is most gracious, and in such a desolate land as this Goshen, it is only with considerable effort and expense that such happiness can be found. And for you, my Hebrew friend, I would spare no effort in filling your desire at a most favorable price. Shall she pour for you again?"

After the second glass of the sweet mixture, negotiations proceed. I end up buying a half seah of roasted beans, a small mortar, a dalli and three small glasses, for two Tyrian shekels and three denarii. In modern equivalents, it equates to about seven pounds of coffee beans and utensils for around fifteen hundred dollars - priceless.

Once the sale is sealed, a third glass of Al-Qahwa is poured, indicating the meeting is over. Immediately, the coffee tray is removed. We offer our thanks for his generosity and rise to leave.

"We leave on the morning the day after tomorrow," he says. "Please be at the gathering place before dawn. If you wish, you may eat and sleep with us the night before."

"Thank you," Barosh says. "Shalom aleikhem, Abdul-Hakeem, and may Yehovah bless you."

"Salaam aleikum—Peace be unto you, Hebrew."

After we are back on the main street, I ask Barosh how he thought it had gone.

"Good," he replies, "we overpaid for everything, of course, but that's of little concern. He's getting money for camels, guards and equipment he already has, and only has to supply some water and a little food."

"Is he to be trusted?"

"Yes, his reputation is on the line. Pilgrims and travelers comprise a great profit for the caravans, and he will do all in his power to ensure our safety. But if we fail him, he'll cut our throats or abandon us in the desert in an instant. That's why I got the second camel, so Mark can ride, giving Abdul-Hakeem no reason to leave us behind. You're in for a treat Mark. You'll have your own private limousine."

Mark didn't seem excited about it.

"He's making a good profit," Barosh continued, "and is immensely pleased, and that's what's relevant to us right now, and you have your coffee, which makes you happy. I only wish we were leaving sooner. We've lost so much time."

Jesus or coffee? For me the choice was clear, it was worth the wait – I had my heaven.

***

We walk past a stone wall, where tall, alabaster columns and extensive buildings rise behind. The nasal notes of flutes and the thumping of drums come from within. Two guards stand outside a set of wide gates. It is the entrance to the Temple district where the upper class resides.

Glancing through the gates, the district looks organized and rich. Compared to the houses outside the wall, the ones inside are large, open air mansions, having wide porches, multiple stories and rooms. People, dressed in the whitest of linen, sit on actual chairs. Open homes are furnished with couches and decorated with lapis-lazuli and turquoise; walls are decorated with painted frescoes and have heavy rugs and decorative textiles over them. Incense burns in braziers and gardens with flowing streams wind through the district. Some girls are playing a form of badminton with a crude, feathered shuttlecock.

It is a stark contrast between those inside and those outside the walls. Things would not change much in two-thousand years; I thought.

***

We spend the night with the rabbi Barosh had met the day before. He lives in a small community of Hebrews, on the edge of the city, and most of the community has gathered to meet us and exchange news.

The meal is a sumptuous feast, featuring roasted lamb. They ask Barosh, as the visiting rabbi if he would invoke the blessing:

"*Barukh atah Adonai, Eloheinu, melekh ha-olam, ha-motzi lechem min ha-aretz.* Blessed are you, O Lord our God, King of the universe; blessed is He who brings forth bread from the earth."

The other rabbis nod in approval.

We eat and talk; while in the city, people worked and played into the night. This is a stark contrast from the fellahin camps we had slept in, where everyone was asleep at night and back in the fields at first light. Here, artisans continued to work into the night, and people lingered, eating and drinking. Numerous lamps, consisting of shallow pots and saucers filled with castor berry oil and floating wicks, were lit up and down the streets. Salt was added to keep the smoke down, and the lamps burned throughout the night, creating an exotic orange glow over the city, flickering and quivering like an eerie fog.

Music and dance fills the streets. Strumming harps, pulsing drums, flutes and oboes merge together in vibrant rhythms echoing and resonating in the alleys. Female acrobats perform, dancing to the rhythm of castanet, sistrum and tambourine. Women, dressed in revealing, transparent sheaves, linger in doorways, their perfumes beckoning in the night air.

Barosh asks the rabbi about the Jewish community in Goshen.

"We are a small group. A larger group resides in Alexandria. Some of us are descendants of those who fled Nebuchadnezzar's conquest of Israel, but the majority of us trace our lineage to the wars, following Alexander's death, over his empire. Our fathers were uprooted from Israel and brought to Goshen, forced into service as soldiers. God has been merciful to us. The Goshen authorities accept us, and we have little interference from the Romans as long as we pay their taxes."

"I have not seen the Romans here," Barosh says.

"They keep a low presence. Their garrison is north of the city, and they train constantly. At night they frequent the taverns and streets seeking entertainment. If one sees soldiers during the day, it usually means someone is going to be arrested—or killed."

"Is it the same in Israel?"

"It is worse Ben Barosh; you must be careful in Jerusalem," the chief rabbi says, "there is considerable unrest and some rise to enflame the people. The Zealots cause the Romans to look for troublemakers. Many have fled Israel to live here with us in Goshen."

"The soldiers are mean and angry," another says. "They do not like being there and have a dislike for our people. Things will erupt someday. My advice is to finish your pilgrimage quickly and go back to your home. Do not linger there; it can only result in things not good for you."

"Have you heard of a prophet named Yeshua, from Galilee?" Barosh asks.

"Yeshua? No, I've not heard that name. There was a rabbi who came here last year and spoke of a wild man, named John, who was in Judea preaching immersing in water. Some said he was a prophet, but I do not know what became of him."

An old man, who had been sitting quietly in the corner, spoke up.

"There was a man, many years ago, who came here with a wife and child. Joseph, his name was. He said they were fleeing Israel. I remember the child well; there was something about him, even being so young, that caught one's attention. He looked at you like no other child did."

The old man stops and pauses, "The child's name was Yeshua."

"Do you remember why they fled Israel?" Barosh asks.

"Of course, Herod was king and had gone quite mad; killing everyone he thought was a threat to his throne. The mystics told Herod a young child would grow up to take his throne. Herod didn't know who that was," the old man shook his head, "so he sent his soldiers to kill all the young boys in the village."

"Did this really happen? Or did Joseph tell a story?" I ask.

The chief rabbi looks at me sternly.

"David Bar Kalaid, Joseph was not a man to make up stories. The killing of the children in Bethlehem was not unusual for such a man as Herod."

"My apologies chief rabbi, I meant no disrespect, but I had not heard of it talked about before."

"Why would you? Herod was mad; he killed thousands, including his own family. A few small boys from a tiny village would be but a ripple on his sea of blood."

"What happened to the family?" Barosh asks. "Are they still here?"

"No, they are gone. Joseph stayed with us for a few years, and then one day, he took his wife and young son and returned to Israel."

"Why? Was there trouble here?"

"There was no trouble, Joseph worked hard and paid his taxes to the Romans and the Egyptians. Herod died, and Joseph returned."

"Did they return to Bethlehem?"

"I know not; we never heard about them again."

***

We sleep in real beds that night, made with wooden frames and legs, having strips of leather crisscrossing the bottom and mattresses made of cotton sacks packed tight with feathers and covered with linen sheets. The beds slope slightly from the head towards the foot end and have a head rest, covered in layers of wool.

Coffee and a bed—in one day – for sure I'm an atheist in heaven.

10

Finding the caravan encampment was quite easy. They told us to head northeast and follow our noses. They were right.

I had never smelled a camel before. Did not have a clue what one smelled like, but I immediately knew it was camel, when I smelled it. Strong, ripe with urine, it reached out as a tangible declaration of camel existence, snagging our noses and reeling us in. Intermingled amongst the odious smell were whiffs of things cooking – ripe aromas of vegetables boiling, meats roasting and some kind of burning fruity fragrance, reminding me of mincemeat pie. Above all, the earthy scent of camels overpowered everything.

Before long, we could hear them belching, braying and bellowing in protest to the voices of men yelling and berating the animals.

The compound was enclosed by a low stone wall shaped in an enormous oval the size of three or four football fields. It was bustling with activity. Two men, dressed in the same royal blue haiks as Abdul-Hakeem, and having long sweeping scimitars in their girdles, blocked the entrance. Looking at them, I had no doubts they knew how to use those swords and would have little hesitancy in doing so. Next to the entrance, a short, pudgy man sat on a low, three-legged stool behind a small table, making marks on a long scroll.

"Shalom aleikum," Barosh greeted them.

"Salaam aleikum," the man on the stool said. The two guards only stared.

"I am Rabbi Ben Barosh ha-Rav. These are my companions, David Bar Kalaid ha-Rav and Mark Levi ha-Roshini. We have contracted passage with the train of Abdul Rahman bin Omar al-Ahmad Hakeem."

The man skimmed through the scroll then stopped at a line, nodding his head.

"Ah yes, it is here—Rabbi Ben Barosh ha-Rav and two companions, passage to Kadesh-Barnea; two camels and certain provisions. Yes, good, welcome Rabbi Ben Barosh ha-Rav. You are number eleven, yes, very good."

He made a notation and called out, "Omar."

A young man, dressed in a grey haik and turban, appeared from out of the chaos of the compound.

"Yes Shakol, what is your wish?"

"This is Rabbi Ben Barosh ha-Rav and his companions. They are eleven. Show them their place and ensure everything is in order." He turned to Barosh and asked, "You are new to the train, Ben Barosh?"

"Yes, we are pilgrims to Jerusalem."

"Yes, of course, a holy journey. Omar, show our guests the way of the camel." He smiled knowingly and nodded to Barosh, "Salaam. We leave on the morrow."

Omar bowed slightly at the waist, "Please to follow me."

Passing through the entrance into the arena, camels and men, everywhere, were in various stages of preparation. Makeshift booths and stalls littered the compound, providing last minute repairs to saddles, harnesses and pack carriers. Everything from sandals and scimitars, to food and water bottles was being sold. Many of the dromedaries roamed free, but were hobbled, keeping them close to their assigned areas. They stood, knelt and wallowed in dirt, braying loudly and farting profusely. Camel dung, in flat pancakes or oval chunks, was scattered everywhere. Boys roamed around, collecting the driest pieces in sacks.

We passed an area where date sized argan fruit was being stripped off and placed on flat sheets of iron over several fires. The roasted fruit was rolled into balls and packed away as camel food. This was the source of the burnt mincemeat I smelled.

The camels shocked me. During my weeks of cramming, I had briefly read about them and dismissed them as of little importance. Now, standing among scores of the beasts, they weren't so easily dismissed. With their long, looping necks, and heavy bodies perched atop spindly legs, they towered over me.

Being cud chewers, they have the most atrocious breath in creation. You could smell them coming and going. It was a toss-up which end was worse.

In addition to being smelly and noisy, they did not budge. Push and shove as I would, they'd just turn and look at me with their smiling, long faces. I didn't know animals could smile, but they smiled, and did so as if they knew secrets no human would ever know.

Camels are the lifeline of Egyptian trade: gold and incense from Nubia; olive oil from Israel and Jordan; salt from Timbuktu; timber from Byblos; aromatic resins, ebony, ivory, and wild animals from Punt; tin and copper from Anatolia; the prized blue lapis lazuli stone from Afghanistan; all came into Egypt via caravan. In turn, Egypt exported grain, jewelry, artwork, linen and papyrus, in addition to the coveted Fraise, ceramic, stone and glass works, on the backs of camels. With the invention of the 'Arabian saddle', a camel could carry loads over sand and wilderness and across rivers and mountain passes for days on end needing little water and food.

Simply because, they could travel farther and longer than any other pack animal, the camel was the 'ship of the desert'. Able to last four to nine days without water and much longer without food, retrieving energy from the reserve of fat stored in its hump, nothing compared to it. Donkeys, mules, and oxen could neither endure the desert and its heat, nor walk across it easily. The camel's foot was a wide pad, making it ideal for plowing through the desert sand without sinking in.

The Egyptians did not control the trade. The deserts and the wilderness were the province of the Arabs. Numerous Bedouin tribes vigorously and viciously defended their territories. Caravans, loaded with immense riches and wealth, could be easy prey for swift attacks. Rome attempted to oust the Arabian control of the Sinai and the Sahara, but quickly learned the deserts were not agreeable to the heavy armored legions. In its wisdom, Rome formed alliances with the largest tribes. Not only did this end having to fight long costly wars against the people of the desert, it put the onus on those tribes to keep the smaller ones in line.

Omar led us around the enclosure. Numbers were painted on the wall, with supplies and cargo piled in front of each numbered area, staged for loading in the morning. Some had guards stationed, their long, curved scimitars prominently displayed to discourage thieves.

"Balek, Balek!" A man yelled, leading two camels directly at us. "Out of the way!"

We jumped aside as the camels passed. One of them gave me a long look and then released a massive discharge of gas directly in my face as it walked away—smiling. The smell is forever burned into my memory.

We passed traders from many countries and walks of life. Africans, Nubians, Persians, Egyptians and Romans were all contracted with the caravan for travel to their destinations. Abdul-Hakeem had been busy.

"How many passengers are there?" Barosh asked our guide.

"Nineteen people, thirty-two camel," Omar replied promptly. "Travel is down. Hakeem most unhappy."

"How large is this train, Omar?"

"This not big, have only one-hundred-twenty-seven camel."

"So, the rest of the camels belong to Abdul-Hakeem?"

"Beg pardon, Abdul-Hakeem is most honored khabral-bashi, train master, but he not own camels. Owners live in Damascus."

"I see; he is the captain of the ship then," Barosh said.

"Beg pardon?"

"Nothing, sorry."

He stopped walking. "We are here, number eleven. You are most fortunate; Abdul-Hakeem has put you up front." On the wall, a large "11" was painted, and a stack of provisions was piled against it.

"Please see all is as agreed. I find camels."

Checking the supplies, everything was there, a leather bucket, blankets and cleaning cloths, bags of camel food, saddles, a tent, utensils, harnesses and six saddle-bottles for water. I felt stupid, not having a clue how to use these things. Omar returned, holding the reins of two hobbled camels.

"This is Sudaas. She has twenty-two seasons and is gentle to ride. And this is Al-naab, who is youngster of seven seasons, but is learned in way of the train. They will be most good for you. Come, say hello."

We approached the camels and following Omar's lead, stroked them.

"No be afraid. You must talk to them; let them hear you so they will follow you."

Stroking the younger camel's neck, I began talking to it, calling it by name and saying stupid things like, "Nice camel." Al-naab lowered his head to my level—smiling at me. He chewed loudly, and his breath was hideous. I held my own breath and grimaced while he took me in. Just when I could stand it no more, he pursed his lips together and spit a thick gob of gooey, sticky slime, in my face, before raising his smiling face.

"Ah, he likes you," Omar beamed.

Is it possible to pass out while vomiting?

***

Omar showed us how to harness and pack the supplies on the camels, secure the saddle on the hump, where to fill the water bags and how to load them, three to a side, on Al-naab.

The watering trough was located in the center of the compound, fed by a well. An ox worked a wheel, similar to the one on the river, raising water from the well. The water looked clean. The saddle-bags held around nine gallons each. We filtered the water as we filled each bag and added five pills to each, as a precaution, before securing the tops.

Omar showed us how to mount the camel.

Barosh volunteered—me—to go first.

Omar smacked Sudaas on her hind legs, and when she did not respond, he began cursing at her and using a short rod; he rapped her hard just above the inside of her knee. She sat down, folding her legs under herself front first, then rear, like a see-saw. Omar easily and fluently climbed onto the camel. Dismounting, he beckoned me to do likewise.

Following Omar's example, I stood on the front, folded leg of Sudaas. She looked like a mountain to climb. Grabbing the saddle, I heaved myself up, throwing my leg over the rear of her high back behind her hump. As I did so, she decided to stand up, thrusting her rear high into the air, pitching me forward. I was hanging upside down, half on and half off defying gravity staring at the ground that was rapidly growing more distant. Then the beast lurched back, lifting its spindly front legs, throwing me backwards while I desperately clutched at the saddle to hold on. Once the camel was standing, I crawled over the back of the saddle and fell into the seat.

"Yes, that is good," Omar said.

The saddle was high on each end and deep in the middle, and sitting on top of the hump, it was weird and nothing like riding a horse, where you are even with his head. All I could see was the top of the creatures head, far out in front and below me. It was even further to the ground. When the animal began walking, it was choppy, like a boat cutting across incoming waves. She did not walk like a horse but moved both front and rear legs of one side forward together. Getting 'seasick' was a real possibility, especially after they spit in your face.

Omar watched each of us mount and dismount the camel and seemed satisfied we were ready for train travel. He left us, laughing.

Mark is welcome to his 'limousine'—I'll walk.

***

That evening, dinner was served at the far end of the compound. We followed the others. Large pots, suspended over fires, spewed out stomach gurgling aromas, while bread was baked over metal domes. Several large platters holding roasted meat, cooked vegetables and fish, surrounded by chunks of broken bread were laid out on mats.

Finding an open mat, we squatted on the ground. A bowl of water was passed around, and everyone washed their hands in the bowl. We followed their lead carefully, not wanting to violate some custom by mistake. Food was taken off the tray either by the right hand directly, or by pinching it between a piece of bread. Only the right hand was used as the left hand is considered unclean, used for hygiene purposes. Pitchers of camel milk, with its watery, walnut flavor, were served to drink.

The food was excellent.

There was much talk about the next day's activity. Most centered on the Roman Cohort that had left earlier. It was clear there was a lot of concern regarding bandits. Apparently, a train had been recently attacked and overrun by bandits. The entire train had been lost and everyone murdered. Because of this, our train consisted of eighty-one people. In addition to Abdul-Hakeem, there was Shalen (the Daleel – pilot); eighteen Mukowwems (camel drivers), nine laborers and nineteen passengers, including three females. The remaining thirty-three men were warriors from Abdul-Hakeem's tribe, who would guard the train.

While obviously an attack was of concern, I had an insider's knowledge about crossing safely—my name was on a tablet in Israel.

***

Trays of figs, dates, fruits and nuts were brought out, following the main course, along with bowls of sugared camel's milk. While we feasted on these, bonfires were lit and stoked high.

Men carrying flutes, drums and stringed instruments began playing. Two men, wearing flowing white smocks, accented with scarlet red girdles and turbans, moved among the caravan, sprinkling oil on man and beast alike, chanting blessings on the train and praying to the gods for a safe journey.

Once they completed their blessings, they left, and the music took on a different tempo and virility. Women appeared from out of nowhere, dancing and flirting. They were Egyptian women, wearing revealing wisps of clothing and playing cymbals, tambourines and strings of tingling bells. Men began dancing in circles with them, swinging their scimitars over their heads in time with the music.

Fortune tellers moved through the encampment. The camel drivers and laborers eagerly sought to know their fates on the caravan, but none of the warriors wanted their fortune told. They would make their own destiny or submit to the will of the gods. They preferred the company of the women.

An old man spread out a mat and laid out some crude tools. I watched as he emptied a bag on the mat and spread the contents out. A man came and sat across from him, obviously in pain. After haggling back and forth, two assistants came out, held the man down while the old man began working on his mouth with the crude tools. He was a dentist, and the bag contained the teeth he had extracted as his calling card. Others came, waiting their turn.

Extraction was the cure for all complaints.

We set our tent against the wall and tried to sleep in preparation for the morning.

We didn't.

11

Falah 'al Din stood on the windy, craggy cliff and watched the long line of camels and men pass by. His family had grazed sheep and goats on the sparse desert grass for generations watching the caravans trek across the wilderness. He wondered from where did they come and to where did they go to? He sometimes thought of leaving his goats to follow the tracks in the sand, but quickly brushed such thoughts aside, knowing his fate was fixed by the gods to raise his goats.

He waves.

Walking beside the huge camel, I gaze across the barren land and see the figure of a man standing on a high bluff watching us. Shrouded in his blowing desert robes - he looks like the eternal image of the desert. He waves and I wonder what he thinks.

I wave back.

It was the fourth day of our journey, and the excitement of going on caravan had given way to fatigue, boredom and sore feet.

The morning we left the compound was bustling alive before sunrise, and after a breakfast of *tedj* (sour milk mixed with sugar) and *jamiid* (goat cheese soup), the camels were rousted and prepared for travel.

Cargo was secured and tested for stability. Tethers were set, from the tail of one camel to the lip of the next, forming strings of three to eight camels. A mukowwem managed each string. Laborers tested loads for balance and tightness.

I struggled with the tether on Al-naab, not knowing how to connect it to the camel's lip. He protested my ignorance loudly and nipped at me twice while jerking back.

I detested his know-it-all smile.

The train formed, and under the guidance of the Daleel-pilot, number one exited the compound, with each succeeding number falling in behind.

Abdul-Hakeem, looking splendid and royal in his blue haik and turban, sitting atop a large white camel adorned with colorful blankets and tassels, scrutinized each group carefully as they passed through the exit. Every number was ready when their turn came, or they would be severely reprimanded. As number six passed by, a mukowwem was struggling with an ill-tempered camel. As it kicked and yanked against the mukowwem's tether, Abdul-Hakeem cursed and quickly galloped over. He began whipping the man viciously, causing him to drop the tether, cowering under the blows. Immediately another mukowwem picked up the tether and led the string away. Abdul-Hakeem continued beating the fallen driver, ordering him out of the compound. The man protested loudly, throwing himself at his mercy, begging not to be dismissed. Abdul-Hakeem spat at him and turned away, resuming his scrutiny of the procession.

I began to panic, not able to control Al-naab, who had gotten more belligerent sensing my inexperience and fear. The mukowwem from number twelve saw my plight and ran over, taking charge. He quickly calmed Al-naab down, connected the tether and showed me how to lead the camel. I thanked him profusely, and he smiled wide, laughing, showing large, white teeth.

"Salaam Hebrew, I am Jamal."

When number ten filed out, we were ready and fell in line. The two camels were loaded and tethered together; Barosh led Sudaas with Mark bouncing high on his perch. Al-naab and I followed. As we exited the compound, Abdul-Hakeem nodded his approval.

***

There was no road—we headed due east on a course set by Shalen, the Daleel-pilot. There had been much discussion regarding the route to take. It was a compromise between the shorter Northern Route, and the longer Southern Route across the desert and around the mountains. Abdul-Hakeem wanted to avoid bandits but make good time, and water was a foremost concern. Since we moved during the hot, dry season, the camels needed to be watered at least every second day, to keep them at peak condition and travel speed. Shalen wanted them watered and fed well during this "easy" portion of the journey—across the Sinai. Their next segment, across the deserts of Arabia, would be demanding. He knew a secret watering place in the mountains that his people had made by cutting channels collecting runoff in a hidden cistern cut out of rock. Arches were built over it, hiding it from bandits and Romans. But first we had to cross a section of desert. Water for man and camel would be what was carried.

"This was the shortest route for Moses to lead the people from Egypt," Barosh said, "but it was not the way God wanted. Instead, He led them south, across the Red Sea.

> '. . .when Pharaoh had let the people go that God led them not through the way of the Philistine, although that was near; for God said, 'Lest peradventure the people repent when they see war, and they return to Egypt. But God led the people about, through the way of the wilderness of the Red Sea. . .'"

"Sooner or later, I expect to run into Charleston Heston," I said. When he didn't respond, I asked, "How did God lead them?"

"By a pillar of cloud during the day and a pillar of fire at night. What should have been a two-week journey took 40 years."

"You believe that? Wandering around out here for 40 years? Following a pillar of fire? You actually believe these stories."

Barosh shook his head, "After everything you've seen; you're still skeptical about what you don't understand. So too were the Israelites. They too were cynical and skeptical of God. . .until He got their attention."

"Or until He gave them a compass."

***

After crossing a mosquito ridden swamp, we left the Delta behind and soon found ourselves in the desert. Caravan is walking twelve to fifteen miles a day, dependent on the terrain and weather.

This desert is barren and empty. There are no pyramids or tombs dotting the skyline. There is only dune after dune of rolling, sweltering sand. Some are hard, baked and crusty. Some are fine and powdery. The camels labor mightily climbing these shifting dunes, before lurching down the other side as their large padded feet sink up to their shins in the hot powder, enlisting spine jolting curses and cries from Mark as he struggles to hold on.

Small dunes—high dunes—deep dunes—an ocean of dunes. Sand, fine like dust, hot like fire—swirls—stings—and burns. Walking the dunes holds a touch of mystery, not knowing what was on the other side of each ridge. Usually it is only scorpions.

We have no thermometer, but I know it's well over a hundred degrees and despite what they say in Arizona about a dry heat—it's hot.

A herd of goats and mules travel with us. I wonder about them, questioning why Abdul-Hakeem allows them, knowing they can't traverse the desert and will slow the train down.

Caravan isn't a nine to five day. Travel time varies dependent on weather and Abdul-Hakeem's intuition. Usually camp was made around midday, resting and eating during the hottest part of the day. Shortly before dusk we'd break camp and travel during the night and morning. Not only did this spare the camels, but Abdul-Hakeem felt safer traveling at night and better prepared for attack during the day. The Daleel-pilot set the course by the moon and stars. The sky was a roadmap for him.

There is a rhythm to caravan. The singing of the mukowwems; the soft padding of the camel's feet slicing across the dunes; the creaking of saddles and sloshing of water in the saddle-bottles; all mingle together with the tingling of the tiny bells attached to the camel's necks and blankets. It makes for a relaxing sound in which to walk and think as we follow the broad, camel tracks.

A skeleton protrudes from the sand. It is the long skull and high ribcage of a camel that made its final passage across the dunes.

Mark is learning key words and phrases of the language, and during those times he walks, I work with him, teaching him. Sometimes I walk with Barosh, and he would talk about Moses and the Israelites wandering around in the Sinai for forty years. It is all too mythical and depressing for me, so I'd leave him to his musings and walk with Jamal.

I marvel at Jamal and his people – the Bedouins, and how they've adapted to this world. Their clothing is perfect for the desert; blocking out the sun, allowing the breezes to flow around their bodies, keeping them cool and sweat free. It's loose and flowing, not sticky, bulky or constraining. The kafiya turban protects their heads and necks while making a decent pillow at night. Our tunic and mantle is no match, even with the advantage of twenty-first century technology.

Guards, equipped with bows and arrows, in addition to their curving scimitars, travel alongside the length of the caravan, riding strong, fast war camels. A large force protects the rear. Jamal said this is wise as bandits like to make hit and run raids, nipping off a few camels before defenses could be mobilized.

I find I prefer traveling at night. The desert makes for a miserable bedroom. It's an upside down place, having no logic and making no sense. Blistering hot during the day—it's freezing cold at night. The wind scorches me in the blazing sun and frost bites me in the dark of night. The warmth of traveling is welcome compared to the cold of sleeping at night. I'll never understand how the largest mosquitoes I've ever seen can be in the middle of the desert on bitterly cold nights.

Gathering around the dinner mat on the third day, in addition to the daily fare of vegetables, soup and bread, strips of roasted meat are served. They are excellent and satisfy my stomach like no calabash could. I ask Jamal where the meat came from and he points to the goats and mules, and then I understand. They're not on caravan to cross the desert—they are walking food. As they weaken – they are butchered.

***

The fifth day dawned on the horizon. We'd been traveling all night, and it was unusually calm. Mark had left his perch on Sudaas, preferring to walk alongside the great beast. The sores on his thighs and backside out-voted his ankle. I walk alongside of Jamal, who has become a friend and companion during these long nights. He has told me many things about his people, living in the desert and about his dreams of someday owning his own train. He is a happy man, full of energy and laughter, and I enjoy traveling with him.

A silver moon, crisp and sharp, lit up half the sky, while the other half held so many stars, there was not room to squeeze in a single additional one.

The sun breaks around the rim of the earth, extinguishing the stars one by one, and casting rays of glowing fire across the crests of the dunes. It is eerie and has an unnatural look to it. The glowing, orange disk rises across the horizon, expanding outward in a jagged, disconcerted way. It grows long and wide and seems alive, pulsing from within. I stare, confused, it isn't the glorious sun, but is a swirling luminous yellow mass of ugly anger filtering the sun, and it is moving—across the desert—directly at us.

"*Irifi! Irifi!*"

Shouts sound all along the caravan as men begin running, pointing at the horizon. Panic breaks out. The camels begin braying and grunting, breaking out of formation, running scared. They pull and jerk against their tethers, making wild noises, growling and gnashing their stained teeth, sensing the danger in the air. Mukowwems tug on harnesses, shouting guttural commands and cries, fighting for control while the frightened, angry beasts snap back at them. Using hard raps to their rumps and legs, they force the giant animals to sit down with their sides to the horizon while laborers hurry unloading and stacking the cargo against the down-wind side of the camels. Men pull their haiks and turbans tight around themselves and hunker down behind the cargo and the camels.

With our camels down and unloaded, Barosh and Mark crouch behind Sudaas. I take one last look at the towering wall screaming down on us, before cowering down next to Al-naab's protective ribs.

Irifi roars in from the east; a monstrous desert sandstorm that blackens out the sun, the moon and the stars of heaven.

It hits like a tidal wave.

Horizontal spears of sand slice into me like knife blades. I crouch down deeper, on my stomach, trying to escape the onslaught; my eyes squeeze tight to keep them from being blasted out of my head. I can't breathe, inhaling gulps of gritty, sand-filled air through the scarf wrapped around my head. The sound is deafening—a mind-shattering roar from the beast of the desert.

Camels are designed to survive. Their deep-set shaggy ears and long, protruding eyelashes protect them against the swirling sand. Their nostrils collapse adding moisture to the air they breathe. They have thin eyelids and can see through them while their eyes are closed. Al-naab only lowers his head while continuing to chew his cud.

It lasts for over three hours, seeming an eternity. At one point, I think I am going crazy from the unrelenting assault of the sand and nonstop roar of the wind. I lose it and cannot stop myself from pushing up out of the sand. I need to run – to get away. Jamal jumps up and pulls me down, holding me tight and covering my mouth with his turban. I lay trembling, barely able to breathe. Jamal holds tight and doesn't let go.

Finally, it stops abruptly, and the silence is as deafening as the storm had been.

The caravan slowly comes to life. Men push up out of the sand like corpses rising from graves. Shaking myself loose, I look around at a colony of camel necks sticking up from mounds of sand. Barosh and Mark slowly emerge. They are dazed and in shock, but otherwise appear unhurt. Mark is coughing hard, his throat raw.

I look down where Jamal lay—a mound of sand—not moving. Scooping the sand away, I uncover his leg and begin digging frantically. Others run over, joining me in excavating him.

It is of no avail; Jamal is dead; his mouth, eyes and nose plugged with sand.

He had given his life to save mine.

***

Abdul-Hakeem decides to make camp, allowing everyone to regroup after the violent storm and to honor Jamal and two others who have died. He declares a 'feast'. The remaining mules had died; so he has them butchered along with a lame camel.

We water the camels and shake the sand out of everything. A light breeze has settled in behind the sandstorm, and men remove their turbans, allowing them to unfurl in the wind knocking the sand loose. They are ten to fifteen feet long, blue, red and white streamers waving in the wind. Standing back and watching, it strikes me as a final tribute paid to our fallen comrades.

Using dried camel dung for fuel, the cooks start a series of fires. They produce a pile of "cooking" rocks from somewhere and proceed to roast the meat and bake the bread. Once a bed of rocks is hot, they whisk away the ashes and drop a slab of raw dough on the hot rocks, searing the bottom. Meanwhile, they build a second fire, close to the first and turn the dough over, searing the other side on the hot rocks, as well. They then cover the bread completely with sand and push the second fire on top of the sand, forming an oven. When finished, they pull the bread out, and whack it with a stick to remove the grains of sand.

The baked bread, served with '*dwaz*' dip of vegetables and spices, is better than any bread from the twenty-first century, although the sand is hard on the teeth.

Before we sit down to eat, Barosh admonishes us not to eat camel meat.

"It is forbidden for us to eat camel," he says.

"Why do I care about that?" Mark asks. "I'm not Jewish."

"You are to these people, and don't ever forget that. Remember, we're Hebrews on pilgrimage to Jerusalem. They know that, and they watch everything. If they thought we were deceiving them, it would be disastrous for us. Do not even touch the meat."

"I thought it was permissible to eat animals that chew their cud," I say.

"The Torah forbids eating camel because it doesn't have a separate hoof."

"What a crock!" Mark mumbles.

"Call it what you want. That's the way it is," Barosh replies firmly. "There's enough mule meat."

The feast looked fabulous, but I had little appetite.

***

Talk turns to bandits. Abdul-Hakeem is everywhere, making sure everyone is prepared for any surprise attack. He fears an attack could come while we're recovering from the storm. The guards are extra vigilant, on their camels and showing a strong force of arms to discourage such an attack. Scanning the horizon on all sides, I wonder where an attack could come from. As far as I can see, there is only sand.

Some mumble we should head to a garrison for protection. Garrisons and outposts had been constructed by the pharaohs to secure the gold and precious stone mines in the mountains and wadis of the Sinai. The Romans had taken them over, patrolling the trade routes. Their pretense is to protect the caravans from bandits, but Abdul-Hakeem claims their true purpose is to extract tolls and help themselves to the goods from the trains as payment for 'protection'. Talk of seeking Roman protection sends Abdul-Hakeem into a rage.

"I'll fight all the bandits in the Sinai rather than pay homage to Roman dogs."

Following dinner, the musicians come out, and the night is filled with music and dancing. I'm amazed at the openness of these hardened, brutal men and desert nomads dancing without restraint or embarrassment.

They live with death and, therefore, relish the joys and passions of being alive. Something, I think got lost along the way to the twenty-first century.

While the caravan danced in the joy of living, I sit, dejected and hurt.

Jamal had died, giving up his life and his dreams for. . .me and. . .my fear.

12

We stayed two days at the storm site. Abdul-Hakeem was insistent on the proper time to honor the dead and to appease *Hubal*.

Upon resuming the journey, the desert dunes give way to uneven rocky wasteland. Ahead are the jagged peaks of rugged mountains.

Approaching the steep peaks, walking becomes precarious and difficult. Instead of plowing through hot, blistering sand, we dodge sharp rocks and boulders protruding haphazardly from a ground blanketed in stones, turning and twisting our feet. In small crevices and coves, tamarisks and patches of coarse bushes sprout. Isolated patches of green hattab, the prickly juiceless bush of the desert mountains are scattered about, and the camels eat them eagerly.

Mark reclaims his perch atop of Sudaas. With his ankle almost healed, we don't want to risk re-spraining it on the unfriendly ground.

Shalen leads us into the bleak and barren mountains, past the craggy cliffs and overhanging boulders. Weathered trees, covered with sharp, piercing thorns and briars seem to sprout from the rocks themselves, towering over our heads. Riding high on Sudaas, Mark dodges and ducks, to avoid being shredded.

Entering a narrow pass, we journey into the heart of the mountains. It is joy to get out from under the scorching sun into the shadows of the mountains. We are down to our last skin of water. The filtering and pills have worked well. Other than some minor cramping and diarrhea, none of us has become ill. The camels haven't complained either. Shalen is leading the train to the concealed cistern his people had built, where we can replenish our water supply.

The pass opens into a small clearing. Upon entering it, we are backed up by the camels and men ahead of us, who are all clustered together, not moving. At the front, Abdul-Hakeem and Shalen argue. . .with a Roman centurion, who, along with a company of soldiers, is blocking both the cistern and the pass.

". . .have no right!" Abdul-Hakeem shouts.

"We have the right of Imperial Rome," the officer shouts back.

"This cistern has been in my family for generations!" Shalen yells. "My people built it. It does not belong to you! You have no right to deny us that which is ours!"

"It belongs to the Emperor. You want water; you pay like everyone else."

"This is an outrage!" Abdul-Hakeem shouts. "The water and the mountain belong to the gods. You cannot make us pay for what the gods provide."

"The Emperor is your god. Drink the Emperor's water and travel the Emperor's road and you have the privilege to pay the Emperor for the protection he provides."

"Road!" Abdul-Hakeem screamed. "This is no road, this is a pass cut by the god of the mountain. Rome gives no protection! Bandits roam freely. . ."

"Enough! Continue that talk and you'll scream from the inside of prison. The Emperor owns this land, this pass and this water. Out of his goodness he gives you the protection of his Imperial army. For such benevolence, a fee of one-half denarii for each man and beast that passes is required. . .and for your treasonous talk, we will pick out two camels, with their goods, for Rome's service."

Abdul-Hakeem turns red with rage, but the officer isn't finished. "And if you desire to drink the Emperor's water, a fee of one-half denarii for each saddle-bottle will be paid." He placed his hand on his sword's hilt and the company of soldiers jolted to attention. "Now, if you continue to bellow like a mule, we will requisition this entire caravan in the name of the Emperor. Otherwise, turn around and go back to the hole from where you came."

Abdul-Hakeem is silent, appraising the situation. *This dog dares to speak to me like that, about the land my ancestors have owned for all time? 'Go back to the hole from where you came'! I come from here you hyena!*

The Centurion has only a handful of soldiers with him. He could overpower and defeat them. But it would be at a cost of men, and he'd then be pursued by the entire garrison. He knew the Romans would not stop until he and his entire family were captured, thrown in prison and executed. He must not start a war with Rome until he has consulted with the owners and his family. He has no choice but to submit—for now.

***

Abdul-Hakeem has us fill our water skins in order. Approaching the cistern, the fee is paid first and then the skins are filled under the watchful eyes of the soldiers. Abdul-Hakeem stands to the side, ensuring each transaction is recorded.

Shalen burns with hatred and anger. This is his water! His ancestors built this cistern to collect the water. The insult was too much for him to bear, and Abdul-Hakeem had three of his guards hold him and take him away before he got himself killed.

The soldiers form a line bordering the cistern. They stand in full armor, holding their shields and spears, ready to attack or defend at a moment's notice. Their spears are light shafts, having long, thin, iron points, perfect for throwing, and the Romans have a reputation for being extremely accurate with them. The points were made to bend when striking the ground so that they couldn't be thrown back against them. The soldiers aren't glamorous and colorful as shown in the movies. Their short tunics and leather breastplates are faded, stained and dirty; helmets streaked with tarnish. They are crude, hard men with whom violence and brutality are their daily fare. They are not happy being in this desolate, barren land, and I didn't think it would take much for them to show just how unhappy they are.

Simply stated—they scare the hell out of me.

We fill our skins and proceed to the far side of the clearing, where a second line of soldiers is formed. They collect the toll from each person entering the pass. Abdul-Hakeem's assistant stands with a bag of money and pays out the coins for his camels and men. It will cost him a tidy sum for the train to proceed. We are expected to pay our own fare, and when our turn comes, Barosh gives the soldier the coins, and we enter the pass. The soldiers lean on their high, rectangular shields watching us, contempt evident on their faces. One, in particular, follows my every move. Whenever I glance at him, he is staring at me; his face is one of male beauty, lean, smooth but having a dark, evil hue surrounding it.

He looks the same as the soldier who almost ran me down outside of Pithom.

***

Strung out, single file, in the mountain pass, we travel through the night. It is difficult moving in the dark, climbing the narrow ridges, followed by steep descents on loose, uneven rock. The shimmering quarter-moon is our only illumination and creates flickering shadows. My eyes continually deceive me, as I see the face of the soldier in crevices and from behind rocks. The face haunts me.

Abdul-Hakeem does not like the train strung out. He positions guards along the way, keeping everyone moving.

Exiting on the far side of the mountains, we are greeted by the dawn, unfolding as a splendid yellow-orange sunrise. Abdul-Hakeem rides alongside the train as it exits the pass, yelling and screaming to keep moving. I don't understand the urgency as the guards push us further into the open so as not to block the exit of the pass to those following behind. Finally permitted to stop, I fall to the ground, exhausted.

Screams shatter the air.

I jump up; mukowwem are pulling camels back against the mountain. Looking beyond them, I see more camels. . .running. . . fast. . .bearing down on us. . .carrying riders. . .screaming and waving scimitars.

We are being attacked!

They come from around the side of the mountain and have timed their attack while much of the guard force is still inside the mountain pass. Abdul-Hakeem quickly mobilizes the guards he has to meet the attackers. Using the mountain as a rear defense, Shalen orders the cargo camels down against the steep wall while hurrying the remainder out of the pass.

Brays and bellows fill the air as camels growl and grunt, lurching forwards and backwards, squatting under their heavy loads. We hunker behind Sudaas and Al Naab; our only weapons are our daggers. Pulling mine out, it feels small and insignificant compared to the long curving swords the bandits are waving as they gallop closer and closer. My stomach heaves and I vomit.

"If I had my rifle, this would be over quick," Mark complains.

"And when it was, they'd take it from you, along with your head," Barosh says. "Trust in God; we'll be okay."

"You trust in your god; I'll trust in mine."

"I didn't know you had one."

"You're looking at him."

The bandits charge. There are scores of them. Six swordsmen, headed by Abdul-Hakeem wait for them, their sharp scimitars out and ready. Behind them, a row of nine archers sit mounted, arrows nocked, bows poised. While appearing calm and confident, the defense looks small and inadequate against the charging horde. At a command, in a single fluid motion, the archers draw and release their arrows at the oncoming bandits. Immediately they nock and release another round, and again and again, and yet again. I'm amazed—within a span of seconds the nine archers filled the air with over forty arrows. Many find their mark, as men and camels collapse in clouds of dust and spewing stones. Riders catapult into the air smashing against rocks or crushed by their own falling beasts. Camels stumble and skid through the dirt and stone like locomotives run off their tracks. Others trip over them sending their riders smashing into the mountain. In seconds, the odds are improved.

The horde is too close for further shooting, so the nine archers abandon their bows, draw their swords, and together with the front six, charge into the oncoming bandits. Behind them, the mukowwem and laborers are lined up holding swords and daggers, as the last line of defense.

The fighting is fierce and bloody. Powerful blows of sharpened steel slice through flesh and bone. The guards carry small, round shields made from wood and bronze on their forearms and wear leather armor. The long, curving scimitars swing wide and cut deep. Strikes finding their mark are fatal or incapacitating. Camels bark and roar in fear and confusion crashing headlong into one another.

Animals topple. . .men are mangled. . .both fall, trampled underneath.

The guard force is well trained and skilled, but the bandit force is large. Their losses are heavy, yet still they come. A bandit breaks loose and charges into the waiting mukowwens. They fight back valiantly, but are no match for the warrior until one of the camel's legs is disabled, bringing the beast down. They converge on him, beating him until another bandit gallops up, slashing at them, driving them away from the fallen bandit. More bandits begin to break through and attack the line of mukowwem and laborers.

I don't see the blow coming until it hits me, sending me hard into Sudaas's solid body. A searing pain screams through my body from the force of the camel ramming into me.

I can't breathe and falling against Sudaas; I see an arm raising a sword aimed at my head. I see the bandit's face—it's the same face as the

Roman soldier's! Lean and beautiful, but with a dark, evil cast about it. It's the face of death, eager to take my life. I stand frozen, unable to move.

The arm begins the downward swing, and suddenly the bandit folds in halve, flying off the high saddle. Mark runs to the fallen man and using the staff he had dislodged him with, he crushes his throat. He picks up the outlaw's fallen scimitar and rushes into the melee. The bandit the mukowwem had pulled down had risen back to his feet and was slashing at the laborers. With a quick swing of his sword Mark kills him and then runs at another bandit sitting atop a camel, slashing at the mukowwems. Mark jabs at him with his staff and when the bandit moves to deflect the staff, Mark brings his sword down on the bandit's leg, cutting deep to the bone. Screaming, the bandit collapses from the saddle. As he falls, Mark strikes him again, killing him. Another bandit charges Mark, who ducks the charge, and as the camel surges past, he strikes the camel from the rear, cutting through its hamstring. It collapses in a bellowing heap, and Mark jumps over the kicking beast and quickly dispatches the bandit struggling to get out from under the camel.

The remaining guard force has cleared the mountain pass and joins in the melee. The added reinforcements overpower the remaining bandits, who retreat and flee.

The battle is over.

The ground is soaked in blood and littered with the bodies of men and camels alike; some lie still while others whither in pain. The bandits timing was late by minutes, giving the train time to prepare a defense, and allowing the rest to exit the passage. Just a couple of minutes earlier and they would have picked us off one-by-one as we came out of the mountain pass.

The victors move around the battlefield, claiming swords, saddles, blankets, pouches—anything of value from the fallen. Wounded bandits are dragged away or dispatched on the spot, depending upon their wounds. Seven of our guards are dead, along with three mukowwems and four laborers.

I crawl to the fallen bandit who almost killed me, needing to see his face. Rolling him over, he has a full, black beard and thick mustache; it is not the same face I had seen when he was about to sever my head. *Am I going mad?*

Abdul-Hakeem calls for camp to be made and guards posted. He doesn't expect a repeat attack, but he takes no chances. The bandits suffered heavy losses, with thirty-nine dead and eight captured. The dead bandits are stripped and thrown outside the camp for the jackals and buzzards to feast on. Our dead will be given proper burials.

The wounded are treated by stitching the flesh together and bandaging them with a piece of raw meat wrapped in a linen cloth soaked in honey. I observe a white powder being given to those in agony. I assume it is opium.

Great fires are built, and the dead camels are butchered for a victory feast. Soon the flutes, lyres and drums come out, and the camp celebrates its victory.

***

At the height of the celebration, aides carry a lounging couch, along with a smoking blazer full of flaming coals with a metal rod protruding from it, to the center of the camp. In a flourish, Abdul-Hakeem enters and takes his place, reclining on the couch.

The eight captured bandits are dragged out and pushed to the ground in front of Abdul Hakeem. A guard stands behind each bandit. The first is given the opportunity to become the property of Abdul-Hakeem, as his slave. He crawls forward and kisses Abdul-Hakeem's feet. The guard yanks the man's head back by the hair while another takes the red-hot iron from the blazer and burns Abdul-Hakeem's mark on the man's forehead. He is taken away.

The ceremony is repeated with the next man.

The third man remains defiant, not moving to accept Abdul-Hakeem's offer. The guard draws his scimitar and beheads him on the spot.

When the sentencing has been completed, five of the captives have been taken away, branded as slaves, and three have been beheaded.

The bodies are removed, thrown outside of the camp's perimeter to join their comrades as vulture fodder. The heads of the three dead bandits are spiked on top of poles stuck in the ground as a warning.

Two guards approach us, and motion for Mark to follow them. I rise, ready to defend him, but Barosh grabs my arm. With Mark walking between them, they take him and push him down on his knees, in the blood-stained sand, in front of Abdul-Hakeem. The coals from the blazer glow brightly, even in the fading sunlight. I can feel the tension in Barosh's hand.

Abdul-Hakeem stands and nods to an aide, who approaches, carrying an outstretched cushion. On it, a dagger rests. Abdul-Hakeem takes the dagger and pulls the blade from the sheaf. It glistens in the firelight. He motions for Barosh to come forward.

"Your deaf and mute friend is a mighty warrior, and I, Abdul Rahman bin Omar al-Ahmad Hakeem, pay him homage for his courage and skill."

"Thank you Abdul Rahman bin Omar al-Ahmad Hakeem, I shall tell him, and he will be most grateful for such an honor from one so mighty."

"This scared blade has been in my family since the beginning of time, given by the god *Hubal* himself. I give it to you, Mark Levi ha-Roshini, who speaks, not with words, but with the sword. By this, all men will know you are friend to Abdul Rahman bin Omar al-Ahmad Hakeem, and you will be always welcomed in my tent."

With both hands, he holds the dagger out to Mark. The hilt looks to be solid gold and has a large red ruby anchored on the top. The sheaf is covered with jewels and looks to be made of gold also.

Mark glances at Barosh, who nods for him to take it. He takes the dagger and bows his head in respect. Abdul-Hakeem nods, turns and leaves. His assistants follow, carrying the blazer and couch.

***

Barosh thought I had a couple of cracked ribs under the dark purple bruises on my side. He wrapped linen tight around me to aid in mending. I was lucky; I could have been killed.

Boiling water for coffee and watching Mark fondling the dagger, I try to understand him. After the battle, covered in blood, he had washed but had insisted on doing so alone, out of sight from anyone. Ever since, he had first changed clothes at the pyramids, he had been paranoid about his privacy when dressing or bathing and I wondered what he was afraid of. . .or hiding.

"Why did you save my life?" I ask.

"Don't get sentimental; it was self-survival. You think that goon was going to stop after killing you? I figured I'd better move while I had the advantage. It was instinct." He looked up and smirked, "Besides, you're my ticket out of here. I can't let anything happen to you, can I?"

I spent that night thinking about the things that had happened. I wondered if a curse was on me: the crocodile, the Roman horseman, the sandstorm and now this bandit. And—the little boy, the old man, Jamal and now Mark. It seemed death was stalking me, and if I dodged it, someone else took my place. Everything was upside down. We pay Romans for protection, but Mark, who wants to kill me, ends up fighting my battle. And I think about men who would rather lose their heads than submit to another.

There was much to think about.

13

With the mountains behind us, we cross a small section of desert before the shifting dunes give way to a hard baked rocky terrain. A skyline of razor-toothed cliffs and hills bordering deep ravines nestles among mountain runoffs. The east wind carries the scent of fresh water and foliage as we approach one of the richest springs in the Sinai at Kadesh-Barnea. The camels pick up their pace, smelling fresh vegetation ahead. With grunts and barks, they rush to the patches of prickly, green hattab.

Camp is made, and while the cooks prepare dinner, Barosh wants me to climb a steep slope with him. Reaching the summit, we look out across a fertile valley below, and Barosh once again wanders back into his history.

"It was here David, in Kadesh-Barnea, on such a peak as we now stand that Moses looked across into the land of Negev. He sent out a group of men, one from each of the twelve tribes, to scout the Promised Land. They were gone for forty days, and when they returned they brought a report of a land rich in bounty and blessings."

"But they also said the people were giants and strong, and that they could not capture the land. Only two men told the people they should take the land because God was with them. The people rejected them and turned back in fear. It was for this reason God caused them to wander in the Sinai until all the adults of that generation had died. Only Caleb and Joshua, the two who stood for God, didn't die in the wilderness."

"And that David is why they wandered forty years in the Sinai. One year for each day." Placing his hand on my shoulder, he looks directly at me.

"Sometimes God has to get our attention."

***

We begin the descent back to the camp. The smells of vegetables and roasted meat rise on the air currents and cause my stomach to rumble. I haven't eaten much since Jamal's death and the battle in the desert. Seeing those things on a screen, with their glamorization and special effects, was one thing. Experiencing them in life, was not glamorous, and the heads stuck on spikes were not special effects – they were real people.

A laborer meets us on the way down, saying Abdul-Hakeem looks for us and wishes to speak with us. He turns back down the hill, and we follow directly behind him.

"Aieeeeeee! Aieeeeeee!"

Kicking and flailing wildly, the laborer jumps back, knocking my injured ribs hard against a large rock, bringing a cry of pain from me. I grab his arms, trying to restrain him, not knowing why he is screaming.

"His feet!" Barosh yells. "His feet, look at his feet."

On the top of his left foot, a thin, snake withers and coils, still attached by its fangs. His right foot has blood running from two sets of puncture marks where vipers have bitten him. I scramble back in horror; the ground in front of the man is covered with copper-colored vipers slithering in frenzy. Using my staff, I knock the serpent loose from his foot and drag him back away from the snakes, all the time looking at the ground in dread.

Guards, hearing his screams, come running. Barosh yells at them waving them away from the nest of vipers.

"No—not there! There are serpents!"

The men beat the vipers with their staffs and spears.

Two guards take the stricken man from us and carry him back to the camp. He has stopped thrashing, and his body is turning a hideous bluish-black color.

Barosh and I follow.

At the camp, I slump down, shaking and trembling. There had been dozens of them. And they had been directly in our path. . .

. . .where I would have walked if the laborer had not come.

***

"This is where you leave us," Abdul-Hakeem says.

He had bought back Sudaas and Al-Naab, along with the saddle skins, saddles, blankets and tent.

"We turn south in the morning, to Aqaba. Your path is there," he points northeast. "That is the way to Jerusalem. The way is clear. There will be others traveling, as well. Be careful on your journey, the Canaan is a troubled land."

He turns to leave, but stops and turns back. "Forgive my rudeness, but I feel a deep disquiet around you. You are different from others. You speak having an accent I know not, and you do not pray as pilgrims pray."

He looks at Mark, "You are a mighty warrior, and I honor your skill and bravery; yet I wonder much about a 'holy man', who does not speak, having such abilities. There is much to know about you."

He looks at me, "I am deeply troubled for you, my friend. Death is your companion. I sense great distress and trouble ahead for you. You should make sacrifice to your god to lift the evil that stalks you."

He folds his hands, touches his lips and forehead, and bows his head to us.

"Salaam aleikum, may you find that which you seek."

***

That night, Barosh and I sit, starring into the heavens, watching the stars that brought us here, twenty centuries ago. I search my mind trying to understand all that has happened.

"Barosh, have you ever heard of snakes like that?"

"There is an incident In the Torah about a time when the people of Israel rose up against Moses."

"They seem to have done that a lot," I interrupted.

"Yes, they did. And God continually had to correct them for it. This one time He sent hundreds of serpents among the people, biting and killing them."

"Do you see a connection?"

"The serpents on that hill today weren't there minutes before, and if the servant hadn't come to get us, we would have walked into them ourselves and would be dead."

"Are you suggesting God sent the snakes to kill us?"

"No, I'm not, I don't understand this, but I don't believe it was coincidence."

I sat thinking about what Barosh had said.

"What happened?" I ask.

"To whom?"

"To the Israelites, when the snakes came."

"God told Moses to make a bronze serpent and raise it on a pole, and anyone who looked upon it would be saved."

"I don't want to see anything else stuck on a pole, thanks," I shake my head. "What was that about? A bronze serpent on a pole? Some kind of magic or something?"

"It signified looking to God for salvation. The Jews believe it to be a prophecy of the coming messiah being raised on a pole for salvation." Barosh sighs deeply before continuing, "Christians believe it represents Jesus being raised on the cross."

"Jesus? The same Jesus we're looking for?"

"The same."

I am silent, wondering what we've gotten ourselves into. "I don't get it. I thought we were going to meet Jesus, a preacher. All this violence and death. It's not what I expected."

Barosh nodded his head, "No—it's not what I expected either. It makes me wonder if we're something more than only passive observers."

"You mean participants?"

Barosh doesn't answer.

14

"There are always prophets in Israel; it is our curse," the old man said.

We had crossed into Israel two days ago. The change from the barren, hostile wilderness of the Sinai to the fertile hills of Judea is remarkable. Valleys burst with life, ringed by pyramid shaped Grecian Junipers and groves of olive trees. Winding rows of vines are accented by large clumps of distinctive, blood red *dam hamakabin* flowers. In the distance, a low range of brown cliffs borders a tan wasteland strewn with loose shale and protruding boulders.

We are in a village called Hebron. The old man sits cross legged, in front of a low stone building. His back is bent; his fingers gnarled and crooked from years of labor in the fields, and his heart is broken from a life of awaiting a messiah to deliver him from his harsh life. Along with the Romans have come an increasing number of messiahs, most of who ended up on the business end of a Roman sword, faded into obscurity.

"This old one, having dull eyes and a weary heart pays no attention any longer," he mumbles.

We have traveled through a handful of small villages since crossing into Israel and have not found anyone who has heard of Jesus of Nazareth. Traveling is becoming extremely difficult for me with the pain increasing in my side. The bandit encounter has left me with at least one cracked rib, probably more. Breathing is hard, and I can't hold food down.

Mark's ankle has healed, and he looks healthier than he had in the twenty-first century. No shots, no pills, no preparation for the trip, and now, the hero of a sword battle—go figure.

"Maybe Jesus doesn't exist," Mark said.

"Would that make you happy?" Barosh asks.

"No way! I'm no atheist you know? I got no axe to grind with Jesus. I come from a Catholic family. . .we even had a crucifix hanging on the wall when I was a kid. You think I want to go back and tell my mom Jesus never existed? She'd kill me."

"Well, you won't have to tell your mother," Barosh says. "Jesus is real enough. This is what it is like to live without modern communication. No cable TV, no internet and no smartphones to tweet around the world when a miracle happens. It's word of mouth – by people who seldom travel far from their own village. Even major events are known by the fastest a man can ride, for those rich enough to own a horse. They struggle to survive; so if something doesn't affect them, they don't care. Most of Jesus ministry was in Galilee, not here in Judea. As we get closer, we'll hear things."

"How are you holding up?" He asks me.

"Not good. . .it's hard to breathe."

"Let's find an inn for the night; does the aspirin help?"

"Doesn't matter, there's none left."

***

That evening, over coffee, we talk about Israel. I wonder about Barosh and his people. They are a mystery to me. They think differently, whether now or two-thousand years from now. I see Barosh in a different light than I had before, a light not clear.

"Barosh, what do you believe?"

He gives a dismissive shrug, "We already went over that. I told you back. . .".

"No, you didn't," I interrupt him. "You told me what you *didn't* believe, that Jesus isn't the messiah and that you were out to prove that. That's fine, but this thing about a messiah, for thousands of years. I mean, here we are somewhere around the year 30, and that old man spoke about messiahs, and there you are, twenty centuries later, still talking about a messiah. What's changed? Anything? You tell these stories about Moses, but you don't talk about anyone since those days. Is your faith only for the past? Is there a future in it? That makes me wonder – what do you believe? You are a rabbi and an informed leader of your people – do you believe in a messiah? Are you still waiting for one? I don't know anything about what you believe."

He sat for a long time, pondering what I'd said. I wasn't sure if I'd insulted him, hurt his feelings or made him angry, none of which were my intentions. He seemed to sense this, and it appeared I had touched something inside of him. The normal authoritative Barosh, with the quick response, wasn't home tonight. Instead, a different Barosh answered.

"Ask that of five different Jews, and you'll get seven different answers. Understand, my faith in God as the one, true God is unwavering, but the question of a messiah is unclear. We've argued, speculated and debated it ever since Moses. Do we believe in a messiah, you ask? There are different answers for different times. Here, in the year 30—they believe and pray for a messiah, a savior to deliver them from the Romans. It is the consummate hope that sustains these Jews. They recall and tell their children about the glory days of David's kingdom. The prophets foretold of the ten tribes, scattered over the earth, returning to the Holy land. They believe those prophecies will be fulfilled in their time, and the Kingdom of God will reside, once again, in Israel under a king—the anointed one— the messiah."

"In the twenty-first century, do we believe in the messiah? No, not really. Maybe some do, but most don't – they don't think about it – don't even know about it. They think it was for their ancestors, not for them. Since the temple was destroyed, they've replaced blood atonement with *teshuva, tefillah* and *mitzvoth*—repentance, prayer and good deeds—those that even care, that is. They've changed God's system to a man-made one, and as such, they don't see the need for a savior. They follow the oral customs and traditions and are more concerned with their earthly lives. You'd be surprised while the impression is strong that Jews follow the Tanakh, most have never read it."

"God's voice has been still for centuries. There's been no prophets, no Elijah, no Jeremiah, and if one had come, most of my people would close their ears. Yes, the Tanakh is clear; we will have a messiah, and I believe that. He isn't meant to free us from earthly bondage. He's meant to free us from ourselves and to bring us back to God."

"There's a mystery about it. The prophets had a conflict in describing the messiah. Some described him as being meek and suffering and others as conquering and powerful. For hundreds of years, leading to the age we're in right now, scholars believed there were actually two messiahs that will come, Messiah 'Ben-Joseph' and Messiah 'Ben-David'. The first would be sacrificed and killed, preparing the way for the second, who would then resurrect the first, and together they'd reestablish Israel to its former glory." He stood and turned to leave.

"I believe a messiah will come, David, but I don't know when. I leave that in God's hands. But this man here, called Jesus, has caused too much pain and suffering for my people for over two-thousand years, and it's time to show the world the truth and expose him for what he isn't— the messiah."

He strode off—alone with his thoughts.

"He's crazy," Mark said, turning to sleep—alone with his thoughts.

I stare at the wall—alone with my thoughts.

Outside, in the shadows, a cloaked figure waits—alone with his thoughts.

***

Barosh couldn't contain his excitement. He talked nonstop and kept hurrying the pace. If it wasn't for my busted ribs, he'd be running.

We are following a centuries old track leading to Jerusalem. Low mountains and grey knolls, covered with patches of shale rock and sparse trees, rose along the horizon on both sides. Between them lay fertile hills and hummocks organized with rolling terraces of olive, fig and date trees. Scattered, in-between are large patches of wild grasses and flowers, brightening the hills with clumps of yellow dill, pink sage, blue chicory and purple nepeta.

As each crunch of stones underfoot, draws us closer, he expounds on the glory of the temple, explaining everything: the sacrifices, the rituals, and the worship. He describes the outer and inner courts and the holy of holies. This will be the greatest moment of his life, when he will see worship as his God had decreed it. I thought he might burst, exploding from the emotion boiling inside.

The road is filled with workers, craftsmen and farmers carrying their wares to the city. Pilgrims come from all over the known world, carrying offerings of fruits and vegetables. Many lead sheep, goats and rams for sacrifice or carry babies for dedication. It is the time of *Shavuot*—the Festival of Weeks, and many are going to the temple.

The first glimpse of Jerusalem is the Temple itself breaking on the horizon, like a golden crown. The day is clear and hot, with a gentle breeze giving the rows of palm and date trees the slightest sway and the Temple glows within the city, sitting atop two hills rimmed by a great wall with towers and gates. Compared to the tiny villages we'd passed through, Jerusalem was startling. Many pilgrims break into chants and song at the sight.

Approaching the walls, we pass an ugly outcrop of rock to our right. Although people are everywhere now, none go near the place. Wooden poles rise from it, like pins in a pin cushion, and people don't look, lowering their heads and hurrying past.

"Golgotha," Barosh says, "the place of the skull."

I turn to look at it. On one of the upright poles, a crossbeam is attached. Hanging from the crossbeam are the remnants of what once was a person – male or female—I can't determine; limbs and bones picked over by vultures and magpies. The stench of death drifts on the breeze.

"Golgotha?" Mark asks. "Isn't that where they crucified Jesus?"

"Did – or will," Barosh says.

***

Lepers, forbidden to enter into the city, are massed outside the gates, beseeching alms. The local people ignore them while many pilgrims, throw putras to them. I wondered how they could trade and use them. They keep a respectable distance from the flow of people, but other beggars aren't so discrete and get right into our faces, grabbing at us, trying to intercept any coins thrown to the lepers. I am shocked at the number of sick, maimed and disabled people, but of course, there are no hospitals.

Passing through the high, thick gates of Jerusalem is like entering the Twilight Zone. Tight, narrow streets, bustling with shops, people and animals are a dramatic change from the stark, barren wilderness and desert. Women dominate the markets and side streets, buying food, cloth and the needs of their households. Children hang onto their mother's tunics or are carried in sacks on their backs and shoulders. Many women carry clay jars on their heads. Some jars are tall; others are short. I notice people are detouring around the short ones.

"They usually carry waste being disposed of," Barosh says. "Avoid them, sometimes they spill."

I steer clear of short jars.

From the studies, I know that Israel stands unique in the empire. Jews are exempt from compulsory military service, and Rome allows them to govern themselves, within limits and as long as the taxes are paid. Rome installed a Procurator, who is headquartered in Caesarea, a city built in Roman style by Herod to appease his mentors. While an engineering feat of magnificence, with its enclosed harbor, circus arena and racetrack, it is offensive to the population with its temples and statues of Roman gods.

A four day journey from Jerusalem, the Procurator rarely came to Jerusalem, preferring his luxury on the sea coast. When Herod died, the country was divided into four territories overseen by tetrarchs, who are puppets of the Roman Emperor. The High Priest, presiding over the 71 member Sanhedrin, is recognized as the cultural and religious leader of the Jewish nation. Caught between these forces of military, civil and theological powers, like meat in a grinder, are the people.

We pass Herod's palace, enclosed by additional walls and towers from where guards carefully watch the crowds, searching for signs of trouble or insurrection.

It's a cosmopolitan scene, with merchants, travelers and soldiers; rich and poor alike filling the streets. Jew, Arab, Greek, African and Roman rub shoulders indiscriminately. The common language is Koine, but strands of many different languages mingle together through the streets.

Behind open doors, craftsmen work making what they sell. Strings of dried fish, batches of figs and bunches of dates are strung across stalls. Baskets of pomegranates, apricots and grapes are stacked high. Cotton and linen from Egypt, fine colored fabrics from Babylon and exquisite leather goods from the Arab counties fill the shops. Dealers squat amongst trays of bright, aromatic spices and herbs.

Beggars line the streets in alleyways, leaning against walls and sprawled along the side of the streets. They are filthy, wearing dirty, tattered rags with long, unkempt hair and beards in long greasy knots. They lay on filthy mats, hobble on tree limbs and crawl on all fours. They are ignored by the local people, dependent on the pilgrims and travelers for subsistence.

Unlike Pithom, soldiers are evident. Swaggering about in groups of three or more, they move for no one, and everyone avoids them.

A beggar is sprawled on a mat in an alley, his feet protruding into the street. A group of soldiers is stomping down the street, rowdy and laughing. He hears them and scampers to get out of their way, but he's not fast enough and a soldier bumps his leg. Exploding in anger, he stomps the beggar and kicks him hard in the chest, sending him sprawling into the shadows. Laughing, they continue on. I stare into the dark alley searching for the beggar when a cloaked man emerges from the shadows. He looks at me and pulls the hood back from his face. It is lean and smooth. The eyes stare at me, and the mouth curls in a smirk before he fades back into the shadows. My heart pounds in my chest and my breath becomes labored.

"David, what's wrong? Are you all right?" Barosh grabs my shoulders, turning me away and shouting into my face.

"The face. . . .it's. . .," I stutter, ". . .it's him."

"What face? Who? What are you talking about?"

I shook my head, not able to speak, but in my heart I knew.

***

The Temple sits on the eastern ridge between the Kidron and Tyropoeon Valleys. Set on the foundations of Solomon's Temple, I am awestruck by its size, covering a substantial portion of the entire city. It rises above us, gleaming and shining. White alabaster, limestone and marble adorned and inlaid with gold towers above the high outer walls. A wide esplanade, hundreds of feet long, leads the way to the entrance.

People move up and down the esplanade across its entire length. Those bringing animals for sacrifice enter through a separate set of gates, after purifying them in the Sheep Pool.

At the top of the esplanade, we pass through an enormous bronze gate, gleaming with gold panels, so large it takes a force of men to open it. We enter into the Royal Portico.

I'm surprised at the noise. The high walls had kept it contained. It is a large area, teeming with people and animals. We pass through and enter the Court of the Gentiles. Holding pens are filled with oxen, sheep, goats and rams. Others roam free. Cages full of pigeons and doves are stacked and lined up along the walls. Long rows of tables are set up before the entrance to the inner courts, where scribes sit, recording transactions. Other priests inspect the animals presented for sacrifice. Listening to the bartering and discussions, many sheep and rams are rejected due to blemishes or age. Arguments are everywhere with many people claiming their animal is not blemished, while priests offer replacement animals. Overall, it's an unpleasant, noisy, dirty marketplace.

"This place stinks," Mark says.

He's right; there's the foul stench of dung and urine permeating the entire area. Barosh doesn't move, frozen in place as his eyes dart from one scene to another. I feel bad for him; his enthusiasm and joy has been stolen by the reek of sheep manure and goat urine.

Without saying anything, he turns and leaves.

We follow.

15

We stayed in Jerusalem for several days. It was *Shavuot*, the Feast of Weeks, which meant we had spent far too much time getting here, missing the Passover by a wide margin. Barosh wanted to get his bearings before proceeding any further as there was no hurry; the execution of Jesus was either long over or yet to be.

Barosh paid for a week in advance at an inn, and we spend the time getting familiar with the city and the culture. Being festival time, the city throbbed, packed with Jews from across the known world, here to present themselves to God, at the temple. There was such a wide variety of peoples and cultures; it was a historians dream. Unfortunately, my health prevented me from enjoying it.

"I'm going back to the temple tomorrow and would like it if you would go with me," Barosh said the day before the Sabbath. "If you are not well enough, I understand."

"I'll go."

***

Leaving before dawn, we merge with a flood of people moving towards the Temple. I am surprised at the throngs of people and animals waiting at the doors this early hour. We climb the steps of the esplanade to wait.

Before long, the massive doors swing open, smooth and quiet. Again, we enter the Royal Portico. This time Barosh takes a direct route across the Court of the Gentiles, avoiding looking to the right or left at the animal pens and money tables, already busy.

"We must purify ourselves before we enter the inner courts," Barosh says, leading the way to a stairway going down to a lower level pool. Men, in various stages of undress, enter the water, immersing their feet and hands.

"How does this clean us?" I ask.

"It's not a matter of cleanliness; it's ritual purity. We cannot enter the temple area unless we're purified first. We only need to immerse our feet, hands and head. Just do as I do."

Following Barosh, we remove our sandals and head coverings, dip our hands into the water, sprinkling some on our heads, gather our cloaks and tunics about us and step into the pool. It is a couple of feet deep and we walk the length of the pool, emerging on the opposite end. After sprinkling more water on our heads, we cover ourselves with a prayer shawl from a stand and take another set of stairs back up.

We stop at the *Soreg* – a low, inner wall surrounding the temple called 'The Wall of Partition'. A sign is posted at the entrance:

No stranger is to enter within the balustrade around the temple and enclosure: Whosoever is caught will be responsible to himself for his own death, which will ensue.

"What's a stranger?" I ask.

"A non-Jew," Barosh says and laughs. "You've impersonated a Jewish pilgrim for two-thousand years now, what's another day?"

Passing through the wall, we enter another open area surrounding the temple. While not like the outer court, the area is crowded and priests sit along the wall conducting business. Coins from different nations and cultures are being exchanged for the silver, half-shekel required of all men as the Temple Tax. There is arguing about the rate of exchange and quality of coins being presented.

Barosh stops, watching, and I can see anger rising in his face before he turns away and climbs the *Chel* steps to the Beautiful Gate.

And beautiful it is. Over seventy feet high, it's set between marble columns, inlaid with bronze, silver and gold. Passing through the gate, we enter the Court of Women and move through a double row of marble columns, called 'Solomon's Colonnade', leading to the Court of Israel. We aren't allowed to go further, but we have a front row seat for the Temple ceremony.

Standing one hundred-fifty feet high, adorned with golden spikes to keep birds from rousting and fouling the roof, the Temple is massive. Circular steps lead up to the entrance which is open. Looking in, there is a large golden candlestick, and an altar having incense burning on it. Behind the altar is another opening, lined with polished wood, and over which hangs a heavy, embroidered curtain.

"The Holy of Holies," Barosh whispers.

I watch, transfixed, as a scene from Hollywood unfolds before me. A massive altar, the size of a small house dominates the Court of Israel. One entire side is a long incline to the top, where priests are raking and cleaning. Priests carry bundles of wood up the ramp to a large, square blazer in the middle of the altar. In addition to the altar, the courtyard contains a colossal bronze basin, the size of a backyard swimming pool, resting on the backs of four bronze bulls, and butchering tables for the sacrifices. Around the court, under the cedar roofs, hundreds of men wait.

It is very quiet. Only the sounds of priests moving about, shuffling and raking and the occasional bleat of a sheep or bellow of a ram breaks the quiet pantomime.

The sun begins to rise on the horizon over the Mount of Olives. A moment of absolute stillness and quiet hangs in the air; not even the animals stir, sensing a change, and then it is abruptly shattered by the loud clattering sound of the cleaning priests slamming their rakes to the marble floor, signaling the altar is prepared for *Shavuot*.

Immediately, shofar horns blast out from a row of priests standing on the steps leading to the inner sanctum. The sound echoes across the walls and resonates through my body, causing goose bumps and tingling down my spine. Priests ignite plates of incense on bronze censers throughout the court. The fragrance fills the court and is almost intoxicating. Seven priests, standing above the shofars, sing the *Shema*:

> *"Shema Yisrael Adonai Eloheinu Adonai Echad"*
> Hear O Israel: the Lord our God, the Lord is One

Followed by the *Vea Hafta*:

> *"Love the Lord your God with all your heart and*
> *with all your soul and with all your strength"*

A large choir, led by seven cantors and accompanied by musicians playing lyres, harps, and cymbals begin singing psalms. The fire of the altar is lit and flares blazingly. Priests, in the butchering pens, ceremoniously sacrifice the two lambs of Shavuot. The High Priest, easily identified by his multi-colored tassels, head covering and breastplate of jewels, carries two loaves of bread up the long ramp. He is followed by priests carrying the sacrificial lamb parts. The High Priest ceremoniously makes the wave offering, and the sacrificial offering is given to the fire.

Men bow, kneel and prostrate themselves, chanting in thanks for the harvest and praying for a—messiah. In the Court of Women, men dance carrying scrolls of the Tanakh tight in their arms.

Priests begin slaughtering the sheep, rams, pigeons and doves, brought by the people for various dedications and atonements. The offerings are carried up the long ramp to the fire where they are consumed. The smell of fire and roasting flesh mingles with the incense, creating a scent forever burned into my mind, that is connected with the rhythmic singing and the shofar's spine chilling blast. Long rows of men move slowly towards a line of priests stretched across the Court of Women. They carry baskets containing the first fruits of their harvest from across Israel: wheat, barley, grapes, figs, pomegranates, olives, and dates. They present the offerings to the priests and recite the Shavuot verses from the Torah.

Having lost myself in the ceremony and rituals happening on all sides, I had forgotten about Barosh. Turning to him, he is prone on the ground, and his body is convulsing. Fearing he suffered a seizure of some sort, I move to help him, when I hear him sobbing deeply.

I back away allowing him his time with his God.

***

Leaving the temple, the narrow streets are crowded and difficult to maneuver through. We stop at an inn. Seated on a squat bench at the end of a table, we're served pieces of flat bread and honeycomb, along with a watered down bluish wine.

Barosh is quiet and has receded deep within himself. After long moments of silence, I ask him:

"Was it what you had hoped for?"

He sighs before answering.

"It sickens and saddens me to see how the Temple is more a place of business and less a place of worship. The animals should be kept outside the walls, and only brought in through the side gates to the slaughter area. Taxes and tithes should be conducted separately, away from the presence of God. But, despite that, it was the most marvelous event of my life – to actually witness the worship God directed his people to do to atone for our transgressions. So much has been lost, and we've moved so far away from what God wants his people to be." He pauses and looks at me, "Did you feel it David? The spirit? The anointing?"

"You know how I feel about this stuff, Barosh," I shrug. "But I can't lie neither – it was moving. I felt that, although it could have been a reaction to the music and the atmosphere."

"Or the presence of God."

"Or a well-rehearsed show, hitting all the right notes to evoke emotion," I bristle, not allowing that door to open. "I don't want to rain on your parade, but it seemed barbaric to me. The court was a pig-sty, and it baffles me 'purifying' myself stepping in sheep dung."

Barosh shakes his head, "How sad life is, when one only sees the sheep's dung and not the sheep."

I don't respond. I am feeling too weak and in too much pain to argue. Besides, what is the point? Let him believe his fantasies if it gives him peace.

We sit in silence nursing our drinks and egos. The honeycomb is especially tasty, after the fare we'd grown accustomed to. Three men, sitting next to us, have been talking in agitated voices, growing increasingly louder. In the silence between Barosh and me, we can overhear them clearly.

". . . it's not the intent of God that these vultures take our money! How do I pay the infidel Roman now? I have nothing left. They took all from me."

"A half shekel Temple tax! And they want it every year! It was paid once in a man's life; not every harvest."

"They wouldn't even take my money for it! Made me exchange my coins for their shekel and at twice the rate."

"If only the Galilean was here, he would stop this again."

Barosh turns to the man who had spoken.

"Shalom friend, but did you mention a Galilean?"

The men stop talking and stare at Barosh, suspicion and fear on their faces.

"Please, forgive my rudeness. I am Rabbi Ben Barosh ha-Rav. My companion and I travel from a far country, to worship the One God in the Temple. We heard there is a Galilean miracle worker, and I wondered if he is the same man you speak of."

"Shalom rabbi, I am Elizar Azariah from Jericho. The man I spoke of is indeed a prophet and a healer from Galilee."

"Do you recall his name?" Barosh asks.

"Of course, how could one not remember the name of the man who stood up to those robbers and thieves? He called them vipers and sons of the evil one. Imagine! Calling the Pharisees the sons of the evil one! And he drove them out, whipping them and overturning the tables. Oh, it was a sight to behold! Their precious coins flew everywhere."

"People ran in all directions," his companion adds, "Most tried to get out. Others, like me, scurried for the coins. The guards didn't know what to do."

"What was his name?" Barosh asks again.

"His name is Yeshua."

"When did he do this thing?"

"Two Passovers ago. The Pharisees were afraid to arrest him because the people cheered him, and they feared a riot."

"Ah, but they've waited for him ever since," Elizar says. "At each festival the Temple guards look to arrest him, but they can't find him. He comes and teaches right under their noses, and then disappears before they can get him."

"He is still alive then?"

"He was seven weeks ago. I saw him here during Passover."

"Do you know where he is?"

"In Galilee, of course. The danger is great for him here; the Sanhedrin have put a price on his head, and Herod also seeks him."

"I'd be fearful of that one; he beheaded the Immerser, and he fears the Galilean is a magician stirring up the people."

"Does Yeshua stir up the people?"

"He claims to be the messiah. There are many who wait for him to expel the Romans and claim the throne of David for Israel."

***

The next day we begin the journey to Galilee.

Following a twisting road, we skirt around a rocky wilderness and cut through the green oasis of palms and sycamore trees marking Jericho. On the far distant horizon, the sun rises over the purple mountains of Peraea.

Before us stretch wide, fawn colored hills, spotted with clusters of stone and isolated groves, accentuated by the green, winding ribbon of the Jordan Valley. Bright yellow patches of Sabra prickly pear flowers dot the area and almond trees are loaded with soft green almonds. Picking them, they are edible though not as tasty as the ripened nuts will be in a couple of months, but they are a welcome change in diet.

Barosh is energized. He has seen and felt the Temple, and he knows Jesus is alive.

Mark is solemn, withdrawn and has developed a habit of reaching into his cloak.

I'm having difficulty walking, breathing, and I keep breaking out in fever sweats.

We head to Galilee.

16

The bright sun illuminates the sky, reflecting in shimmering ripples off the surface below. The lake is a blue jewel, sparkling amongst the lush, gentle rolling hills and green fertile valleys surrounding it. A soft breeze, blowing off the water, tastes fresh and ripples through the wheat fields like waves on a golden ocean. Groves of dates and pomegranates cover the hillsides, interwoven by rows of grape and berry vines bathing in the life-giving light. On the far shore, mountains, bathing in an iridescent glow, peek out from wispy clouds stretched across the sky.

We stand on a grassy hilltop overlooking the Sea of Galilee. Surrounding us, farms are stitched together by low stone fences. Small hamlets and clusters of buildings are scattered about the countryside. Birds flit between the bushes, and flocks of magpies swoop amongst the waving grain.

Men and boys work the fields, cutting, bundling and loading donkeys with sheaves of wheat. Women cluster around gardens and domestic livestock. On the water, boats drag and haul in nets; while on shore, fishermen clean catches and mend nets. It's a scene right out of the Bible.

"I've stood on this very same hill, two-thousand years. . .from now," Barosh muses. "Except for the cars, roads and buildings, it looks the same."

"That's a lot of excepting," Mark snickers.

"Not really," Barosh says, "electricity and gasoline is all."

"Where are we?" Mark asks.

"We're on the edge of the Sea of Galilee."

"Do you know where we're going?"

"On the other end of this lake is a town called Capernaum. It's his staging base. If he's in Galilee, they'll know where," Barosh said. Looking to where I sloughed down against a tree, he added, "We need to get David someplace to rest."

"I don't think he's going to make it," Mark said. "I think it's time you let me in on how we get out of this hole. Anything happens to you I'll be stuck here."

"Then you had better make sure nothing happens to me," Barosh snapped back.

"That's not good enough Goldberg. Not this time. Look at him; he's dying, and that would only leave you knowing how to get out of here. That doesn't sit with me. Look, I've played ball with you two lunatics; now you need to give me something. You owe me that."

Barosh's face flushed scarlet red. "You better get your head out of the clouds, Rosino. You're no hero to me, and I don't owe you anything. Nothing's going to happen to David, you hear? And if you want to ever see the twenty-first century again, you had better see that nothing does. He just needs a little rest. He didn't have a camel to ride on like you did." He paused, forcing himself to calm down.

"Look, we've been here over two months already, time is moving fast. I'll tell you this; the gateway will open again on the Spring Equinox, right where we were standing, between the paws of the Sphinx."

"So, we do have to go back to Egypt? I thought as much."

"And we need David to go back; he knows how, so I suggest we take care of him."

"It's that drink, isn't it? It's some kind of magic potion."

"That's right, some kind of magic potion and David knows how to make it."

Mark nodded, "Yeah, and let's not kid one another, so do you. There's no way you'd come here with only him knowing."

Barosh shrugged, "One thing we both know is that—you don't. And it's clear to me, once you did know, and thought for a minute you didn't need us—one or both of us would die. So, let's just leave it at that, why don't we?"

***

The hamlet was too small to have a stand-alone inn, but a large, mud-brick house served as a gathering place for the local fishermen and farmers and took in travelers. Barosh mostly carried me the last hundred yards.

The room was dark, lit by a dim, olive oil lamp. It had a dirt floor and no furniture. They laid out a straw mat on the ground, against the wall, and I collapsed on it. I was burning fever, sweating profusely and gasping for breath. Barosh checked my bandages, and though he tried to hide it, I saw the look on his face. I looked down at my ribs. They were black and scabby. Pus leaked out from open sores and carried a foul smell. It was putrid—the smell of rotting flesh—gangrene.

"I'm dying Barosh."

"No, you're not. You're running a fever is all. Rest and I'll see if they have any kind of doctor around here."

I shook my head; no doctor was going to help me.

After he'd gone, Mark knelt down next to me.

"Listen. . .Kincaid. . .tell me how to make the magic drink. You don't want to die with it on your conscience that you left me stranded here in this god forsaken land, do you? Come on, do the right thing; I saved your life. . .you owe me. . . ."

I passed out.

***

The room is spinning.

The walls, window and door roll pass in an unending cycle, swirling, twirling, turning upside down, faster and faster. . . . Objects flicker in and out of the spinning whirl. . .a giant crocodile snaps at me. . .horses gallop over me. . .bandits laugh, swinging swords at my head. . . snakes hiss and strike. . .bright lights flash and flicker. . .followed by total blackness. . .bursts of brilliant flares. . .I am smothering. . .suffocating. . .unable to breathe. . .I'm lost in the blackness. . .blinded by the brightness. . . .

Explosions detonate all around me. . .lights and colors burst above and below. . .fireworks fill the blackness. . .A volcano erupts spitting red-hot lava high into the blackness. The flaming fluid doesn't fall back but rises into the heavens, igniting the constellation of Leo with bursting fire and shooting flares. . .The constellation breathes. . .looks at me, and roars. . .it's plucked out of the heaven by a hand. . .the hand connects to a dark, hooded figure in a long black cloak. . . .He turns to me. . . .it's the lean face of the soldier. . . .It changes to the bandit. . . .Then into a snake. . .It changes back to the hooded man. . . . He holds the breathing constellation of Leo out to me. . . .'*jump*' he says. . . .

I'm inside the earth, passing through layers of rock into the depths. . .to the core of liquid fire. . . .I float in the fire. . .screamIng. . .burning. . . but not consumed. . . .

I stand on the ocean's floor. . . freezing. . .my bones ache. . .I breathe ice-water. . .it freezes in my lungs. . . .I no longer can breathe. . . .Gigantic sea monsters swim past. . .growling. . .roaring. . .huge mouths. . .row upon row of sharp teeth flash and gnash at me. . . .Gigantic squids slither by. . .eyes glare. . .they snap their immense incisors at my face. . . .they leave a murky, red cloud behind. . .a shadowy figure drifts through the cloud towards me. . .floating through the water. . .leaving a redder swash in his wake. . . .He draws closer. . . .Stretches out his hands to me. . . . In one are the heavens and stars. . .in the other he holds the earth. . . .He stares into my eyes. . .his face is beautiful. . .his eyes shine red. . . . His lips move. . . ."*Jump*" they speak. . . .blood drips from them. . .

I stand above the earth. . .the civilizations of earth are below. . .Ba bylonians. . .Persians. . . Egyptians. . .massive armies. . .Greeks. . .Rom ans. . .Chinese. . .all in full battle armor. . .Japanese soldiers cover the plains. . .Napoleon heads an enormous force on one side. . .Hitler stands in front of a staggering army of tanks and planes on another. . .there are armies I don't know, wearing armor and carrying weapons of great power. . . . Overhead rockets and flying orbs soar in vast fleets and num- bers. . . . Among these armies towering giants roam, having enormous bodies of men, but heads of lions, bears and falcons. . . . They strut like gods. . .all the armies bow to them. . . .as they pass, they turn to me and bow. . ."*Jump*". . . they say. . . .*join us*. . .

I am in the mud house, lying on the straw mat.

All is still and quiet. I can breathe. I'm not burning. I'm not freezing. I feel the pain in my side. I sense a presence in the room. I am afraid to open my eyes to look. . . .

. . .but I do. . . .

He sits on a throne made of gold. . .cloaked in bright red robes, his face buried inside the folds. The throne floats in a pool of blood. He levitates to me. The hood falls away revealing the most beautiful face I've ever seen. Smooth, clean, golden locks, ruby lips, shining blue eyes. He smiles. His face hovers over mine. His eyes bore into me, deep and knowing, the blue fades, they are dull and dead.

The face moves back. He's wearing a thousand crowns, gold, dia- mond, ruby and emerald. His hands open. . .he holds the earth. . .the oceans. . .the heavens and all the armies. . .He holds them out to me. . . He opens his mouth and speaks. . .

"Follow me."

"Your beauty is a lie," I say.

I'm standing on the railing of the river. . .it surges past. . . .I fall into the turbulence. . . .I am spinning. . .tumbling. . .in a sea of nothingness. . .feeling all the hurt, pain and emptiness of life. . . .There is no hope. . .no caring. . .no feelings for anyone or anything. . . .It's the pain of existing. . .with nothing except—nothingness. . . .I stop spinning. . . .In the blackness. . .the shadowy figure appears. . .he moves to within inches of my face. . . .the lips open and a long, scaly, forked tongue flicks at my face. . . .The face is a viper. . .hissing and spitting. . .the tongue touches my mouth. . .It burns and tastes of death. . . .The smell of rot and decaying flesh fills my nostrils. . . .Its mouth opens. . .revealing enormous fangs dripping with venom. . . .The face merges with mine. . .flames burn my flesh while streaks of cold freeze my spine. . .It transforms into a sickening, hideous green. . .having large ragged scales, and mold. . .eyes are black and cold. . .from its mouth blood gushes forth as it screams in agony. . . .It holds my hand. . .pulling me with it. . .to suffer. . .along with it. . . .I am in hell. . . .All is black. . .empty. . .nothing. . . .I suffer the greatest of physical pain. . .It's excruciating. . . .I twist and turn but have no relief. . .My body screams. . . .I have full intelligence. . .but without knowledge. . .I have full awareness. . .but without anything to be aware of. . .only pain. . .emptiness. . .nothingness. . . .

. . .and the greatest pain of all. . .is somehow knowing. . .it could have been different.

I scream. . . .

I am in the small mud house, on my mat.

All is still and quiet. I can breathe. I am not burning. I am not freezing. I feel the pain in my side. I sense a presence in the room. I am afraid to open my eyes to see. . . .

. . .but I do. . . .

A face looks down at me. It is not the face in the hood. It is the face of a man. There is peace in his eyes. Stretching out his arms to me, he opens his hands. They hold nothing. He gazes into my eyes, and he speaks in a quiet voice:

"Beneath the turbulence, David – peace is found."

He places his hand on my side. He touches my head. He places his hand over my heart.

I close my eyes and sleep.

17

I open my eyes.
A mantle of stars cover the sky—thousands and thousands of them. I see galaxies and clusters of thousands of stars in every direction. The deeper I look, the more I see. So vast, so large, it can't be measured or fathomed by my mind. There are so many stars that there is almost no darkness.

Shifting my eyes to the side—a mud wall borders my vision. I'm in the house—lying on the straw mat—on the dirt floor. There is no roof. I'm not dreaming.

Turning my head, Mark lays sleeping against the far wall.

I'm hungry. No, I'm starving. I could eat a camel, with or without a cloven hoof. Then I realize, other than the intense hunger, I have no pain. My hand moves to my ribs. I feel no bandages. Surprised, I search for them. I cannot find them. I try to look, but cannot raise my head far enough.

I slowly force my legs to move and struggle to get into a semi-sitting crouch. I look down at my ribs. There are no bandages; there's no black, rotting flesh, no bruises and no foul smelling pus. The only smell is the crisp night air. I sit up. My fingers explore my ribs. There is no pain.

"Welcome back."

Across the room, Mark sits, watching me.

"I thought you were a goner," he says.

"What happened?"

"Beats me. One minute you were dog meat. . .the next you were okay. I never seen anything like it."

"Where's Barosh?"

"Gone."

"Gone? Gone where?"

"After Jesus."

"After Jesus," I lay back down. "What's going on?"

"The people here told Barosh there was a 'healer' in a town called Tiberius, not far from here. Barosh went to get him while I stayed with you. I'll tell you Kincaid; you were a corpse, for sure. Man, how you stunk!"

"Just keep to the story please."

"While he was gone, you were in la-la land. Kept mumbling about some beautiful man and saying "Jump! Jump!" Over and over. I thought about putting you out of your misery, but I didn't think Barosh would like that too much," he chuckled.

"Anyway, one day, when I came back from getting water, you were lying still and had stopped moaning and mumbling. I thought you had finally kicked the bucket, but when I checked, you were alive and breathing easy, and the infection seemed to have worked itself out. I couldn't believe the change. It was night and day. The rotting flesh and pus was gone, as was the smell, thank God. Even the black and blue was gone. There was only some redness, and each day, that is fading. You sure heal quickly, Kincaid. I don't know how you beat that thing; you should be dead."

"How long have I been here?"

"Three weeks."

"Three weeks! That's not possible."

"Trust me; it is. Anyway, when Barosh returned, your wounds were healed, and you were recovering. He was amazed. When he asked what happened, they told him Jesus had come and healed you."

"Jesus? Was here? Did you see him?"

"I didn't see anything."

***

A young boy brought me a bowl of soup. It wasn't much more than water boiled with some vegetables and fish heads, but I wouldn't have traded it for a king's feast. It was like a magic elixir. I could feel the warmth of life flow through me and couldn't get enough water. I fumbled through my cloak searching for the water pills.

"This what you're looking for?" Mark held up the zip lock bag of pills. "Hope you don't mind, but I needed to treat water." He tossed the bag to me as I continued to search.

"Looking for this?" He held up the heat sealed polypropylene bag of white powder. I stopped searching and stared.

"Yeah, I know all about it. Stand between the paws of the Sphinx, during the spring equinox, drink the magic potion, and—'KAZAMM! We're back. This is it, isn't it, the magic potion?"

"You went through my things."

"Hey, I needed the water pills. Besides, you were dying," Mark said.

"Don't be so sentimental about it. So you know everything?"

"Not quite, but enough to get by. I need to find out the exact date of the equinox, but that shouldn't be too hard. And I'm assuming I just mix this concoction of yours with water. Think that's all it was back then. I'll hang on to this for safe keeping if you don't mind," he tucked the bag away.

"Don't worry," he laughed, "I'm not going to kill you. If I wanted to, it'd be over by now. And when the time comes, you'll get half of the potion too. I wouldn't leave you here. Actually, I've become rather fond of you guys. I can't go anywhere until spring anyway, and I'd hate to be here alone until then. It would be boring without all the excitement surrounding you, and I'd miss your smiling face." He chuckled, "Hey, you're not terrorists; so I have no reason to kill you anymore, and when we get back, we'll have one heck of a story to tell, won't we? Oh, by the way, I took some of your money too. Not much, just enough to buy some food."

***

That night we ate with the family of the house, along with most of the village that came out to see me. They were convinced I had been healed by the prophet 'Yeshua' from Nazareth. Apparently this wasn't unusual around here. The area was known for healings. A series of hot springs bubbled up not far from here, and many believed they held magical 'healing waters'.

While we ate, they recited stories of healings and miracles they claimed Yeshua had done. Seemed like anything good that happened got the Yeshua label put on it. A grandmother had been healed of bleeding; a miraculous catch of fish had occurred; rains came when needed and winds stopped blowing when commanded. It sounded like a Sunday school lesson—one that could all be explained by science, coincidence or exaggeration—*could be*.

Some people expressed doubts, saying it was the 'healing waters' that brought about my recovery. Only problem was; I hadn't been in any 'healing waters'. Others said I hadn't been that sick, and it was a natural healing. Most didn't accept those answers; they wanted to believe, and so they did. They pointed at me as proof of their beliefs. I don't know how good a proof I made. Sure I was better, there was no denying that, and I did believe I was dying, but stranger recoveries have occurred – at least, so I kept telling myself.

I said nothing about the visions I'd seen or the beautiful man. Had that actually happened? Or was it a dream? Hallucinating while my body fought off the infection? I wanted to believe this, but it had been so real, and still was. It wasn't fading like dreams do, but remained as vivid and real as it first had been. I could see the face clearly, and it was the same face I'd seen on those other men who tried to kill me. I didn't understand it.

And I couldn't get that other face out of my mind, either, and the quiet voice that spoke those words *"Beneath the turbulence David, peace is found"*. How did he know those words? Was he the one who sent the message for me to come here? Had that been real? Was that Jesus?

More than anything, I couldn't forget the peace I had after he said those words.

It turned out the only person who had seen Jesus was the grandmother. She said he was in the house for only minutes. She kept staring at Mark, who wouldn't look at her.

"How long ago was that?" I asked.

"Over a week ago," she answered.

"Do you know where he went?"

"He followed the road north."

***

I sat alone that night, watching the stars. I wondered if they had things to tell me, but I couldn't hear them. What is this thing I'm so tangled up in?

So many diverse peoples and cultures: Egyptians, Arabs, Romans and Jews. All so different from one another, yet all so much the same. Each searching for answers; worshipping the gods they think will provide those answers. Some search the heavens; others seek a messiah, and others worship the sword.

Not all that different from the twenty-first century.

"Waiting for your friend 'Leo' to come and take you home?" Mark sat down next to me.

"No, just wondering what it's all about."

"And you expected to find the answer here, didn't you?"

"Yeah, I guess maybe I did."

"Well, don't hold your breath; if you didn't find it back home, you're not going to find it here. These people are too busy just trying to stay alive to know anything."

"I wish it were that simple."

"Maybe it is, and you're just making it hard."

I looked at Mark, for the first time, as a person.

"You seem to have adjusted to it," I said.

"What choice is there? Can't do anything until spring."

He pulled out the jeweled dagger, "I go back with this little beauty as proof of this whole thing; I'll be on top of the world."

"Is that what's important to you, Mark, being recognized? Fame? Glory?"

"I can think of worse things. Hey, I didn't ask to come along on this ride, ya know; so don't blame me if I see a way to make good on it. You know the old saying: 'you get lemons, you make lemonade'."

"What do you believe in Mark, I mean seriously? After all, you are a Christian, raised to believe in Jesus. Now, you are here, and he is here. Not as some intangible concept, but for real, walking around out there somewhere. Does it do anything to you being so close to him?"

He sat for a while without answering, when he did; his voice and tone were different from at any time before.

"Actually, I try not to think about it. It scares me. Religion is something I never gave a second thought about. Yeah, I went to Mass when I was supposed to, was baptized as a baby and did the first communion thing. I did all the things required of a good Catholic boy growing up. I listened to my grandmother tell me all the do's and do not's and bowed to the nuns and priests when I was supposed to. Then I grew up and moved on. Joining the agency, I left all that behind."

"Being here and knowing he is here, for real, not like a church play or anything, it scares me. I worry, should I have said more 'Hail Mary's' and 'Our Fathers?' Should I have gone to confession and Mass a few times during the last fifteen years? Will he know who I am? Will he condemn me? I don't know what he'll do. You guys are on a mission to meet him— not me. I'm hoping never to see him and to just get out of here and back where I belong in one piece. I should have carried a rosary on me, or at least a Saint Christopher medal."

We sat for a while in silence; each lost somewhere, either in the heavens above or in the depths below. Mark was no different from the rest of us, scared and looking for answers—and afraid he'll find them.

"Tell me about Barosh," I said.

"Well, when he heard what had happened, he checked you over and saw you were okay. He told me to stay with you and keep giving you water. Said he was going to find Jesus, and we should follow when you were able to. Then he left. Do I assume you're going after him?"

"Is there another option?"

"You could just hang around until spring."

"That's not an option."

"I didn't think so."

"You coming with me?"

"Is there another option?"

"You could just hang around until spring."

"That's not an option."

"I didn't think so."

I looked at him and chuckled, "Capernaum is at the north end of the lake. We follow the shore around, and we'll come to it."

"You think you're up to traveling?"

"Let's give it a few days, and I'll take advantage of those 'healing waters' they said they have here. What is this place called anyway?"

"Ammathus."

My mouth fell open.

"Ammathus?"

"Yeah, that mean something to you?"

"Yeah. I wonder if you can do something for me."

"What's that?"

"Could you get some of those flat stones a foot or so long and wide?"

"Yeah, there's no shortage of them lying around. What're they for?"

"I got to do something. I need some writing clay too."

***

Mark watched intently while I carefully etched the stylus in the clay.

κάτω από την αναταραχή - ειρήνη είναι βρέθηκε

"That looks like Greek."

"It is."

"What's it say?"

"Beneath the turbulence – peace is found"

"What does that mean?"

"That Mark, is what I've been trying to figure out since I came here."

I turned the tablet over and again etched into the clay.

David Alden Kincaid
31 CE

"Hey, these are those tablets!" Mark said. "Holy cow, that's what started this whole thing. Man! This is blowing my mind."

Placing the tablet inside the pitcher, I fitted the top on tight and melted a thick layer of wax over it.

Using my knife, I scraped at the wall next to where I've laid sick and began digging a hole. I had dug about a foot under the wall when I jumped back in shock and fear. A snake shot out, striking at my hand. Behind it was another and another. I had uncovered a nest in the wall—right next to where I had laid for three weeks.

Mark thrust his staff into the nest, again and again, killing them. Some tried to slither away, but he was adept at hitting and crushing each one. When he finished, he looked at me, his face ashen in shock and disbelief.

"Did I get them all?"

"Yeah, I think so. I think I'll sleep somewhere else anyway."

"You were sleeping right next to them for weeks! You got to be kidding me! You are one lucky son-of-a. . . ." His face was in complete astonishment, "Someone wants you dead my friend."

After carefully disposing of the ugly things, I knelt down and gingerly continued digging. There were no more snakes.

Finishing the hole, I inserted some flat stones, forming a box. Placing the pitcher carefully inside of the stone tomb, I covered it with a stone lid, followed by a layer of dirt. Next I formed a second stone box on top of the first one and placed a second pitcher inside. I filled the hole back in and packed it down tight.

Inside the second pitcher was another clay tablet, written in Hebrew.

תרצנמ ושי לש

"What's that say?" Mark asked.
"Jesus of Nazareth."

***

Waves of emotion cruised through my mind and body.

I wanted to laugh – to cry—to jump up and down! Tears filled my eyes, although I wasn't sure why. I shouted to the stars.

"Yes! Yes!"

Across two-thousand years, I had done it. I do not know how, and I do not know why I was chosen to do this. I didn't understand it, but I felt it and knew what I was doing was going to change the world, and the weight of what I was doing sat on me like the weight of each of those two-thousand years.

I also knew that whoever the man was with the beautiful face, he didn't want me to do what I was doing, and he would stop at nothing to keep me from finishing whatever I was chosen to finish.

***

Outside, the wind blew hard and cold, moaning as it ripped through the village and around the stone house. Villagers scurried inside their houses, bolting the doors.

A cloaked figure slunk around the corner and stormed the street in madness.

Across his face, darkness and fury rippled. The eyes shone red and overflowed with hatred.

Around him, creatures, half men—half animals, roared and raged. Winds blew, demons howled and the sky shook with thunder as streaks of lightning flashed across the face of the earth.

Yes, he thought, *it had to be that you buried those tablets – but you won't bury the third one – I shall see to that.*

18

We crossed a verdant plain, passing farmers and oxen going and coming from the harvest fields and threshing floors. The barley harvest was over, and the wheat harvest was in full swing. People were everywhere, working, gathering or tilling. If ever there was a season to visit this land, it was now. Everything was either harvested, being harvested or ready for harvest; sheep were fat; fruit and nut trees were full, and grapevines strained under heavy bunches of velvety, purple fruit.

The Jordan Valley was a veritable jungle of papyrus and palm trees. Sugarcane, henna, and sycamore fig populate the valley in vast numbers. Stands of balsam trees sway in the fresh breezes, filling the air with their musky scent. Yellow mullein, resembling the menorah, blooms throughout the region. Shepherds herd flocks of fattened sheep, covered in thick tangles of wool, up and down slopes and valleys. The tinkle of sheep bells mingled with the haunting notes of the shepherd's flute.

It was our second day since leaving Ammathus, and we approached a small town, located along a feeder stream to the lake.

"Barosh was right; take away electricity and gasoline and this place has not changed at all. The Dead Sea is still the Dead Sea; the Jordan River is the Jordan River, Jerusalem is Jerusalem and the Sea of Galilee is still the Sea of Galilee; all pretty much the same as when I was here in '82. Or should I say, will be here? Just replace a lot of this vegetation with roads and towns."

"How come they call this a sea, it's not big?" Mark asked.

"I guess they never saw Lake Michigan. Why don't you ask Jesus when you meet him?"

"Not funny."

"There should be an inn here. Let's stop and get our bearings. Maybe someone has seen Barosh."

***

The town is called Gennesaret and has a house that serves as a gathering place.

"Shalom sister, may we sit and rest?" I ask the woman of the house.

"Please do sirs."

Sitting on low stools, she brings us mugs of watered down wine.

"Could you tell us how far it is to Capernaum?" I ask her.

"It is not far, only a short walk. Have you come far?

"We travel from beyond the Nile."

"That is a long journey to visit Capernaum. It does not see many visitors."

"We seek a rabbi who may have passed this way. Perhaps you have seen him; his name is Ben Barosh ha-Rav."

"The rabbi who seeks Yeshua? Yes, he passed this way."

"How long ago was he here?"

"Four days. He did not stay long, anxious to get to Capernaum."

Finishing our wine, we left for Capernaum.

***

"Why do they speak that language? Don't they speak Hebrew?" Mark asked.

"They do, among themselves. Each country has its own language, creating obstacles for travel and trade. *Koine* is a common language spoken just about everywhere. It goes back to Alexander the Great, hundreds of years before the Romans. All the conquered nations learned a mixture of Greek and Aramaic, and it became the common language. When Rome came along, they figured it best not to change anything. Each culture has its own language, but it's usually not spoken to outsiders."

"When I grew up," Mark said, "everyone spoke English, but when the family got together for Sunday meatballs, it was all Italian."

"Yup, same thing. Learn *koine*, and you'll get by just about anywhere. You're doing good; I'm surprised how fast you pick it up."

"I'm a fast learner, but it doesn't matter."

"Why not?"

"Train's coming."

"What train?"

"The Equinox Express—departing from Sphinx Station—destination—twenty-first century."

***

Capernaum sits directly on the shores of Galilee. It's a small village, with winding, narrow streets, lined with fieldstone houses, built on foundations of basalt rock. The walls are rough, unhewn, held in place with mud and animal dung, and covered with a clay-mud mixture. Windows are situated high, allowing for maximum light and air into the closed, tight quarters. Common courtyards connect houses together, distinguishing it from the other villages we'd passed.

It's a clean village. The lake keeps a crisp, fresh smell in the air. Gentle waves lap at the shoreline, licking the high rocks protruding from the bluish-green water. Silhouettes of distant mountains shadow the skyline across the lake.

Walking along rows of cypress trees, surrounded by red-orange flowers, we watch fishermen working their nets along the shore. As we come into view, they stop talking and follow us out of the corner of their eyes. Three men sit at a table, repairing nets. They look down as we pass by.

It's the same everywhere we go; people stopping their conversations and looking away, but following our progress carefully.

"What's going on?" Mark asks. "We got a disease or something?"

Approaching a large, grain mortar in the middle of the road, there are two women working the grain while a donkey turns the large stone. The sound of stone crunching grain, is broken only by the sound of our sandals crunching the stony road.

"Shalom, peace be to you," I say. "Is there an inn here?"

One woman points to a building across the road.

"Thank you."

Once again, the 'inn' isn't much more than an enlarged house with a room set aside for visitors. When there aren't any (usually), the goats call it home.

After shooing out the goats and laying down fresh straw mats for us, we're invited to the communal 'dining' table.

Sitting on low benches around the table, the food consists of baked fish and boiled vegetables, along with the traditional bread and wine.

The food is. . .good.

The hospitality is. . .bad.

We eat in silence; no one talks; avoiding us. When we dip our sop into the bowl, they turn the bowl so as not to dip from the same side we did.

***

Following the awkward meal, Mark and I walk down to the shore of the sea. Night is falling, leaving an eerie, orange cast rippling across the surface. A slight breeze creates a pleasant and relaxing ambience as the waves softly break against the shore.

Sitting on the ground, I'm wondering what to do next.

"Why are they acting like they are?" Mark asks.

"I don't know. It's as if they're afraid of us for some reason."

"Do you think Barosh is here?"

"I'm sure of it. It's the only reason I can think they're. . . ."

"Who are you?"

The voice is loud and harsh; angry, with an undertone of fear. It belongs to a group of men coming from the village behind us. We rise to greet them.

"Shalom friends. Peace be with you," I say.

"Who are you?" The voice asks again.

He is a big, burly man; weathered face, hair windblown, having big, meaty hands. Appraising the men as they approach, I don't sense a threat. They're more of a group than a mob, staying close together, fearing us more than we fear them.

Mark doesn't sense the same thing, or his instinct doesn't take chances. He backs up, raising his staff in a defensive position while reaching inside his cloak. I quietly hold his arm while addressing the group.

"We are pilgrims who mean you no harm," I say to the man who spoke.

"Who sent you?" A tall man, having a thick black beard framing a sharp face, shouts. His eyes have a hard, cynical look to them. "The Romans or the Sanhedrin?"

"No one sent us. We come of our own accord."

"You lie!" The man shouts back, "You spy on us."

"I am David Bar Kalaid ha-Rav, and my companion is Mark Levi ha-Roshini. As I have said, we travel in peace and mean you no harm. We've been sent by no one and seek only to find our friend. Now, we have traveled far, and you are being rude. If you are robbers, then we shall take up arms against you. If not, then conduct yourselves properly."

The man stares back, deciding what his next step would be.

"I am Judas, son of Iscariot. What is the name of this friend you seek?"

"Rabbi Ben Barosh ha-Rav, who has traveled this way."

"Why would he travel here, to Capernaum?" The burly man asks.

"He seeks the teacher, Yeshua."

A murmur or fear ripples through the group. *What are they so afraid of?*

"Why does this rabbi seek Yeshua?" He asks.

"To speak with him. Now, enough of your rude questions; have you seen my friend or not?"

They huddle together, talking and gesturing at the same time. Some voices are angry and strident, but most carry fear. Judas appears to lead the angry voices and a man they called Thomas, the fearful ones. After a discussion, the burly man turns back to us.

"We are not robbers. My name is Andrew. We apologize for our rudeness. Your rabbi was here; come, follow us." He says, turning and heading into the streets of Capernaum.

"What language was that?" Mark asks quietly as we follow.

"Hebrew."

"Why did he change to it?"

"A test, to see if we understood—to see if we're really Jews."

***

The lead us down a winding, narrow lane to a small house. The inside is dimly lit and sparsely furnished. We're offered a seat on the floor. We're not offered drink, food or any amenity that is required of good manners.

The others sit in a semi-circle around us. There are nine of them, and they fidget, glancing at the door often.

"From where do you travel, David Bar Kalaid ha-Rav?" Andrew asks.

"From a land beyond the Nile."

"And your friend, Rabbi Ben Barosh traveled with you?"

"Yes, we travel together."

"And you come seeking Yeshua too?"

"Yes."

"They know of Yeshua from so far away?"

"He is known in all the world." This caused a rippling among them.

"Tell us, how did you lose your Rabbi friend?"

"I was sick, injured from an attack by bandits, and could not travel any further. While unconscious, they said Yeshua came, and Rabbi Ben Barosh left to find him."

With this, they begin talking and gesturing among themselves, pointing at me.

"Was it at Ammathus that you were sick?" A tall man asks; short curly hair unceremoniously falling across his forehead.

"Yes, it was."

"You are the one," he says.

"I don't understand."

"The teacher wished to see his mother, so we had traveled to Nazareth. Earlier, he had told us a man would come, through whom the teacher would give the world a great blessing. In Nazareth, he told us this man was now in Ammathus, and that he would die unless he went to him. We wanted to go with him, but he would not allow it, and told us to return to Capernaum where he would join us."

I stared at the man, my mind struggling with the words he spoke. *Was Jesus the man I saw? I thought it had only been a dream, 'a great blessing to the world'. What did that mean?*

"The master knows many things people do not understand, Ben David," Andrew says.

"You say Yeshua came and healed me?"

"It would not be so strange; we have seen many marvelous things. And. . .you are alive are you not?"

"What happened next?" I ask, wanting to shift the focus away from me.

"We returned to Capernaum, and the teacher joined us there. He told us another would come, seeking him. As always, he was right and in a few days a man came seeking Yeshua. He said his name was Rabbi Ben Barosh ha-Rav."

"So, Rabbi Barosh is here. Take me to him, please."

"He is not here, Ben David. He left with Yeshua—into the mountains."

"The mountains? Why? How long ago?"

"Three days now. They traveled north to Mount Hermon."

"It is very dangerous there," Thomas spoke, "there are many bandits and the Zealots hide in the mountains."

"Then we must go and find them," I say.

"Yesterday, Peter, James and John left to find them."

"And I also am going to find them," I say.

"Your friend is safe with Yeshua," a thin man, with a gaunt, sunken face and pointy beard says. "I am called Simeon, and I know the Zealots well. They are not the ones who seek to harm Yeshua. They seek only for him to join with them and declare the kingdom with them."

"Who does seek to harm him?" I ask.

"The Judeans, of course," Andrew answered, vehemently.

"Not all Judeans," Judas interrupts, "we are no different from you Galileans. It is the Sanhedrin who wants him dead. They despise him for the things he says and teaches." He looks around at the others "Shackles they have placed on all of us, Judeans and Galileans alike. What the Romans leave, they take. And worse, they do it in the name of God."

"Hush, Judas," Thomas says, "we know your feelings, and there are hidden ears around."

"Hush yourself Thomas, it is time we stop fighting among ourselves, Judean against Galilean. We are the chosen ones; the messiah comes for all of us. Together we'll overthrow them and be rid of them. Any day now, Yeshua claims his crown." Judas points at me, "Maybe this man is the one Yeshua has been waiting for."

I didn't like the way this was going. "I do not know anything of that. If your Yeshua is waiting for someone, it is not me. All we want is to find our friend, Rabbi Ben Barosh. If you can direct the way, we will leave immediately."

"It would be extremely dangerous for you to travel alone. There are bandits and revolutionaries that call the mountains home," Andrew says.

"I see no soldiers in Capernaum."

"Why would there be? There is nothing for them in Capernaum. They only come to collect taxes, isn't that right Matthew?" Judas says while directing a sneer at a well-dressed man who doesn't answer.

"Yeshua would not approve of us allowing you to go alone," Andrew continued. Looking around the room at the others, they nod. "We will go with you. We will leave at first light. Let us eat now and prepare for the journey."

19

Leaving the Sea of Galilee behind, we cross a rich, fertile delta where the upper rivers and streams enter the lake. Everywhere, there's an abundance of trees, foliage and vineyards. Low, squat-bodied palms form a dense canopy over our heads, almost entirely blocking out the sun.

We travel winding trails skirting the river and streams flowing from the high country. Every step is not only one further, but one higher, as well. The water had carved strange looking gorges and canyons as the streams wound their way through the volcanic basalt covering the limestone plateau. Caverns and crevices dot and line the walls as they rise higher and higher the further we travel. It is rough, jagged rock, hard on sandals and feet. The river, that was placid in the Jordan Valley, is alive and turbulent, with the cold mountain runoffs, forming swift rapids, sending sheets of dancing water high into the air where they sparkle and shimmer like falling diamonds.

I observe the men closely. This is the group who Thaddeus said would show us what Jesus was truly about; who would take the teachings of Jesus and change the world with them.

I'm not impressed. These guys are not going to change anything.

It's not that they're crude—that would be unfair to them. They lived in crude times; life was crude and hard here, and they struggle to survive. What they are is— ordinary. There is nothing remarkable about any of them. They are fishermen, farmers and tradesmen, struggling under the yokes of oppression and law. Their education consists of oral and cultural myths, and what they learn in their lifetime.

I don't see how they are going to change the world. They are not articulate and are cloaked in biases and dislikes about everything, including one another. They are not the harmonious brotherhood of men so often portrayed. Many seem introverted, having not said a word since meeting them. Matthew is out and out disliked, and there are different cliques and inner groups, each having separate agendas. The only thing they hold in common is fear.

I am confused about his small group of dysfunctional followers. On one, hand, they have no doubts about the supernatural things they say he does, but, on the other hand, are divided about who he is and what he's doing. They speak of kingdoms and thousand year reigns, yet glance over their shoulders and jump at every loud sound. They are not united, arguing among themselves constantly.

I know from my studies that Christian lore teaches these men would all die violent deaths. I do not believe it, not this group. Christian history has certainly taken a lot of liberty with the mythology of these 'martyred' apostles. *Amazing what a few hundred years can do to enhance a person's reputation,* I think. If Jesus is depending upon this group to spread his teachings—he's in trouble.

I wonder how Barosh is faring in his private mission to discredit Jesus. And why did Jesus take him up to this mountain? Alone? Could Barosh be in danger?

***

We reach a small lake that is the main feeder of the river, and stop to eat. Chewing dried bread and fish, watching the waves break against the shoreline, everyone is quiet, lost in their own thoughts.

Some are first century thoughts, about Romans, messiahs and 'what's next'.

Others are twenty-first century thoughts, about gateways, white powder and 'what's next'.

One thing the centuries hold in common is—'what's next'?

"Why did Yeshua come here, to this mountain?" Thomas breaks the silence.

"Why does Yeshua do any of the things he does?" Andrew answered. "He is Yeshua, and he does what he does, for his purpose."

"How do we know he came this way, or that he's up there?" Thomas replied.

"He said this is where he was going. He does what he says." Andrew said.

"But it's been days since he's left. I wonder if the others have found him."

"It won't matter if they have," Judas said, "they won't tell us anyway. They're the special ones."

"You should stop that talk Judas. It serves no purpose. My brother is. . ."

"What if he's been killed by the Zealots?" Someone said, interrupting Andrew.

"They won't kill him," Simeon yelled, agitated, "I've told you, they want him to join them."

"He can't be killed, and he'll join no one," Judas shouted over everyone. "He's the Messiah; no one can kill him. They tried, and they couldn't. You saw it; we all did. When they wanted to stone him, he walked away, untouched, and when they try to arrest him, he disappears. Kill him? They can't even catch him! Don't you see yet? He is the Messiah and will rise up against them. He'll overthrow the Romans, and we'll be his generals to share in the glory of his kingdom."

"And how will he do these things Judas?" Philip asked. "He has no army, no weapons or wealth to buy them with."

"He doesn't need an army," Judas answered. "He has the host of heaven at his fingertips. He just speaks the words, and it will be done. Did not the sea and the wind obey him? Did he not make bread and fish enough to feed thousands out of air? Yeshua comes from God; he has the power to destroy the entire Roman Empire with a wave of his hand. We will have our revenge."

"I don't sense that from him," Matthew replied, "he speaks not of armies and conquest. He speaks of love and compassion."

"Love and compassion?" Judas responded with a sneer. "Something you know all about. . .tax collector."

"I am not that any longer. I follow Yeshua only."

"Tell that to those you robbed while you made yourself rich."

"I give what I have to our way. It is you who cares about coins, Judas. You would sell your mother for a denarii."

"I am not the traitor here. It is not I who betrayed my people, putting them in debtor's prison."

"Enough of this bickering," Andrew scolded. "Whatever Yeshua's plans are, we will know soon enough. He's made it clear the time is near. As for now, he said this is where he was going with the rabbi, so this is where he will be. If the others have found him, then they will be there also." He stood, "Come, we should go now."

So much for the men who changed the world, I thought, rising to follow.

***

We spend the night in Caesarea Philippi, on the southern slope of Mount Herman. It's a growing town, with new homes and buildings having finished walls and roofs. They were built with a higher level of craftsmanship than seen in Capernaum. Inside, walls are plastered and decorated with mural designs and ornaments.

"Fill your water skins here, and there is a bath house if you so choose," Simeon tells us. "Tomorrow we climb the mountain."

Most of the men don't follow his advice regarding the bath house. They needed to.

***

The following morning, leaving the fields and groves behind, we enter a mountainous wilderness. The stately rows of fruit and nut trees, decorating the rolling hills, give way to gnarled, bent and crooked trees bearing thorns and needles.

This is such a strange land. It changes between lush hills and valleys to barren remoteness and hostile wilderness in the blink of an eye. One second—paradise, the next—desolation.

And the people mirror the land. While a segment of the population lives in luxury and wealth, the rest wallow in squalor, struggling to stay alive. How could this kaleidoscopic place and time have the greatest impact upon mankind through all time?

The questions burn my mind.

We begin ascending the mountain. The men don't talk. Only the shuffling of sandals and clinking of staffs on stone interrupt the natural sounds of birds and trees rustling in the wind.

We are about half way up, when we hear noises above us. Rocks rolling, branches breaking—men are coming down. Our group freezes in place, fear registering on their faces as they strain to see who is coming. Is it bandits? Or Zealots? Mark reaches inside his cloak while I brace myself with my staff.

"Shalom brothers, peace be to you," a man, looking very much like Andrew, greets us. With him are two others. There is something about them that immediately catches my attention. They seem fazed, disassociated, almost as in a state of shock.

"Shalom brother," Andrew hugs his brother. "James, John—shalom, peace to you."

Greetings are exchanged between the two groups. Standing to the side, it's evident only cursory greetings are exchanged with Matthew and Judas and, surprisingly, with John. I sense there's animosity towards him. He is the youngest of the group, and I wonder if it is his youth they resent.

"What is it Peter?" Andrew asks. "What is wrong? What has happened? Where is the Master? Has something happened to him?"

"No, the Master is well. He said he will join us in Capernaum in a few days."

"Then what is it?"

"Not now brother."

"But where is the Master?" Thomas asks.

Peter approaches me, "You are David Bar Kalaid ha-Rav?" He asks.

"I am."

"Shalom David and your companion," he nods to Mark. "I am called Simon Peter; your friend, Rabbi Barosh, sends his greetings and says to tell you he is well and that he will meet you in Nazareth."

"Nazareth? I thought he was here, on the mountain."

"He is not here he went with Yeshua," John interrupted. Peter gave him a stern look, and John shrunk back.

"Rabbi Barosh was here, with the Master," Simon continued. "He and the Master left early this morning, for Nazareth. He wishes for you to join him there."

"What happened on the mountain?" I ask.

He looks at me, and I could see a desire to speak brimming on his face, but it clouds over, and he turns from me and addresses the group, "We should go now."

***

Heading back down the mountain, I approach James and John. They had been talking low between themselves and stopped when I get near.

"Did you speak with Rabbi Barosh?" I ask.

"No," James answers, "when we reached the summit, the rabbi was with Yeshua, and we did not interrupt. When they left, Yeshua instructed us to wait for him in Capernaum. He was going to Nazareth with the rabbi."

"Something happened on top of the mountain; what was it?" I ask.

"It was amaz. . ." John quickly answers and is cut off by James.

"We cannot speak of it, Yeshua said."

"James, I respect your obedience to Yeshua regarding your silence, but my friend was there, and I know something happened with him."

"In that case," James said in a measured, thoughtful response, "You should speak with your friend about it." Grabbing John's sleeve, he moves away.

Again, we spend the night in Caesarea Philippi as the hour had grown late for travel. At the inn, we are offered porridge of wheat and barley, laced with cucumbers and onions. There is no meat.

As the bowl is passed around, and we dip pieces of flat bread into the mixture, I try to remember what a medium-rare T-bone steak tastes like.

I can't.

20

Leaving the disciples in Capernaum, we head to Nazareth where Jesus is. I am confused why, if Jesus is in Nazareth, do they remain in Capernaum. But it is clear; they will do exactly what he told them to do. Despite their bickering among themselves, they were united in their loyalty and following of Jesus.

Peter said it would be safest to stay close to the lake and follow it around until we reached Magdala. He gave directions to a house there and asked if I'd deliver a message from him.

"Tell the woman there, Yeshua is in Nazareth."

"That's all?" I asked.

"That's all."

***

Retracing our steps around the lake, I fill Mark in on everything. He's learning the language quickly and had picked up a lot on his own. His biggest obstacle is hearing two different languages, koine and Hebrew. I sympathize with him; neither is easy, and I have to give him credit; he's intelligent and a quick learner.

"So, Barosh is in Nazareth now. When we hookup with him there, we'll be done, and we can leave for Egypt and the Sphinx, right?"

"There's plenty of time Mark, don't worry."

"You don't worry—I worry. I won't be late for our appointment with Leo. I'll be on the train out of here—with or without you."

***

Magdala is a level above Capernaum. Houses are hewn and finished in limestone and plaster. They aren't stacked up with common courtyards but consist of one and two story dwellings. Roman roads lead into and out of the village, and the streets echo with the hammers and tools of workmen. Markets sell fresh vegetables, fruits, nuts and strings of honey-based 'candy'. The downwind side of the town holds a cluster of smokehouses and fire pits where baskets of fish are smoked or hung up for drying. On the outskirts of town, a textile industry is located for making and coloring fabrics. Unlike Capernaum, soldiers are visible, in groups of never less than two.

Following Peter's directions, we work our way around the winding streets populated with shops and shoppers. The further we go into town the bigger and higher the houses become.

Locating the address, I knock on the door. After a long wait, it's cracked opened by a woman who appears to be in her late twenties.

"Shalom aleikhem sirs, may I help you?"

"Shalom, sister. I bring tidings from Peter." At the mention of the name, she perks up and opens the door wider.

"Simon Peter, of Capernaum?"

"The same."

"Come in, please."

She opens the door, and we enter. It is spacious and bright inside. Large windows, high on the walls, let the light in. Brightly colored tapestries and wall decorations adorn the walls. The room has actual furniture, chairs and tables arranged on a mosaic, tiled floor. The house is perfumed having a warm, pleasant scent to it. I recognize it as the 'ud' fragrance I liked earlier.

"My name is Mariamme, welcome to my home."

She is dressed in a haluk undergarment of pure white linen, covered by a turquoise sleeveless tallit, embroidered and laced with beads and tassels. Around her neck is a long shawl of royal blue with white stripes and plaited with gold colored silk cords. She leaves a fragrant trail behind her.

"Thank you Mariamme. I am David Bar Kalaid ha-Rav, and my companion, who has certain infirmities with speech, is Mark Levi ha-Roshini."

She looks at Mark inquisitively, and I see compassion reflected in her eyes.

"I too, once had such infirmities."

"I am sorry, Mariamme."

"Do not be David Bar Kalaid; if not for my infirmities, I would not know the Master."

"You have recovered well, Mariamme."

"Thank you, but I did not recover; the Master healed me. Is Simon Peter well?"

"He is well, yes."

"Good. May I offer you drink and food? You must be weary from your journey."

"Thank you, you are most gracious."

"Joanna! Susanna!" She called, and two women appeared from a back room. I assume they are servants.

"This is David Bar Kalaid ha Rav and his companion, Mark Levi ha-Roshini. They come from Simon Peter and will dine with us."

Greetings are exchanged, and they leave to oversee the food preparation.

"Please, sit and be comfortable." Mariamme gestures to a low divan. She stands until we are both seated before sitting herself.

"So, what news do you bring from Simon Peter?"

"He and his brethren are in Capernaum where they wait for Yeshua's return."

"Where is the Master?"

"He is in Nazareth."

"He visits his mother then. I am surprised he did not stop here. I shall go to him." I wonder if there is more here than meets the eye. This is the area Alex had said to explore.

"He is not alone," I say, watching her face closely for any hint of disappointment, "my friend, Rabbi Bar Barosh, is with him." She shows no interest, other than curiosity.

"Where do you and your companions travel from David?"

"We travel from beyond the Nile."

"From Alexandria?"

"Beyond Alexandra."

"And why do you journey so far?"

"To meet with Yeshua."

"And have you?"

"I have not."

"But your rabbi friend has. Are you traveling to Nazareth?"

"Yes we are."

She sits silent for a while, digesting this information. I can see questions on her face, but out of good manners, she doesn't ask them.

"You travel far to speak with the master; I trust you will find what you seek. You will stay here for the evening, and we can leave together in the morning."

"We would not want to be a burden. We can find an inn."

"You are not a burden David. I serve Yeshua and those who seek him. We have ample room, and it can be dangerous for you to wander in the city at night. It would offend me if you were to refuse."

"I would not wish to offend you Mariamme."

"Would you like to refresh yourself, after your journey?"

"That would be most appreciated."

"Good, please follow me."

She leads us to a stone staircase in the back of the building.

"Below is a cistern where you can refresh yourselves. When you are finished, we will have food prepared."

"Thank you Mariamme."

The stairway leads down to a rectangular room. In the center of the room, a sunken rectangular basin, around ten feet long and five feet wide dominates the room. Looking to be a couple of feet deep, lined with mosaic tiles, it reminds me of a shallow swimming pool in a hotel. To one side are four smaller basins and along the walls of the room, huge, stone pitchers are lined up, each filled with fresh water.

It looks more appealing than the spa at the Waldorf Astoria.

"After you," Mark said. "I'll wait upstairs."

***

Refreshed and settling back in the divan upstairs, I feel better about myself, and I realize I'm starving. Even onion and barley soup sounds good.

Joanna comes into the room carrying a tray heaped with bread and sliced cucumbers, celery, olives, leeks and onions. Susanna follows, bringing a large bowl of steaming stew. The aroma is irresistible, bursting with herbs and meat. A servant girl brings a mixed tray of smoked, salted and dried fish.

I am unable to hide my lust for this feast. Mariamme comes into the room carrying another tray loaded with vials of olive oil, dishes of spices and a stack of stone bowls, cups and spoons. Joanna returns, bringing a pitcher of wine.

Bowls, cups and spoons! We'll eat like real twenty-first century people.

To my surprise, all three women sit down to eat with us.

"Would you offer our blessings David ha Rav?" Mariamme asks.

Blessings? How does an atheist offer a blessing? What was it Barosh had said when he gave that blessing in Pithom?

I close my eyes, hold out my open hands and wing it.

"Barukh atah, Eloheinu, melekh ha-olam, ha-motzi lechem min ha-aretz. Blessed are you, King; who made the bread from the earth."

Opening my eyes, Mariamme is staring at me, her eyes slicing through me like a knife. Not dropping her eyes, she hands me a bowl. All three women wait until I dip into the stew and take a portion and then wait for Mark to do likewise. Only after we have placed food into our bowls does she break her stare and take a portion for herself.

"This meal is more than we deserve Mariamme. We are profoundly in your debt."

"It pleases us that you enjoy our offering. Please try each of the fish; Magdala is known all the way to Alexandria for the flavor and texture of our fish. Perhaps you have had it there?"

"I'm sorry no; I have not. What is the name of the fish?"

"It is called mousht. It is most delicious."

"Have you spoken with the Master?" Joanna asks. By the style and material of her clothing and the jewelry, she is not a servant or of the common folk.

"You may speak freely, David. Joanna and Susanna are my friends and follow the Master."

"I have not," I answer Joanna. "It seems I'm always where he just was. I expect to see him in Nazareth, his birthplace." I deliberately tested the Bible narrative.

"He was born in Bethlehem David; The Master grew up in Nazareth," Susanna answers.

"Mariamme, you said earlier that Yeshua would visit his mother in Nazareth. You did not mention his father," I said.

"Yeshua's father is dead."

"I'm sorry, I didn't know. Was it an accident?"

"It was no accident," she answers, and I look at her questioningly.

"There have been many who have stood to drive the Romans from our land. These rebellions have cost us many good men."

"Yeshua's father was a revolutionary?"

"Oh no, Joseph was a kind and gentle man. He was just in the wrong place at the wrong time. There was a man, named Judas, the Galilean, who had led a rebellion and was killed by the Romans. His son, Menahem, was bitter and sought revenge for his father's death. He had a large following, which exists today as the Zealots. They attacked the Romans wherever they could, and it was in a valley, just outside of Nazareth where the soldiers met up with him. Mariam's husband, Joseph, had delivered a plowshare he'd made for a farmer in that same valley, and was returning home. Menahem conscripted him, along with any other travelers on the road, and forced him into his 'army'. Joseph was given a sword and told to fight. He refused, and Menahem laughed, placing him in the front row facing the approaching Romans, saying, "Either fight or call on your son, to save you."

"Onlookers said, when the Romans attacked, Joseph threw the sword down."

"It must have been devastating for Mary."

"It was; she misses Joseph greatly; there was a special bond between them. Her other sons blame Yeshua for their father's death."

"So, Menahem knew of Yeshua?"

"Of course, all of Galilee knows of Yeshua."

"Why is that?"

"Why, for the things he says and does," Joanna said, "the healings and miracles."

"What do they think about him?"

"Many are anxious for him to proclaim himself king," Mariamme answers. "Some say he is a sorcerer who has magic and powers. Still others, such as Menahem, call him a charlatan, deceiving the people."

"What happened to Menahem?"

"He was killed, and now his son, Barabbas, leads the Zealots and continues the fight."

"Peter and the other disciples appear divided and confused."

"They do not understand Yeshua. They think they do, and so they squabble among themselves, about their status with Yeshua. But they are men, and men do not see what women see. They want things and follow a single path to them. Yeshua's path is not as they see it."

"Hush Mariamme. . .these are our guests. You shouldn't say such things," Joanna chastised her.

"Yes, I forget myself. Please forgive me; I mean no insult."

"And none is taken. I know, full well, the shortcomings of men, myself included."

Mariamme looks at me appraisingly, "You are a strange man, David, to say such a thing. You and Yeshua will have much to talk about."

While we talked, a servant cleared away the trays and bowls and came back into the room carrying another tray overflowing with figs, dates and honeycomb. In the center was a mountain of sliced melons.

"Would you like some more wine David? It's been sweetened with honey."

Melons! If ever I believed in heaven, it's now.

I glance at Mark and know by the look on his face. . .he is a believer too.

***

We're given a room upstairs having genuine beds. The servant placed fresh feather bundles on the leather straps and covered them with linen sheets.

After the long day's walk, capped off by the sumptuous meal, Mark falls immediately into a deep sleep. I have too many unanswered questions and troubling emotions swirling in my head to sleep. I go out onto the flat roof, and sit holding my knees.

Watching the millions of stars overhead, I wonder if Barosh and Mark will safely find their way back home. I know I wouldn't be going. I don't know where I'll end up, but I know I won't leave this time. While advances in technology and comfort filled in those thousands of years, nothing changed man's questions and fears.

I feel a presence and turn to look. Mary of Magdala is standing a few feet away. I hadn't heard her approach.

"May I sit with you?" She asks.

"Yes, of course, please do. Have you been standing there long?" I say, rising.

"Thank you. I did not want to disturb you. You were very far away."

"I was in the stars, following their course over time."

"That's a strange answer David. Most men aren't concerned with the stars or the passage of time. They're more concerned with where their next meal comes from and how to pay the Roman tax."

"Tell me Mariamme, do you believe Yeshua is the promised Messiah?"

"He is not the Messiah his disciples expect. He does not come to conquer the Romans. He has said he will die. His disciples do not believe him and are confused, but I believe him. I also do not understand his path, but yes, he is the Messiah. He speaks of a different kingdom, the kingdom of God, and he comes to bring us into that kingdom. He says it clearly, but men only hear what they want to hear."

"You make it sound personal."

"It is personal. He healed me of my infirmaries and demons. He is from God, and I will follow him and provide for him, and his disciples, even though men like Simon resent my support. I will be patient; all will be known in time."

"Time? Yes, everything is about time."

"Where do you come from David? It is clear you are different and more than just from a foreign land. There is something about you that does not belong here." She pauses and smiles, "It is also clear you are not a rabbi, and I question if you are even Hebrew. I think you know many things you don't speak of. I don't sense you threaten the master, but I feel a disturbance around you. What do you seek?"

I thought a long time before answering. It was clear she believed in Jesus as more than a man, and she provided financial support to him and his followers. I would have liked to tell her the truth about myself, and about the impact that Jesus would have on the world, but I may as well be explaining Allen's theories on Quantum physics.

"When Yeshua was born," I answered, "do you know if learned men came seeking him?"

"Yes, Mariam told me some learned men, who studied the stars in the east, came to Bethlehem seeking the newborn child. They brought gifts and worshipped him." Her face lightens, "The stars! Of course, you are those men, come again!"

"No, we are not those men Mariamme, but we are learned men from the west, who have studied the stars and other things, and now come seeking the grown man. We mean him no harm and only wish to speak with him, something I suppose, Rabbi Barosh has done," I look at her and smile, "and he is a real rabbi."

We sit for a while, enjoying the night air and the silence of the heavens. It feels good to sit with a woman again. She reaches out and places her hand on top of mine. It is soft and warm.

"You have a destiny with Yeshua David. I pray you will find your peace."

21

We left Magdala, skirting the lake, heading south. Johanna and Suzanna had wanted to come, but Mariamme feared for their safety.

"It is too dangerous with the Romans about. Three women would be too tempting for them to ignore should we happen upon them. Go to Capernaum, where Yeshua said he would return. I will join you there."

Prior to reaching Tiberius, she turned off onto a small, dirt path following a stream feeding the lake. The day was hot and dry, but a fresh breeze blew off the lake making the walk comfortable.

We followed the path until it intersected with a road. This road was paved with large stones.

"These are the only good things the Romans have given us—their roads," Mariamme says. "But they come with a heavy cost. We must be alert as they travel their roads, and bandits roam them seeking prey. I'll walk between you and Mark." I had wondered why she had dressed in a plain cloak and head covering; now I understood.

The paved road made for good travel, and we covered the low rolling hills and stretches of flat fields with ease. The harvest has finished, and many fields are being plowed by man and beast alike. We pass large stands of cedar, giving off a rich fragrance.

I am surprised so few people travel the road. Off to our right, a single high hill rises, looking out of place among the low bluffs. It stands like a ruler overseeing its kingdom.

"That is Karnei Hittin," Mariamme says, seeing my stare. "In ancient times it was a volcano. For me, It Is a sacred place."

"Why is that Mariamme?"

"It is where I first heard Yeshua speak," she paused, "and it is where he healed me."

"Would you mind talking about it?"

"I will never mind talking about something so wonderful," she said. "He had come to this place, and an immense crowd followed him. There was so much talk among them. Some knew him from his home, not far from here, and scorned him. Others from stories about the miracles and healings he had done. Many came out of curiosity and hope. He sat up there," she pointed to a high rock on the side of the mount, "and people covered the entire side of the hill to see and hear him. When he spoke, I will never forget his words. He blessed the meek, the humble and the weary. He spoke of love and compassion, of doing good and not judging others. He said to ask, and you will receive; seek and you will find, and knock and it will be opened. I listened, and I believed. When he came down from the hill, I waited, and he came to me. He never touched me. He looked at me; at my hand and my foot; at my mouth that could not speak, except to blasphemy; and my arms that bore the marks of the ones inside me who wanted me dead. 'Lord, I believe.' I lisped."

'Receive according to your faith daughter,' he said."

"I went home knowing something had touched me. When I woke the next morning, my foot and hand were straight, my mouth was no longer deformed, I could speak clearly, and no spirits raged, telling me to cut myself. I have followed and served him ever since and will continue to do so. Unlike Simon Peter, I do not believe he is here to establish a kingdom. He's here to change the hearts of. . ."

Grabbing my arm, she yanked me back hard. We had turned a sharp bend in the road, and in front of us a group of soldiers were set up alongside the road. There were seven of them. One stood on each side of the road, holding spear and shield while four others relaxed on the ground. The seventh, looked like an officer, and sat on a small folding chair, holding a tablet. A large chestnut horse was tethered to a small tree.

"Toll collectors! That is why the road is so empty today. I should have known," she looked at the perplexed look on my face and answered my unasked question. "They set up randomly along the roads to collect tolls. It is too late now; they've seen us and will come after us if we try to go another way. Just stay calm, and pay whatever they demand."

I glanced at Mark and motioned for him to do nothing.

As we approached, the two guards watched us carefully while the other four snickered and laughed. I've seen nothing glamorous or to like about Rome and its soldiers.

"You travel the Emperor's roads," the one with the tablet said. "The cost is one denarii for each one of you."

While I counted the money out, one of the men sitting on the ground nudged another and nodded towards Mariamme. After paying the toll, we begin walking away.

"Hey, Jew girl! Come over here!"

The shout startles us while the soldier jumps up, charging Mariamme.

"Let's take a look at you!" He yells.

Mark instinctively reached inside his cloak and the two soldiers on guard, instinctively reacted to the disturbance, moving towards us. I grabbed Mark's arm and held up my hand in an effort to defuse the situation.

"We're no threat. We're leaving."

"Stop where you are!" The officer yelled, and the men on the ground struggled to their feet.

The soldier, who started it, grabbed Mariamme's head covering, yanking it off, revealing her face and long hair.

"Whoa! What a beauty we have!"

He grabbed the front of her cloak and began jerking on it.

"Let's see what else she's hiding under there."

Swinging my staff with both hands, I struck him full in the face, sending him sprawling to the ground. He rolled in the dirt, letting out a howl of pain and rage. The officer jumped up, spilling his bag of money and drawing his sword while the guards raised their spears into throwing positions. I knew I had seconds to live.

BOOM! BOOM! BOOM! BOOM!

The explosions shattered the stillness of the air, and both guards flew backwards while their spears sailed in wide misses. The soldier I had struck struggled to his feet. . . .

BOOM! BOOM!

. . .he stopped struggling, looked down at his stomach and collapsed, blood soaking his tunic.

The other three soldiers froze in place, confused and startled, at seeing their comrades bleeding and dying, without anyone touching them.

BOOM! BOOM! BOOM! BOOM!

Two of them crumpled, withering in death. The third, his instinct to survive overcoming his fear, rushed at Mark with drawn sword. Mark pointed a pistol at the soldier and pulled the trigger.

Click Click

Moving backwards, Mark fumbled inside his cloak searching for something. The soldier raised his sword and rushed past me, focused on Mark. Stretching my staff out, I tripped him, sending him sprawling into the dirt. He rolled with the fall, regained his feet and continued charging Mark.

But, the fall had given Mark enough time to pull out his prized dagger. The soldier came at him swinging the sword like a pendulum. Mark dodged, ducked under the arm, embraced the man in a bear hug, thrusting his dagger through the leather amour deep into his chest. Blood and life flowed out of the man in one stream. Mark withdrew the dagger and the soldier slid to the ground.

The officer had mounted his horse and was riding away. In one fluid motion, Mark ejected the empty magazine from the pistol, slammed a new one in and crouched in the classic two-handed, sharpshooter stance, aiming at the receding figure on the horse.

BOOM! BOOM! BOOM! BOOM! BOOM! BOOM! BOOM! BOOM! BOOM! BOOM!

The officer jerked in the saddle, stooped over but continued riding away.

I glance at Mariamme; she knelt on the ground, trembling, in shock as to what was happening. Turning to Mark, I glared at him. Despite knowing he'd just saved my life, I felt the heat rising inside me. He stared back, waiting for the outburst.

It didn't come.

"That's what you've been hiding all this time—a pistol, in a shoulder holster probably."

"No good agent would be without one," he said, and then, gestured at the bodies, "and you better be glad about it too. Another second, you were a dead man."

I wanted to be mad, to shout, to smash his face in (although I knew that was easier said than done after seeing him in action), but I couldn't. He was right. For whatever reason or by whatever destiny was directing us, I certainly would have been dead—again, if Mark hadn't intervened.

"What now?" I ask. "You have the powder; you know the way back, and you have a gun. What happens now, Mark?"

"Nothing," he said. "Look, I've had the gun all along. I could have used it anytime I wanted to. And I've had the powder ever since you were sick.

If I wanted to kill you, I would have. As far as I'm concerned there's no difference now than there was five minutes ago."

"How many rounds do you have?"

"Not many. I only had four, ten-round clips, and I just used two of them."

"You had a lot more than that in those pouches."

"Those were for the rifle, which you so handily destroyed. They're back there, buried in the desert, just like Barosh wanted. They're no good in this pistol."

"You can't just go around shooting up the countryside."

"Would you rather I hadn't?"

I couldn't answer.

"Look, I didn't want to do it. I didn't use it on the bandits, did I? Now, there're only twenty rounds left and the way I figure it we're going to need them to keep those Egyptian sky worshippers away from the Sphinx while we wait for Leo."

He made a good point; they'd be there and wouldn't like us butting in on their festivities. I had to admire Mark for thinking ahead. Apparently he'd done a lot of thinking.

"David," Mariamme spoke, "what is happening? What is that weapon he has, and what is that language you speak? Who are you?"

"We are who we said we were Mariamme, travelers from a far place. A place that speaks that language and has those weapons. That is all."

"I have never heard such a language or of such weapons. You scare me. Do you also have such a thing? How do I know you will not use that weapon on Yeshua?"

"No, Mariamme, I do not have such a weapon. Rabbi Barosh has been with Yeshua for many days, and Yeshua is at ease with him. We are not here to harm him or anyone."

"Their blood speaks otherwise," she pointed at the bodies.

"I am sorry for that," I looked at the ground, where six first century Roman soldiers lay dead by twenty-first century technology.

"We must leave," Mariamme said, "people will come, hearing the noise."

"Should we bury them?" I asked.

"No, the jackals and buzzards will only dig them back up. We should leave and get away from here before we are seen." She looked at Mark, "Can I trust him?"

"You can. He is not a threat to you or to Yeshua. What he did he did to protect you."

"Yes, I know that, and I am grateful, but still I fear him. Come, we must hurry and leave the road now."

She moved off the road, headed into the hills, staying away from Mark. I turned taking one last look behind and stopped dead in my tracks, my heart rose to my mouth.

"What's the matter?" Mark asked.

"He's here," I mumbled under my breath.

Mark followed my gaze across the road to the far hills. "Who is he?" He asked.

I jerked around, staring at him, "You see him?"

"Yeah, he's standing in the open, why wouldn't I? Do you know who he is?"

I turned and stared at the beautiful face in the dark cloak, standing openly on the rocks staring back at me. He wasn't trying to hide his presence any longer. That scared me.

"Yes, I know him," I said, "he's the one who's been trying to kill me. Come on, let's get out of here."

***

The large chestnut stopped running, walking slow; approaching a group of men it felt comfortable with—soldiers.

They pulled the prostrate officer from the horse and examined his wound. Blood drenched the back of his tunic where his leather body armor had plugged a small hole in his back.

As they spread him on the ground, he reached up and grabbed a soldier's tunic, pulling him down to his face.

"Jews," he whispered, "two men. . .woman. . .Zeus's thunder. . . .all dead. . . ."

He died.

22

We enter Nazareth behind a donkey.

It plods along, a high burden of flat bread, tilting precariously, side to side with each step. Each of us plods along as well, loaded down with our own thoughts. I can tell by the occasional glances from Mariamme she is trying to figure out who (or what) we are, and if we can be trusted.

On the other hand, I sense a feeling of freedom from Mark, now that his big secret is out, and once again, he's a 'hero'.

My thoughts are simple: who (or what) is the beautiful man, and why is he intent on killing me?

Nazareth is small, a tiny speck on the landscape of Galilee; locked away, deep in the hills surrounding a wide, yawning valley, distinguished by dense oak forests. It is a good location for a carpenter and his sons.

The buildings are single story and of stone-mud construction, with thatched reed roofs. Many buildings have had a coating of plaster on them at one time, although most are in need of a new one. A communal courtyard containing a well, an olive press and a row of ovens, dominates the village. Women are drawing water and baking bread, and a large group is gathered at the olive press.

Olives are the heart of Israel. Unlike most produce trees, they stay green year round and produce fruit every year. The first harvest is collected in cloths as they beat the trees with sticks. This 'beaten oil' is sacred and is taken to Jerusalem to be burned in the menorah at the temple.

I watch as the stone wheel mashes the olives into a pulp, and the oil is separated into vats by purity. The purest is given to the priests; the remainder separated for cooking, heating and burning in lamps while the sludge will be used for balms, soaps and medicines. Nothing is wasted, and it's a time of community togetherness.

A dirt road runs down the middle of the village where a number of shops and stalls scratch out a meager living. At the center of the street, a small synagogue stands. I hear the children inside, reciting the rhyming verses of the Psalms.

It's hard to believe from this insignificant, backward village comes the world's most influential man who ever lived.

People notice us as we walk through the village. Mariamme opens her headpiece so that they can recognize her, and it satisfies their concerns.

"They are cautious," she explains, "they worry we could be spies."

"Spies?" I ask. "For who?"

"For the Sanhedrin—for Herod—for the Romans. Even the Zealots and the Sicarii keep their eye on Yeshua. He arouses much attention, and they all spy on him, looking for something to accuse him of or some weakness to exploit. Mariam says many strange faces visit Nazareth since he has gone forth."

"That must be hard on her."

"Being the mother of Yeshua comes at a heavy cost. Joseph was her strength, and since he was killed, she has had to endure the trials and scorn alone. She finds comfort in her children."

"Who scorns her, and why? I thought Yeshua was revered."

Mariamme looks at me in surprise, "You truly are from far away David. Yeshua is *my* master and to those who follow him. There are many who do not accept him or his teachings. These people here reject him, saying he's only the carpenter's son. His brothers reject him."

"You said thousands follow him."

"When they want something, to be healed, fed or to hear pleasant things. Once their stomachs are filled and their sicknesses healed, and the Pharisees come around, they fade away. Israel has had many holy men David. What is one more, unless he gives them something?"

Stopping in front of a doorway, she turns to Mark and looks at him hard. "I don't know who you are or where you come from, but I know you are a dangerous man. If you mean to do harm to Yeshua, then you will have to kill me also."

Before I can translate what she said, Mark answers her. It's slow, disjointed and not every word is correct, but he speaks.

"I. . .hurt. . .not. . .Yeshua."

Reaching under his cloak, he pulls out the pistol. Mariamme jumps back in fright. He holds up his hand to calm her and ejects the magazine from the pistol. He works the pistol's action showing there is nothing in the chamber. He hands it to me, and I gingerly take it. He holds his open hands out to Mariamme. I am sure she doesn't understand any of it, but he's made his point. Mariamme looks at me; I tuck the pistol away and nod that it is okay.

She knocks on the door.

***

The door is opened by a young woman of Mariamme's age.

"Shalom aleikhem, may I. . . .Mariamme! Shalom! How are you?"

"Shalom Ruth, I am well thank God. I trust you are well?"

"Yes, yes, please enter. Mother is at the press. I will send for her."

The interior is plain but clean. The walls are plastered, and the floor is stone. Tapestries hang across two doorways leading to back rooms. A long, low table accompanied by seven stools dominates the room. Oil lamps hang on each wall, and wooden shelves hold various stone cups, mugs, bowls and storage vats.

We follow Ruth through a doorway, across a room lined with large, covered stone vats and various baskets and pouches filled with clothing and household items, into a large room where the smell of fresh wood mingles with oil. A bearded man is working an adz along the smooth curves of a plow yoke. He stops as we enter. When he sees Mariamme, he bristles.

"He's not here."

"Shalom James. Have you lost your manners? I have guests with me."

"More friends of Yeshua I suppose. As I said, he is not here."

"James, I am embarrassed for you. You would not speak so if your father were here. Apologize."

The voice is soft, feminine yet strong and firm. I turn in its direction, and a woman stands in the doorway. She wears a blue, sleeveless mantle over a grey, cotton tunic. Her once dark hair is streaked and sprinkled with grey and is tied up under her shawl. She is slender; her face bears the lines of age and her hands the years of work, but her eyes shine with understanding and compassion. A shroud of calm surrounds her.

"Forgive me mother. Shalom Aleikhem, Mariamme." James says and turns to Mark and me and repeats the greeting.

"Shalom Mariam, it is so good to see you again." Mariamme hugs her, kissing her on the cheek. Stepping back she motions to us, "These are friends of Rabbi Bar Barosh who accompanies Yeshua."

"Shalom Mariam, I am David. . . ."

"Bar Kalaid ha-Rav. Yes, I know. Rabbi Barosh told me you would be coming. Please forgive my son for his rudeness. Ruth, would you prepare refreshments for our guests?"

"Yes mother."

"James, please join us."

"Yes mother."

She leads us back into the main room and motions for us to be seated. Another young woman comes in carrying a stone bowl, a pitcher of water and a towel. She kneels in front of me and begins removing my sandal.

"No, please, you don't. . . .," I start protesting, but Mariamme cuts me off.

"David, this is Elizabeth, Yeshua's sister. She shows you honor. Do not deny her that." Removing my sandals, she places one foot at a time into the bowl, pours water over them, washes and dries them. She repeats the process for Mark and Mariamme. By the time she's finished, Ruth has brought in a small tray of food and wine. James has also joined us.

"Yeshua is not here," Mariam says, "he left yesterday, returning to Capernaum."

What? My mind races. *What kind of wild goose chase is Barosh playing? We just came from there!*

"Rabbi Barosh is not with him."

"Then where is he?" I ask, rudely.

"I do not know, David. Yeshua sent him away and did not tell me where."

I sit stunned. How was I going to find him? He could be anywhere. What was I supposed to do now?

"Don't feel alone; that's what he does," James smirks. "Turns everything upside down and then walks away, leaving a mess behind."

"James! Stop such talk."

"I speak only the truth mother. Someday you will see that."

"It is you, my son, who someday will see the truth of your brother."

"The only truth I know is we are here working to pay the Roman tax while he is running around the country playing messiah. All my friends laugh at us because of him."

"Then they are not friends. Now that is enough." She turns to me.

"Rabbi Barosh said he would meet you in Jerusalem. You should return to the same inn you stayed at before, and wait for him there. He has something to do first. And Yeshua told me to tell you that he will see you when the time arrives. He told me to answer any questions you have of me."

When the time arrives? What does that mean? Any questions? Where do you begin asking questions of the mother of Jesus?

"Blessed. . . .are. . .you. . .among. . .women."

The words come staggered, and they amaze me. It is Mark who has spoken.

His face is enraptured, transfixed on Mary. I am stunned and confused at the same time. Mark is a hard, cynical man; I've watched him kill, efficiently and without any sense of remorse. What was happening?

I think of his Catholic upbringing and wondered if their veneration of the 'Mother Mary' has affected him. A twenty-first century Catholic was sitting next to the Holy Madonna. Hardened killer or not, I guess I could understand his reaction. I only hope he doesn't break out a rosary and start reciting 'Hail Mary's'.

"I am but a vessel; Yeshua is the wine, but I thank you for your kindness." She turns to me.

"David, what would you want to ask me? Your friend, Rabbi Barosh, asked me many questions."

"Then it would be rude of me to do so again."

"Then ask me instead," James interrupts, "I will tell you about my bother—the 'messiah'."

"You do not like your brother?" I ask.

"Like? That is the wrong word. He is my brother, and I do not dislike him. But I do not respect what he has done to our family."

"What has he done?"

"He's made us the laughing stock of Galilee, that's what he has done! He has caused my mother shame and undue grief!"

"James, I suffer no shame or grief for Yeshua. Any shame in Nazareth is on the people who scorn him, when he does only good to them. I hold my head high to be his mother as should you, to be his brother."

"My father was killed because of him."

"Your father was killed by Roman soldiers, and he was given to them by Menahem, a fellow Galilean, who had him murdered for his own selfish cause."

James jumps to his feet, "I have work to do, shalom to you." He storms out of the room before anyone can say anything.

"Forgive him; it has been difficult for him, and he does not understand. His ability to see the 'messiah' is clouded by his seeing the 'brother'."

"I am sorry about your husband, Mariam. The circumstances of Yeshua's birth must have been very hard on him." I closely watch her face, looking for any sign of betrayal or remorse.

"Thank you," she replied, "but you are mistaken, Yosef was a good man, and he welcomed the birth of Yeshua." She looks at me, leaving no doubt as to her understanding of the question.

"Yosef knew who Yeshua was and where he came from. He was honored to raise him. Yosef was chosen by God, and he feared God in all he did. What would you like to ask me David?"

"Mariam, I have only one question for you if that is agreeable with you."

"Please ask David."

"Mariam, do you believe Yeshua is god?"

"No, I do not believe that, David; I know. Yeshua is the Son of God. I conceived him by the power of God. I have heard from his messenger, as did my husband. I know he will suffer greatly, and I also know because of his suffering, he will be the salvation for all the world, to all people. I know he is on this earth for a much greater purpose than to only free us from the Romans. He is here to reunite mankind with God. Yes, David, Yeshua is God."

***

Mariam directed us to a house that served as an inn where Mark and I could stay for the night. Mariamme would stay with her. When we were ready to leave, they walked us out.

"I will be traveling to Capernaum on the morning," Mariamme said.

"Is it safe for you to travel alone?" I asked.

"Do not worry for me David, I will follow the back roads and avoid the main road. Once I reach the Sea, there will be no danger to me. It is you who must be careful."

"We will be Mariamme. Thank you for your kindness and assistance."

"May God go with you David." Squeezing my hand, she looks at Mark, more confused than before.

"And with you also Mark," she steps back as Mariam approaches us.

"Shalom be with you Mark; may the blessings of God go with you." She turns to me and takes my hand in hers. It is warm and soft, yet the grip is surprisingly strong.

"Be strong David Bar Kalaid ha-Rav. May you have the strength to accept God when He calls upon you." She squeezes my hand tight, "I will see you at that time."

***

That night, Mark and I are quiet; each lost in thought.
Mark doesn't ask for the gun.

23

I leave Nazareth in a sourly mood.

Running all over Israel, chasing after Barosh, while he tramped around with Jesus was bad enough. Being told to go back to Jerusalem without knowing what he was doing, was downright irritating, to say the least. How long would he be? How would I know if he was in trouble or not?

Too many questions—too many unknowns. And it disturbed me that he didn't seem concerned about me, or how I was making out with Mark on my own.

"I'll take my gun now," Mark said.

He inserted the magazine into the handle, chambered a round, put the safety on, and holstered it under his arm.

"What is it, anyway?" I ask.

"It's a modified Beretta Px4 Storm, Special Duty .45. You know anything about firearms?"

"Not really, just wondering. I wish you hadn't had to use it."

"I didn't want to, but we weren't going to beat seven armed soldiers with our staffs. There wasn't any other choice."

"I know, but it scares me. There's so much we don't know about this time travel."

"Tell me about it; I'm still trying to figure out how I got here. Don't worry; I'm not trigger happy. I need to keep what's left for the Sphinx. I wasted a whole clip trying to stop that guy from getting away."

"You hit him."

"Yeah, but if he survived, he'll identify us."

"Let's hope he didn't."

"Do you know how to get to Jerusalem from here?"

"Somewhat, it shouldn't be hard to find. Nazareth is around 70 miles north of Jerusalem. We'll follow these trails going south, and the closer we get, it should become clear. We're entering the Plain of Esdraelon now. Do you know what that is?"

"No."

"It's the valley of Megiddo. It's where all the gloom and doom folks say the battle of Armageddon will happen."

"Apocalypse now," Mark laughs. "You seem to know the geography and history. Did some studying, did you?"

"Yeah, those weeks when you sat out there trying to listen. If I'd known you'd be coming along, I'd have passed a few books your way."

"Probably would have been more exciting than sitting out there with stone face Rodgers."

"You ever think about him?"

"Sometimes. He's probably in hot water. You know; I was going to shoot you back in Athens."

"Glad you didn't."

"Sorry, anyway. They'll be putting the professor through the wringer."

"We've been here for a while, should be over by now," I say. "Of course, it hasn't happened yet, not for another two-thousand years. You could go crazy trying to figure it out. Don't worry about the professor; he'll be okay; he's a tough old bird, and it'll be worth it when it's over; I left him a calling card."

"Those pitchers you buried back there?"

"No—a tea cup and I still need to leave one more before it's finished. Boggles the mind, doesn't it? All the things we've done—haven't happened yet. Just think of the story you'll have when you get back. You'll be the hit of the talk shows."

"Well, you too."

I smile; there remains a few secrets he does not need to know.

"What's going on with your pal, Barosh? What's he doing anyway?"

"I wish I knew. But guys like him are like bloodhounds. Once they're on a scent, nothing else exists."

***

We stop in a small village called Nain, where we buy a loaf of bread and some salted fish. Washing it down with a weak, bland wine, I over hear two men arguing close to us.

"I tell you, I was there, and I saw it with my own eyes!"

"You drink too much wine, is what I think, my friend."

"Say what you want, but I know. And not only me, there were many who saw it."

"Well, there was a mistake, and he was not dead."

"Then he must have been able to hold his breath for two days! Listen, the boy was dead! We were burying him! He was prepared for the tomb. Then Yeshua walks up, takes hold of his hand and tells him to get up—and he did!"

"If this Yeshua has such powers, why is he not using them to free us from these Romans?"

"He will. We wait for his call. Be alert my friend, for when the day comes, we must be prepared to join with him."

"We cannot kill Roman soldiers!"

"With him, we can! The hosts of God will come down and destroy the Romans. Spread the word and be ready, the day approaches."

***

Skirting Mount Gilboa, there is little traffic on the narrow roads. The hills are covered with wildflowers, creating a living canvas of reds, yellows and blues. Sabra cactuses are sprinkled amongst the cypress and carob trees, swathing the hillsides. Almond trees have ripened with full masts of fruit. Asphodels and cyclamen emerge on rocky hillsides, waving in the warm breezes, straining their faces to thank the sun. Birds, butterflies and bees flutter and hover among them.

I understood why people love this land as much as they do. As barren and desolate as the wildernesses are, the valleys and hills abound with richness and vitality, unlike any other.

We hadn't seen a village in quite some time after leaving Nain, when we come upon a large stand of trees where impromptu shelters and tents are set up for travelers to rest. We decide to spend the night there.

Settling in, there's a buzz in the camp. Men are talking in low, excited voices. They move from group to group, spreading and seeking new information. A man approaches us.

"Shalom, may I sit with you?"

"Peace be with you. Please sit."

"Thank you, my name is Chandrah. I come from Tyre and travel to Jerusalem. From where do you come friends?"

"We journey from afar, from beyond the Nile."

"And do you travel to Jerusalem?"

"We do."

"Then you should travel with us. It is safer in greater numbers. The Romans are everywhere, seeking the prophets."

"Prophets? What prophets? Why do they seek prophets?"

"For revenge. Have you not heard of the massacre?"

"Massacre? What massacre?"

"On the road to Tiberius. Seven soldiers, collecting tolls, were killed. The Romans say a large band of Zealots attacked them, but it is known that the prophets killed them."

"Did someone see it?"

"There were travelers, who saw it. They saw three persons, who killed the soldiers by only pointing at them! They called on the power of God, and God brought thunder down and stuck them dead."

"Maybe these men were Zealots, and the travelers are confused."

"There is no confusion, friend. The soldiers attacked, and they died without being touched. One tried to escape on a horse, but the prophet knelt and pointed at him and the thunder came and he fell in the saddle! They are from God and are prophets or angels. They just walked away, leaving everything. Zealots would have stripped the soldiers of their weapons, armor, and the toll money they collected."

Chandrah finished talking, staring at me intently. I take a deep drink, buying time to calm my beating heart.

"Where do people think these prophets went?"

"Jerusalem, of course! That's where we are all going, to meet them and share in the triumph. The kingdom is being restored! The Romans are being destroyed!" He stood up.

"The messiah has come! Rejoice pilgrim! The time of Rome is finished! We all travel to Jerusalem to be there and greet him!"

He returned to his place next to a large tree, where he sat, watching us carefully.

"How much of that did you understand?" I asked Mark.

"Enough to know it's not good."

When I'd finished explaining it, we sat in silence for a long time. I was scared. Not only of the Romans but this is exactly what Allen and everyone had feared. We were impacting the events and becoming part of the history of the era. We had to extricate ourselves, now before it escalated. How do I stop history?

"Other than getting killed by a Roman sword, what're your concerns?" Mark asked.

"Something called a time paradox. It's a theory of how time travel could cause world history to unravel. Have you ever heard of it?"

"Vaguely. Lay it out for me." I explained it to him, and he picked up on it quick.

"Yeah, I remember hearing about that stuff. It was all science fiction," he said. "If someone is killed who's not supposed to be, then everything that happened after him is nullified."

"Pretty much, and everything unravels, and the universe self-destructs."

"If things were going to unravel, shouldn't it have happened already? Back at the pyramids or on that road?"

"Maybe—maybe not. I don't know; that's the issue; no one does. Could be, you only killed people who died in history without leaving any kids or anything to unravel. But suppose that officer was supposed to become the next emperor? At what point does a paradox occur? I don't know. Allen said history is fixed, and it cannot be changed. Hopefully, he's right. I only know it was easy for him to talk about it back there, but he's not here; we are."

"Well then it just means we have to get back to Egypt, and the Sphinx, so we can get back to where we belong before we do something wrong."

"True, but we have to wait for spring when the gate opens." I didn't want to tell him about Allen's problem with manipulating the gate. No point in rocking that boat. "But there's another problem."

"What's that?"

"In all my studying I did not come across any revolution that occurred during Jesus' life. There was one before and one after, but none during. And none involving prophets or angels."

"Well, that's because there are no prophets."

"That's my point. We know that—these people do not. They see prophets, and their long-awaited messiah, and they're moving towards a revolution that never happened."

"Meaning?"

"Meaning we're caught in a catch-22. Either we're going to unravel history, or for history to remain intact, these 'prophets' had to have disappeared before it got started."

"Yeah, okay, that's cool, like I said we go home and disappear."

"Maybe, or. . . ."

"Or what?"

"Or. . .the prophets die."

We're quiet for a long time. The man by the tree is watching us.

"What now?" Mark asks.

"I wish I knew. Him and his buddies are suspicious of us. First thing we need to do is get out from under their scrutiny. Tonight, while everyone is asleep, let's slip away. We need to avoid people. They're looking for two or three strange men traveling together; that makes us suspects. I don't know about going to Jerusalem."

"But that's where we're supposed to meet Barosh."

"I know."

***

Staying off the roads, traveling the hills and woodlots, avoiding towns and villages, our travel is slow, and it takes us a number of days to cover the distance to Jerusalem.

Activity has increased, most of it being men in groups ranging upwards of ten and more, traveling to Jerusalem.

Roman soldiers are moving as well. Stationed at various locations around villages, they are in groups of no less than ten and upwards of fifty and more. They're fully armed, looking mean and spoiling for a fight. They're clearly not happy about any 'prophets' bringing the 'thunder of God' down on their comrades.

The Jews avoid the soldiers, taking wide berths around them, but not lowering their heads as usual. Instead, they walk heads held high, looking at them derisively, almost in a challenging mode.

The soldiers swagger, proud, arrogant, feet stomping out the strong cadence of battle hardened men, itching for an excuse to lash out. The air is charged with tension, crackling and sizzling, ready to erupt.

***

"Wish I had my binoculars now," Mark says squinting.

We're sitting inside a tree line, on a hill giving us a view of Jerusalem. Pilgrims, travelers, merchants and residents move about like ants on an anthill. We could blend in with them easily, but there are squads of soldiers stationed at each gate, checking everyone who enters. I don't think we could slip by them.

The Sabbath is approaching, and the shofars sound, warning people that dusk is almost here. People hurry to where they need to be. Soon all travel and movement will stop, except for the gentiles. We need to get settled for the night because we wouldn't be able to travel much after that. Two Jewish pilgrims, traveling on the Sabbath, would attract everyone's attention, Jew and Roman alike.

A large group of men has gathered just outside the city's south gate, making camp there. There are three or four hundred men in the group, and I have a thought of joining them to blend in, but quickly dismiss it when I recall the way the man at the last camp had watched us.

We stay in the tree line where we have good cover on three sides and a clear view of the city on the other. If any soldiers are going to come, we want to see them first. We have food and water, so we'll just settle in, rest and wait the Sabbath out while figuring out what our next step will be.

Where is Barosh when I need him?

24

It was once asked of the Chief Pharisee if, on the Sabbath, one might cover a scorpion with a pot, to prevent its sting. No, the Pharisee answered, that was too much like hunting, and hunting is forbidden on the Sabbath.

Thus did the people drown in the ever widening ocean of oral traditions and interpretations of the Torah and Mishnah that comprised the Talmud.

The sixth day of the week came to a close, heralded by a single, long blast of shofars blown from the temple walls. Work and travel stopped.

In homes across Israel, mothers lit the clay Sabbath lamps, inviting God's spirit into the house for the next 24 hours. Families gathered around tables or sat on the floor while fathers pronounced the blessing and broke bread, and then spoke the Shema and told the stories of Israel's glory to their sons and daughters.

The change in the city is astounding. The residents of the city are in their houses; thousands of travelers and pilgrims are holed up; the merchant's shops are closed; no children play or run the streets. Only goats, dogs and beggars wander about.

In the morning, they will gather in the Temple or local synagogue to listen to the readings from the sacred Torah scrolls, written in the ink of plants and minerals.

The Jews rested on the Sabbath. . .

. . .the Romans didn't.

***

Passing before me in rapid succession, they come down from the heavens one moment and out of the earth the next.

Giants—striding the earth—flying through the heavens—having the bodies of men and the heads of beasts—bears—eagles—crocodiles. They bellow, roar, snarl and howl. Behind them, spreading across the horizon, the beautiful one rises: his face dark and brooding, eyes unblinking, unwavering. . .

"David, wake up! Something's going on."

The beautiful face smiles—an evil smile—a sneer. The eyes narrowing into slits, turn orange; the mouth opens; blood drips, falling to the earth.

"Their blood is on you!"

"David! Come on, wake up!"

I am being shaken, hard. My eyes open; it isn't the face of the dark one looking at me—it's Mark. His face is excited—and scared. Brushing the images from my mind, I hear the words coming from him.

". . .get up; there's something going down. . .come on. . .hurry. . .look at the city. . ."

"What? What is it?"

The pre-dawn is just beginning to diffuse the darkness of the night, and the city is still and calm in the early glow.

"Over there," he points, "at that upper gate. See them?"

Clearing my head and directing my gaze to the upper wall, I see movement in the shadows. It's the glint of armor and spears in the torch light.

"Yeah, I see them, looks like soldiers going out on a patrol."

"It's more than a patrol. Look at the bottom gate."

Redirecting my gaze to the eastern wall, I see the silhouettes of a second line of soldiers going out that gate. I guess there are fifty or more in each group. Both groups pass through the gates, turn and head south.

"What's going on?"

"If I had to guess, I'd say they're setting a trap."

"A trap? For who?"

"For that group camped outside the walls."

We watch the lines of soldiers move past the sleeping men, one above and one below. Once the lead soldier of each line is beyond the camp, they turn and start moving towards one another until they meet. The encampment is now completely surrounded. The soldiers face inward, forming a continuous line with their shields and spears.

"Are they going to attack those men?"

"No – not them, they cut off the retreat."

"Retreat? From what?"

"From them!" Mark says, pointing to the Antonia Fortress, where another group of soldiers is moving quickly through the city to the south gate. This group carries no spears or shields – only swords.

"Oh my God! Why?"

"You know why, as well as I do; they're going to stamp out this 'prophet' uprising before it gets going."

"This is because of us?"

Where are Herod and his soldiers to protect his people? Looking at Herod's Palace, the walls are bare. The ever present guards are—absent. *Their blood is on you!*

"We must warn them!" I yell, standing up. Mark grabs my cloak, pulling me back down.

"It's too late. By the time, we get there; it'll be over. Besides, unless you got my rifle under your cloak, there's nothing we could do."

"Maybe they're just going to arrest them and question them."

"Yeah, and maybe I'm the tooth fairy."

The soldiers pass through the gate and form into a tight line. They are precise and disciplined. There's no shouting, no confusion and no rushing.

Men begin stirring in the encampment. They move about in confusion, shaking one another awake. At the sight of the soldiers, fear displaces their confusion and panic ripples through the camp. Within seconds, the entire encampment is on its feet. We hear the voices of fear and panic carrying on the morning's breeze. The soldiers stand, not moving as if waiting for everyone to wake up.

Dawn has fully broken in a golden-orange crescent, igniting treetops and spreading across the horizon. A harbinger of what is to come?

I watch in horror as the line of soldiers draw their swords, and begin advancing on the camp of men. A man steps forward, raising his arms, trying to reason with the soldiers. He shakes his head back and forth, gesturing they have no weapons and are peaceful.

The flash of the blade is quick and accurate. Blood sprays as the man's head lops sideways, and the body collapses to the ground.

Panic breaks loose. The line of soldiers advances, swords slashing and stabbing. Bodies drop and fall on top of one another. Some draw swords from under their cloaks and attempt to fight back. They are no match for the Romans. The men turn, trying to escape, only to run into the wall of Roman spears. Efficient and brutal, it's bloodier than ever portrayed on a screen.

No one escapes, and the screams shatter the Shabbat's dawn. Lights are extinguished inside of houses.

As Mark predicted, it's over before it began. Hundreds of men lie dead. The ground is a red carpet covered with the dead and dying.

A few are kept alive, taken away to the garrison, where they will be tortured to disclose the identity of the 'prophets'.

Soldiers pick through the bodies, taking whatever spoils are there. Short, swift thrusts of swords dispatch those bodies that move.

Within the walls of the city, Jews tremble in darkness, behind closed doors.

***

I am in shock. We had witnessed a massacre. A merciless spectacle of death, by a military power focused on maintaining its standard of living on the backs of the people. An unrecorded footnote in the bloody history of a brutal empire. Hundreds of defenseless men butchered in open view of an entire city, with no twangs of remorse.

And. . .I am responsible.

I am sick and disgusted with myself, my existence. All the reasons for being here are washed away by the blood soaking that ground. Who do I think I am to think I can play games with history? These are people, regardless of what century it is. Coming here was wrong. The beautiful man knew that, but I was too arrogant to listen.

"It's not our fault," Mark says. "There was nothing we could have done."

"I shouldn't be here. It's not natural, not part of nature's way. I'm a disturbance, a dirty wind blowing across their already barren existence."

"A little melodramatic, don't you think? What just happened is nothing new David. Governments, armies and nations, have been slaughtering and butchering one another ever since the beginning of time. This was going to happen whether we were here or not; it was only a matter of time."

Time—everything was only a matter of time.

"If you need to blame someone, then blame that snake in the garden."

Snake in the garden. I thought about the beautiful man with the dead eyes, whose face had merged with mine and turned into a snake, and although I refuse to believe in a devil with horns and a pitchfork, I couldn't help but draw a connection between the two. He was so real! On my sickbed, and in my head, and Mark had seen. . . .

CRACK! A branch snapped.

We both jump and turn around at the sound. Behind us stand a dozen men. Mark instinctively reaches into his cloak and withdraws his pistol.

"No! Shalom! Peace!" The lead man yells, holding up his hands. "Do not kill us!"

Grabbing Mark's arm, I hold it back, shaking my head.

"What do you want?" I ask.

"We seek the 'prophets'."

They're Jews, not Romans, dressed to travel light and fast. They have swords around their waist, and some carry spears and small round shields. They are lean and muscular. The man who spoke is weathered and scarred, tough and hard looking.

"Why do you seek them?" I ask.

"We wish to join with them. They have the power of God."

"Who are you?"

"I am Barabbas Ben Judah, son of Menahem the Galilean." He motions to the men next to him, "This is Azir'el Macabi, and this is Caleb, my son. We fight for Israel."

Barabbas, son of Menahem—the killer of Joseph – Yeshua's father. Is he the Barabbas of 'Give us Barabbas'? Could it be possible they are the same? Why not? I think.

"Are you the 'prophets'?" He asks.

"Did you see what happened there?" I point to Jerusalem.

"You must not stay here. It is not safe. Roman patrols search the villages, hills and valleys looking for you. Come with us where it will be safe."

I turn to Mark and explain what was said. "What do you think?" I ask.

"I don't see a choice. We can't get into Jerusalem, and they'll find us here."

Hearing Mark speak, Barabbas grows excited. "It is the language of heaven they speak!"

"We will go with you," I say.

"We are honored; let us go."

25

Traveling fast, we cut across the dense forested hills and fertile valleys around Jerusalem and enter a barren wilderness. Being the Sabbath, no one stirs in the fields, and we avoid villages. Apparently, the Sabbath has little meaning to Barabbas.

The only person we see is a solitary shepherd boy, tending his flock and practicing with his sling. Perhaps he was recalling David the shepherd boy who killed the giant Goliath with a single stone from his sling. He watches us pass by.

Stopping at a small village, Barabbas tells us to top off our water skins. As we fill the skins from a deep well, I notice a strange looking mound in the distance to our left. It's a perfectly symmetrical cone, rising like a volcano. Along the side is a spiral stairway of white steps leading to the top that is crowned with a ring of towers and splendid looking buildings.

"Herod's grave," Barabbas says, following my gaze, "he built it, and he is buried in it. It was a grand procession. I was a child and watched with my father. Herod's body was draped in purple and gold, with a crown of gold on his head and a gold scepter in his hands. The bier was gold and studded with jewels. It sparkled and glittered in the sun and was followed by hundreds of slaves carrying incense. My father almost killed Herod once and always looked for the opportunity to try again. He was glad he was dead, but regretted it wasn't him who had killed him," he spat noisily. "May he rot in hell."

Behind us is the village of Bethlehem.

It is ironic that the king, who killed the babies in Bethlehem was himself, now buried here.

***

Once again I am struck by the rapid change in the land. This wilderness, so close to the richness of Jerusalem, is intimidating and hostile. There are no trees, no undergrowth and no vegetation. It is desolate and bleak with barren hills as far as I can see. The heat is magnified by the baking hills and reflects back from the sterile surfaces.

"The Wilderness of Judea," Barabbas says, looking out across barren emptiness as far as can be seen.

Crossing the stark hills, I don't think it's possible for land to be any more inhospitable. The hills lose their greyish color, along with their roundness, and become jagged ridges and steep cliffs of hard, tannish rock.

I smell water, but it's not a clean scent, having a flat, stale taste to it.

Cresting a high ridge, there below me lays the bluest body of water I've ever seen. It's a strange blue, deep, without being blackish. It smells of salt, and jagged lines of the dried, white material line the shore, like a miniature mountain range. It's the Dead Sea, the saltiest body of water in the world. I had seen it in 1982 and seeing it again, two-thousand years *'earlier'*, I knew it wouldn't change much, even though everything around it would. Where there are rocks and bizarre salt sculptures, there will be hotels, restaurants, condominiums and beaches packed with tourists covered in the black, 'healing' mud or floating like inflated balloons on the dead buoyant water.

"Yām ha-Māvet – the Sea of Salt," Barabbas says. "The prophet Ezekiel prophesized that someday the waters would, '. . . *be healed and made fresh'*. A prophet will come and touch the water with his staff, and the sea will bring forth new life." He looks at me in an expectant way.

"I am not that prophet," I say.

"Come," he says.

***

Cresting another steep cliff, we come face to face with a wall of stone, perforated by a labyrinth of caves. We follow Barabbas into a large cave, where it opens into a network of caves. Women huddle around communal fires and ovens baking bread and cooking stew. Children play chasing one another between the caves.

As we enter, everyone stops and stares at us.

"I bring the prophets," Barabbas announces.

"We are not prophets," I say annoyed, but he ignores me, and many of the people break into praise to God.

"You will be safe here," he turns and greets his followers. Mark and I find a corner in the shadows and sit down. No one approaches us.

"What now?" Mark asks.

"I don't know. Everything is upside down. We're being hunted by the Roman army; these people think we're prophets come down from heaven to save them; the followers of Jesus are scared of us; we caused a massacre; we don't know where Barosh is, and worse, we don't know if he's aware of the danger he's in. Has he heard about what happened on the road from Tiberius? Does he know about the massacre? Is he in Jerusalem, waiting for us? Or is he in a Roman prison? How did it get so messed up? We were supposed to keep our noses out of things."

"I suppose you blame me."

"No, I don't blame you. You did what you had to. If you hadn't, we'd be dead. If there's any blame to place, it's on us for being so arrogant to think we could tamper with time and history."

"Well, none of that matters now; we're here, and we need to get back. That's all I know. I say we start heading to Egypt."

"And leave Barosh here? If that's what you want, I won't stop you, but you'll go alone. I'm not going anywhere until I find Barosh."

"I figured you'd say that."

***

Later that night, we watch the last rays of the sun recede behind the stark hills as the blackness of night settles over the Dead Sea. My mind grapples with the threads of events, trying to weave our next step. Hearing footsteps on the loose rock, we turn to see Barabbas and some of his men approaching us.

"Shalom. May we speak with you?" He asks.

I nod, and motion for him to sit.

"Can you tell us what you will do?"

I thought long and hard before answering.

"There is a man named Yeshua; you know of him?"

"Yes, we know Yeshua. What of him?"

"We have a companion. His name is Rabbi Ben Barosh, and he travels with Yeshua and is now missing. We seek him."

"What does he have to do with Yeshua?"

"That is not for you to know."

He bristled, not liking my answer.

"Yeshua fancies himself as the messiah. Have you come to proclaim him as king of Israel?"

"Yeshua is not our concern; we seek Rabbi Ben Barosh."

"Is Rabbi Ben Barosh the messiah then? Has he come to proclaim himself as king of Israel? Does he possess the thunder that strikes down the enemies of Israel?"

"You ask many questions Barabbas, son of Menahem. Can you not answer mine?"

Again he bristled. It was clear I wasn't making any friends here, but I thought it best to keep him on the defensive and guessing, so he'd be willing to help me find Barosh.

"We seek to be free of the Roman swine," Barabbas says, "I am Sicarii. The Zealots travel with us because we both wish to kill Romans. If you and Rabbi Ben Barosh have come to free us from them, we will stand with you. We know what you did on the road to Tiberius. You say you are not prophets, yet we know you have great power. I have seen your 'thunder' rod. I think maybe your Rabbi Ben Barosh is the prophet, and you are guardians to protect him." He turns to his companions, and they speak too low and fast for me to follow. He turns back.

"Yeshua travels Galilee. We will find the prophet. You are welcome to remain here as our guests."

After they'd left, Mark asks me, "What's Sicarii?"

"Assassins, consider them Jewish ninjas."

"You're kidding."

"No. They're called the 'dagger men'. They sneak in and slide a dagger into their targets chest and slip away before anyone knows it's happened. They're extremely dangerous people. We must be very careful."

"It doesn't end," Mark sighs.

26

“We can't wait much longer David; time is short. We need to cross the Sinai and get back to Egypt.”

Mark was becoming paranoid about leaving. I feel dirty, holding out about the uncertainty of Allen's time gate. I haven't been able to bring myself to tell him, not knowing how he'd handle it. He spoke of going back as if it was a feat accomplished.

I will not go anywhere without Barosh. Common sense tells me he is dead. I hang onto that slim hope that somewhere, somehow he is alive. But Mark is right. If he's going to catch the Leo Express out of here, he needs to head to the station.

***

Leaving the labyrinth of the caves, I walk among the ridges following the shore of the Dead Sea. Weeks have turned into months while they hunted for Barosh. With communication no faster than the speed of walking, I'm learning things do not happen very fast. What would take a five-minute phone call in the twenty-first century, takes two weeks here.

They had found Jesus easy enough, but Barosh was not with him.

They followed Jesus and reported back on his every move, but they hadn't located the rabbi. Barabbas sent people to the inn we had stayed at, and it did not appear Barosh had made it back to Jerusalem. Had he gotten picked up by the Romans, or could he have gotten caught in the slaughter outside the gate? I couldn't bear the thought of him killed in the carnage I caused.

There's a new report on Jesus every week. One report is that he spoke to a crowd of thousands and fed them all. The two men who reported this said they were there and ate as well, but they didn't know where the food had come from. No one had gone to bring such large amounts to feed thousands; yet everyone ate their fill.

There are reports of healings and miracles. People come, from far distances, to be healed. Barabbas isn't moved by these reports.

"Israel has many healers using tricks and magic to deceive these ignorant fools. The messiah does not come to cleanse lepers, but to free us from Rome and establish the kingdom of Israel."

One day, they reported Jesus was in Samaria teaching people there. This resulted in contempt from Barabbas.

"The messiah is not for the likes of them," Barabbas spat. "Samaritans! Might as well teach dogs! This proves Yeshua is false. He is hungry for followers."

"Even his disciples complain about this. There was great discord among them. Many followers left," Azir'el Macabi said.

"As they should, you cannot proclaim yourself the messiah of Israel and eat with dogs," Caleb added.

"He is but dog himself," Azir'el Macabi said, "the bastard son of the whore Mariam. Those who know say it was a Roman soldier who fathered him."

I jumped up, grabbing him by the cloak. His face went white with fright.

"No, do not kill me! Please, do not use the thunder!" He cried while Barabbas shrunk back in fear.

Releasing him, they moved away, mumbling among themselves. I could care less about the Samaritans, but I had met Mary, and she is no whore.

***

Looking across the ridge, I see more caves in the distance. Men move about the inside of them. I wonder who they are and what they are doing. I start making my way towards them when one of Barabbas's men, who is always not far away, stops me, shaking his head.

"You mustn't go there. They are the Essenes and do not welcome outsiders," he says.

Essenes. I recall reading about them. They were the source of the Dead Sea scrolls, one of the greatest historical finds. Discovered in 1947 by a shepherd boy pitching stones into a cave, they turned the world upside down with the evidence of Old Testament scriptures. I had not realized it was around this time that they had been buried in the caves, but it must have been because the Essenes disappeared after the Romans destroyed Jerusalem, which will happen in just thirty years from now.

It is mindboggling, seeing the men who wrote and buried those scrolls. I want to talk with them and find out if other scrolls will be buried and hidden. To leave such information for Thaddeus would make him giddy.

"They have many strange customs. It would not be wise to attempt to go there."

Watching the men in the distance, I'm tempted to go anyway, but not now; not until I know where Barosh is. These Zealots are my best hope of finding him right now, so it's best not to rock the boat. I'll go after Barosh and Mark have gone home.

Looking at the caves for one last time, a man stands in one of the openings staring back at me. I wave at him. He waves back.

I turn and walk away.

***

Sitting alone on top of the ridge, the last remnants of daylight slide behind the mountains on the far horizon. I had watched an eagle all afternoon, soaring, gliding overhead in lazy circles, making loping dives and dips. Stars appear poking through the mantle as they will for thousands of years to come. What secrets do they hold?

Strange—the eagle continues to circle in the dusk.

A dazzling array of purple and gold, lights up the mountains bordering the Dead Sea. I wonder if I shouldn't attempt to go back to my own time when the equinox comes. Mark is increasingly eager to begin the journey back to the Sphinx. Maybe Allen's been successful and has discovered how to control the gateway. What do I have to lose; there is nothing here but brutality and sorrow? How did I ever think I could make a life here?

Seeing Jesus had been the purpose—two-thousand years ago, but it has been many months, and I have not even seen the man yet and probably will not now. I don't know if Barosh has accomplished anything. He's disappeared, and I'm doubting I'll ever see him again. More and more I'm convinced he is dead. Going back to the railing at Niagara was not an option any longer. I didn't know what purpose I had after all. Maybe it was all just a colossal lie—an illusion I had convinced myself of, to feed my own need for a purpose. If Allen hadn't perfected the time gate, well then who knew, maybe I'd find a purpose in some other time.

The beautiful face was real enough. I've seen it over and over again, and even Mark has seen him. His efforts to kill me have been real enough too. That means something; I just don't know what. And I was dying when the other man came and spoke my own words to me. But was that real or was it a figment of my coma? Was the man in my coma Jesus? But how could that be? Jesus is a real person; here, in Israel, not a figment of a dying, sick mind in a coma.

I don't know what to think or believe. Everything is an upside down jumble.

A star shoots across the sky, bright and fiery. It's not a short flash like a 'shooting star', but streaks across the entire sky, growing brighter and brighter.

It's coming straight at me!

I flinch as it bursts and explodes overhead into an abundance of bright spots. There are hundreds of them, each glowing and growing. They take form, like drops of water, but having living beings inside, looking like men or angels. The drops fall onto a green orb, rich and vibrant. As each hits, it bursts apart, and the being steps forth. They are giants and massive men of stature having the heads of beasts and birds of prey—hawks, crocodiles, bears and bulls. They stride about the orb like gods, and where they step towers, mountains and pyramids spring up.

A being hovers above them all, and they all bow and worship him. The being turns and faces me—it is the beautiful one. The vibrant green begins to fade, and the orb becomes harsh and hostile.

A new speck of light ignites in the celestial distance and moves through the heavens, growing closer and brighter, until it touches the orb. From inside, a naked man and woman step out onto the orb and from them men and women come and spread across the orb. The giants and man-beasts mingle with the men and women, and majestic temples rise for worship and sacrifice to the beautiful one. The orb turns red with their blood.

Water rises from within the orb and falls in powerful torrents from the heavens. All living things are overcome, buried under violent oceans and seas.

But the man and woman rise with the water, and when the waters settle, they stand on dry ground, and again the orb is green and vibrant.

From out of the ground, the beautiful one comes. He holds out his hand to them, and they take it in theirs. The beautiful one smiles. Blood drips from his mouth, and where it falls, the earth dies and withers.

A new star shines in the sky sending a single ray of light to the orb—touching the woman. The light grows within her and spreads across the orb and wherever the light touches—death disappears and life returns. The light overtakes the beautiful one, and he fades.

I shake my head and close my eyes, trying to clear them, but it doesn't help.

When I open them, millions of people fill the orb, of all different colors and types. They delight in filth and slaughter. Demons and man-beasts fly among them spewing famine, disease and war. Men fight and kill one another; women are defiled, and men tortured. Blood flows across the orb. The skies darkened, the stars fall from the heavens. The moon turns red. Earthquakes shake the foundations of the orb. Massive fires and towering waves burn and smash the cities on the orb.

But the people rejoice in their lust and blood. They murder, destroy and plunder the orb. A new man strides across the orb, speaking peace, but spreading hatred among all the peoples. I see the man, and I recognize him from my own time. Armies fill the barren valleys and plains. Millions of soldiers, in different colors and uniforms, armed with weapons of all types and sizes; giant tanks and ships with monstrous cannons roar and fire at one another; rockets streak back and forth across the sky; lights and massive explosions fill the globe on all sides. Gases in red and yellow spew from the ground; everything they touch die—animal—plant – and human. Blood flows in rivers, filling the valleys and covering the plains.

From out of the blood the beautiful one rises again, stronger, meaner, but he's no longer beautiful. He roaring and bellowing; blood spewing from his mouth and splattering the land and the new man I recognized from my time and all the armies and peoples bow and worship him. Those who don't are trodden under. None is spared.

Again I close my eyes. I can't be seeing this. Am I sleeping? Is it a dream? But I am awake. A loud blast sounds, startling me; it's the blowing of a shofar, resonating a single note that shatters the air and stills the orb causing all to look to the sky.

My eyes open. Everything is frozen in place while a new light comes, brighter than all the others. It touches the orb on a high place, and a king comes from within. He is radiant, adorned in white and with a large golden crown on his head. Behind him come a host of millions. They pour unto the globe, sweeping away all the armies. The evil one shrieks and disappears in a ball of flame, and the orb shatters and disintegrates into nothingness.

A new orb grows, greener and more beautiful and vibrant than the one before. On the orb, men and women stand together; around them a bright light shines from a great city. They fly off the orb into the heavens in all directions taking the light with them, and they light up the entire universe. A quiet, still voice speaks:

Beneath the turbulence—peace is found

I close my eyes; my heart is pounding, beating fast and hard; my breath comes in short sharp gasps.

Opening them, the sky is full of stars. There is no orb—no lights—no faces. There are no armies, no ball of flame. All is normal. On the horizon, the mountains are silhouettes across the Dead Sea. Had it been a dream? No, I was awake and still am. I have not slept. I saw what I saw. It was not a dream. What was it? A hallucination? An overactive mind stressed to the limits?

A vision?

I don't know, but I know now that I will never leave this place or time. Whatever my purpose is, it's here, because. . . .

the face of the king was the face. . . .

of the man who had touched my side on my death bed.

Above me, the eagle circles once and then leaves. . .heading east towards Jerusalem.

I know it is time – to follow the eagle – to Jerusalem.

27

The following day we meet with Barabbas.

"Have you learned anything of Barosh?" I ask.

"We have not; he has fallen from the earth."

"I fear for him."

"It is likely he is in prison. Traveling alone, no one would know," Caleb said. "You should not fear; with the 'thunder stick' they cannot harm him."

If only he had one.

"What about the Romans? Do they still look for us?"

"It is quiet," Barabbas says. "Since the 'Prophet's Massacre', the threat has quelled. They believe the 'prophets' were killed."

"We thank you for your generosity Barabbas; we will be leaving in the morning."

"Where do you go? Will you seek your companion?"

"To Jerusalem, if he has been there, he will have left a message."

"Perhaps he thinks you were killed in the massacre."

"Perhaps, there are many questions yet to be answered. But the answers are not found in these caves. Hopefully, we will find them in Jerusalem."

"We will go with you."

"No, we go alone. It is best not to draw attention."

***

We crouch on the same hill overlooking Jerusalem as when we witnessed the massacre. There's no indication it had occurred. The city is busy, people moving about everywhere, with a high volume of visitors and travelers going into the city. Roman guards and patrols move about, but the activity appears normal.

From atop the walls of Herod's palace, guards again watch the crowds. "Looks normal," Mark says.

"It's getting late. Let's spend the night here and go in the morning."

"That plan didn't work too well last time," Marks says.

***

The following morning, we're back on the road to Jerusalem. We're not alone. Travelers from all over the world are coming in for the festivals. The road fills with merchants and farmers rushing their products to market. Once again, many people bring sacrificial goats and sheep.

Approaching the gate, I notice the Roman guards. They don't seem to be looking for anyone in particular, but rather just looking for signs of trouble or suspicious groups of men.

We pass by without a second glance from them.

Knowing Barosh would return to the same inn, we head directly to it. Sitting at the low table, nursing cups of wine, I scan the room. The inn is full of travelers, from all parts of the Empire and beyond. Jewish men, required to come to Jerusalem and present themselves to the temple. Men from Damascus, Egypt, Greece, Lebanon and. . . .

. . .America!

"Barosh?" I yell, jumping to my feet, "Is it you?"

The man jerks his head around at my call.

It is Barosh!

He jumps up, and we lock arms.

"David! I thought you were dead."

"And I, you."

"I feared I would never see you again."

"I know, I know, me too. You disappeared, and I didn't know what happened to you."

"I'm sorry, but so much has happened. I must tell you everything. I thought the Romans had killed you in that 'massacre'. Have you heard about it? How horrible."

"Yes, yes, we know. We watched it. . . .we caused it. . ."

"We? Yes, of course, Mark. Where is Mark?"

"I am here," Mark said.

"Mark? Is that you?" Barosh is uncertain on how to approach him, not knowing what his mental state is. "Your beard has grown – you look Jewish! And you understood me!"

"It's alright Barosh," I say, "Mark is no longer the enemy. He saved my life, more than once."

"Then I am glad to see you Mark," Barosh says, hugging him. "You must tell me all. Come, we must sit and talk."

"Have you been here long?" I ask.

"Only since yesterday. I was afraid you had waited, and given up months ago, but I figured this was the place to start looking for you. And you? How long have you been here?"

"Been here? We just now walked in! I too thought you were dead or had left and came here, hoping for a message."

Barosh nods, "It is God who has brought us together. There is no other explanation." He looks at me fearfully, "What do you mean when you say you caused the massacre?"

When I look around at the crowd, he nods, "Come, I have a room; we can talk there."

***

Barosh is insistent on hearing our story first. I tell him everything; my recovery – following him to Capernaum – meeting the disciples – then to Mount Herman, where we met the followers of Jesus coming down from the mountain. Barosh nods vigorously.

"Yes, yes. I will tell you of that; please go on."

I tell him about going to Magdala and meeting with Mariamme, of missing him again in Nazareth, and of meeting Mary and James.

"Mariam is a very special person," he replies.

I tell him of the incident on the road from Tiberius that resulted in the massacre. Barosh's face grows red as I recount the events. I put my hand on his arm, "It could not be helped, Barosh. We would all be dead if Mark had not intervened, and it proves Allen's theory of a time-traveler's event being part of history."

"I don't follow."

"Mariamme of Magdala would have been taken brutally used and probably killed."

"I understand. Thank you Mark, but we must not allow ourselves to be in such a position."

"Then we need to get to the Sphinx and go home," Mark says.

I recite the events of the massacre and how we had watched it unfold from on top of the hill.

"There was nothing we could do," Mark said, "all those men were slaughtered."

"It would have happened, if not now, then later. We know the history. All this will come to an end, and Jerusalem will be destroyed in only a few years from now. What happened then? Where have you been hiding these months?"

"Barabbas found us and took us to his hidden campsite, and we've been there while his men searched for you."

"Barabbas? The Zealot?"

"The same; do you know him?"

"Yeshua spoke of him, and when Yeshua sent me to the Essenes to study their scrolls, James told me Barabbas was camped not far from them."

"The Essenes!" I yell. "You were at the cave of the Essenes?"

"I have been there these past months, studying the Torah and the scrolls. Why?"

"Four days ago I gazed upon the cave of the Essenes and watched the men there. Barabbas's camp is only a couple of miles south. We were that close to one another all this time!"

Barosh gives me a quizzical look, "Four days ago I had come out of the cave to stretch and look upon the great sea of salt. I saw a man standing on a high ridge in the distance. For a brief moment, I thought of you. He waved at me, and I waved back. That was when I knew it was time to return to Jerusalem."

"That man *was* me Barosh; I saw that man—and I waved at. . .you."

"It truly is God who is directing us."

"Now you must tell us what you have seen and learned. What kind of man is Jesus? Tell me, did you expose him as a false prophet?"

"No," Barosh answers, "I did not expose him." He places his hand on my shoulder, "Yeshua is the messiah David."

28

With mouth gaping, I stare at Barosh, my shock and surprise evident. Is this the same aggressive Rabbi who traveled 2000 years to expose the 'greatest hoax' perpetuated on mankind? Barosh smiles and nods his head.

"I know. I still have a hard time believing it myself. It was not what I had set out to do, but I cannot deny it." Taking a swallow of wine, he begins his story.

"You were in a coma, and I feared you were going to die. I went to Tiberius to find a doctor. When I returned, you were healed! Your fever was gone; you could breathe and, amazingly, the rotting infection was gone! That just isn't possible. Even if, a doctor from our time treated you, it would take medicine and time to recover so completely. When I asked what happened, they told me Yeshua had come and touched you. David this was it; this was my chance to expose him. Whatever magic he used to heal, and deceive people that he was the messiah; this was the opportunity to expose it and him. So when it was evident you were going to be okay, I took off after him."

"I found him in Capernaum. I should say he found me. I had just arrived in the village when this man walked up to me."

"Shalom Aleikhem, Ben Barosh," He said.

"I seek Yeshua of Natz'rati," I said.

"Yes," he smiled. *"I have waited for you."*

"Are you Yeshua?"

"I am," he smiled, *"follow me."*

"Someone might have told him you were coming," Mark said.

"I'd spoken to no one, not even in Ammathus. I knew Capernaum was where he stayed, and I knew that was where I should go. I spoke to no one along the way. Do you understand what those words meant to me? Those simple words he spoke?" He stood and began pacing.

"I Am is the name of God. It's what God said to Moses from the burning bush. God's name is the biggest mystery of Judaism, and he was telling me right up front who he was. I was shaken."

"There was nothing remarkable about him as far as his appearance went. He was a man, like many others. But there was something exceptional about his presence. He had complete self-awareness, not arrogant or condescending but of knowledge. He knew. . . .period. You listened to him and believed him because. . . .he knew. There were no doubts, no gaps and no confusion in him. Everything about him quietly and confidently said, 'I know because. . . . I am.'"

"He led me to a house where his disciples waited for him. When we entered, they looked at me with suspicion and something else. . . .jealousy, I think. No one spoke to me, not even Yeshua. He didn't introduce me, and after a while, it was as if I wasn't in the room. It surprised me how divided they were. When Yeshua spoke they listened intently, but when he didn't speak, they murmured about what he had said. I could see the strife among them. Some even out and out disliked one another."

"We saw that too," I said, "Judas and Simon the Zealot detested Matthew the tax collector, and I thought Simon Peter was jealous of John."

"Yes there is that and more. They expect Yeshua to declare himself king of Israel and deliver them from the Romans, and they argue about who will have what positions in this kingdom. They are horrified and offended when he speaks to Samaritans or other non-Jews, and they resent the women who follow him and support them."

"We met some of them when we stayed at Mariamme's house," I add.

"I have not met her yet," Barosh continued, "but Simon Peter mentioned her and not in a friendly manner. He feels they shouldn't be allowed in Yeshua's inner circle. Anyway, the next morning things heated up. Yeshua told them he was going up the mountain with me. They went ballistic; arguing and bickering about Yeshua going alone with me. They raised concerns of danger, with Peter being particularly vocal, but it was clear; above their concern for Yeshua's safety, was their fear of me taking the top spot from them. They saw me as a threat to their standings with Yeshua. Yeshua was quiet, allowing them their voice. I understood later that was his intention, for me to fully see their weaknesses and shortcomings."

"Why?" Mark asks while I wondered what Barosh meant by the word 'yet'. He needed to head to Egypt; there was no time to visit Mariamme in Magdala.

"Later, when we came down from the mountain," Barosh answered Mark, "Yeshua said to me:

"These men, filled with their weaknesses, will desert me in my hour of travail. Yet, I tell you; each will suffer greatly for my name, and be subjected to lives of hardship. Most will die a death of horror for my sake, and not one will forsake me. You know this to be true. Think upon what you have seen of these men and ask 'How can this be?' What changed them from this to that? When you answer that question, you will know that—I Am."

"How did he know you already knew that?" Mark asked.

"If he is who he claims to be, wouldn't he know who we are and where we came from?" Barosh asked.

"We met the disciples at Capernaum while you were on the mountain," I said. "They're not a happy group. Three of them had already left looking for you. The others came with us to find you, and bickered and argued the whole time. Halfway up, we met the other three coming down. They told us you had left with Jesus to Nazareth, and appeared to be in some kind of trance or something. I asked James what happened up there, and he said to ask you."

Barosh lowered his head and was silent for a long time. When he looked up, his eyes were full.

"I met Moses on the mountain David."

"What?" I yelled.

If it was anyone other than Barosh, I would have laughed and told him he had drunk too much wine, or he had found a stash of loco weed on the mountain. But it *was* Barosh, and he *was not* to be laughed at.

"Yes – Moses and others. They came and spoke with Yeshua." He sat down controlling his composure. "We had climbed to the top of the mountain and sat on a high rock overlooking the wilderness. We could see everything from up there; it was as if we were overlooking the entire world."

"Yeshua had not said anything on the way up, and he did not say anything now. I was wondering why we were there, and if I should say something, when everything went black, so black I could not see Yeshua sitting next to me. It had been full daylight an instant before, and now it was black. I was shocked and speechless when a speck of light in the distance streaked across the blackness like a shooting star, only it came directly at me, growing larger and brighter. I thought it was going to crash into me, when it exploded into hundreds of tiny specks of light. As each fell, they looked like drops of water, but there were things inside, living things. . . ."

I sat spellbound as Barosh described the identical vision I had seen. When he mentioned the *beautiful one*, I sat up rigid.

". . . .he had a beautiful face, but as the giant and half-men worshipped him, his face turned dark and filled with hatred. Blood dripped from his mouth and spread across the ground. . . ."

Was this possible? How could Barosh have seen the same vision I had seen? Every detail was identical, like a film being watched by two people, at different times, in different places.

". . . .he was radiant and had a crown of gold on his head, and a great host followed him. The wicked one vanished in a ball of fire." Barosh was trembling. I grabbed his arm and squeezed hard. He raised his face and looked into my eyes.

"Barosh. . .I saw it all! Sitting on the mountain, overlooking the Dead Sea, not a mile away from where you were in the cave with the Essenes, I saw everything, just the way you described it. How can that be?"

Barosh stared at me.

"You saw it too?"

"Every detail. What does it mean?"

"Remember our discussions with Allen and Alex: the unanswered questions of history, the structures and unexplained mysteries of ancient times and all the myths and stories? I think we were shown what happened."

"I do remember, and I've thought of those things, but what about the rest of it, the armies and the wars? That *beautiful one* who spews blood everywhere? Barosh, I've seen the man with the beautiful face many times. Each time my life was threatened, he was there. He's real; even Mark has seen him. He's not a vision."

"I believe you David," Barosh said.

"Barosh, did you see the other man? The new man from back in our time—who's there now?"

"Yes, I saw him David. It means time is short," Barosh said.

"Is that what happened? Did the other three also see the vision? Is that why they were in a trancelike state?"

"No," Barosh continued, "When the vision was over, it was light again. I turned to Yeshua. He sat as he had before, and when he turned to look at me. . . .his was the face of the king in the vision."

"During the time I was sick and unconscious," I said, "I had a dream, and the *beautiful one* was there too. He wanted me to worship him, to serve him, offering me things. I refused, and then another man came and touched me. I don't know if I was still dreaming or if it was real, but the man who touched me was. . . .he was the same man who was the king in my vision."

"Yeshua," Barosh whispered.

Mark had not said anything during this exchange, and I expected a sarcastic rebuttal, but when I turned to him, he was staring out the window into the open streets of Jerusalem—sobbing.

"Mark? What's wrong? Are you okay?"

He turns, his face is flushed and his eyes brimming. I'm stunned and confused. Crying? Mark? The DHS agent who kills without hesitation?

"What is it Mark?"

"I don't know what's going on," he stutters, "I don't know. This isn't supposed to happen. I'm not supposed to be here. It's all a mistake."

"Mark, what is it? What's wrong?" Barosh asks.

Raising his head, he looks at Barosh and me with imploring eyes, "It wasn't a dream David. The man who touched you—was Jesus."

"How do you know that? You told me you didn't see him."

"I lied," he said. "I saw him when he came into the village. I hid and watched him sit by you and touch you, the old woman seen me, and when he left, he turned to where I hid and looked directly at me."

"Why did you lie about it?"

"Because. . .because he's also the king you saw in your vision."

"How do you know that?" Barosh asks.

"I. . . .I saw. . . .the vision too."

***

We sit in silence. So thick it can be sliced with a knife. The revelation that Mark had seen the same vision shook us to our core. This mission was for Barosh and me. Mark was a reluctant hitchhiker on this train – uninvited, along for the ride. Sure, his attitude had changed during the past few months, but he either had to adapt or go insane. Never in my wildest dreams did I think of him as a part of what we were doing.

What does it mean? I don't know. Everything is confused and upside down. Looking at Barosh, it's clear he's just as confused as I am. I can't think about it any longer; so I change the subject.

"What happened after the vision?" I ask Barosh.

"We stayed on top of the mountain, sitting and talking."

"What did you talk about?"

"He asked me why I persecuted him. Wanted to know why I denied who he was?"

"He knew how you felt?"

"Of course."

"What did you tell him?"

"I told him God is a spirit and cannot be seen, and therefore, could not take human form, which is a fundamental belief of all Jews. You claim to be divine, I said, and that is a blasphemy against God and the Torah. He smiled softly and said,

'Why do you limit the power of God? Who walked and talked with Adam? Who made him clothing? Who was it who ate with Abraham and argued over Sodom? Who was Melchizedek, to whom Abraham paid tithes and worshipped? Who wrestled with Jacob? Who spoke to Moshe from the flaming bush? Who did Joshua meet on the road to Jericho and bow down to? Who did Gideon meet? Who stood in the fiery furnace with Shad-rakh, Meishakh and Aved-N'go?"

"I Am there, in the Torah, Ben Barosh. I Am—'the angel of Yehovah'—I AM 'the Son of Man'— Before Abraham—I Am. You, who study the Torah and the prophets, should know this. It is there for you to see. Why do you accept these manifestations of 'I Am' in the flesh, yet reject the manifestation of 'I Am' in Yeshua?"

"He was right, and there were even more times in the Tanakh where God in flesh form had visited, walked and talked with man. Elijah, Daniel, even Noah. This wiped out my objections of Yeshua, the human, being the messiah." Barosh shook his head, "My number one argument was gone, so I gave him another; 'God gave us the law,' I said, 'yet you come to destroy God's law and replace the law with forgiveness and grace.' Again, he smiled,

'Whose finger was it that wrote the law for Moshe? I Am wrote the law. I do not come to displace my own law, Ben Barosh; on the contrary, I come to fulfill it. On the mount, when I spoke to the multitudes, did I replace the law, or did I show the application of the law? The law without forgiveness is condemnation; forgiveness without the law is moral decay. I do not condemn, and by my coming, I bring true forgiveness for true repentance. The circle is complete; my grace fulfills my law."

"So we spoke. Everything I said, all my well thought out arguments; all my 'proofs'; he dispelled with easy recital of scripture from the Tanakh. He never argued, never raised his voice or demeanor. He wanted me to throw everything I had at him. He left no area untouched. We were on the mountain for two days and two nights. On the morning of the third day, he was standing in an opening surrounded by huge stones—when it happened."

"When what happened?"

"When Father Abraham appeared," Barosh stood and began pacing the room. "Yeshua was standing there, and he started growing brighter! His clothes became white, whiter than the purest of snow, and light began radiating out from him. And then, a man was standing there beside him. I don't know how he got there—he was just there. They spoke in a language I never heard. It sounded more like music rather than words, but I knew that was who he was. He was real David. He looked at me and nodded. He was the first, others followed, some alone, some in groups. I knew each one. I don't know how, but I did. There was Isaac, and Jacob (who limped), and Joseph and David the king. There were the prophets, Elisha, Jeremiah and Ezekiel. They came, and I knew he was showing me all the fathers and prophets that had served him and foretold of his coming. At one point, Enoch and Elijah were with him together, and I could understand what they said—the message was for me."

"What was the message?" I asked.

"That they will be coming back to earth, as prophets, to proclaim the coming of Yeshua's kingdom. They will preach for a time, and there will be great turmoil and suffering, and the kingdom will come after that."

"Enoch left, and Moses appeared. It was at this time that Peter, James and John arrived and witnessed what was happening. They were stunned and wanted to build altars of worship, when a voice came from above. It spoke in that same musical language, but I understood it."

"What did it say Barosh?"

"It said:

'This is my son, whom I love, with whom I am well pleased. Listen to him.'

"The disciples heard it also and fell down in panic, as did I, for I knew the words were meant for me. Yeshua told us not to be afraid, and when I looked up, he was alone."

"David, do you understand what happened? God spoke to me! To me, David, on the mountain. Almighty God spoke to me! And He showed me the fathers of Israel and the prophets and that they all foretold of Yeshua. He told me Yeshua is 'I Am', and that I should listen to Him. He is Yeshua HaMashiach—Jesus the Messiah."

Barosh was crying.

"When we left the mountain, Yeshua told his disciples to wait for Him in Capernaum and not to tell anyone what they had witnessed until after He rose from the dead. They didn't understand at all. He took me to Nazareth, where we met His mother, and she told me of His birth, the trip to Bethlehem and then to Egypt, of Joseph's death and of Yeshua's sinless life. Meeting His mother was remarkable, but wasn't the reason He wanted me to go there. He wanted me to meet His brothers and sisters. They did not have Miriam's knowledge of her son, and they did not believe Yeshua was the messiah. They were outspoken about it, especially James and Jude, who were resentful and bitter. They said Yeshua embarrassed them, and He shirked His responsibilities, as the firstborn, to provide for His mother and sisters. Yeshua could easily have proven who He was to them. I asked Him why He didn't."

'It is for the generations to follow that I do not reveal myself to them at this time. Their belief in me after my death will be a confirmation, for your generation, of my resurrection'.

"He chastised me, for denying Him all these years and for not believing who He was until He showed me. All these things were there for me to see, but my eyes were blinded, and my heart poisoned. All was in the Torah, the Prophets and the Psalms that were fulfilled in Him; there was nothing He had showed me that wasn't already written, but I was blinded to it. The prophets were right; there *are* two messiahs, Messiah Ben-Joseph and Messiah Ben-David. The first would be sacrificed and killed, preparing the way for the second, who would resurrect the first and establish God's plan for mankind. What they failed to see is that both messiahs are one, in Yeshua. He told me to:

'Go to the Essenes. There, read the scrolls. Everything is fulfilled that was written about me in the Torah of Moshe, the Prophets and the Psalms. Read them, Ben Barosh, and open your eyes to truth. Read the Tanakh, and then ask the God of Abraham, Isaac and Jacob if 'I Am' the messiah. Read the prophecies of my birth that my mother told you of; read the prophecies of my death and that all will be as written. When you fully believe, then will I give you a new name, and you will fulfill your purpose for me.'

"He left me there, in Nazareth, and went back to Capernaum, to His disciples. I left for the Dead Sea, to the Essenes, where they were waiting for me. I've been there these past months reading and studying the scrolls."

"All this time? You've studied these scrolls all your life Barosh. What could be new now?"

"David, these are the complete scrolls, all of them with no pieces missing. There were many areas that were new. The discovery of the Dead Sea scrolls in 1947 was earthshattering, but many of the scrolls were not recovered. I read them all and found many things I had never seen before. For example, when John the Immerser sent his disciples to question Yeshua if He was the messiah or not, Yeshua answered by saying:

"Go back and report to John what you hear and see: the blind receive sight, the lame walk; those who have leprosy are cured; the deaf hear; the dead are raised, and the good news is preached to the poor."

"This response refers to a prophecy that Isaiah made, but it's always been used as proof of Yeshua's deception by the inclusion of *'the dead are raised'* which was not in the prophecy as written in the Tanakh. But there, in those scrolls, was the prophecy from Isaiah, and it included that phrase."

"I had been reading the prophets and psalms with a closed mind, unwilling to see that Yeshua was the only person who filled all those prophecies. There are hundreds of them, David, hundreds! The odds are astronomical, impossible, for any person to fulfill them all. Isaiah, Jeremiah, Micah, Zechariah, David, Daniel, Hosea and others, over a span of hundreds of years, prophesized about the birth, life, death and resurrection of the messiah. All the details His mother had told me about, they were all prophesized to happen hundreds of years before His birth.

Then there are the Targums, ancient paraphrases of the scriptures, all completed decades before Yeshua was born and give clear details of the messiah. Only Yeshua fulfills them all."

"Isaiah revealed the manner of the messiah's birth; Micah pinpointed the place of birth; Genesis and Jeremiah specified His ancestry—descendent of Abraham, Isaac and Jacob—from the tribe of Judah and the house of David. Psalms foretold His betrayal, His accusation by false witnesses, His manner of death, the pierced hands and feet (even though crucifixion hadn't been known yet), gambling of soldiers for His clothing, no bone would be broken in His body, and He would not decay but would be resurrected. And that's only the beginning."

"But those things haven't happened, he is still alive." I said, trying to undermine his enthusiasm.

"But they will, soon." Barosh replied.

29

During the next few days, we fill each other in on the events that had occurred during the past few months. And, we discuss our plans.

Mark's revelation puts a new perspective on everything. Up to this point, my focus was to get him to the Sphinx by the spring equinox, without him killing anyone else. At the Sphinx, I'd take my leave. Well, the spring equinox is just around the corner, and they needed to get moving in order to cross the Sinai in time. It was time for me to put the cards on the table.

That evening, I speak the words I've been struggling with.

"I won't be going with you to Egypt," I say, bracing myself for the outburst.

Barosh says nothing and only nods his head.

"You're staying here? In the first century?" Mark asks without rancor.

I have to pause and regroup; my prepared arguments aren't needed.

"Yes, I never intended to go back."

"Wait a minute. Did you say never? I thought being here might have changed your mind, but you never intended to go back? Why?"

"I have my own reasons, but there is something you need to know."

"What's that?" He asks warily.

"You know we came to the first century to meet Jesus, but it wasn't entirely by choice. It was either come at this time, or don't come."

"I'm not following you."

"We didn't select the date that the gateway opened to," Barosh said, "it was predetermined."

Mark considered this information, and as I knew, he wasn't stupid.

"Are you saying you can't select the year it will open back to?"

"Allen was working on how to select it," Barosh said, "and he's had a full year to figure it out. He gave his word he would have the gate open to one year from the date we left."

"So, you're not going because you don't know *when* you'll be going to." Mark said.

"Allen is a genius, and I have complete confidence he'll do what he said." Barosh said.

"But you don't believe he can, do you David?"

"If anyone can, Allen can, and that's not my reason for not going back, Mark. I'm supposed to be here. You just needed to know there's a risk involved."

"Are there any other little secrets?" Mark said turning to Barosh, "Are you staying here too?"

"I came here fully intending to go back and see my family again. I'm going to Egypt, and I have confidence Allen will do what he said he would. I want to see my wife and children and share with the world what I've learned. If Allen doesn't do it this year—he will next year, and he'll know where we are to get us back. I've done what I came here to do."

"Really?" I asked. *"You've done what you came to do?* From what you've told us, you've become a 100% convert."

"Recall David, our goal was to determine *if* he was or was not the son of God. Granted, I had some preconceived ideas. . . ."

"Preconceived ideas! You came here to tar and feather the man, and run him out of Israel on a rail," I exclaimed.

Barosh smiled, "True."

"Let's get back to this gate thing," Mark said, "what does it mean if Allen can't select the date? Where do we go?"

"You mean 'when' not 'where'," Barosh said. "Allen's computer calculated it to open further in the past."

"Great!" Mark said. "So it'll be even more primitive than this. How good is he at what he does?"

"He's the world's expert in the field. As David said, if anyone can do it, he can."

"Yeah, but you're missing one little detail," Mark said.

"What's that?"

"The Department of Homeland Security. They may not exist here, but they sure do back there, and they've been questioning your buddy pretty hard. If they suspect anything, especially with me missing, he'll never have the opportunity to work on it."

Barosh exhaled loudly, "I'm sorry you got caught up in this. I truly am."

"It's not your fault. I've no one to blame but myself. I was going to be the big shot; stop the terrorist plot, single handed; be the world's hero. Guess I'm seeing things a little different now." He laughed a sad laugh, "If Rodgers could see me now!"

The first century Mark is a different man than the twenty-first century agent was.

"What are you going to do?" Barosh asked.

"I'm going to Egypt, with you. Take my chances with, my new best friend, Allen."

"Okay, then we must leave in a couple of days at the latest. I'll make the arrangements. I learned we can hire an armed escort on horseback and cross in half the time," Barosh said. "David, are you sure this is what you want?"

"I'm sure. There's nothing for me, back there Barosh. Besides, I feel it's not over for me here yet. There's something more I have to do. Something that 'beautiful man' doesn't want me to do. I haven't even met Jesus yet, seems like I've been chasing him all around Israel."

"He said he would see you when the time came."

"That's starting to scare me. It's the second time I've been told that."

***

Barosh and Mark made plans to leave in two days. It made for a sorrowful time, depositing a cloud of sadness over us. I had just reunited with Barosh, only to part ways again, this time forever. He made me promise to go to the Essenes and read the scrolls. I told him I would.

It hurt seeing Mark leave as well. It was strange, the way it had gone with us; starting as enemies and evolving into an uneasy truce before developing into a real bond between us. Barosh was still leery and unsure of Mark, but he hadn't been through the things Mark and I had together. Mark had saved my life, more than once crossing the Sinai, and there was the battle on the road to Tiberius, and we witnessed the massacre together, met Mariamme of Magdala and Mary the mother of Jesus which had an enormous impact on him. He could have killed me or deserted me at any time, and he'd shown immense restraint in keeping that gun holstered when he had the upper hand all along. The old Mark would have exploded over the information about the gateway. I've witnessed the metamorphosis of Mark—and a butterfly was emerging from the cocoon.

As for me, I won't lie—I'm scared; I don't know what will happen. Barosh may feel he's accomplished his mission, but I haven't completed mine yet. I'm not even sure what it is. I haven't met Jesus yet. I need to do that, and I need to bury this journal for the professor as I promised I would. (I could give it to Barosh to take back, but not with the uncertainty of the gateway. It may end up in the belly of a Tyrannosaurus Rex.) After that, I don't know. I have a small fortune and will be a rich man here. I'd like to see Athens and Rome. Maybe answer some of the questions we have about history's unsolved mysteries. It would be fun, finding things and leaving clues for the professor to find two-thousand years from now.

I wouldn't mind visiting Mariamme again, either. She said she would see me again, and I think she took a liking to me. She certainly is a beautiful woman. I could try to get her out of Israel before the revolt and the Romans destroy Jerusalem. Jesus will be dead by then so she'd be out from under his spell. Do I dare get involved with anyone in this time era? Would that be pushing the 'paradox' bubble too far? I'll have time to think about that after Barosh and Mark are gone.

But first, Barosh wants to go to the Temple one last time. The Passover is almost here, and it's an exciting time for someone like Barosh in Jerusalem. Both, Mark and I will go with him. We're going in the morning, and the following day, they'll begin their journey back to the future.

It'll be a sad day—I'll miss them both.

***

The streets of Jerusalem are jammed with people, dressed in all styles of clothing, headgear and shawls. There are dark and light skinned races, speaking every known language within the empire. It's loud, busy and full of life.

We approach the Temple as we had before. I can't get over the number and variety of people who enter. I notice the guards on the walls of the Antonia Fortress have doubled and that the soldiers keep a close eye on the activities inside the temple.

Entering the Court of the Gentiles, it is more crowded than our last visit, during the Festival of Weeks. More money changer tables have been set up, along with increased buying and selling of animals. Goats, sheep and bulls, are staged, caged and even wandering free. Animal excrement and urine creates a stench mixing with the strong scent of incense burning in all the censers around the court. What should have been the intoxicating aroma of holiness was the pungent smell of a brothel outhouse.

Glancing at Barosh, I see disgust and anger building on his face—again.

"Ignore it," I say to him, "stay focused on why you're here. Tomorrow you'll be leaving, having seen the Temple, something no one will see again for two-thousand years. Remember the good parts and take those back with you."

He nods, "Thank you, I will."

We've completed the ritual purification and are half way up the steps, leading to the Beautiful Gate and the Women's court, when people begin screaming and running in panic. A crush of bodies push at us from below, where a scene of confusion and panic is unfolding. A man falls on top of a cage, smashing it, freeing a covey of doves. Others fall against wooden pens holding sacrificial animals, breaking them open, freeing the panicking beasts. People stumble and fall.

"What's happening?" Mark shouts. I glance to see if he's reaching under his cloak—he's not.

Tables crash spilling coins in all directions. People jump, duck and run, knocking more cages over. Sheep and goats bray and bulls bellow. Men crawl on all fours chasing after the coins, getting kicked, stepped on and tripped over. Above the din and chaos, an angry voice calls out:

"Get out! Get out!"

I look towards the voice. It comes from a man, fraying a cord, and from whom everyone runs. His back is to me, but stools and tables overturn, as he shouts:

"My house is a house of prayer; you have turned it into a den of thieves!"

The Temple is in total panic. Pharisees flee in disarray calling for guards to arrest the man, but many in the crowd cheer and encourage the man further. The guards hesitate, fearful of the crowd. The man stops, turns, and looks directly at me. His eyes bore into mine. . . .

. . . .it is him! The one who touched me on my death bed. . . .him. . . .the king in the vision.

"Yeshua," Barosh whispers.

"Out of the way! Move! Get out of the way!" The shouts come from the opposite side of the courtyard. Standing on the stairs, I have a clear view as a troop of temple guards are pushing their way through the crowd towards Jesus.

"Move! Out of the way!"

I turn back to where Jesus stands, to warn him, but he is gone. I search the crowd and do not see him.

CRASH!

The sound of a table overturning and coins spilling onto the courtyard comes from a different direction, below me.

I look and see the man, but it's not Jesus. . . .it's. . . .Barosh and he's knocking over the tables.

"There he is!" The guards point to Barosh, forcing themselves through the crowd.

Running back down the stairs, with Mark in tow, I grab Barosh by the arm, jerking him away.

"Come on, let's get out of here!"

Pulling his sleeve, I drag him towards the side exit.

"Come on," I scream, "are you crazy? You're leaving tomorrow, remember?"

The three of us run across the Court of the Gentiles. As we pass through the exit, a squad of Roman soldiers is coming around the corner in double time, responding to the commotion.

"This way," Mark shouts.

"That's them—there! Get them!" The Temple guards yell to the soldiers while pointing at us. The soldiers begin chasing us. People scatter in all directions as we run down the narrow street with the soldiers in pursuit.

We're gaining ground and should escape, when my sandal catches on an uneven stone, and I fall hard to the street. Scrambling back to my feet, my ankle gives out, and I collapse back down. Barosh and Mark pick me up, and together we hobble down the street, but the soldiers have gained on us now and are closing fast.

"Let me go," I shout to them, "or they'll catch all of us."

"No," Barosh shouts, "we can make it."

But we can't. The soldiers have moved fast and will be upon us in seconds. Mark suddenly lets go of my arm and spins around.

Boom! Boom! Boom!

The sound echoes through the street as the front two soldiers fall to the ground. The others stop, and stare at their fallen comrades, writhing on the street. Grabbing my arm with his free hand, Mark starts dragging me back while Barosh clears a way out.

We've gone only a few feet when the soldiers regain their composure, and stepping over their comrades, come after us again.

Boom! Boom! Boom!

Mark fires while pulling me. Two more soldiers fall, but the rest keep coming.

Boom! Boom!

Another falls, but more soldiers have joined the chase and they're throwing spears at us. One hits the street and another crashes off the wall behind us while another grazes Mark's arm, knocking the gun free, sending it crashing to the street.

"Go Mark! You can't stop them. They'll only catch you too. Go!" I yell at him while reaching into my cloak. I pull out the pouch containing the journal and shove it into his hand. "Give this to Barosh. Tell him to finish it. Go—save yourself."

"No, I won't leave you," Mark yells.

"Go! There's no other way. Here, take this," I thrust the bag of money into his hand. "Tell Barosh to buy me back. Go! Go!" I wrench my arm free of him and push him away. The soldiers are close now, almost on us, swords drawn and raised.

"Go!" I yell.

Mark backs away, "David, we'll get you! We'll buy you back! We'll get you!" And he turns to run as a soldier slams into me. The last thing I remember is the hilt of a sword, crushing my face.

These final chapters of David's journal were written by me. They are an accurate accounting of the events following the arrest of David Kincaid. They are based upon the testimony of reliable witnesses, David's own words, and my participation in and observations of the events.

Rabbi Ben Barosh Goldberg

30

D avid awoke, lying in a puddle of filth. It was wet and smelled of urine and feces. His head pounded, and his mouth throbbed. Sitting up, he touched his jaw—pain erupted where a number of teeth were broken. It was total blackness; he could see nothing. He heard movement a few feet away.

"Is someone there?" He slurred. There was no answer. The skittering noise continued. It sounded like a small animal. He felt the floor around him. It was cold, slimy and hard. He was on the floor of a dungeon. The skittering noise was probably a rat. He kicked at it, and it ran. He didn't know if it ran further or closer to him.

Trying to stand up, a burst of pain exploded from his ankle. Ignoring it, he continued rising, only to fall back down hard, when his head slammed into the ceiling. The cell was less than five feet high.

He remembered nothing since the soldier had hit him and had no sense of how long he has been here. His head, face and ankle throbbed. He tried to think and reason what his next step should be. He had no clue. Bribery and corruption were rampant, so he could only wait and hope that Barosh could buy him out.

***

It took a couple of days for me to make contact with someone who had connections at the Antonia Fortress, and could get someone out for the right price. I scrubbed my plans to travel to Egypt. I'll stay another year if I have to, but I won't leave David in prison. Allen promised, if we weren't there this year, he'd do it again the following year, and the next. I knew he wouldn't give up and would do everything possible to get us back. Mark would have to travel across the Sinai alone with the escort. I told him immediately.

There was no hesitation in his response, and it surprised me.

"I'm not leaving with David in that prison," he said, "we're getting him out of there, you hear me? No matter what it takes, we're getting him out. If you can't buy him out, then I'll get an army together and take him out by force. I know Barabbas, the leader of the Zealots, and I have that dagger from Abdul-Hakeem. I can get them to join with us. I know a lot of things about making war these yokels don't have a clue of. I'll go back to Egypt and dig up those pouches."

"What for, you don't have the rifle?"

"Those are high-power rifle cartridges and contain a lot of gunpowder, and there're almost three hundred of them. I can make some sizable bombs that'll blow those doors to smithereens, and those Romans will mess their drawers running all the way back to Rome."

"You're willing to stay here for another year?" I asked.

"Listen, we don't even think about going back until David is out of that prison, you understand me?"

"I got it. . .let's get him out."

***

The guards brought him bowls of bug-infested slop. He didn't know if it was day or night; the only light he saw was from the yellow, smoking torches they carried when they came stomping down the damp corridor.

"Here 'prophet'; food of the gods."

"When am I getting out of here?" He asked. Laughing, they left him in darkness.

He kept count of the number of bowls. He didn't know if that represented days or not, but after three of them, an officer came with two guards.

"Are you the one they call 'the prophet'?" He asked.

"I don't know any prophets," David answered.

"Who are the ones who conspire against the emperor?"

"I wouldn't know."

"What is the 'thunder' stick? Did Zeus give it to you? How does it kill?" David didn't answer.

"We have ways to obtain this information from you. You should be very worried to not displease me."

"It is you who should be worried about mistreating me, and displeasing the gods who have the 'thunder' sticks and can bring their wrath down on you."

The officer made no answer but made no further threats. He turned and walked away.

A short time later, David was surprised to hear the guards coming back.

"Get up. . .follow us," they said, unlocking the door.

Limping gingerly, he followed them up a series of winding stone stairs to ground level; outside he shielded his eyes from the bright sun while they led him to an open pool of water.

"Clean yourself," they said, "you stink."

When he had washed away the layers of filth and blood, he emerged from the pool, with his tunic and cloak clinging to him, but he could tolerate himself a little. They led him back inside the fortress, but not back downstairs, rather to a small room with a window, although it was two feet over his head.

"You're moving up in life 'prophet'," they said, giving him a plate of real food. "Enjoy it while you can."

"How long will I be here?"

"Until the Procurator arrives; he wants to see you, himself."

"When will that be?"

"When he gets here."

***

I learned from my contact that David has been relocated to a holding cell on the ground floor of the fortress. They were afraid of him and did not want to upset the gods by torturing or mistreating him.

That was the good news.

The Roman Governor, Pontius Pilate, was on his way to Jerusalem from his home in Caesarea for the Passover festival, and he wanted to see the 'prophet' personally.

That was the bad news.

With Pilate wanting to see David, no amount of money could now bribe him out of prison. If he was released, the guards would pay with their lives.

***

Mark and I watched Pontius Pilate enter through the Damascus Gate. His trireme had docked at Jaffa two days ago. He had traveled to Gazara on the following day, spending the evening there.

Today, his procession made the grand entrance into Jerusalem. Roman standards of brass eagles rode high above a sea of flags and banners. A double row of twenty trumpeters and drummers led the entourage, followed by five squads of his personal mounted body guard. Next came officials and dignitaries and slaves, carrying placards announcing 'Pontius Pilate – Pro-Consulor of Israel', followed by the Governor himself, sitting tall and straight on a magnificent black stallion adorned in a purple coat with gold trim. Two more squads of mounted body guards, preceded the gold and silver inlaid pilentum that carried Pilate's wife, followed by four additional squads of mounted guards. Lastly, came an entire company of legionnaires on foot.

Studying Pilate's face, as he rode by, I saw nothing encouraging. He looked unhappy, bored and mean. He gave the crowds only the slightest acknowledgment. He had no use for them, or for Israel. To Pilate, being governor here was akin to being exiled. Knowing his history, I knew that he not only didn't want to be governor here but that his benefactor, Sejanus, had recently fallen out of favor with the Emperor in Rome, putting Pilate's future in jeopardy. Further, Pilate, himself had been reprimanded by Rome for excessive brutality. This gave me great cause for concern. If Rome, as cruel and harsh as it was, reprimanded this man for excessive brutality, how would that fare for David? I racked my brain for what leverage I had.

I couldn't find any.

"Have you contacted your Zealot friend, Barabbas?" I asked Mark.

"No one knows where he is. He's disappeared. I know I can get Abdul-Hakeem and the rifle cartridges, but it will take some time."

"Unfortunately, that's the one thing we don't have."

***

He stood before Pilate.

"What is your name 'prophet'?" Pilate asked.

"David."

"That's all, just 'David'?"

"David Alden Kincaid."

Pilate stared at him and then rose from the large, wooden chair that was the seat of Roman authority and power in Israel. He walked around David, studying him carefully.

"That is a strange name, David Alden Kincaid. From where do you come? You do not look or smell like a Jew."

"I come from a land beyond Rome."

"What land? I know all the lands of the world."

"Not this land, it is on the other side of the world."

"The other side? There is no 'other' side of the world. The world is Rome." He stopped and thought, "Or do you mean *the other side*? Are you a god, David Alden Kincaid?"

"I am as you—a man."

"Not like me—Jew. I am the Roman Governor, Procurator of this Providence, as god-forsaken as it is. And you, you're a. . .what are you? Are you—a prophet? Or are you—merely my prisoner?"

"I am a man as you are."

"Don't test me, Jew. I've little patience with all you prophets and revolutionaries in this dung heap you call the 'promised land'."

He sat back down and motioned for the Centurion to come forward. The man carried a wrapped cloth. Unwrapping it, he held it to Pilate.

Pilate reached inside the cloth and pulled out Mark's pistol. He moved it around in his hand, examining it closely. Holding it by the handle, feeling the heft and balance of it, he turned it around and pointed it at his face looking down the barrel, his finger resting on the trigger. He lowered his hand.

"So, this is the 'thunder-stick', you kill my soldiers with. Is it from the gods, David Alden Kincaid?"

David didn't answer.

"Answer me, Jew."

"Yes, it is from the gods, and you should return it to me, and set me free so as not to anger them, and they will honor and favor you."

Pilate smiled, "You toy with me 'prophet'." He motioned to the Centurion, "Bring them in."

A squad of soldiers marched in. Between them, three men were in shackles. David gasped at seeing them. It was Azir'el Macabi, Caleb and Barabbas. They had been beaten severely.

"Ah, I see these are friends of yours," Pilate said. "So, you are a revolutionary, after all. Tell me, prophet, by what power does this 'thunder-stick' work? They said you just pointed it at my soldiers, and they fell down dead. What sorcery is that?"

David didn't answer.

"Let's test it." Pilate raised the pistol and pointed it at Barabbas. He pushed it forward as if trying to push the power out. Nothing happened.

"Will it not work for me, prophet? Only for you?" He asked, turning knobs and levers. He raised it again and pointed it at Azir'el Macabi and pulled a lever back.

Click

Nothing happened. Unknowingly, Pilate had put the safety on. He pointed it back at Barabbas, returning the lever forward.

Click

He turned the pistol over in his hands, trying to figure it out. He pointed it at Caleb.

BOOM!

The gun jumped out of Pilate's hand, bouncing across the marble floor. Pilate jumped back in shock and surprise, as did all the guards, who cowered and instinctively ducked. One guard dropped his spear and ran into the corridor. Barabbas and Azir'el Macabi fell to the floor in fright while Caleb flew backwards, blood spurting from his chest, pooling on the pure white marble.

David got over the surprise of the shot and made a dash for the gun, seizing his opportunity. Half-way there, he was struck from behind and knocked to the floor. He screamed in pain as the guard grabbed him by his swollen ankle, dragging him back.

With the echo of the shot still ringing in everyone's ears and the scent of cordite in the room, Pilate looked at Caleb and then at the gun on the floor.

"It truly is the power of the gods," he murmured reverently, and then he smiled, looking at David, "and it is not any power you have. Whoever owns it has the power." He bent and picked up the pistol, "Now, I have the power."

He turned to the Centurion, "Get him," he motioned to the soldier who had run when the gun had gone off.

The soldier came into the room; his head lowered in shame in front of his comrades.

"You run like a coward? Then by the gods' thunder, you shall die like a coward." Pilate pointed the pistol at his face and pulled the trigger.

BOOM!

The soldier's head exploded. This time, Pilate held the pistol tight and didn't drop it. It kicked in his hand while the spent casing ejected, bouncing along the marble floor, and Pilate's eyes grew wide.

"Such power it has."

He raised the pistol again and pointed it at Barabbas.

"No longer shall you puny zealots and rebels disturb me," and he pulled the trigger.

Nothing.

He pulled it again.

Nothing.

David saw the breeching was open – the pistol was out of bullets.

"What is wrong? Where is the power?" He yelled, shaking the pistol at Barabbas and pulling the trigger.

Nothing.

Pilate picked up the casing. It was warm. He put it to his nose and smelled it. He looked at the pistol and tried to put the casing back in. Managing to insert it into the chamber, he fumbled with the buttons and the breeching slammed shut, starling him. But he smiled, feeling he had reinserted the power. He raised the pistol once again to Barabbas, who cowered, covering his head with his arms, and pulled the trigger.

Click

He pulled it again.

Nothing.

He shouted at David, "Make it work."

"I cannot."

Pilate pulled on the trigger over and over. Nothing happened. He moved the safety back and forth and pushed the ejection button sending the magazine clanging onto the marble floor. He figured out how to push it back in, and pulled on the trigger again and again. In frustration, he turned to David.

"Make it work!"

"I cannot."

He screamed and raged. He was seeing his dream, his power, and his chance at being the next emperor of Rome fading in front of his eyes.

"Make it work—I command you! Bring the power back!"

"I cannot. The power is gone from the 'thunder-stick'. It has no use any longer."

Pilate stopped his rant and stared at David.

"Then, I have no use of you any longer." David's heart surged; he would be set free now. Pilate turned to the Centurion.

"Crucify him."

31

David sprawled on the cell's floor. They had dragged him back, threw him in, and he hadn't moved since. He was in total shock and denial.

This can't be happening he said, over and over. *It's a mistake. . .a dream. . .another vision. Crucify him, Pilate had said. Crucify!? No, no, no, wake up David. You're dreaming.*

How could David from the twenty-first century come face to face with the most infamous Roman of all time and be sentenced to death by crucifixion?

It's not possible—it's just not possible!

Something was all wrong. He was a modern man; he didn't belong here. *Wake up!*

He screamed inside. Any minute now he'd wake up and be back in his bed or even standing on the railing overlooking the Niagara River. Anything—but this.

He pinched himself; he slapped himself in the face – his swollen mouth sent immediate pain surging through his face—it wasn't a dream.

Okay, calm down, it was only a ruse to get me to tell him how the 'thunder-stick' worked. He hadn't meant it. He'll call me back, any minute now, that's all, only a ruse.

***

We had no clue what was happening inside the Antonia Fortress. Since Pilate had arrived, guards had increased, and no word emerged from within the high walls.

"Maybe Pilate will release him," I said.

"Don't count on it," Mark said, "I left five dead Roman soldiers in the streets. They're not going to forgive or ignore that; they want revenge. It's me they want—and David's in prison paying for it."

"Don't go there, Mark; there's plenty of guilt to go around. I'm the one who started it. What was I thinking? I know better than anyone not to get involved in events here, but when I saw Yeshua venting the anger that boiled inside of me, I acted without thinking. If you hadn't intervened, we'd all be behind prison walls right now. We need to stay focused on getting him out. Any headway on your front?"

"None. I got people looking for Barabbas with no luck. Seems he and his son has fallen off the face of the earth. His men are running around trying to find them. And, as far as Abdul goes, he's leading a caravan somewhere between Damascus and Ethiopia. I know I can put it all together, but it's going to take time. How about your end?"

"I can't get to first base. With Pilate in town, no one's taking any bribes. I can't even get anyone to talk to me about it. Maybe we'll get lucky, and Pilate will have other things to worry about; there seems to be a lot of tension in the city."

"Yeah, ever since that riot at the temple, people are on edge. There're soldiers everywhere, probably looking for us, and the guards have doubled at Herod's Palace."

"Same at the Temple. The Passover begins tomorrow, and crowds of foreigners are in town; there's lots of money to be made and the Sanhedrin don't want anything or anyone to rock that cash boat. They don't know what to do about Yeshua," I turned and looked at Mark, "but we know. If I'm right, this is the time."

"What time?"

"The crucifixion."

"Crucifixion? Of Jesus? Like in the Stations of the Cross?"

"The same."

"Oh man, what should we do?"

"Nothing. It's history and has to happen. You keep working on your assault plan to bust David out, and I'll keep working on a bribe. Let's hope Pilate has other things on his plate and forgets about David."

***

"Get up!" The guard shouted, unlocking the door. "You got some friends waiting for you."

Friends? Barosh and Mark. They did it. They bought me out.

Scrambling to his feet, David limped out of the cell. It was dark outside.

A bribe in the middle of the night Thank God!

The guard grabbed him and pushed him ahead. "Come on! I ain't got all night. Let's go." David hobbled down the corridor as fast as he could. He couldn't get out fast enough.

***

"Barosh, wake up; something's happening," Mark was shaking me.

"What? What is it?"

"I don't know, but there's a commotion in the streets."

Looking out the window the sun was just breaking over the city, and while most of the city still slept there were people rushing down the street. Mark was right: something was happening. We left the inn to follow the crowd.

"Be careful Mark until we know what's happening; it could be dangerous. Keep your head covered; we don't want to be recognized."

The flow of people seemed to be towards the Antonia Fortress. We followed, blending in with the crowd. David was inside there, and I prayed whatever was happening didn't involve him.

A large crowd had gathered outside the fortress. There was a lot of mumbling and questions being asked, but no one knew what was happening. We were like a bunch of moths, drawn by the light, but we didn't know why. Mark and I slowly worked our way through the crowd to see.

Outside the Praetorium, high on the steps of the Judgment Hall, stood Pilate. He was talking to a group of men standing below. His personal guards surrounded the Hall, and soldiers lined the walls, top and bottom. Whatever was happening, Pilate was taking no chances.

The group Pilate was talking to was interspersed with Pharisees and Sadducees, who moved through the crowd spurring people on. Pilate shook his head about something and motioned to his guards. They led two men out.

I gasped, "That's Yeshua," I said.

Mark gasped, "That's Barabbas," he said.

Both men had been beaten.

"Who will it be?" Pilate shouted. "Who do you want? This man, the king of the Jews?" he pointed to Yeshua, "Or this man, a murderer?" he pointed to Barabbas.

"Yeshua!" A man shouted. A Pharisee descended on him, and he stopped shouting.

"Barabbas!" The Pharisee shouted, and then another, and another. They urged the crowd to pick up the chant.

The crowd did.

"Barabbas!" they shouted. "Give us Barabbas!"

Pilate raised his hand for silence, "You Jews and your callous religion. I wash my hands of this whole affair. You want Barabbas then you shall have him. What then shall I do with this other man—your 'king'?"

"Crucify him!" a Sadducee yelled.

"Let's get out of here," I said, grabbing Mark's arm.

***

"No wonder I couldn't find Barabbas; they had him in prison," Mark said as we hurried away. "What do you think this means for David?"

"Hopefully he's been forgotten about in all this excitement."

"You think?" Mark asked, and I could hear the hope in his voice.

"Well, Pilate didn't offer David to the crowd, so he must think he's a nobody."

"Or, he thinks he's too dangerous to be released."

"I hope you're wrong about that."

"What now?" Mark asked.

"Well, as much as I hate to say it, it's too big to ignore."

"What is?"

"The crucifixion."

"You're not serious."

"That's the Son of God they're going to put on the cross Mark. Your God and mine now too. This is the biggest event in history; how can we not be there?"

"But, I don't know if I can handle it."

"Neither do I – but I must, I know now; it's what I came for."

"To see him die?"

"That, yes – and then what follows."

***

We sat in the corner of the inn, collecting our thoughts. I told Mark we shouldn't go to Golgotha too soon out of fear of being recognized by any soldiers. That was true enough, but deep inside was another reason—I didn't think I could handle watching them nail Yeshua to a cross.

And, I needed wine, and not the watered down kind.

Mark didn't object.

"I need to find Barabbas," Mark said, "and gather his men. Hopefully, he's more energized."

"You underestimate the Romans," I replied.

"What do you mean?"

"Pilate promised to release him, but nothing says he'll do so in one piece. Don't be surprised if he comes out with no eyes or mangled hands. I don't see them releasing the head of the Zealot's with only a slap on the wrist. At the least, they'll flog him mercilessly."

"We're going to get David out of there, you hear me? With or without Barabbas."

"I know we are, Mark. We'll get him out. Once everything calms down, and Pilate leaves the city, we'll be able to buy him out."

The inn was crowded with pilgrims and travelers. Arguments were everywhere.

"He claimed to be the Son of God; let's see him deliver himself now."

"He's done nothing wrong, only healed people and spoke of love."

"It's not going to be 'love' that'll deliver him from the Romans."

"I don't understand this; when was the trial?"

"When your thick head was sleeping, that's when, during the night."

"They can't do that; he has to have a proper trial. The Sanhedrin needs to rule. . . ."

"It's the Sanhedrin who want him dead, you fool. He called them hypocrites and vipers, in their own Temple. They can do anything they want."

"But the city praised him just days ago. How could they do this now?"

"Most don't know what's happening. They're just waking up like us."

"If he is the son of God, then maybe God will strike them all dead."

"If he's the son of God, why's he being crucified?"

***

We waited until the excitement died down. Sadness and foreboding had descended on the city. People awoke to learn a Jewish rabbi was being executed, one who advocated no violence and had done many wondrous things. Blind and lame men could see and walk; men and women with leprosy and infirmaries had been healed. It's said he even raised the dead. Whether you believed he was the Son of God, a prophet or only a man, he had done no wrong and had only shown goodness and love to the people. They knew that, despite what the Pharisees and Sadducees said about him. He called them out for what they were, and the people knew what he spoke about them was true.

And, if for no other reason, he was a Jew. The Jews had always had prophets, and it was not for pagans to be killing them. As more and more people realized the Sanhedrin was behind it, they turned their anger and hatred against them. To many, the Sanhedrin were worse oppressors than the Romans.

Mark and I slowly began making our way to the Damascus Gate. I wanted to stay with the highest concentration of people. Passing through the gate, we looked to the left where that hill was. Three crosses now stood amongst the poles. On each, a man hung. The raising of Yeshua onto the cross was over, and as the scriptures said, he was crucified along with two criminals.

It was time to go there.

Most people looked away from the mound as they moved in and out of the city, but on the mound itself, a sizable crowd had assembled. We slowly made our way up.

Climbing the dirt path, the crowd blocked our view, and we couldn't see Yeshua. Approaching from the rear, we had only glimpses of the back of the crosses above the heads of the crowd. There was a considerable amount of jeering and mocking going on, and it surprised me to see the number of people who had come to attend the event. Most Jews despised the Roman executions. Then I noticed the Pharisees and Sadducees in attendance. They had come and brought others with them to gloat in the execution of their nemesis. They were scattered about in groups, with smug, self-satisfying looks pasted on their bearded faces, pleased with themselves—having orchestrated an illegal, midnight trial ending with Yeshua hanging on a tree, bloody, torn and dying—among common criminals for all to see.

For the first time in my life, I was ashamed I was a rabbi.

"Come down—son of god," they sneered, "show us your power."

"He saved others, but he can't save himself."

"Hail, king of the Jews! Wear your crown proudly!"

Working our way through the crowd, I saw a man staring at me. He signaled me before disappearing. It was a familiar face, one I'd seen before. I looked around but didn't see him.

"Did you see him?" Mark asked.

"That man? You saw him too?"

"Yeah, that's him. This way," Mark said, pushing through the crowd.

We worked our way to where he had stood.

"Over there!" Mark said, pointing to where a man stood. He wore a dark cloak, covering his face. The cloak fell back, revealing his face. It *was* him, the *beautiful one* in the vision.

"It's him," Mark said, "he's the man I saw in the vision."

"Yes, in mine too – the evil one – he is real."

The man sneered at us, and his face broke into an evil smile. Slowly raising his arm, he pointed up—to the cross. I followed his gaze and looked.

"OH MY GOD. . . . IT'S DAVID!"

"NOOOOOO!" Mark screamed, falling to the ground.

***

There was no acceptance to what I saw. The shock of it will forever direct my life. Never will I be able to close my eyes and not see David hanging on that cross. We'd traveled two-thousand years together, and I had come to regard him as a brother—no, as a son. Guilt flowed over me like a tidal wave. I had put him on that cross—me and my anger. It should have been me hanging up there, not him. I was the one who lost control; I was the one who had pushed him to make the decision to come here. We were only supposed to be seeing and not participating. We weren't supposed to interfere with history or the people of the era. He had been careful to follow the rules; I was the one who broke them.

Now, he was taking my place in a horrendous death.

I forced myself to look at his face. It was a face from the agonies of hell. Anguish and torment were permanently carved into it. He was conscious, but not aware. I looked at his hands and his feet where the nails fastened him to the cross like some kind of bug on display. Dear God why? Why David?

His body was torn and ripped. They had flogged him. I saw the cuts and whelps across his back, sides and legs. His hands and feet had turned dark blue, almost black. Streaks of blood had run down and pooled into dark congealed puddles. His shoulders were pulled from their sockets giving him a gruesome, macabre pose. He was naked and stained; they couldn't even leave him that dignity.

I looked for Mark. I didn't see him. I didn't know when he had left. The last thing I remembered was him backing away from the horror in front of him.

I fell to my knees, and wept loudly for my friend.

***

A hand touched my shoulder. I turned and looked into the beautiful face—of a woman. It was wracked with grief. Her eyes were swollen, red and brimming, tears leaving rivulets down her cheeks.

"Are you Rabbi Ben Barosh?" She asked.

"I am." I said, rising.

"I am Mariamme. I know your friend David Bar Kalaid ha-Rav. He came to my house while seeking you, and we traveled together to Nazareth."

"Yes, he told me. He thought highly of you."

"My heart is torn for what's happened," she said, her voice breaking and sobbing. "I too liked David and was hoping to see him again, but not. . .not like this." She collapsed into my arms. Comforting her was good for me. It eased my own grief. My heart was broken, and it helped to share in that grief.

While holding her, I looked up and stared into the eyes of—Yeshua. My legs gave out again, and I fell back to the ground, pulling Miriamme with me. I couldn't take my eyes off of him. He was barely recognizable. They had beaten him ruthlessly, much worse than David. His entire body was ripped and torn. Open cuts and gouges vibrated from quivering muscles. He was entirely covered in blood, some dried and black, some fresh and red. His face was bruised, sliced and caked with blood running down his face from thorns jammed deep into his head. His body was twisted and hung in a horrifying manner. He didn't resemble anything human.

But his eyes were aware as he looked into mine, and he knew me. I saw a slight nod before he shifted his gaze from me.

"Come," Mariamme pulled my arm. I staggered to my feet and fol-lowed her to where a small group stood together. In the middle of the group, Mariam, the mother of Yeshua knelt on her knees. She spoke to no one and only stared at the bloody body of her son.

Thunder roared from the heavens and ripped across the sky. Lightning cracked and streaked in blazing flashes and blinding flares. People screamed and began running back to the city. The Pharisees and Sadducees ran with the crowd. The sky turned black as the thunder and lightning continued assaulting the earth, while the soldiers huddled together, cowering and fearful.

No rain fell.

Just as soon as it began, it stopped—the thunder and the lightning; but the darkness remained – thick and heavy. I looked up at Yeshua and David. I was grateful for the darkness; it covered their bodies making it easier for me to look on them. I felt guilty and ashamed for thinking this, but I couldn't help it.

Yeshua looked to where we stood.

"Mother, behold your son."

He looked at John.

"Behold your mother."

"Baa. . .rrrosh," I hear a voice, hoarse and rasping.

"Ba. . .rrosh."

It's David. I move to stand below him.

"David, I'm sorry. I'm so sorry."

"The. . .jour. . .nal," he rasped, "Fin. . .ish. . .it. . . .bury. . .wall. . ."

"David, please. . .forgive me."

"The jour. .nal. . .finish. . .tell. . .world. . .the beaut. .iful one. . .liar. . .Jesus. . . is God."

A woman moved to the cross, and bent to kiss David's feet.

"Peace is yours David," it was Mary, the mother of Jesus. "You have chosen God, and He has given you the strength to finish the task He has asked of you."

David looked at Mary, and in the midst of his torment, the agony of hell left his face, and peace settled over him. . .the peace he so desperately sought all his life.

He smiled.

He looked at Yeshua.

"For. . . give me. . . You are. . . the true. . . God. Remem. . . ber me. . . in. . . your. . .kingdom."

Yeshua looked into David's eyes.

"Your peace. . . . is found. . . .David. . .I tell you. . .this day. . . .you will. . . be with. . . .me in. . . . paradise."

Thunder pealed, and lightning flashed.

In the flickering glares and blinding bursts, I saw the beautiful one, but he no longer was beautiful, his deception was stripped away, and he was dark, ugly and in misery.

He howled and screamed and roared.

He had lost David – forever.

***

The darkness continued for hours. Only our small group and the soldiers remained. All others had fled. No one in the city ventured out. I saw the evil one over and over again. He was everywhere, on the ground, in the air, at the side of Yeshua, at the base of the cross. He goaded him, mocked him and tried to provoke him to call on the Father and leave the cross. During all his taunts, I saw a continuous stream of dark mists coming from all directions across the world to Jesus. There were millions and millions of them. As they merged into His body, he wilted and sagged more, and the dark one roared louder and louder in rage and frustration.

They were the sins of mankind, being taken by Yeshua.

"Elohi! Elohi! L'mah sh'vaktani?" Yeshua cried out in anguish.

My God, My God, why have you forsaken me?

Pilate had sent an envoy to speak with the Centurion in charge. There was a lot of arguing back and forth between them. I could overhear bits and pieces of the argument, enough to understand that Pilate had called the Sanhedrin to task for the darkness, thunder and lightning, saying his wife claimed they had upset the gods with their unjust execution of this man. He no longer wanted to drag it out, but wanted it finished quickly before the gods punished him for what he'd done.

The Centurion gave the order to break the legs of the men on the cross to expedite their dying.

"Father. . .into your. . .hands. . .I commit my spirit!"

"What's he saying?" The Centurion shouted, running over, "Is he calling the gods down on us?"

"He isn't doing anything," a soldier said, "he's dying. Dead people don't do things."

"It. . . is. . . finished."

Immediately thunder pealed and rolled across the sky as the lightning streaked profusely upon the earth. The ground shook all around us. Huge rocks and boulders broke loose and rolled down Golgotha's mound. The ground snapped and popped, opening in long, jagged cracks. The crosses shook – but stood.

It lasted for long minutes, and when it abruptly stopped, the darkness was gone, and it was light.

"Surely this man was God," the Centurion said. "Let's finish here and be gone."

A soldier broke the legs of Azir'el. He screamed a howling scream that faded into croaking gasps as he suffocated. As the soldier approached David, I covered my ears, not able to bear seeing them break his legs.

The soldier swung the hammer.

David screamed.

I fell to my knees, screaming and vomiting.

The soldier swung the hammer again.

David choked, gasping for air, his throat making a harsh, gurgling sound, and. . . .

. . . .David died.

When the soldier came to Jesus, the Centurion stopped him.

"He's dead; leave him."

"We must make sure sir," the soldier said, "It is required."

The Centurion stared at the soldier and wanted to reprimand him for questioning him, but he knew he was right. If word got back to Pilate he hadn't verified death, he'd be in trouble.

"Give me your spear," he said to another.

The Centurion stepped up to the cross, and thrust the spear deep into Yeshua's side, piercing his heart. Water and blood flowed down his side.

"We're sure now," he said, tossing the spear to the ground. "Let's leave this place."

A man ran to the cross where Yeshua's lifeless body hung and dropped to his knees, wrapping his arms around Yeshua's feet.

He wept bitterly.

It was Mark.

32

Alone man walks up the path to Golgotha. He's dressed in fine clothes and carries himself with authority. We are the only people there, clustered together at the crosses. Mariamme and other women comfort Mariam, the mother of Yeshua. I am surprised when Mariam comes to me.

"Rabbi Ben Barosh, I am sorry for David; he was a good man with a good heart."

"Yes, he was."

"Do not weep rabbi, Yeshua promised him life in paradise. He has found peace."

I am amazed by this woman. She has just witnessed her son's brutal murder, and yet she feels compassion for a man she hardly knew. She also has absolute faith that her son was more than only a man and would fulfill his promise. She did not have the benefit of knowing what I know, but her faith is unwavering.

She leaves me and walks over to Mark. Upon seeing her, Mark falls to his knees and breaks into sobs. She kneels and comforts him.

The man has reached us and approaches Mariam, offering his sympathies. I move over to hear, believing I know who this man is and had been hoping to see him.

". . . .place his body in my own tomb," he is saying. "With your permission, I will go directly to Pilate and request he release the body to me. With his desire to put this behind him, I do not see that he will deny me."

"That would be most kind of you," Mariam replies.

As he turns to leave, I stop him.

"Are you Joseph of Arimathea?"

"I am," he answers.

"I am Rabbi Ben Barosh, and it is my friend who was also killed here today."

"Yes, I know," he says. "He is the 'prophet', who killed soldiers with the 'thunder-stick'. What is that to me? I have no sympathies for the Zealots or for those who seek God through violence."

"David has killed no one," I reply, "he is innocent of those charges. He traveled here to meet with Yeshua. He was not a Zealot or a revolutionary. He had no part in any violence."

He looks at Miriam, and she nods.

"It is as he says, Joseph; he performed a service for Yeshua, and Yeshua blessed him."

"What is it you seek from me, then?" He asks me.

"Only that you ask Pilate to release his body as well. He should not be left up there for the buzzards to defile. He has suffered enough. I will find a resting place for him."

"You have my sympathy for your friend, Rabbi Ben Barosh. I will do as you say. Pilate wants this whole affair finished; he will honor my request as he does not want the bodies of either of these two men on display. And I know of a site where he may be buried if you desire."

"Thank you, I am most grateful. I can pay whatever costs there are."

"That will not be necessary, I do this for Yeshua." He turns to Mariam, "I will return with servants and clean linens to wrap them in. I must hurry, to finish before the Sabbath."

***

True to his word, he returns with a group of servants, carrying two litters and a basket. I am startled to see a Pharisee among them.

"Do not be alarmed," Joseph says, "this is Nicodemus; he is a believer in Yeshua and can be trusted. He has brought spices and oil for the bodies."

Removing David's body from the cross, is almost as painful as watching him die on it. Luckily, Joseph's servants handle it, or it would be a matter of horror for me.

They lay David on clean linen and Mariamme cleans and anoints his body with oils, before wrapping him.

They clean Yeshua's body as best they can and the women anoint his body with a mixture of myrrh, aloes and oils whlle Mariam kneels by his side.

When they are finished, they place both bodies on the litters, and we move from Golgotha.

They carry David's body to a small specter, located among a number of older ones.

"Your friend may be buried here," Joseph says as they place his body inside. "I leave you to your grief. We will be just over the rise. When you are ready, please join us, and my servants will come back and seal the tomb."

"Thank you Joseph; you have been most kind."

***

We sit by David's body for a long time. I want to leave his journal with him, but Mark stops me.

"He made us promise to finish it and bury it under the wall of the house."

"Do you know which house?" I ask.

"The house you left him in, in Ammathus. He buried two pitchers under the wall."

"Yes, of course, the tablets that started this whole thing."

"He said he left a message for the professor that he'd leave the journal under the opposite wall. He wants you to finish his mission."

"He wants to tell the world,"

"Yes, to tell the world. . . ." Mark said, ". . . .that Yeshua is God."

***

He was our friend—he was our brother—he suffered and died in our place.

We both weep for him. . . .

. . .and say good-bye to him.

***

When we rejoin the others, they are leaving the tomb. It is a large tomb, having a stone bench inside where they laid Yeshua's body. I survey the scene carefully, wanting to have the image firmly in my mind.

Kneeling down at the bench, I touch the shape of His body under the linen.

This is Yeshua, the Son of God come to earth in the flesh. I had spoken with him. He had turned all my logic, all my reasoning, doctrines and beliefs into so much vain ramblings. He had shown me the truth as seen all along in the scriptures and as lived in his life.

He had not spoken to David until they had died together, but had been there with him, from the very beginning. That day, standing on the railing of the Niagara River, Yeshua had stood next to him, and promised him 'peace'. Yes, he said there would be 'turbulence', but beneath that turbulence there is 'peace' —for eternity – for each of us.

I look at Mark, kneeling by Yeshua's side. I had watched this cynical, arrogant policeman, who killed without hesitation change into a sensitive, caring man who felt compassion and love for his fellow man.

Yeshua had changed each of us—in a different way—using different methods, but with the same results—knowing Yeshua is truly the Son of God.

Mark is quiet for a long moment and then asks, "You know what happens next?"

I nod my head, "Yes – the resurrection of Yeshua HaMashiach."

He looks at me and smiles – I smile back.

Rising together, we walk out of the tomb. The others are waiting. Mariam takes my hand.

"Do not despair; He will live again."

"Yes, I know. He will live again, and He will be the salvation of all mankind for all time. He is the Messiah—not only of the Jews—but of the whole world – not only for now – but for all time."

"Soldiers are coming!" Joseph yells.

Everyone is excited and worried when they see them coming, but I tell them not to fear; they are only coming to seal the tomb and guard it. They look at me as if I am crazy.

"Is this the tomb where the body of Yeshua is laid?" the Officer demands.

"It is. I am Joseph of Arimathea, and I have received permission from Pilate for the release of. . . ."

"We know," the soldier cuts him off, entering the tomb. He comes back out, "He's in there. Seal the tomb," he orders.

They roll the stone across the opening. They tie ropes across the stone, dipping the knot into a pot of hot wax and pressing a seal into it.

"We are posting guards at this tomb," the Officer says.

"Guards? For what reason?" Joseph asks.

"To prevent anyone from stealing his body."

As we walk away, I can't help but laugh, and the others look at me in amazement.

"Why do you laugh? And how did you know the soldiers were coming to seal the tomb?" Joseph asks.

"Forgive me Joseph, but that is not important. Let us go back and rejoice, for the plan of God has been fulfilled, and the world will see salvation."

33

Y ou, who are reading David's Journal know the rest of the story.
Yes. . .Yeshua came out of the tomb—alive.

I was there—I seen it.

Yes. . .He stayed on this earth for forty days, walking and showing Himself to hundreds of people.

I know—I was one of them—as was Mark. He spoke with us alone and in groups. He changed my name as He said He would.

Yes. . .His disciples were a frightened, divisive group who hadn't understood what Yeshua's mission was or where and when His kingdom would be, and. . .

Yes—after His resurrection, He spent much time with them, teaching them and showing them what they had failed to understand before he was killed.

Yes. . .His brothers had rejected Him while He lived, and. . .

Yes—after His resurrection, He visited with James, Jude and the others and revealed His truth as the Messiah.

Yes—they changed—disciples and brothers alike—they'll suffer immense tribulations, tortures and death. They will be beaten, jailed, stoned, beheaded, tortured and crucified, and. . .

. . .not a single one will turn away from Yeshua.

Because Yeshua is God. He defeated the grave—He rose from the dead, and showed them and us that we too, can defeat death. He showed us that. . .

beneath the turbulence—peace is found.

Yes—He ascended into the clouds—I was there, and I saw it.

Yes. . .I was in the Temple on the Day of Pentecost, with the others—the disciples, Mariam (his loving and blessed mother), Mariamme of Magdala, and Mark too, and. . . .

Yes—the promised Holy Spirit of God descended and filled the whole Temple with the presence of God. Thousands had come for the Festival of Weeks, from all over the known world and we, the followers of Yeshua, became filled with the Holy Spirit of God and witnessed to them of the glories of Yeshua HaMashiach—Jesus the Messiah—in their own languages. Thousands were converted and accepted Yeshua as their Savior. Many of the disciples and followers went away with the converts to their lands and cities and spread the gospel of Yeshua, and so the church began.

Yes. . .there was a great disturbance in Judea. Try as they wanted to, the Sadducees couldn't kill the truth that Yeshua had risen from the dead; no more than they had been able to kill the man Himself.

They couldn't produce his body, and there were many witnesses and proofs of His resurrection they couldn't squash. Word spread that the veil of law in the Holy of Holies had ripped in two when Yeshua died, and when the Holy Spirit descended on us, in the temple, a new veil was given to cover us—a veil of grace.

The Sanhedrin knew then, their only recourse, in protecting their power, was to destroy those who believed in Yeshua.

Yes. . .the beautiful one is still here as he is with you there, in the twenty-first century. He is no longer beautiful; his lie has been revealed, and he knows he has lost. His days are numbered, and there is no salvation for him. And so. . . .

. . .he continues to roar and howl, like the beast he is, but his howling is the abandoned cry of the condemned and doomed, after all. . . .

. . .what's a couple of thousand years. . .compared to eternity?

***

We will bury this journal now, Mark and I, as David had instructed, under the opposite wall of the house in Ammathus—opposite the wall of vipers—for Thaddeus as promised, and for you—as the proof and the truth of God's plan for the world and for your salvation.

Along with David's journal, we've placed the bloodstained nails that punctured David's hands and held him to the cross. David's DNA is on file – check them and explain that to the skeptics.

No. . .I'll not be returning to my former time. Yeshua isn't finished with me yet.

Miriam – my dear, sweet wife—know that I love you dearly—and I do not do this lightly. Missing you is the hardest part and cuts through my heart.

My children—I love you more than life, and I give that life to Yeshua. Read what is here, dear wife and children—know and believe that Yeshua is your savior, accept Him as I have.

I wait for you to join me.

Neither is Mark returning. He knows of Yeshua's death and resurrection, having witnessed them firsthand; now he spends time with Simon Peter, to learn of Yeshua's life. The fame he sought—he's found in Yeshua, for he will write a book that all the world will know as 'the Gospel of Mark'.

I know I'll be seeing him again as we'll be taking many journeys together. . .for you see. . .

. . .Yeshua gave me my new name. . .

. . .I am Barnabas, and I go to find Saul of Tarsus.

We have much work to do.

***

Thaddeus – Allen—Jennifer—Alex. . .my dear friends. . . .

. . .feel joy and gladness at what you've done—for through your hard work, the world now has the proof that Yeshua is—the Lord God.

Find Him—He's always been there—all we had to do was look.

Don't wait! Time is short – the man in our visions is there, among you as I write. . . .

. . .and the evil one knows his time is short.

Farewell friends—may the peace that Yeshua gave to David—be yours.

Epilogue

D avid's Journal rocked the world – and the skeptics came out in force;
Those who refused to believe even before seeing the evidence. . .

Those world leaders who breathed hatred and death for their neighbors. . .

Those religion and secular founders who've amassed immense power and wealth. . .

Those atheists, agnostics and humanists who refuse to accept a higher authority. . .

The scientists and philosophers who saw their own theories and writings being dispelled. . .

Yes, each of them came out, looking for detail and nuance to discredit the journal's story. . .

. . .to justify their own disbelief and denial.

They discounted the science; ridiculed the theories; belittled the witnesses; made a mockery of the story; labeled the journal a fraud and scorned Thaddeus's group.

The Department of Homeland Security denied they ever investigated such a group; denied the existence of the original tablets; and claimed Agent John Markus Rosino wasn't missing but was on a 'secret' assignment.

The United Nations raved and ranted, calling it a militaristic scheme perpetuated by the United States and Israel to justify invading the Middle East, and called for preemptive strikes immediately.

But try as they would, they couldn't deny the evidence, the films, the date testing and the witnesses who were there when the 'journal' was discovered.

So, as they do—they lied.

All sorts of lies and distortions flowed about the group, the discovery, the tablets, the archeological site and, of course, the journal—most from people who never read a page of it or spoke to anyone involved. . .

. . .all to prove the journal was a fraud—because. . .

. . .if they accepted the journal as fact, they had to accept Jesus as God.

They tried to destroy the book. Nations banned it and burned it by the thousands. But still it spread, and they couldn't stop it.

A great tribulation followed. The *beautiful one* went on a rampage. He knew his time was coming to an end, and he roared and howled against God and creation.

He revealed his true self—and it is an ugly self.

***

But the people read the little book, and many believed, and there was. . .

. . .the greatest worldwide revival ever seen in history.

***

Three men. . .
    David Alden Kincaid,
      Rabbi Barosh Ben Goldberg,
        John Markus Rosino,
          looked down from above and. . .
            . . .smiled.

"Therefore, if any man be in Christ, he is a new creation; old things have passed away; behold all things are become new."

2 Corinthians 5:17

About the Author

Raised as a 'river-rat' on the Upper Niagara River, in Western New York, Duane spent time in the military and then earned his college degrees while raising a family in New York.

Having both, a strong love of the outdoors and of studying history and humanity, he spent many hours pursuing them separately or combined, reading a book while sitting in a blind in the woods.

A desire to understand human existence and purpose dominated his mind with the same questions that haunted men and women down through the centuries – haunting him. Studying, searching and exploring, his life consisted of sorting out the pieces of the puzzle. After decades of resisting and denying the evidence of creation and of an overall plan and purpose for humankind, he recognized that there is a Creator and a purpose. Fascinated with the idea of 'time travel', and with writing, it was only a matter of time for all three to merge and express themselves into a single entity. This story is that expression. It's a work in progress; no one has figured out the whole puzzle yet, but many of the pieces have been put in place over the centuries framing and forming the picture. A few of them have been 'forced' into places they don't quite fit, and as time continues on, we learn to reposition them, and the clarity of the picture increases.

Always enjoying a good read, this story he gives to you and he hopes that you found something of value in it and enjoyed it as much as he did writing it.

Duane would like very much to hear your thoughts.

Connect with DK LeVick On-Line:

Wordpress: http://dklevick.wordpress.com/
Twitter: http://twitter.com/#!/dk_levick
Email: duanelevick2011@gmail.com
Face book: http://www.facebook.com/pages/
Bridges-DK-Levick/157243617667780

CPSIA information can be obtained at www.ICGtesting.com
Printed in the USA
LVOW11s1816090315

429805LV00002B/424/P